Using
Harvard™
Graphics

Stephen W. Sagman
Jane Graver Sandlar

CORPORATION

LEADING COMPUTER KNOWLEDGE

Using Harvard™ Graphics

Library of Congress Catalog No.: 88-63850

ISBN 0-88022-407-X

92 91 90   8 7

Interpretation of the printing code: the rightmost double-digit number is the year of the book's printing; the rightmost single-digit number, the number of the book's printing. For example, a printing code of 89-1 shows that the first printing of the book occurred in 1989.

Using Harvard Graphics is based on Harvard Graphics Version 2.12.

DEDICATION

To Eric and Artie
for their love and support.

Publishing Manager

Lloyd J. Short

Product Director

Karen A. Bluestein

Production Editor

Sandra Blackthorn

Editors

Kelly Currie
Kelly Dobbs
Gregory Robertson
Alice Martina Smith
Richard Turner
Steven L. Wiggins

Technical Editor

Ron Holmes

Indexed by

Sherry Massey

Book Design and Production

Dan Armstrong   Joe Ramon
Cheryl English   Dennis Sheehan
Lori A. Lyons   Peter Tocco
Jennifer Matthews

Composed in Goudy Old Style and Excellent 47
by Que Corporation

About the Authors

Stephen W. Sagman

Stephen W. Sagman is a technical writer and PC educator, based in New York. He has written hundreds of articles and product reviews, which have appeared in *PC Week*, *PC Magazine*, *PC Computing*, and other publications. Mr. Sagman has lectured extensively and trained thousands of people on a variety of computer topics, including Harvard Graphics. Prior to that, Mr. Sagman edited *MIDI Marketer*, an electronic musical instrument marketing newsletter, and served as marketing manager for several high-technology companies. Mr. Sagman works closely with Jane Sandlar in developing user documentation, training programs, and custom courses on PC topics.

Jane Graver Sandlar

Jane Graver Sandlar is the president of Support Our Systems, Inc., a documentation and training company in Red Bank, New Jersey. During the last two years, she has taught more than 1,000 students in many corporate environments to use Harvard Graphics. Ms. Sandlar's company produces users' guides, training guides, and other systems-related documentation for the corporate and government audience. In addition, the company trains users on a variety of personal computer and mainframe software packages. During the course of her 10-year career in data processing, Ms. Sandlar has written for computer users and taught in a myriad of computer environments.

Support Our Systems, Inc., 10 Mechanic St., Red Bank, NJ 07701, offers a symbol library of invaluable documentation symbols for technical writers. Please contact Support Our Systems for more information.

Contents at a Glance

TABLE OF CONTENTS

I Learning the Basics

II Making Charts

6 Creating Graph Charts: Area, High/Low/Close, and Pie.................................... **211**

III   Adding Pizzazz

ACKNOWLEDGMENTS

The authors want to thank Ira Kaye, Ron Ridgeway, and Lisa Christopher of Software Publishing Corporation for their valuable assistance.

The authors especially want to thank Karen Bluestein, Sandy Blackthorn, and Lloyd Short of Que Corporation for their hard work, patience, and encouragement during the development and production of this book.

TRADEMARK ACKNOWLEDGMENTS

Que Corporation has made every effort to supply trademark information about company names, products, and services mentioned in this book. Trademarks indicated below were derived from various sources. Que Corporation cannot attest to the accuracy of this information.

1-2-3, Freelance Plus, Lotus, and VisiCalc are registered trademarks of Lotus Development Corporation.

COMPAQ is a registered trademark of COMPAQ Computer Corporation.

Encapsulated PostScript is a registered trademark of Adobe Systems, Inc.

GEM Draw is a trademark of Digital Research Inc.

Hewlett-Packard is a registered trademark and LaserJet is a trademark of Hewlett-Packard Co.

IBM is a registered trademark and PS/2 is a trademark of International Business Machines Corporation.

Microsoft Windows is a registered trademark of Microsoft Corporation.

PageMaker is a registered trademark of Aldus Corporation.

PFS is a registered trademark and Harvard Graphics is a trademark of Software Publishing Corporation.

Ventura Publisher is a registered trademark of Ventura Software, Inc.

Windows Draw is a trademark of Micrografx, Inc.

Xerox is a registered trademark of Xerox Corporation.

CONVENTIONS USED IN THIS BOOK

The conventions used in this book have been established to help you learn to use the program quickly and easily. As much as possible, the conventions correspond with those used in the Harvard Graphics documentation.

Names of commands, menus, and overlays are written with initial capital letters. Options in overlays and on-screen messages are written in a special typeface and capitalized exactly as they appear on-screen. Words and letters that the user types are written in *italic* or set off on a separate line.

Introduction

If you draw graphs by hand or use a typewriter to type overhead projections, you will be amazed at the helping hand a computer can provide. And whether or not you already use a computer, you will be delighted when you try Software Publishing Corporation's Harvard™ Graphics. No other business graphics software can give you a larger helping hand in creating interesting and expressive business presentations.

Harvard Graphics is one of the computer industry's most popular business software packages because it makes creating professional-looking, expressive business charts as easy as choosing a few options from your computer's screen. When you try Harvard Graphics, you will find that you have a host of easy-to-use tools for creating charts and equally easy methods for presenting your masterpieces on paper, on slides, or in animated desktop presentations.

Harvard Graphics can create just about any visual aid you can imagine to enhance a business presentation. Many people use Harvard Graphics to make slides, transparencies, and printed handouts, but you may want to use the program to create a printed agenda for your meeting or to draw a map that directs attendees to their locations. You also may want to use Harvard Graphics to create the cue cards you will use at the podium during your speech and to create the awards you will present at the conclusion of your presentation. The potential uses for Harvard Graphics are limited only by your imagination.

Harvard Graphics is certainly not the only business graphics program available, but many other graphics programs require that you be a proficient artist or an experienced computer user. Harvard Graphics imposes no such limitations. In fact, even if your formal art education stopped in the fourth grade, you will be able to turn out well-designed and attractive business graphics with Harvard Graphics. Simply leaving the default options will yield beautiful results for your charts.

1

The program's capacity to guide you in creating a chart makes Harvard Graphics unusual. By following its built-in chart recipes, you let the program make many of the aesthetic decisions—both major and minor—that might otherwise confront you in designing a chart. If you decide to create a bar chart, for example, Harvard Graphics automatically picks an appealing combination of colors, adds descriptive information to the chart's axes and legend, and even scales the size of the chart title to fit your needs. If you are happy with the scheme Harvard Graphics uses and the chart looks satisfactory, you can stop there. To complete your work, you can save the chart on disk and reproduce it with your printer, plotter, or slide maker. If your sense of aesthetics suggests a few changes, though, you easily can edit any aspect of the chart's design. You may even want to elaborate on it by adding lines, boxes, arrows, or predrawn pictures from the included libraries of available symbols. All these possibilities and more are at your fingertips with Harvard Graphics.

What Is in This Book?

In the chapters that follow, you will find detailed information about how to accomplish specific charting tasks and how to control the many features of Harvard Graphics. Topics are organized logically, so they build on the information contained in prior chapters.

Part I of this book examines the basics of Harvard Graphics. Chapter 1, "Introducing Harvard Graphics," provides information on the benefits of Harvard Graphics, the applications of the program, and the other graphics packages available on today's market.

Chapter 2, "Getting Started," provides all the information you will need to install and start the program.

Chapter 3, "Quick Start to Harvard Graphics: Taking a Guided Tour," takes you on a comprehensive tour of the program's most important capabilities. In this quick tour, you get to try your hand at making a text, bar, and pie chart.

Part II of this book provides in-depth information about making charts. Chapter 4, "Creating Text Charts," Chapter 5, "Creating Graph Charts: Bar and Line," and Chapter 6, "Creating Graph Charts: Area, High/Low/Close, and Pie" provide detailed descriptions of all the options available for making text and graph charts. These chapters offer you the chance to create sample charts of each type.

In Part III, you add refinements to your charts and put it all together. Chapter 7, "Drawing with Harvard Graphics: Draw/Annotate," focuses on the pizzazz you can add to charts with the Draw/Annotate feature. Chapter 8, "Using Step-Savers: Templates and Macros," gives you information on how to speed your work greatly. And Chapter 9, "Producing Stellar Output," describes all the ways to take the masterpieces you have created on-screen and reproduce them as pages, slides, or screenshows.

Who Should Use This Book?

Even if you never have used a computer, you will be able to follow the simple step-by-step instructions that this book provides. If you have used other software, such as a word processor or database manager, you will learn in this book about what makes Harvard Graphics different. And if you have used other graphics software, or if you have been using Harvard Graphics already, you will find details about getting the most out of the more sophisticated capabilities of Harvard Graphics.

How To Use This Book

All learning is done best in small, frequent doses. Don't try to get through this book or learn everything that is in it in one sitting. Do try to find time to work with this book and your computer when you will not be distracted by the routine uproar of your business or home.

We assure you that you will learn the most if you have the chance to try the procedures and exercises in each chapter while you're sitting at your computer. And when you finish *Using Harvard Graphics*, you will want to keep the book handy as a ready reference. You will find that this book's comprehensive index and table of contents will be helpful guides when you want quick refreshers about how to accomplish specific tasks.

Part I

Learning the Basics

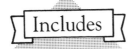
Includes

Introducing Harvard Graphics

Getting Started

Quick Start to Harvard Graphics:
Taking a Guided Tour

1

Introducing
Harvard Graphics

Harvard Graphics is so versatile that the types of charts you can create are virtually unlimited. Nevertheless, you may find yourself routinely picking from one of the preprogrammed popular business charts that Harvard Graphics provides. This chapter presents an overview of the basic charts you can create with Harvard Graphics. In addition, it introduces some of the advanced tasks you can perform, such as drawing and enhancing charts, creating slide shows and screenshows, and combining chart types on a single page. Also in this chapter, you will learn about the benefits of Harvard Graphics and how it stacks up against other graphics software packages on today's market. Finally, you will examine the Harvard Graphics approach to creating charts, an approach that makes Harvard Graphics easy and fun to use.

Making Text Charts

Text charts are useful for creating handouts or slides to be used during a presentation when concepts are better conveyed with words than with pictures. Text charts can list a presenter's key points or show lists of goals and objectives. Text charts are also ideal for making comparisons or for presenting the benefits and drawbacks of an issue.

Text charts can be simple and unadorned or numbered lists of items. Text charts can include bulleted points to call to attention the equal emphasis of all items on a list. Text charts also can contain two or three columns to help the viewer compare information side by side. Figure 1.1 shows a sample text chart with bullets used for a presentation to elicit donor contributions to a nonprofit organization.

7

Fig. 1.1.

A sample text chart.

S & J Foundation
1988 Achievements

- Endowed four chairs at two major universities
- Provided scholarships to 48 college students
- Established Tinton Falls Community Center
- Created Charles Street Theater
- Instituted Writers' Crisis Hotline

Creating Graph Charts

Graph charts are ideal for conveying numeric information, and they come in a variety of familiar designs. *Bars charts* depict the relationships among discrete numbers, and *line charts* eloquently express trends. *Pie charts* and *column charts*, other popular graph chart styles, show the relative percentages of the components of a total.

Harvard Graphics provides still other graph chart types. *Point charts*, also known among statisticians as scattergrams, show the correlation between two sets of results. *Area charts* emphasize total quantities. *High/low/close* charts fulfill the need of Wall Street watchers and other financial professionals by tracking the high, low, and closing prices of stocks and bonds and other financial instruments.

With Harvard Graphics, unlimited variations are possible on these basic themes. By making such changes as altering the scale of the axes of a chart or altering the bar style, you can create a never-ending variety of new charts to satisfy any need. Figure 1.2 shows some of the basic Harvard Graphics chart types.

With Harvard Graphics, you can enter numbers you have calculated for graphing, or you can enter raw data and instruct the program to perform the calculations and then graph the results. Harvard Graphics provides nearly two dozen mathematical and statistical calculations that you can use to make your data more meaningful. For statisticians, the statistical calculations Harvard Graphics provides are primarily linear, but a number of standard regression curves are also included.

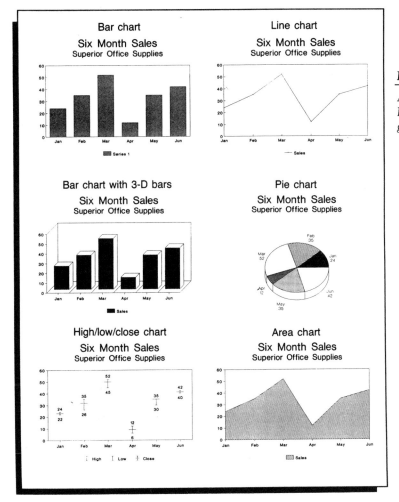

Fig. 1.2.

An assortment of Harvard Graphics graph charts.

Creating Organization Charts

Keeping track of the ever-changing personnel in most companies is a task that only a computer can manage. Using the special *organization chart* feature of Harvard Graphics, you can depict the reporting structure among employees or among the divisions of an organization.

With Harvard Graphics organization charts, setting up hierarchical diagrams with multiple levels and complex relationships is easy. You merely enter a list of managers, each manager's subordinates, and any staff assistants level by level until the entire organization or division is diagrammed. Figure 1.3 shows a typical organization chart for a small company or department.

Fig. 1.3.

A typical organization chart.

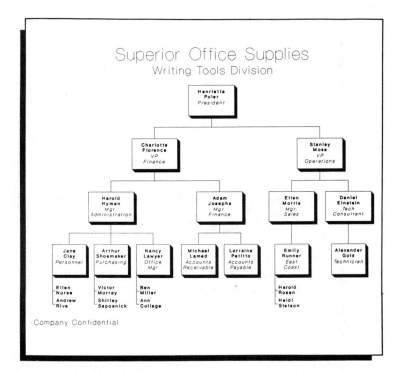

Drawing and Enhancing Charts

Once you finish creating either a text or graph chart, you can embellish it with a special Harvard Graphics feature called Draw/Annotate. Figure 1.4 shows a chart both before and after it has been enhanced with Draw/Annotate. You also can use Draw/Annotate to draw a chart or illustration from scratch.

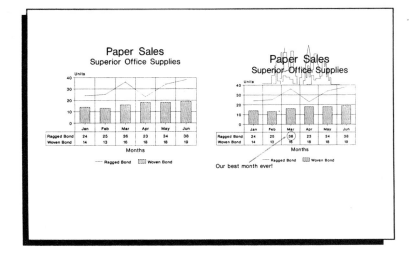

Fig. 1.4.

A chart before and after Draw/ Annotate was used.

The Draw/Annotate feature provides you with a complete set of drawing tools so you can transform charts from the ordinary to the extraordinary. Using this versatile feature's simple commands, you can add lines, arrows, boxes, circles, and other shapes to a chart. And you can move, copy, or resize any of the chart's components and add text to comment on any particular aspects of the chart.

Perhaps the most useful feature of Draw/Annotate is its capacity to adorn charts with preexisting drawings, called *symbols*. You can use symbols to dress up charts and add meaning with pictures. You also can use symbols as the starting point from which to create your own custom graphics files for later use with desktop publishing programs. Harvard Graphics comes with a comprehensive starter set of symbols in a variety of libraries, each pertaining to a specific theme—buildings, cities, people, industry, and so on. You can have more symbols by creating your own in Harvard Graphics or by purchasing additional symbol libraries from the makers of Harvard Graphics (Software Publishing Corporation) and from third-party companies that produce graphics files that you can import into Harvard Graphics.

Creating Slide Shows

Most often, you will create and then reproduce charts one by one. But Harvard Graphics provides *slide shows* for reproducing or viewing charts a group at a time.

By collecting a group of charts into a slide show, you can display your charts one after another on the computer's screen or send your charts consecutively to an output device for reproduction. If you're planning to use the charts you create as part of a stand-up presentation, you also can make cue cards for when you're at the podium or practice cards for when you're rehearsing your speech. Practice cards can hold notes and comments about the charts in your presentation. Slide shows are also the means by which you create screenshows, described next.

Creating Screenshows

Many people use Harvard Graphics to produce only printed pages, overhead transparencies, and slides. But you can take advantage of the program's capability to create a special type of dazzling desktop presentation called a *screenshow*.

Instead of creating slides, which are projected on a screen one after another, you can create an animated presentation right on your computer screen that uses movie-like special effects to change from one chart to the next. At your disposal is an entire arsenal of wipes, fades, overlays, and weaves that provide spectacular transitions between images. For a boardroom meeting or small presentation, you can use a screenshow on a large-screen monitor as the visual accompaniment to a presentation. For large audiences, you can project a screenshow onto a large screen with a high-resolution computer projector.

You can even use a screenshow to create an informative presentation that the viewer can control. A screenshow can display different segments based on the keystroke input of anyone watching the screen. Screenshows used in this fashion are ideal for demonstrations and sales presentations and even for rudimentary computer-based training.

Mixing Chart Types on a Page

With Harvard Graphics, your presentations can include more than one chart displayed on a single page or slide so readers or viewers can compare charts easily. In Harvard Graphics, two or more charts on a page, even if you're mixing chart types, is called a *multiple chart*. Once you create a multiple chart, you can pull it into Draw/Annotate to add text comments and arrows that point out the similarities among charts. Figure 1.5 shows a typical multiple chart.

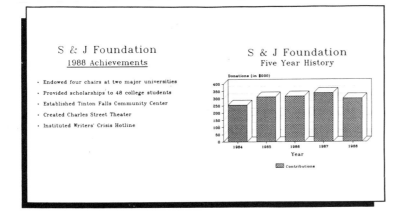

Fig. 1.5.

A typical multiple chart.

Examining the Benefits of Using Harvard Graphics

The suitability and flexibility of Harvard Graphics for creating top-quality presentation graphics is enough to make this program the leading business graphics software for IBM® standard computers. But Harvard Graphics offers added benefits in its elegance of design and ease of operation.

Harvard Graphics was designed to blend effortlessly into a preexisting computer setup, regardless of the combination of hardware in use. Harvard Graphics is well known for its remarkably broad selection of drivers for the bewildering array of printers, plotters, slide makers, graphics displays, and other output devices available. Unless you own truly obscure (and probably obsolete) equipment, Harvard Graphics should be ready to exercise the maximum capabilities of both your graphics display and output devices.

Harvard Graphics also provides carefree compatibility with a variety of other software. To avoid retyping existing data into a chart, you can pull data from a 1-2-3® spreadsheet or ASCII file just as easily as you can pull the data from the files of other Software Publishing Corporation products, such as PFS®:Professional Plan. Harvard Graphics also imports and exports directly one of the most popular computer graphics file formats: Computer Graphics Metafiles (CGM). Popular desktop publishing software such as Xerox® Ventura Publisher® and Aldus PageMaker® can read CGM files directly, which means that you can use Harvard Graphics to create the illustrations and graphs used in newsletters, brochures, and other documents created by desktop publishing software. For software that does not accept CGM files, Harvard Graphics offers you a choice between two other output file formats: Encapsulated PostScript® (EPS) files and Hewlett-Packard® Graphics Language (HPGL) files.

All of these methods of interchanging files between software have in common their object-oriented graphics file formats. *Object-oriented graphics programs*, also known as vector-based graphics software, create images out of dozens, hundreds, or even thousands of individual lines, boxes, and curves. A bar chart, for example, is composed of a tremendous number of individual lines, each forming a segment of one of the bars or one of the axes. Any text added to a chart, in its title or legend, for example, is also composed of objects that are combinations of curves and straight lines.

Paint programs, the alternative to object-oriented graphics programs, act on a representation of your display in the computer's memory in which each point on the screen (a *pixel*) corresponds to one computer "bit" of information. Each pixel is mapped to 1 bit—hence the name bit-mapped graphics. When drawing an image on-screen, bit-mapped graphics programs illuminate patterns of pixels in a specific shape. To draw a box, for example, a bit-mapped program illuminates a box-shaped pattern of pixels.

Object-oriented graphics programs provide several benefits over bit-mapped graphics software. First, because all the figures on-screen are composed of individual objects, you can modify each object separately from the others with ease. If an arrow pointing to a chart needs adjustment, for example, you can shorten or lengthen the arrow or change its position on-screen without affecting the chart's other components. With bit-mapped graphics, you need to turn off the pixels that form the arrow's shape by using an "eraser" tool. In the process, though, you easily may erase pixels that form part of another chart component underneath the arrow.

Object-oriented graphics also maintain their crisp resolution even if you vary the size of the overall chart or use a different output device. To increase the size of a bit-mapped image, a graphics program needs to add new pixels by calculating their position mathematically. To lengthen a box by 20 percent, for example, a bit-mapped program needs to add 20 percent more pixels, positioning them according to the program's own calculations. A new, larger image is created from the existing image. Moreover, as it increases the size of an image, a bit-mapped program thickens the lines of an image as the program tries to magnify everything proportionally.

To lengthen the same box, an object-oriented program needs only to increase the length of the box's four lines by 20 percent. The object-oriented program's modification is precise, adding no distortion to the image. The new, longer lines maintain the same thickness as before, so the lines look as thin and crisp as they did earlier. Figure 1.6 gives you a simple illustration of the difference between using these two approaches.

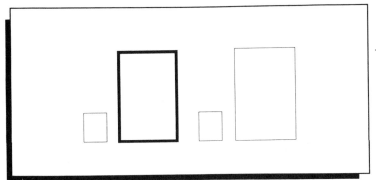

Fig. 1.6.

A box magnified by a bit-mapped program (left) and an object-oriented program (right).

Harvard Graphics offers still other technical benefits that you will experience in the chapters that follow. You will find immediately that Harvard Graphics operates quickly. Harvard Graphics has been designed to incorporate a quick and responsive feel just as a sports car has been designed for power and agility. The menus and screens appear on-screen with a satisfying snap instead of the sluggishness of other graphics programs. In addition, the authors of Harvard Graphics designed its menus and program options with ease-of-use in mind. You can pick any of several methods available for selecting from a menu at any time. As you work with Harvard Graphics, you can choose the method that is easiest and most convenient at the time.

Harvard Graphics is also impressive for its myriad of charting options. The program offers you a broad array of ready-made charts and graphs and enormous flexibility for tailoring its preexisting designs for your needs.

The people who designed Harvard Graphics knew good graphics design, and they incorporated their knowledge into the program. This feature has captured the imaginations of more users and reviewers than any other. Start a bar graph chart, for example, and Harvard Graphics automatically chooses a color scheme, positions the legend, sizes the axes, and arranges the titles. What's more, the program performs all these tasks with what appears to be unerring judgment. Thus, Harvard Graphics is both a graphics tool and a graphics authority. In fact, one reviewer commented accurately that it's "hard to be tasteless" with Harvard Graphics.

This built-in safety-net approach has two advantages. First, it can keep you from embarrassing yourself by creating a chart that's less than attractive. Second, it lets you create a finished chart more quickly because the program does much of the work automatically.

To augment the capabilities Harvard Graphics provides, you can purchase five separate enhancements from Software Publishing Corporation called ScreenShow Utilities, Quick-Charts, Designer Galleries, US MapMaker, and Business Symbols. ScreenShow Utilities adds a capture program that can copy any screen display, even from another program, to a bit-mapped PCX-format file for incorporation into a screenshow. ScreenShow Utilities also provides methods for you to manage slide show files on disk and a tool to project Harvard Graphics slide shows easily and quickly without using Harvard Graphics. Quick-Charts and Designer Galleries offer predefined popular charts and templates that you can use by supplying your own data. Designer Galleries provides 12 special attractively designed color-coordinated palettes not available in the standard Harvard Graphics package. US MapMaker lets you create color-coded maps that can display financial or statistical data regionally. You can display all the United States, select regions, and choose from 32,000 major cities and towns. Business Symbols provides more than 300 predrawn symbols grouped into 20 libraries.

Learning about the Competition

Now that you know some of the background and benefits of the Harvard Graphics package, you may be interested in how the program stacks up against the competition. This section examines some of the other graphics software packages available on today's market.

Other Business Graphics Software

Harvard Graphics is only one of a dozen or more common business graphics packages, but Harvard Graphics is generally regarded as one of the leaders in the category. Even if another program handles one aspect or another of charting with slightly more aplomb, Harvard Graphics overwhelms them all with its well-rounded strengths and generous assortment of features.

Perhaps the prime competitor to Harvard Graphics is Freelance® Plus from 1-2-3's progenitors, Lotus Development Corporation. Freelance Plus offers more typefaces for chart text than Harvard Graphics and a horizontal bar menu that mimics the well-known 1-2-3 menu system. But the Harvard Graphics user interface is logical and, in our opinion, simpler to use. Further, Harvard Graphics offers a wider variety of statistical functions and text and graph chart types than Freelance Plus, and Harvard Graphics' symbol libraries are far more diverse. Harvard Graphics also creates automatic organization charts, unlike Freelance Plus.

The other business graphics software offered by Lotus Development Corporation, Graphwriter II, excels in gathering data from a 1-2-3 spreadsheet and graphing the data visually. Graphwriter II also uses a highly automated approach to generating charts in volume. But Harvard Graphics offers Graphwriter-like data links to 1-2-3 charts, also, and it surpasses Graphwriter's features that allow you to embellish charts and draw charts and graphics from scratch. You would need to use both Graphwriter and Freelance Plus for all that Harvard Graphics can do in one package.

Perhaps the most formidable competition in both flexibility and ease-of-use is GRAPH Plus from Micrografx. GRAPH Plus runs under the Microsoft® Windows graphical user interface so its presentation on-screen is highly visual. Instead of listing possible graph types from which you can choose, for example, GRAPH Plus shows miniature versions of each of its built-in graph designs. Modifying a GRAPH Plus chart is easy, too. With a mouse or similar input device, you can simply point to the object you want to resize and then pull and stretch the object to a new shape or position.

Harvard Graphics provides many of these same capabilities with its Draw/Annotate feature. And despite the benefits that Microsoft Windows bestows on a program that is, by definition, graphically oriented, Windows exacts a price, too. Windows requires a significant amount of disk space to operate and a high-performance computer to run its graphics. With Windows, you need at least an IBM AT-class computer with its fast 80286 microprocessor computer chip. Harvard Graphics runs as comfortably on a less-expensive PC or XT as it does on a faster AT or even a super-fast 80386 computer. The only requirement Harvard Graphics imposes is the use of a display system (a graphics card and monitor) capable of graphics. That enables you to set up a low-cost but effective graphics workstation.

Two other popular entries in the business graphics software category are distinguished by their use of three-dimensional graphics to impart real pizzazz into a presentation. Both Boeing Graph and Enertronics' EnerGraphics allow you to graph numeric data in full three dimensions by plotting information along a third axis rather than along the usual two axes offered by most graphing programs. As a result, the depth of bars or lines is a measure of the data they represent. The three-dimensional effect offered by Harvard Graphics simply adds the appearance of depth to objects on-screen to give them a more interesting appearance. In

Harvard Graphics, the depth of bars or lines has no significance; data is still graphed on only two axes. But for all the spectacular output these other packages can create, they are incapable of making plotters produce their three-dimensional graphics (plotters, by nature, cannot reproduce 3-D graphics). So users with plotters may create and reproduce two-dimensional graphics only, and for that, Harvard Graphics offers more options.

Harvard Graphics stacks up well against other programs dedicated to the task of creating business charts and graphs. Harvard Graphics also compares remarkably well with graphics software in several other categories, discussed next.

Draw Packages

Although a majority of purchasers probably buy Harvard Graphics for its capacity to create business charts, many purchasers now rely also on the program's drawing capabilities. Before Harvard Graphics, the most popular method of freehand drawing on a computer was with "Draw" programs such as Windows Draw™ from Micrografx and GEM Draw™ from Digital Research. Draw programs, by nature, offer the same object-oriented graphics offered by Harvard Graphics.

Harvard Graphics incorporates all the essential elements of Draw software in its Draw/Annotate module, accessible right at the Main menu. If your goal in purchasing graphics software is to gain Draw features, Harvard Graphics fits the bill ideally, providing complete charting and desktop presentation capabilities as a no-cost extra. If your goal is to produce business charts or desktop presentations, you will be acquiring superb Draw capabilities in the bundle.

Spreadsheet Graphics

When 1-2-3 first appeared, one of its most valued attributes was the addition of both database management and graphing capabilities to the electronic spreadsheet design introduced by VisiCalc®. At the time, the ability to graph data in the same package that you managed it sounded like a promising idea.

But the 1-2-3 graphics module paled in comparison to the dedicated graphics programs that soon appeared, some designed solely to create charts based on 1-2-3 spreadsheet data. These programs offered more graphics versatility and power than 1-2-3 and created charts with far more style and appeal.

More recent spreadsheets, such as Microsoft Excel, offer charting capabilities that are far superior to those that 1-2-3 delivers. Some of these spreadsheets' charts even compare favorably with the charts generated by the graph chart module of Harvard Graphics. But Harvard Graphics allows you to embellish these basic charts considerably by using the Draw/Annotate feature. With Draw/Annotate, you can add adornments and transform bland charts that are simply communicative into stylish graphics that are truly expressive. Moreover, with Harvard Graphics, you get complete text layout capabilities, described next.

Text Layout Packages

When software authors recognized that computers and computer printers were quickly replacing typewriters on corporate desks, they decided to create computers that have one of the typewriter's more uncommon but indispensable features: the capacity to produce text pages, usually with a large type of ball, that can be turned into overhead transparencies or slides.

A number of software packages have appeared, dedicated to the task of word charting, but none could be easier to use than the text chart capabilities of Harvard Graphics. And creating text charts in Harvard Graphics means that you can bring the charts into the Draw/Annotate portion of the program and add its potential embellishments, so you don't physically have to "cut and paste" the pages to combine both pictures and words.

With the incorporation of complete text charting capabilities in many business graphics programs, word charting software as a category has become outmoded.

Slide Show Packages

Unlike word charting programs, slide show packages are still popular. These packages enable users to capture bit-mapped graphics images from the screens of other programs or assemble the output files of other graphics software into fun desktop presentations. IBM's PC Storyboard kicked off the category with its simple paint program capabilities and rudimentary charting skills. What truly distinguished PC Storyboard was its capacity to create animated presentations that combined images and provided movie-like transitions from one screen to the next. You had in PC Storyboard an entire arsenal of wipes, pans, fades, weaves, and other transition effects. Show Partner FX, another slide show presentation package, provided superior graphics capabilities and even more animation capabilities.

Harvard Graphics screenshows provide the same array of eye-catching special effects, but the images can be full-blown Harvard Graphics charts, with all the bells and whistles. If you have created bit-mapped graphics in paint programs, you can even incorporate those graphics in a screenshow, perhaps as the background for a Harvard Graphics chart.

Understanding the Harvard Graphics Approach

To understand why people who use Harvard Graphics find it so easy to use and logically organized, you need to understand more about the Harvard Graphics approach to creating charts. Every graphic that Harvard Graphics creates is called a *chart*. A chart is a screen of text or a screen of graphics or a screen that combines both. You begin a new Harvard Graphics chart by entering raw text or numbers onto a text or graph chart's data screen or by importing the data from another program. That alone is enough to produce a chart. Immediately, you can press the F2 (Draw Chart) function key option to preview the simple chart Harvard Graphics creates automatically.

Inevitably, you will think of a few changes and additions you will want to make to the basic chart Harvard Graphics produces. If you're working with a text chart, you can make changes right on the data screen you have filled in. To make changes on a graph chart, you simply tick off the alterations you want by changing the selections on the chart's Titles & Options pages. Each graph chart type has its own specific set of options on its Titles & Options pages. Now your chart is far more informative, embellished with labels, legends, special formatting, and other additions. Charts carried to this stage are sophisticated and have the quality you would expect in a professional business presentation. So far, you have done no actual drawing, but you have created professional-looking charts.

If you have the time and inkling to adorn your chart with more graphics or if you need to highlight some aspect of the information that the chart conveys, you can pull either a text or graphic chart into the special Draw/Annotate feature of Harvard Graphics. Of course, those of you who are truly artistic can skip the earlier steps and jump right to Draw/Annotate to create a new chart by hand. Most people, however, use Draw/Annotate to add lines, boxes, arrows, text comments, or predrawn graphics to a chart. You can bring a text chart into Draw/Annotate to add graphics or bring a graph chart into Draw/Annotate to add text, but otherwise text and graph charts do not intermix unless you combine charts in a multiple chart.

Finally, you can send your chart to a printer, plotter, or slide maker. Or you can create shows that display your chart on-screen.

You can think of using Harvard Graphics as involving four principal activities:

❑ Making text charts

❑ Making graph charts

❑ Drawing new charts or annotating existing charts in Draw/Annotate

❑ Producing output by reproducing charts on paper, on film, or on-screen

All the other uses for Harvard Graphics embody some variation of one of these four activities. In fact, Harvard Graphics offers so many variations that it's the great chameleon of business graphics programs, blending inconspicuously into any environment. Put Harvard Graphics in a corporate art department and churn out professional slides and graphs. Use Harvard Graphics in a marketing department and generate superb sales presentations. Integrate Harvard Graphics into a desktop publishing workstation and serve up professional-quality illustrations and graphics for newsletters and brochures.

Before you finish reading this book, you will become expert at all four activities and you will be ready to discover your own variations. The makers of Harvard Graphics have done an extraordinary job at automating the type of artistry that before has always required the services of a trained professional. But Harvard Graphics, like any fine computer software, is an instrument that you must learn to master. Only after you have become proficient with the program can its subtleties and nuances appear.

Chapter Summary

In this chapter, you have learned about the capabilities of Harvard Graphics. Now the time has come for you to see Harvard Graphics in action. In the next chapter, "Getting Started," you will learn important information about setting up, starting, and using Harvard Graphics, and in Chapter 3, you will take a comprehensive tour through the program.

2

Getting Started

Chapter 1 described the benefits of using Harvard Graphics and some of the philosophies that underlie the program's design. This chapter provides much more pragmatic information, from how to install and start Harvard Graphics to how to navigate through the Harvard Graphics menu structure.

Harvard Graphics is highly regarded because of its simple, intuitive user interface. *User interface*, one of the computer vernacular's newest additions, refers to the methods a software package offers you to control its operation. Some software packages require that you use your keyboard's function keys to issue commands. Some programs provide menus of choices that appear on the screen. Harvard Graphics provides you with a *combination* of approaches to issue commands. More often than not, you can use any of a number of techniques to tell Harvard Graphics what to do next. Later in this chapter, you will learn about the various ways you can control Harvard Graphics. Which method you decide to employ will depend entirely on your personal style.

This chapter also presents a detailed look at other aspects of the Harvard Graphics user interface, such as summoning help information to the screen. It also provides some fundamentals that you will find helpful when joining the Harvard Graphics quick tour in the next chapter.

Installing Harvard Graphics

The complete Harvard Graphics software system, ready for installation into your computer, comes on six disks if you use 5 1/4-inch disks or three disks if you use 3 1/2-inch disks. The Harvard Graphics users' manual gives detailed instructions about how you can install the program either manually or by running the

23

INSTALL program on the disk labeled Utilities. The INSTALL program makes Harvard Graphics do most of the work of setting itself up on your computer's disk drives.

Although you can run Harvard Graphics on a computer without a hard disk, you will find that being able to keep all your Harvard Graphics files readily accessible accelerates your work. Hard disks have become relatively inexpensive, so acquiring one is almost certainly worth the cost.

If you use INSTALL to set up Harvard Graphics on a hard disk, you will find that it copies all the Harvard Graphics files to the directory you specify when you start the INSTALL program. Most likely, this directory will be C:\HG. To start INSTALL, insert the Utilities disk into drive A, type *a:* at the C:\› prompt, and press Enter. Then type *install*.

When you install Harvard Graphics, you may want to create a separate directory in which to store the actual charts you create. By setting up a separate directory for your work—C:\HGDATA, for example—you can use DOS commands to back up or archive your data files easily. In addition, Harvard Graphics can present a list of the charts you create much faster because it does not need to search through as many files, including its own program files, to pull out your charts.

To create a special directory for your work, follow these steps:

1. Make sure that the DOS prompt is on-screen.

2. Type *cd* \ and press Enter to be sure that you are at your hard disk's root directory.

3. Type *md* *hgdata* and press Enter to create a directory for your work. (If you want to name the directory something other than HGDATA, type the name you desire after the backslash.)

Figure 2.1 shows how your screen appears as you carry out this sequence of steps. After you create a new directory, the screen doesn't appear any different, but a new directory now exists to store your data files.

Placing your data files in a subdirectory of the Harvard Graphics program directory provides an additional measure of protection from the hands of inexperienced DOS users. By hiding your work two directory levels deep, you will keep others from accidentally wiping out your work because they will not go near it in their day-to-day use.

To make a subdirectory for your work under the Harvard Graphics directory, follow these steps:

```
C:\>cd \

C:\>md \hgdata

C:\>
```

Fig. 2.1.

Creating a directory for your work.

1. Make sure that you are at the DOS prompt after installing Harvard Graphics with the INSTALL utility.

2. Type *cd \hg* and press Enter to change to the Harvard Graphics directory. (If you chose a name other than \HG for your Harvard Graphics directory, substitute that name instead.)

3. Type *md \hgdata* and press Enter to create a directory for your work called HGDATA under the current directory (C:\HG).

4. Type *cd * and press Enter to return to the root directory.

Figure 2.2 shows how your screen appears as you carry out this sequence of steps.

If you set up \HGDATA under C:\HG, the new directory name is C:\HG\HGDATA. If you choose to place all your charts in a special directory, such as C:\HGDATA or C:\HG\HGDATA, you should modify the Harvard Graphics defaults so the program always uses that directory to retrieve files or to save new files. To specify a directory as the default data directory, select Setup from the Main menu and then select Defaults from the Setup menu. For detailed instructions, see the section called "Setting up Defaults" later in this chapter.

Certain output devices require a special installation procedure even after you complete the standard Harvard Graphics installation. These devices are distinguished by their use of the Virtual Device Interface (VDI). The VDI is special software written to manage the exchange of data between software like Harvard

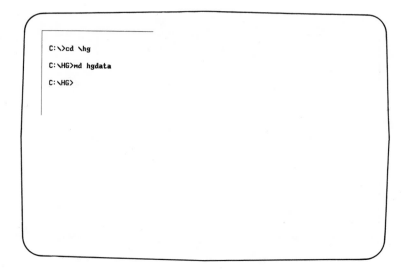

Fig. 2.2.

*Creating a
subdirectory for
your work.*

```
C:\>cd \hg

C:\HG>md hgdata

C:\HG>
```

Graphics and certain output devices. If your output device requires the VDI, its operating instructions will say so. You also will need to carry out the VDI installation if you plan to create Computer Graphics Metafiles (CGM files) for export to other graphics programs or to desktop publishing software. CGM files are discussed in Chapter 9. You will find information about setting up the VDI in an appendix of the Harvard Graphics users' manual.

Starting Harvard Graphics

After you install Harvard Graphics, you can start the program by changing to the directory that contains Harvard Graphics and typing *hg*. Assuming that you have a hard disk, follow these instructions when you see the C:\> or C> DOS prompt:

1. Type *cd \hg* and press Enter to change to the Harvard Graphics directory.

2. Type *hg* and press Enter to start Harvard Graphics.

Note: You can use upper- or lowercase letters or a combination of the two when typing commands.

Those of you who know DOS well may prefer to set up a batch file that automatically changes to the data directory and then loads Harvard Graphics from its own directory. Assuming that the data directory is C:\HGDATA and the Harvard Graphics directory is C:\HG, such a batch file may look like the following:

```
ECHO OFF        ;Turns off DOS echo
CD \HGDATA      ;Changes to the HGDATA directory
C:\HG\HG        ;Loads HG from the C:\HG directory
CD \            ;Returns to the root directory after you quit
                ;Harvard Graphics
```

The comments to the right, preceded by semicolons, are optional.

The Harvard Graphics opening screen, shown in figure 2.3, leaves little doubt about whether you started the program successfully. After the opening screen appears, the Harvard Graphics Main menu appears (see fig. 2.4).

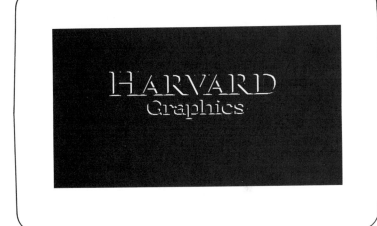

Fig. 2.3.

The Harvard Graphics opening display.

Using the Harvard Graphics Menus

Many user interfaces offer only one method for you to choose program commands. You use the arrow keys to pick an on-screen option, select from a menu by pressing the number corresponding to your choice, press a function key to run a command, or use any one of several other popular approaches. With Harvard Graphics menus, you can use a combination of all these techniques, deciding which to use spontaneously as you work.

If you haven't installed and started Harvard Graphics already, do so now so you can try the methods of selecting from menus, the focus of this section. After you

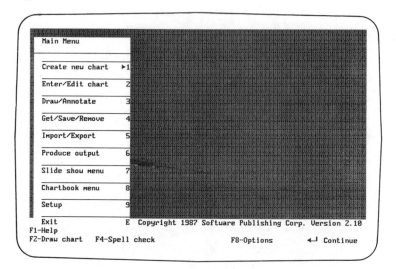

Fig. 2.4.

*The Harvard
Graphics Main
menu.*

pick a menu option, you can press Esc at any time to return to the Main menu to
try another option and another approach.

- ❏ *Selecting with the arrow keys.* Move the highlight up and down the menu
until your choice is highlighted. Then press Enter.

- ❏ *Selecting with the space bar.* Press the space bar to move the highlight down
the list and then press Enter to select an option. If you continue to press
the space bar, the highlight cycles back to the top of the menu.

- ❏ *Selecting with numbers/letters.* Press the number (or letter) to the right of
each menu option. With this approach, you don't need to press Enter after
selecting a menu option.

- ❏ *Selecting with the first letter of the menu option.* Press the first letter of the
menu option you want to choose and then press Enter. If more than one
option share the same first character, press the same key again to move to
the next option with the same first letter.

As you work with Harvard Graphics, you will find a surprising intelligence at
work in its menus. When you first start Harvard Graphics, for example, the highlight is positioned on the Create New Chart option because that option may be
your next logical choice. After you retrieve a chart created earlier, you will find
the highlight automatically positioned on the Enter/Edit Chart option.

Most Harvard Graphics menus are in the same vertical list format as the Main
menu. In addition, most Harvard Graphics screens include a separate horizontal

menu of function key options located across the bottom of the screen. Each function key option includes a one- or two-word reminder of that key's purpose. As you work with Harvard Graphics, you will notice that although the F1-Help option nearly always calls up help information and the F2-Draw chart option nearly always previews the current chart on-screen, most other function key options perform only short-stint jobs, such as setting the size and placement of text or changing from one file directory to another. What a function key does and, therefore, what the menu at the bottom of the screen reads at any one moment depends on the current activity you are performing in Harvard Graphics.

Using a Mouse

If you have a mouse, you have even more ways to use Harvard Graphics menus. By moving the highlight with the mouse and pressing the left mouse button, you can select from among menu options. Pressing the left button is equivalent to pressing the Enter key. To back out of a menu and return to the preceding menu, you can press the right mouse button. Pressing the right mouse button is equivalent to pressing the Esc key. To choose from among the function key choices at the bottom of the screen, you can press both mouse buttons simultaneously; then highlight a function key choice and press the left mouse button. Pressing both mouse buttons together switches between choosing from the vertical menu on-screen and choosing from the horizontal function key menu at the bottom of the screen. Here is a summary:

Mouse Operation	Keyboard Equivalent
Left button	Enter key
Right button	Esc key
Both buttons	Toggle to/from the function key menu

Later, when you learn about using the Titles & Options pages, you will find that moving the mouse cursor off the top or bottom of the screen moves you to the preceding or next Titles & Options page.

Navigating through Harvard Graphics

By examining the Harvard Graphics Main menu, you can get a sense of how the program is organized and how the task of creating business presentations logically flows.

Everything you do in Harvard Graphics starts at the Main menu. Once you leave the Main menu by selecting one of its options, you may not return until you finish creating a chart, assembling a slide show, printing a series of charts, or performing any of the other tasks Harvard Graphics makes possible.

Take a look at the Main menu and notice that its entries are arranged top to bottom in order of their frequency of use. Creating new charts is the task you probably will carry out most frequently, and so the Create New Chart option is positioned at the top of the list. The task you will perform least often is setting the program's defaults, and so the Setup option is located at the bottom of the list.

Choosing the Create New Chart option from the Main menu takes you to the Create New Chart menu, which offers a choice from among a variety of chart types. Although this list looks bewildering at first, it holds only two basic chart types: *text* charts (text and organization charts) to communicate concepts and textual facts and *graph* charts (pie, bar/line, area, and high/low/close charts) to convey numbers and numeric information. The other three options, Multiple Charts, From Chartbook, and Clear Values, are for advanced features covered in later chapters.

Choosing the Enter/Edit Chart option lets you make changes to the current chart in your computer's memory—usually the last chart you were working on in the current Harvard Graphics session. If you just started Harvard Graphics, you will need to create a new chart or retrieve (or "get") a preexisting chart from disk by first using the Get/Save/Remove option from the Main menu.

After you finish a text or graph chart and save it on disk, you can bring the chart into a special Harvard Graphics mode called Draw/Annotate by choosing the Draw/Annotate option from the Main menu. Draw/Annotate mode enables you to embellish your chart by adding hand-drawn graphics, text, or symbols from a library of drawings already created for you. Also, you can start at Draw/Annotate with a blank screen and draw your own chart from scratch.

The next two Main menu options, Import/Export and Produce Output, provide facilities for you to manage the flow of data into and out of Harvard Graphics. By choosing Import/Export, you can bring data into Harvard Graphics from other programs and create special output files to transfer Harvard Graphics charts to other software, such as desktop publishing programs. By choosing Produce Output, you can reproduce your charts on paper or on film.

Choosing the Slide Show Menu option or Chartbook Menu option gives you access to two special Harvard Graphics features. *Slide shows* enable you to create on-screen presentations called *screenshows* or to send sets of charts to an output device, such as a printer, plotter, or film recorder, for reproduction. *Chartbooks* allow you to organize Harvard Graphics *templates*, files that you create to hold the formats for your standard charts.

Setup is the final option on the Main menu (other than Exit, which stops Harvard Graphics altogether). By choosing Setup, you can specify a variety of important settings, such as the type of output device you will be using to print your charts, the type of graphics display you have, and the color palette used by your video card and slide maker. You also can set certain standard characteristics for all your charts, such as whether they will be oriented horizontally or vertically on the page. The next section discusses the Setup options in detail.

Setting Up Defaults

Before you begin working in earnest, you should set up Harvard Graphics for your needs and for the particular combination of equipment you will be using. You can set up these defaults by using Setup on the Main menu. When you select Setup, the Setup menu appears (see fig. 2.5).

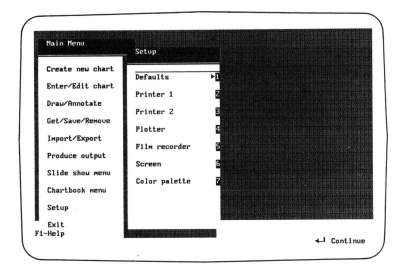

Fig. 2.5.

The Setup menu.

The Setup menu allows you to inform Harvard Graphics about the types of hardware you will use for this session and future Harvard Graphics sessions. From the Setup menu, you can specify the brand of output device you will employ to reproduce your charts, the type of graphics display you have, and the variety of colors —called the *color palette*—used by your video card and slide maker.

The Defaults option is the most important option on the Setup menu. When you select Defaults, the Default Settings screen appears (see fig. 2.6). The options on the Default Settings screen let you set certain starting conditions for all subsequent charts, such as the disk directory for chart storage, the orientation for charts (either vertical or horizontal), and the typefaces used for chart text. This section describes all the Setup options and covers setting up Harvard Graphics for your equipment. The first option, Defaults, is covered next. This option lets you set the default chart directory.

Fig. 2.6.

The Default Settings screen.

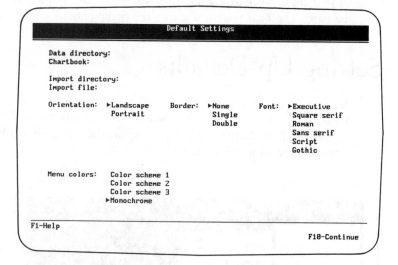

Note: If you change the defaults according to the instructions that follow and find that they don't "take" (the next time you load Harvard Graphics, the defaults are back to their original setting), you must reinstall Harvard Graphics from the disks. This condition indicates that Harvard Graphics has been moved from one directory to another on your hard disk. Therefore, Harvard Graphics no longer knows where to look for the configuration information you updated when you changed the defaults. To move the Harvard Graphics program files, you must delete them from their original directory and reinstall them in a new directory. When you move your data files to the new directory, be sure to copy the file HG.DIR to the new directory, too. This file holds a table of contents and the descriptions you supplied for the data files on your disk.

Changing the Chart Directory

Unless you specify otherwise, Harvard Graphics saves all the new charts you create in the same directory that holds the Harvard Graphics program. If your hard disk is drive C, that directory is probably C:\HG. By specifying a special directory to store your work, you can instruct Harvard Graphics to save new charts there. When you tell the program to "get" a chart (retrieve a chart that has already been created), the program automatically looks in that special directory, too.

Before you specify a new directory for charts, that directory must already exist on your hard disk. You can create a new directory by using the Make Directory (MD) DOS command or by using any of the popular disk management utilities that allow you to manage the files and directories on your hard disk. See "Installing Harvard Graphics" earlier in this chapter for a simple procedure to set up a directory for your work.

To specify a different default data directory, follow these steps:

1. Select Setup from the Main menu.

2. Select Defaults from the Setup menu. The cursor will be positioned next to the Data directory prompt. Unless you already specified a different data directory, this entry will be blank.

3. Type the name of the new directory for your charts—*c:\hg\hgdata*, for example—and press Enter.

Now you can make more changes to the Default Settings screen by pressing Tab to move from field to field, or you can return to the Main menu by pressing F10 (Continue).

Selecting the Chartbook To Open

By entering a chartbook name on the Default Settings screen, you can have Harvard Graphics open a specific chartbook automatically each time the program starts. Chartbooks are special Harvard Graphics files that store collections of pre-formatted charts, called templates. You will find detailed information about both templates and chartbooks in Chapter 8. If you haven't created a chartbook yet, leave the Chartbook entry blank.

After you do create a chartbook that you want Harvard Graphics to open at the beginning of each session, select Setup from the Main menu and select Defaults from the Setup menu; press the Tab key to move the cursor to the Chartbook prompt and enter the name of the chartbook to open. Harvard Graphics will always look for the chartbook in the data directory you specified on the first line of the Default Settings screen.

Specifying an Import Directory and Import File

Later, when you start to build graph charts with numeric information, you will learn that you can import data from the files of other software—from a 1-2-3 worksheet or an ASCII file on your hard disk, for example. By using the Import directory and Import file settings on the Default Settings screen, you can specify the directory in which Harvard Graphics always looks for an import data file and, if you want, the specific import file to use.

To enter a default import directory and import file, move the cursor to the Import directory and Import file prompts by pressing the Tab key, type the appropriate entries, and press Enter after each.

If you regularly import data from Lotus® worksheets, for example, and you keep all worksheets in a directory called C:\LOTUS, you can enter *c:\lotus* at the Import directory prompt. If the worksheet you nearly always import data from is called DATA.WK1, you can enter *data.wk1* after the Import file prompt. Note that you must specify the file's three-character extension in addition to its file name. Of course, when you import data into a graph chart, you always can override the current Import directory and Import file settings. But by providing defaults, you can instruct Harvard Graphics to suggest the most likely directory and file name candidates and save yourself a little time and energy.

Setting Defaults for Orientation, Border, and Font

The next three entries on the Default Settings screen enable you to establish three important starting settings for all future charts. Unless you choose a setting that differs from one of these defaults when you actually create a chart, Harvard Graphics uses these settings for all new charts.

Orientation

By establishing a default chart orientation, you can determine whether the new charts will appear horizontally or vertically on the page. Figure 2.7 illustrates the difference between landscape and portrait orientation.

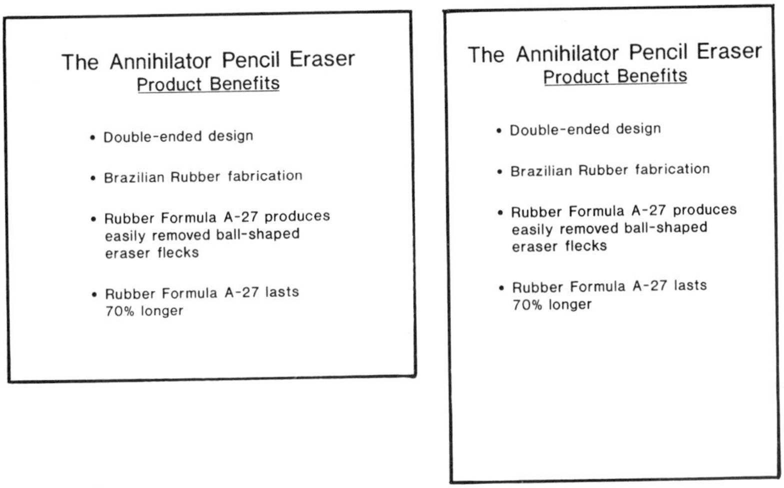

<table>
<tr>
<td>
The Annihilator Pencil Eraser
<u>Product Benefits</u>

• Double-ended design

• Brazilian Rubber fabrication

• Rubber Formula A-27 produces easily removed ball-shaped eraser flecks

• Rubber Formula A-27 lasts 70% longer
</td>
<td>
The Annihilator Pencil Eraser
<u>Product Benefits</u>

• Double-ended design

• Brazilian Rubber fabrication

• Rubber Formula A-27 produces easily removed ball-shaped eraser flecks

• Rubber Formula A-27 lasts 70% longer
</td>
</tr>
</table>

Fig. 2.7.

Landscape and Portrait chart orientations.

The Landscape option produces a chart sideways on a page. Landscape is appropriate for many printed charts and graphs and for displaying charts on the screen. It is especially useful if you intend to create slides that are oriented horizontally. Unless you change the setup default when you first use Harvard Graphics, you will find that the program is preset to produce all charts in landscape orientation.

The Portrait option produces a chart vertically on a page. Portrait is particularly appropriate for text charts designed for printed handouts.

To set the default orientation, press the Tab key repeatedly until the cursor moves to the Orientation prompt on the Default Settings screen. The entry with the small pointer to its left is the current setting. Landscape is the initial Harvard Graphics default, so the pointer should be just to the left of the Landscape option. To move the pointer to the next entry, press the space bar, press the first letter of the entry, or use the up- and down-arrow keys. When the correct entry is highlighted, press Tab or Enter to move to the next setting or press F10 (Continue) to return to the Setup menu. When you create a new chart, you can decide to override the default orientation setting by pressing F8 (Options). Information about the F8-Options selection is provided later in this chapter.

Border

With Harvard Graphics, you can add either a single- or double-line border around each chart or include no border at all. Both borders are illustrated in figure 2.8. A *border* is a box that encloses a chart, adding accent. The initial default is for no borders. You may choose to add a single- or double-line border by pressing Tab to move the cursor to the Border option and selecting an option by using the space bar, pressing the first character of the option, or using the up- or down-arrow keys to highlight the option. If you need to make no further changes to the defaults, press F10 (Continue) to return to the Setup menu. To continue to modify the defaults, press Tab to move to the next entry on the Default Settings screen.

Later, when you begin creating charts, you will learn that you can preview charts on-screen by pressing F2 (Draw Chart). When you preview a chart with a border, though, the border does not appear on-screen. To see the border, you must preview the chart just before you print it by choosing Produce Output from the Main menu and then pressing F2 (Preview). You will find more information about printing in Chapter 9.

Even though you have established a default on the Default Settings screen, you can override your choice for a border later, when you actually create a new chart. To override your choice, press F8 (Options), which is discussed later in this chapter.

Font

Normally, Harvard Graphics allows you to employ only one font for the text in each chart. A *font* is a particular style of character. You may be more familiar with the term *typeface*, but the two terms are interchangeable in Harvard Graphics. Harvard Graphics provides six different fonts, illustrated in figure 2.9. The initial default font is Executive. To choose another font for all text on future charts, move the cursor to the list of possible fonts and choose from among them by using whichever selection method you prefer. To confirm your selection, press F10 (Continue) or press Tab to move the cursor to the Menu colors option at the bottom of the page.

When you are ready to create a new chart, you can select a font other than the default font by pressing F8 (Options).

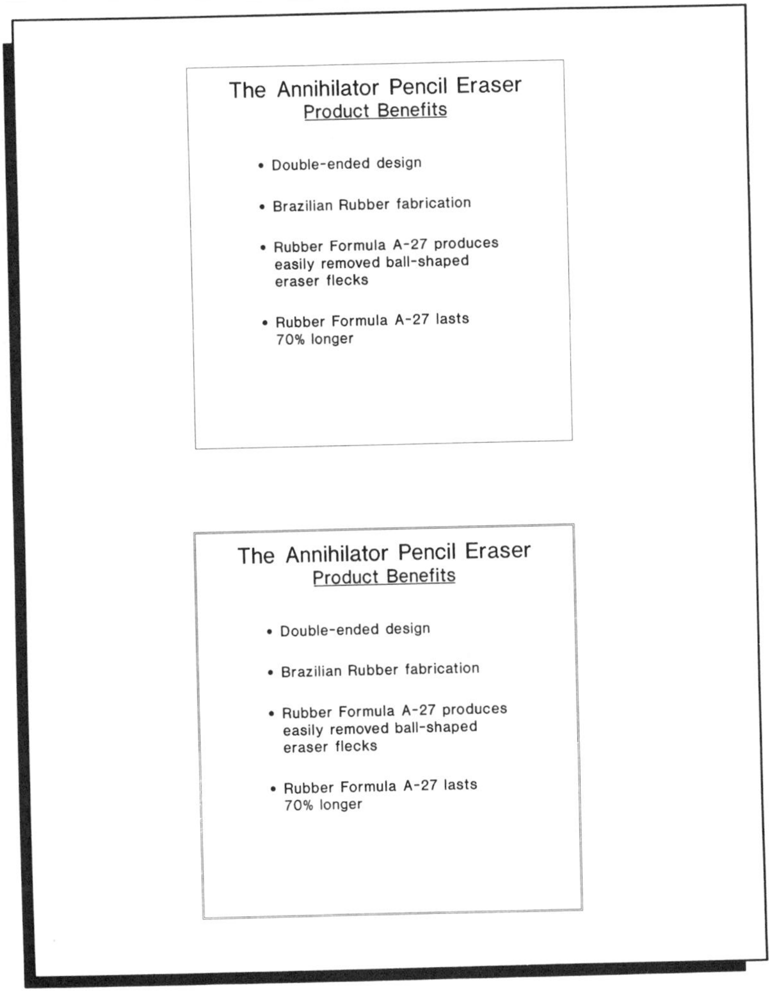

Fig. 2.8.

A single- and double-line border.

Setting a Menu Color Scheme

Even if you have trouble color-coordinating the outfits you wear, you should be able to achieve a pleasing combination of menu colors on-screen because Harvard Graphics lets you choose from only three tastefully selected menu color schemes other than monochrome.

Fig. 2.9.

The six Harvard Graphics fonts.

Executive

Square Serif

Roman

Sans Serif

Script

Gothic

To choose a color scheme, move the cursor to the Menu colors prompt at the bottom of the Default Settings screen by pressing the Tab key repeatedly. Then select the option you want and press Enter. You will see the effect of the change as soon as you press F10 to return to the Setup menu. Of course, as soon as you leave Harvard Graphics, the screen will revert to its original colors. You may find that Monochrome is the preferred setting if you use a monochrome monitor with a color/graphics card. Some of the earlier COMPAQ® computers use this combination.

Specifying Hardware Options

Harvard Graphics supports a wide variety of output devices and video options, but the program will not know what you have attached to your computer unless you tell it. The next four options on the Setup menu let you configure Harvard Graphics properly for the particular combination of hardware you use.

Your system may use a standard dot-matrix or laser printer to produce text and a color printer for graphics. You can configure printer 1 and printer 2 separately if you have two different types of printer connected to your computer. When you print a chart, you can specify which of the two printers Harvard Graphics should prepare output for.

To configure Harvard Graphics for any combination of two printers, a plotter, and a film recorder, follow this approach for each device:

1. From the Setup menu, select the hardware device for which you want to set a configuration.

2. On the setup screen that appears, use the arrow keys to highlight the choice that matches the make and model of your equipment. Figure 2.10 shows the Printer 1 Setup screen. On some computer screens, you cannot see highlighting properly. If your choice does not become highlighted on your computer's screen, you can look at the bottom of the screen to see your current choice.

3. Press F10 to continue.

4. From the Parallel/Serial overlay that appears next (see fig. 2.11), choose options according to the type of connection to the printer you are using. Then press Enter.

```
                        Printer 1 Setup

IBM  Graphics Printer    EPSON   FX,LX,RX      TOSHIBA  P1340,P1350,P1351
     Proprinter,XL,II            EX,JX                  P321,P341,P351
     ProprinterX24,XL24          MX                     P351C
     QuietwriterII,III           LQ 800,1000            PageLaser12
     Color Printer               LQ 1500
     Color Jetprinter            LQ 2500       QUME     LaserTEN,+
     Personal PagePrinter        GQ 3500
                                               AST      TurboLaser
HP   LaserJet,+,500+,II  OKIDATA ML 84,92,93
     ThinkJet                    ML 182,183    APPLE    LaserWriter
     QuietJet,+                  ML 192,193
     PaintJet                    ML 292,293    CALCOMP  ColorMaster
     DeskJet                     ML 294
                                 LaserLine 6   MATRIX   TT200
NEC  P5,P6,P7
     P5XL,P9XL,CP6,CP7   XEROX   4020          TEKTRONIX 4696
     LC-860 (LaserJet)           4045
     LC-890 (PostScript)                       UDI      Printer
     Printer: LaserJet,+,500+,II

F1-Help                                        F10-Continue
```

Fig. 2.10.

The Printer 1 Setup screen.

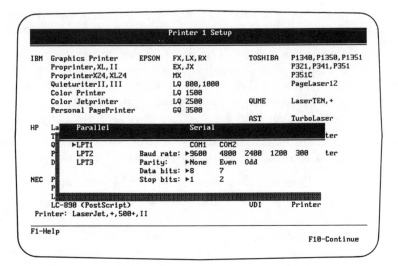

Fig. 2.11.

The Parallel/Serial overlay.

If you are communicating with an output device through a standard parallel printer port, choose the appropriate port (either LPT1, LPT2, or LPT3). If you are communicating with an output device through the serial port, you need to specify whether the port is COM1 or COM2, and you need to select appropriate communications parameters (Baud rate, Parity, Data bits, and Stop bits). The default communications parameters probably will work with your serial output device, but you should check the device's users' manual for specific recommendations.

If your printer or plotter communicates with Harvard Graphics through the Virtual Device Interface (VDI), a communications protocol that interprets between graphics software and certain hardware, you will not see the Parallel/Serial overlay when you select VDI Printer or VDI Plotter and press F10. But your installation is not yet complete. You need to set up the VDI device driver provided with Harvard Graphics. For information on setting up the VDI driver, see Appendix D in the Harvard Graphics users' manual.

If you use a plotter for your output, bear in mind that plotters, as a rule, are incapable of printing three-dimensional graphics. In addition, some of the symbols discussed in Chapter 7 are not supported by plotters.

To configure Harvard Graphics for the graphics card and monitor you're using, select Screen from the Setup menu. Harvard Graphics has automatically configured itself for the screen you are currently using and has made it the default screen. You will need to select an alternate screen only if you have a second graphics card in your system and want to use it rather than the default screen.

You also may need to change the default screen if you plan to display screen-shows. Certain graphics card and monitor combinations will not display screen-show effects. If you have an IBM PS/2™, a VGA card, or VEGA Deluxe, you must select EGA color from the Screen Setup screen to display screenshows prop-erly. If you have any of the Toshiba gas-plasma portables (T3100, T3200, T5100, or T5200), you must choose CGA color or CGA monochrome to see screen-show effects.

If you plan to use a monochrome card with an EGA or a VGA, you will not see screenshow effects at all. The same holds true if you use a VDI or DGIS graphics adapter.

Modifying the Color Palette

The final option on the Setup menu is Color Palette. With this option, you can alter the palette of colors Harvard Graphics uses when it displays charts on an EGA, VGA, VEGA Deluxe, or DGIS graphics card or sends chart output to a film recorder to create slides.

Overriding the Defaults with F8-Options

The selections you make on the Setup menu remain in effect until you want to change them. Suppose that you're creating a chart one day, and you decide that you want to vary from the orientation, border, and font defaults established on the Default Settings screen. You can use the F8-Options selection to change the defaults for the current session. Pressing F8 summons the Current Chart Options overlay (see fig. 2.12). When you quit Harvard Graphics after setting the options on this overlay and start the program again later, the defaults will revert to the settings on the Default Settings screen.

Make a habit of checking the F8-Options selection before starting any new chart to make sure that these defaults are properly set for the chart you want to make next. If someone else uses Harvard Graphics before you, that user may use the F8-Options selection to vary the default settings for his or her charts. There's no need for you to find that out when you preview the chart later.

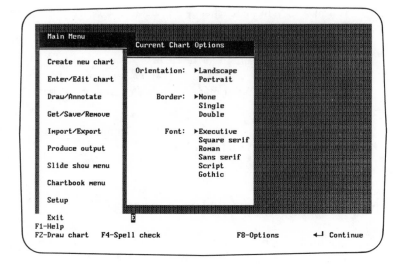

Fig. 2.12.

The Current Chart Options overlay.

Getting On-Line Help

At any point as you work, you may summon help information to the screen by pressing F1 (Help). The help information that appears pertains to the current action Harvard Graphics is carrying out. This is called *context-sensitive help*. Check the bottom right corner of the help screen. If you see PgDn-More help, you can see more help information by pressing the PgDn key. To return to your work and clear away the help information, press Esc.

Chapter Summary

In this chapter, you installed and set up Harvard Graphics. You also learned how to use the Harvard Graphics menus. That information will be invaluable to you when you join the quick-start tour of Harvard Graphics in the next chapter. The tour gets you up and running quickly and shows you how easily you can create expressive and appealing charts with Harvard Graphics.

3

Quick Start to Harvard Graphics: Taking a Guided Tour

In the chapters that follow, you will examine the nitty-gritty aspects of creating graphs and charts of all types. But first, in this chapter, you will receive an overview of how Harvard Graphics works. Before you complete this guided tour, you will learn some of the most appealing features of Harvard Graphics. In just a few minutes, you will see the program's wide range of uses and its impressive simplicity. And you will see how Harvard Graphics' built-in chart blueprints can help you achieve good graphic design.

With Harvard Graphics, you can create sophisticated charts even if you don't have knowledge of computer programming or training in artistic design. In fact, even Harvard Graphics users who have never before used a computer can start fashioning eye-catching charts almost immediately.

In this tour, you will prepare several text and graph charts, and before you're done, you will enhance these charts with Harvard Graphics' special Draw/Annotate feature. Of course, you will need to set up Harvard Graphics before beginning, so follow the installation instructions and starting procedures covered in Chapter 2, "Getting Started." Then rejoin this tour.

After you start Harvard Graphics and the opening graphic display appears, you are taken to the Harvard Graphics Main menu.

Imagine that you are on the board of a well-known office supply manufacturer. Suddenly, you learn that the presentation to tomorrow's stockholders meeting has fallen into your lap, and no one is available to assist you in your preparation.

Harvard Graphics is already on the office computer's screen, however, so you decide to use the program to assemble the visuals to accompany your presentation. Good decision.

For tomorrow's speech, you will need to describe (in *positive* tones) the following criteria:

❑ The corporation's objectives for the fourth quarter

❑ The corporation's second-quarter revenues

❑ The projects with the largest effect on the second-quarter's profits

Harvard Graphics is the ideal choice for presenting all this information visually. You decide that a list of bulleted points will be perfect for your first chart, showing corporate objectives. Harvard Graphics can provide a chart called a *bullet list*, which is an ideal tool for listing a series of points or summarizing the key issues that you will elaborate on in a speech.

The rest of your presentation conveys numeric information calculated from the data you have on-hand. Using the program's bar or line charts, you can present numeric information visually and even have Harvard Graphics perform financial calculations on your data as the program prepares a series of charts.

So with the help of Harvard Graphics, you can prepare comprehensive and creative charts for tomorrow's presentation, a task you will accomplish as you complete this tour.

Selecting from the Main Menu

The Harvard Graphics Main menu (see fig. 3.1) is the starting point for nearly all the program's major functions. The Main menu appears immediately after you see the Harvard Graphics logo screen when you start the program. From the Main menu, you can select the type of chart to create, save a chart on disk, send a chart to a printer or plotter, or import data files from other software applications into a chart. You also can use the Main menu options to assemble charts into slide shows, create multiple charts, and produce *chartbooks*, collections of commonly used charts.

To make a selection from the Harvard Graphics Main menu, you can choose from among many methods:

❑ Move the cursor by using the arrow keys to highlight a menu choice and then press Enter.

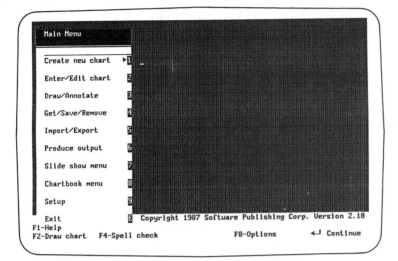

Fig. 3.1.

The Main menu.

❏ Press the number or letter to the right of a menu choice.

❏ Press the space bar until your menu choice is highlighted and then press Enter.

Using the space bar to select from among options is a method that works consistently at nearly every menu and overlay that Harvard Graphics presents to you.

Using a Mouse or the Keyboard

The assumption in this tour is that you are controlling Harvard Graphics with your keyboard only. If you want to combine a mouse with the keyboard, you will find these three hints helpful:

❏ Press the left mouse button to make a selection (same as pressing Enter).

❏ Press the right mouse button to back out of a function (same as pressing Esc).

❏ Press both mouse buttons simultaneously to select from among the function key choices at the bottom of the screen. Point to a command and press the left mouse button to choose it.

Checking the Default Settings

As a rule, before you create your first chart, you should examine the current session defaults by pressing F8 (Options) at the Main menu.

Defaults determine how Harvard Graphics draws a chart if you do nothing more than enter data and let the program create the chart. By changing the defaults, you can determine how all subsequent charts in your current session are created. For example, you can decide whether you want all charts to be in portrait (vertical) or landscape (horizontal) format, and you can set a font—or typeface—for the text in your new charts.

For the first chart in this tour, you will select a portrait orientation and leave all the other standard settings as they are. Portrait orientation is appropriate for the overhead transparencies you are creating. After all, you may make this same presentation at corporate regional offices later. At the corporate regional offices, you can count on having nothing more sophisticated than an overhead projector.

To select a portrait orientation, follow these steps:

1. Press F8 (Options) at the Main menu. The Current Chart Options overlay appears (see fig. 3.2).

2. At the Orientation field, use the space bar to highlight Portrait and press Enter. The cursor moves to the Border field. A *border* is a line or set of lines that surrounds your chart, serving as a frame for your graphic. For this set of charts, you do not need to include a border because your charts eventually will become transparencies. The cardboard holder that you use for transparencies hides the border. (For the curious among you who turn on the border anyway, be forewarned that it will not be displayed when you use the F2-Draw chart selection.)

3. Press Enter to move to the Font options and press F10 (Continue) to return to the Main menu and save your changes.

The Executive font option works well with the text and graph charts you will create in this tour because it is a clean typeface that is easy to read. Therefore, leave this default font option.

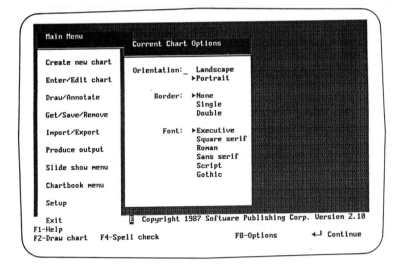

```
Main Menu
                 Current Chart Options

Create new chart
                 Orientation:_  Landscape
Enter/Edit chart                ▶Portrait

Draw/Annotate        Border:  ▶None
                              Single
Get/Save/Remove               Double

Import/Export         Font:  ▶Executive
                              Square serif
Produce output                Roman
                              Sans serif
Slide show menu               Script
                              Gothic
Chartbook menu

Setup

    Exit          ▢ Copyright 1987 Software Publishing Corp. Version 2.10
F1-Help
F2-Draw chart    F4-Spell check            F8-Options       ↵ Continue
```

Fig. 3.2.

The Current Chart Options overlay.

Creating a Text Chart

Now you are ready to create the first chart in your presentation: a bullet list showing marketing objectives for the next quarter. The marketing objectives follow:

- ☐ Increase sales of mechanical pencils by 10 percent.

- ☐ Add 10 distributors to the roster.

- ☐ Improve corporate image with advertising.

- ☐ Increase sales by instituting a corporate training program for distributors.

In the sections that follow, you will learn how you can make this list into a presentable bullet chart.

Selecting a Bullet List Chart

To create a bullet list chart, follow these steps:

1. Select Create New Chart from the Main menu. The Create New Chart menu appears.

2. Select Text from the Create New Chart menu. The Text Chart Styles menu appears (see fig. 3.3).

3. Select Bullet List from the Text Chart Styles menu.

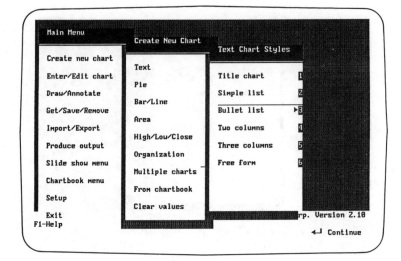

Fig. 3.3.

The menu path to the Text Chart Styles menu.

Because you changed the F8-Options settings earlier (from Landscape to Portrait orientation), an overlay appears and you see the message Latest changes have not been saved. Press Enter to continue; Esc to Cancel. This warning message is helpful when you finish one chart and begin another. If you press Enter, the current chart is removed from the computer's memory and, therefore, the screen. Of course, if you have already saved the chart on disk, you can ignore the warning and press Enter to continue. In this case, however, you have changed only the orientation setting without actually creating a new chart. Because you didn't create a chart to save, simply press Enter to continue. The Bullet List data screen appears.

Use the Bullet List data screen to type in the actual text you plan to include in the finished chart and to make changes to the chart's appearance. Harvard Graphics lets you change both the size of the letters and their attributes (italic, boldface, underline, and so on).

Now you will complete the Bullet List data screen so it matches the sample completed screen shown in figure 3.4.

Because this chart lists the marketing objectives for the next year, use the first three lines of the Bullet List data screen to enter a title, subtitle, and footnote onto the chart. Use the Tab key to move from line to line after you have entered each item. For a title, use *Marketing Objectives*. For a subtitle (in a slightly smaller type size), use *Superior Office Supplies*. Use the footnote line to specify the date *as of November 1989*. Including a note to the reader, such as *Company confidential material*, is another common use of the footnote.

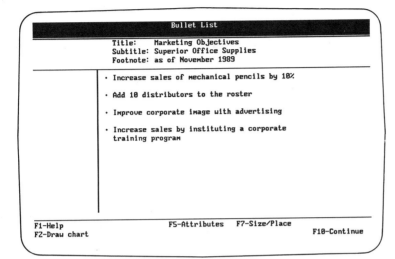

Fig. 3.4.

The Bullet List screen with text entries.

Enter these titles now. Now tab down to the open area below and type your first bulleted item after the bullet that appears. Bullets appear on every other line in a bullet chart. To create a new bullet, be sure to press Enter twice at the end of a complete bulleted item. If a bulleted item consists of two lines (see the last item in fig. 3.4), just press Enter once at the end of the first line to type in the second line of text for the same bullet.

If you make a typing mistake, use the Backspace key to delete the character you just typed or press Del to delete the character at the cursor's location.

After you finish entering text, press F2 (Draw Chart) to preview the chart with its current settings.

Your chart should now look like the one shown in figure 3.5.

After you examine your work in progress, press Esc to return to the Bullet List data screen so you can continue working on the chart. This is the standard iterative process of creating a Harvard Graphics chart. You enter data into the data screen, preview the chart, and then return to the data screen to adjust the chart's appearance. After several iterations back and forth (previewing the chart and modifying its appearance), you decide when the chart is ready and save it on disk.

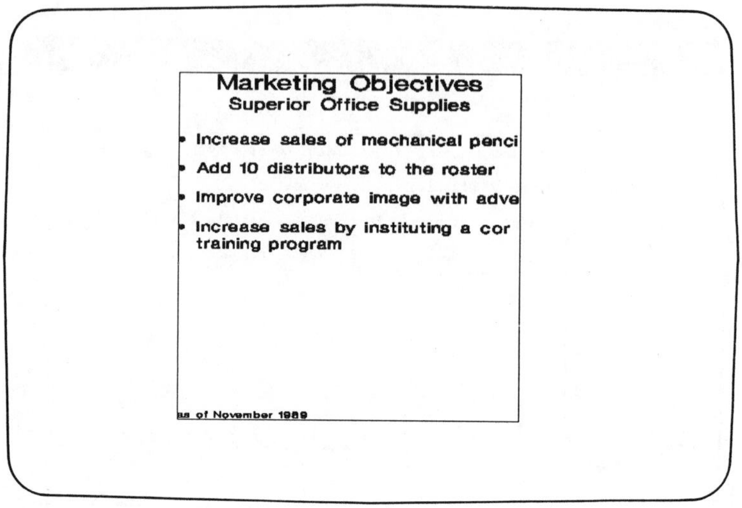

Fig. 3.5.

Previewing by pressing F2 (Draw Chart).

Adjusting Text Size on a Bullet List

When you previewed the chart by pressing F2, you no doubt noticed that something was seriously wrong. Some of the lines of text overflowed the portrait page. No problem. With the Size/Place command, you easily can adjust the size of text characters to fit the available space.

To call up the Size/Place overlay while viewing the Bullet List data screen, press F7. Figure 3.6 shows the Bullet List data screen with the Size/Place overlay visible.

With the Size/Place overlay in view, follow these steps:

1. Type over the Size number to the left of the title, changing the number from 8 to 6.

2. Use the Tab key to move the cursor to the Size number to the left of the first bullet. This number sets the size of all bulleted items on the list. Press Ctrl-Del to remove the number 5.5. Use 4 as the new size. As you work with Harvard Graphics, you will get a feel for the relationship between the Size settings and the actual size of the resulting text.

3. Use the Tab key to move the cursor to the five possible bullet shapes on the menu and press the space bar to select the checkmark bullet.

4. Press F10 (Continue).

5. Press F2 (Draw Chart) to view the chart. The result is shown in figure 3.7.

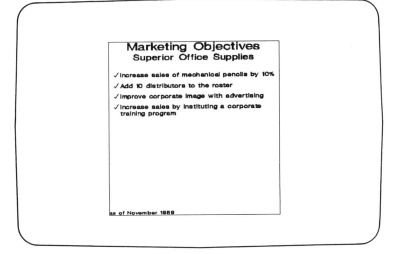

```
 Size    Place              Bullet List
 8      L ►C  R    Title:    Marketing Objectives
 6      L ►C  R    Subtitle: Superior Office Supplies
 3.5    ►L  C  R   Footnote: as of November 1989

 5.5    L ►C  R    · Increase sales of mechanical pencils by 10%

 Bullet Shape      · Add 10 distributors to the roster

 ►·  -  ∫  ■  #    · Improve corporate image with advertising

 Indent: 0         · Increase sales by instituting a corporate
                     training program




 F1-Help                    F5-Attributes   F7-Size/Place
 F2-Draw chart                                       F10-Continue
```

Fig. 3.6.

The Bullet List
screen with the Size/
Place overlay.

Marketing Objectives
Superior Office Supplies

√ Increase sales of mechanical pencils by 10%
√ Add 10 distributors to the roster
√ Improve corporate image with advertising
√ Increase sales by instituting a corporate
 training program

as of November 1989

Fig. 3.7.

A bullet list with
the correct text sizes
and a new bullet
type.

Regardless of whether you decide that the chart is now complete and ready for printing or that you need to make additional changes to its format, you should save the chart on disk before proceeding. To save the chart, return to the Main menu by pressing Esc twice.

Saving the Chart

To save your chart, follow these steps at the Main menu:

1. Select Get/Save/Remove.

2. Select Save Chart from the Get/Save/Remove menu. Figure 3.8 shows the Save Chart overlay.

3. Type a name of up to eight characters for the chart and press Enter. An example name is OBJECTVS. Don't worry about typing the CHT file name extension. Harvard Graphics adds the extension for you when you save the chart.

4. If you want to replace the description Harvard Graphics derives from the title line of your chart, simply type a new description over the old. For now, leave the current description.

5. Press Enter to save the chart. The message Saving... appears on the lower right corner of the screen.

Fig. 3.8.

Saving the chart.

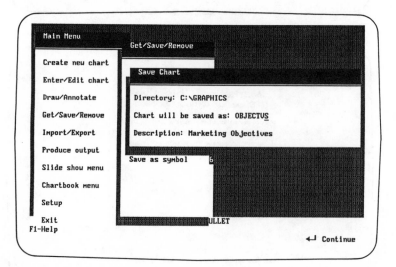

Now you have saved your chart, but you have forgotten to emphasize the bulleted item about increasing sales. After all, increasing sales is the point of your whole presentation. Why not italicize the words "Increase sales" for emphasis? With Harvard Graphics, you can italicize selected words easily by using the Attributes command, discussed next.

Using the Attributes Command
To Set Text Characteristics

Even after you save a chart, you can still revise it. As long as you have not started a new chart, the current chart is still available for immediate editing. If you have started a new chart already and you want to return to the saved chart for editing, you can retrieve it by using the Get/Save/Remove command. At the Main menu, select Enter/Edit Chart to change some of the current chart's text attributes to italic.

At the Bullet List data screen, follow this procedure to change the attributes of selected words:

1. Tab to the first bullet and position the cursor at the first letter of the word Increase.

2. Press F5 (Attributes). The Attributes menu bar appears at the bottom of the screen (see fig. 3.9).

3. Use the right-arrow key to highlight the words Increase sales.

4. Use the Tab key to move the cursor on the Attributes menu bar to the Italic option and press the space bar to turn on the italic attribute. A small pointer appears just to the left of the Italic option to indicate that the italic attribute is on.

5. Press F10 (Continue).

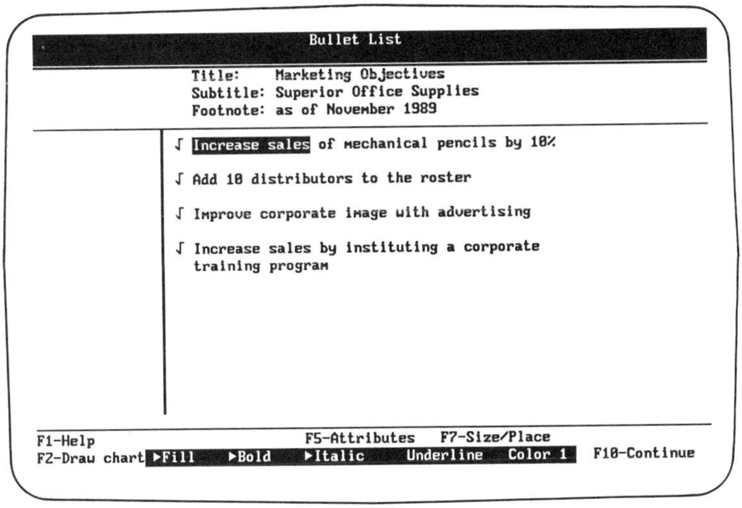

```
                        Bullet List
        Title:    Marketing Objectives
        Subtitle: Superior Office Supplies
        Footnote: as of November 1989

     √ Increase sales of mechanical pencils by 10%

     √ Add 10 distributors to the roster

     √ Improve corporate image with advertising

     √ Increase sales by instituting a corporate
       training program




F1-Help              F5-Attributes    F7-Size/Place
F2-Draw chart ▶Fill    ▶Bold   ▶Italic   Underline  Color 1   F10-Continue
```

Fig. 3.9.

The Attributes menu bar.

Nothing appears to happen on the screen, but when you press F2, you will see the result of the changes you made.

Press F2 to see that the italic attribute really worked. Save the chart again with the same name, OBJECTVS, by returning to the Main menu, selecting Get/Save/Remove, and then selecting Save Chart from the Get/Save/Remove menu.

Now the first chart in your presentation is complete, and you are ready to communicate your enthusiasm about a new topic, the remarkable strength of last quarter's revenues. To do that, you will create a second chart, a bar chart.

Creating a Bar Chart

The next chart you will create in this guided tour presents the organization's second-quarter revenues. You will create a bar chart that displays three months of sales for several products so others can see easily which product was the leading seller.

Bar charts are perhaps the most visually appealing and elegant charts in the repertoire of Harvard Graphics, and they are probably the most familiar type of chart, too. Bar charts provide the opportunity for the reader or audience to visualize and compare numbers displayed graphically. To create a bar chart, select Create New Chart from the Main menu and then select Bar/Line from the Create New Chart menu.

Setting the X-Axis

When you select the Bar/Line option, the X Data Type Menu overlay appears. In this overlay, you make choices about how you want the X data segregated. This chart will segregate data by month, so along the x-axis of your chart, Harvard Graphics will display the results for month 1, month 2, and month 3. Actually, because you will display monthly results for several products, each month will consist of a set of bars—one bar for each product in the Superior Office Supplies line.

To set the Month option on the X Data Type Menu overlay, follow these steps:

1. Use the space bar to select Month for the X data type prompt and press Enter. The cursor moves to the next option, Starting with.

2. Type *Apr* and press Enter. The cursor moves to the next option, Ending with.

3. Type *Jun* and press Enter.

4. Press Enter at the Increment field to leave it blank.

The Increment field determines how many units Harvard Graphics increases each new X data setting. Suppose, for example, that you set X data type to Day and specified *Sun* and *Sat* as your x-axis data starting and ending points. Setting the increment to 2 will give the result of *Sun, Tues, Thurs,* and *Sat* only. Every other day will be listed on the x-axis because you chose 2 for the increment. If you leave the Increment field blank, Harvard Graphics assumes an increment of 1. That's the reason you pressed Enter without specifying an increment at this prompt.

Entering Data on the Data Screen and Previewing the Graph

After you complete the X Data Type Menu overlay, the Bar/Line Chart Data screen appears (see fig. 3.10), which performs the same function as the text data screen. The Bar/Line Chart Data screen allows you to enter the exact data you want charted.

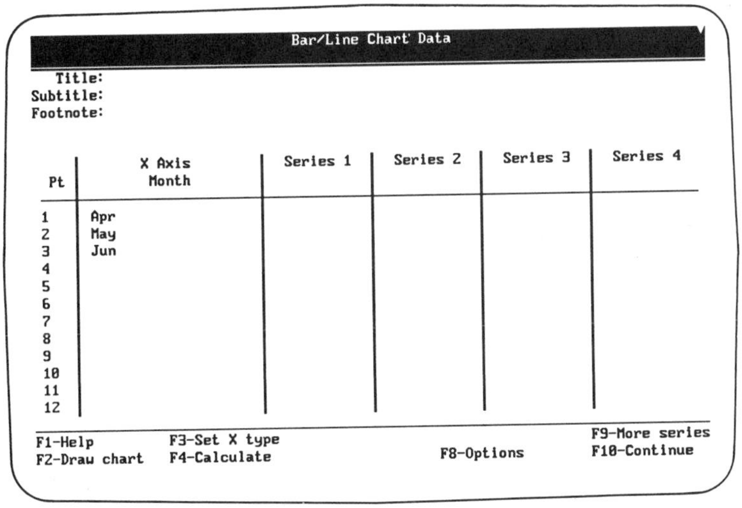

Fig. 3.10.

The Bar/Line Chart Data screen.

Notice that the leftmost column is labeled X Axis Month. Harvard Graphics already has entered *Apr* through *Jun* based on the information you provided on the X Data Type Menu overlay. In fact, if you had typed the full month names on the X Data Type Menu overlay, Harvard Graphics would have supplied full month names (April, May, and June) rather than abbreviations.

On the Bar/Line Chart Data screen, you will see also four columns labeled Series 1, Series 2, Series 3, and Series 4. Pressing F9 (More Series) shows the next four series (5 through 8). To return to Series 1, 2, 3, and 4, press F9 once again. This is where you will enter your actual sales data.

A *series* is a related set of data about one subject, such as the growth in population of a county over a period of years. In bar charts, series are represented by a set of bars of one color or pattern.

Harvard Graphics lets you enter eight series, so you can graph eight separate sets of information. But using more than four or five series in a chart can make the chart look cluttered and less graphic.

With this chart, you want to show the revenue from sales of Mechanical pencils, Swirly pens, and Annihilator erasers. In the chart that you need to produce for Superior Office Supplies, each product's sales over the course of the second quarter will be a single series.

You assemble the data as follows:

Months	Mechanical Pencils	Swirly Pens	Annihilator Erasers
April	3,993	6,995	12,878
May	4,318	5,937	10,698
June	4,957	8,490	13,639

The set of data about Mechanical pencils is Series 1. The data about Swirly pens is Series 2. And the data about Annihilator erasers is Series 3.

Because this bar chart shows the second-quarter revenues by product of three writing tools, give the chart the title *Pens, Pencils, & Accessories*. The Title, Subtitle, and Footnote fields shown on the data screen function the same as they did in the bullet chart you completed earlier. Use the Title line to give the chart a title, the Subtitle line to add definition to the name, and the Footnote line to give relevant supplemental information about the chart—the date, for example.

Enter the title *Pens, Pencils, & Accessories* onto the data screen but leave the Subtitle field blank because the title is a complete description. For a footnote, type *Company Confidential*.

After you enter the title, subtitle, and footnote, press F2 (Draw Chart) to pre-view the blank chart. Notice that the title, subtitle, and footnote are all in place, and a box indicates where the actual graph will appear once you have typed in the graph's data. Press Esc to return to the Bar/Line Chart Data screen to type the sales data into the chart.

The Tab key moves the cursor on the Bar/line Chart Data screen from one series to the next. Press Tab to move the cursor to the right and Shift-Tab to move the cursor to the left. Pressing Enter moves the cursor down one line in the same column. Pressing the up-arrow key moves the cursor up one row. To complete the second-quarter revenue chart, type in the numbers as they appear in figure 3.11.

```
                      Bar/Line Chart Data                        ╲
    ───────────────────────────────────────────────────────
        Title: Pens, Pencils, & Accessories
  Subtitle:
  Footnote: Company Confidential


                X Axis      Series 1   Series 2   Series 3   Series 4
     Pt         Month

     1     Apr              3993       6995       12878
     2     May              4318       5937       10698
     3     Jun              4957       8490       13639
     4
     5
     6
     7
     8
     9
    10
    11
    12
  ─────────────────────────────────────────────────────────────────
  F1-Help          F3-Set X type                    F9-More series
  F2-Draw chart    F4-Calculate        F8-Options    F10-Continue
```

Fig. 3.11.

The second-quarter revenues chart data screen.

Next, preview the chart once again by pressing F2 (Draw Chart). You will see the chart shown in figure 3.12, with x- and y-axis labels, bars, and even a legend.

Using the Titles & Options Pages

Now that you have previewed the chart created by Harvard Graphics, you can customize the result to suit your needs and aesthetic values. Press Esc to return to the data screen and press F8 (Options) to see the first of four Titles & Options

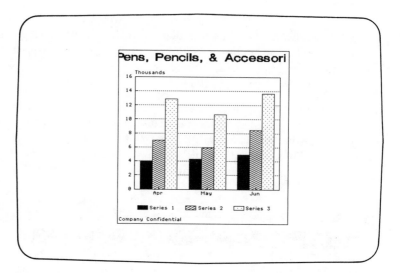

Fig. 3.12.

The second-quarter revenues chart preview.

screens. *Options* in Harvard Graphics are used to change the appearance of the current chart. Each type of graph chart has its own series of Titles & Options pages unique to the attributes you can set for that type of chart.

Titles & Options pages for bar/line charts, for example, give you the ability to turn flat bar or line graphs into snazzy, three-dimensional charts. Once the options are set to your satisfaction, you can press F2 (Draw Chart) to preview the chart.

Right now, you should be looking at the first Titles & Options page. The top line of the page displays Page 1 of 4, and two triangular arrows on the sides of the screen point up (left side of screen) and down (right side of screen) to indicate that additional pages are available to you. You can use the PgDn and PgUp keys to move between the pages. Each page sets another visual aspect of the completed chart. Figure 3.13 shows the first Titles & Options page.

Using the First Titles & Options Page

The first Titles & Options page determines the overall appearance of the series in the chart. You can use this page to specify such characteristics as whether the series are shown as lines or bars. On this page, you also can name the series something other than Series 1, Series 2, and so on.

Notice that the first three lines are set up much like the first three lines of the Bullet List screen, with Title, Subtitle, and Footnote lines. The current

```
┌─────────────────────────────────────────────────────────┐
│  ▲    Bar/Line Chart  Titles & Options  Page 1 of 4   ▼  │
│       Title:          Pens, Pencils, & Accessories        │
│       Subtitle:                                           │
│                                                           │
│       Footnote:       Company Confidential                │
│                                                           │
│       X  axis title:                                      │
│       Y1 axis title: Thousands                            │
│       Y2 axis title:                                      │
│                            Type        Display │ Y Axis    │
│   Legend                                Yes No │ Y1  Y2    │
│   Title:          Bar  Line Trend Curve Pt                │
│                                                           │
│  1 │ Series 1           Bar              Yes      Y1       │
│  2 │ Series 2           Bar              Yes      Y1       │
│  3 │ Series 3           Bar              Yes      Y1       │
│  4 │ Series 4           Bar              Yes      Y1       │
│  5 │ Series 5           Bar              Yes      Y1       │
│  6 │ Series 6           Bar              Yes      Y1       │
│  7 │ Series 7           Bar              Yes      Y1       │
│  8 │ Series 8           Bar              Yes      Y1       │
│                                                           │
│  F1-Help           F5-Attributes   F7-Size/Place          │
│  F2-Draw chart                     F8-Data      F10-Continue│
└─────────────────────────────────────────────────────────┘
```

Fig. 3.13.

The first Titles & Options page.

entries in these lines are borrowed from the data screen you completed a moment ago. You can change these lines by typing over them if you have changed your mind about the contents.

Complete the rest of this page so it resembles the completed Titles & Options page shown in figure 3.14. Use the Tab, Shift-Tab, and Enter keys to move from option to option and use the space bar to make your selections. To name the series, tab to Series 1 and press Ctrl-Del to remove the words Series 1. Then type the words *Mechanical Pencils* in their place. Continue filling out the page until it is complete, with all the series names.

Sizing and Placing Text on the Titles & Options Page

You can alter the size and position of the chart's title, subtitle, and footnote by using the F7-Size/Place option on this page, just as you did earlier when creating the bullet list. By changing the size of these lines, you can vary their importance on the page. Altering the size of the title lines also affects the size of the actual graph portion of the chart. Smaller title lines leave more room for a larger graph.

Press F7 (Size/Place) to summon the Size/Place overlay and change the Title line size to 6. Tab to the Subtitle line and change the settings of both lines to 0. Then press F10 (Continue) to save these changes. Even though no subtitle is in this chart, a setting of anything other than 0 reserves some space above the graph for a subtitle. A size setting of 0 eliminates this space and increases the size of the graph. Figure 3.15 shows how the Size/Place overlay appears with the new Size and Place settings.

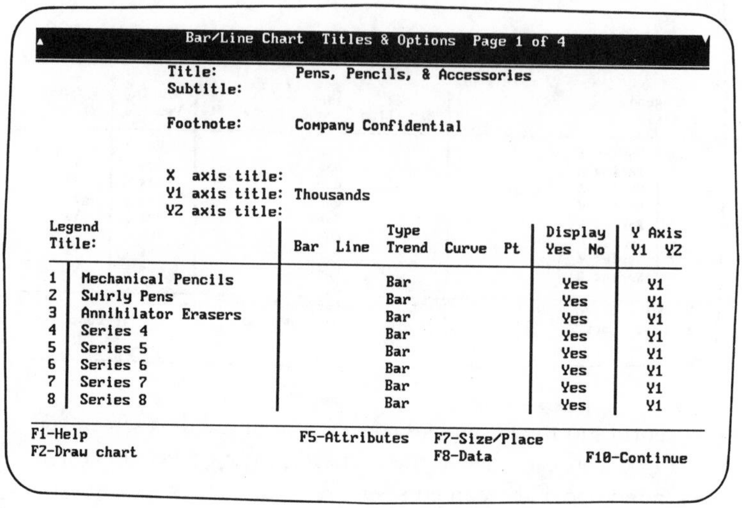

Fig. 3.14.

The complete Titles & Options page.

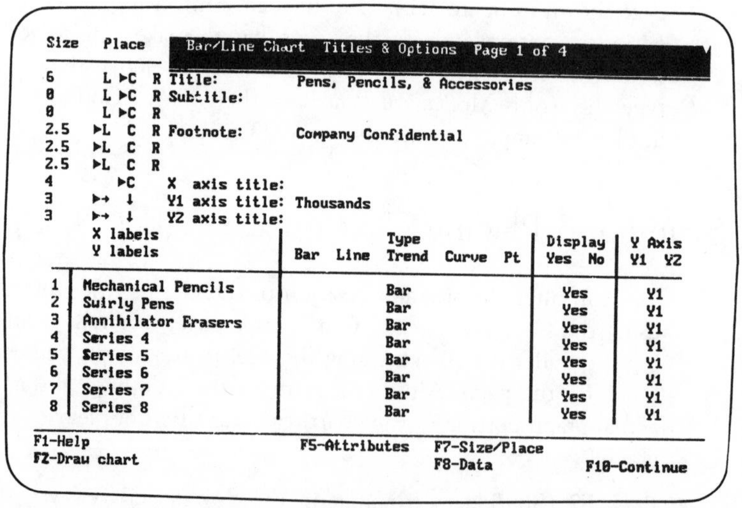

```
                 Bar/Line Chart  Titles & Options  Page 1 of 4
 ▲
                   Title:       Pens, Pencils, & Accessories
                   Subtitle:

                   Footnote:    Company Confidential


              X  axis title:
              Y1 axis title: Thousands
              Y2 axis title:
 Legend                                   Type              Display   Y Axis
 Title:                        Bar  Line  Trend  Curve  Pt  Yes  No   Y1  Y2

   1  │ Mechanical Pencils              Bar                  Yes        Y1
   2  │ Swirly Pens                     Bar                  Yes        Y1
   3  │ Annihilator Erasers             Bar                  Yes        Y1
   4  │ Series 4                        Bar                  Yes        Y1
   5  │ Series 5                        Bar                  Yes        Y1
   6  │ Series 6                        Bar                  Yes        Y1
   7  │ Series 7                        Bar                  Yes        Y1
   8  │ Series 8                        Bar                  Yes        Y1

 F1-Help                    F5-Attributes    F7-Size/Place
 F2-Draw chart                              F8-Data            F10-Continue
```

Fig. 3.15.

The Size/Place overlay on the first Titles & Options page.

```
 Size   Place   Bar/Line Chart  Titles & Options  Page 1 of 4
                                                                        ▼
  6    L ►C  R  Title:       Pens, Pencils, & Accessories
  0    L ►C  R  Subtitle:
  0    L ►C  R
  2.5  ►L  C  R  Footnote:    Company Confidential
  2.5  ►L  C  R
  2.5  ►L  C  R
  4       ►C     X  axis title:
  3     ►→  ↓    Y1 axis title: Thousands
  3     ►→  ↓    Y2 axis title:
          X labels                         Type              Display   Y Axis
          Y labels               Bar  Line Trend  Curve  Pt  Yes  No   Y1  Y2

   1  │ Mechanical Pencils              Bar                  Yes        Y1
   2  │ Swirly Pens                     Bar                  Yes        Y1
   3  │ Annihilator Erasers             Bar                  Yes        Y1
   4  │ Series 4                        Bar                  Yes        Y1
   5  │ Series 5                        Bar                  Yes        Y1
   6  │ Series 6                        Bar                  Yes        Y1
   7  │ Series 7                        Bar                  Yes        Y1
   8  │ Series 8                        Bar                  Yes        Y1

 F1-Help                    F5-Attributes    F7-Size/Place
 F2-Draw chart                              F8-Data            F10-Continue
```

The first Titles & Options page is now complete, so now is a good time to preview the chart and admire your work. Press F2 (Draw Chart). The chart looks fine, so now name your chart P&P-2Q (for "pens and pencils second quarter").

You will learn about saving your chart shortly and then move to creating the third chart in your presentation. But first, take a few minutes for a quick look at the second, third, and fourth Titles & Options pages to see what other changes you can make to a chart's appearance. With the Main menu on your screen, select Enter/Edit Chart to return to the Bar/Line Chart Data screen.

Viewing the Second Titles & Options Page

Press F8 (Options) to call up the first Titles & Options page. Then press PgDn to see the second of four Titles & Options pages (see fig. 3.16). This page lets you set the characteristics of the *elements* of the current chart. For example, on the second Titles & Options page, you can set the width of the bars in a bar chart and decide whether they will be displayed as three-dimensional bars. The second page also defines the appearance and positioning of the *legend*. A legend is a visual key that correlates series with their bars. With Harvard Graphics, a legend is optional. If you decide to include a legend, you can place it above, below, inside, or outside the actual graph.

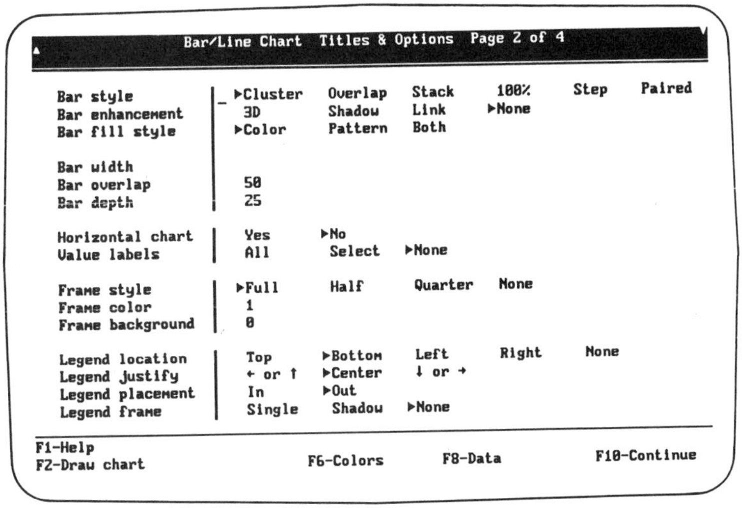

Fig. 3.16.

The second Titles & Options page.

```
▲        Bar/Line Chart  Titles & Options  Page 2 of 4        ▼

   Bar style          |_ ▶Cluster   Overlap   Stack    100%   Step    Paired
   Bar enhancement      | 3D         Shadow    Link     ▶None
   Bar fill style       | ▶Color     Pattern   Both

   Bar width            |
   Bar overlap          | 50
   Bar depth            | 25

   Horizontal chart     | Yes        ▶No
   Value labels         | All        Select    ▶None

   Frame style          | ▶Full      Half      Quarter  None
   Frame color          | 1
   Frame background     | 0

   Legend location      | Top        ▶Bottom   Left     Right   None
   Legend justify       | ← or ↑     ▶Center   ↓ or →
   Legend placement     | In         ▶Out
   Legend frame         | Single     Shadow    ▶None

   F1-Help
   F2-Draw chart              F6-Colors     F8-Data        F10-Continue
```

Viewing the Third Titles & Options Page

Press PgDn at the second Titles & Options page to summon the third Titles & Options page, shown in figure 3.17. Use the third Titles & Options page to change the underlying structure of the chart's appearance. You can set up grid lines behind the bars, for example, or you can set minimum and maximum values for both of the chart's two axes (horizontal and vertical).

Fig. 3.17.

The third Titles & Options page.

```
┌──────────────────────────────────────────────────────────────────────┐
│ ▲          Bar/Line Chart  Titles & Options  Page 3 of 4             ▼ │
│   Data Table        │  Normal    Framed   ▶None                        │
│                     │                                                  │
│   X  Axis Labels    │ ▶Normal    Vertical  %         None              │
│   Y1 Axis Labels    │ ▶Value     $         %         None              │
│   Y2 Axis Labels    │ ▶Value     $         %         None              │
│                     │                                                  │
│   X  Grid Lines     │   · · · ·   ────    ▶None                        │
│   Y1 Grid Lines     │ ▶ · · · ·   ────     None                        │
│   Y2 Grid Lines     │ ▶ · · · ·   ────     None                        │
│                     │                                                  │
│   X Tick Mark Style │ ▶In        Out       Both      None              │
│   Y Tick Mark Style │ ▶In        Out       Both      None              │
│                     ├─────────────────┬──────────────┬──────────────── │
│                     │   X Axis        │   Y1 Axis     │   Y2 Axis       │
│   Scale Type        │ ▶Linear   Log   │ ▶Linear  Log  │ ▶Linear  Log    │
│   Format            │                 │               │                 │
│   Minimum Value     │                 │               │                 │
│   Maximum Value     │                 │               │                 │
│   Increment         │                 │               │                 │
│ ────────────────────┴─────────────────┴──────────────┴──────────────── │
│ F1-Help                                                                 │
│ F2-Draw chart                            F8-Data          F10-Continue  │
└──────────────────────────────────────────────────────────────────────┘
```

Viewing the Fourth Titles & Options Page

Finally, press PgDn at the third Titles & Options page to display the fourth and last Titles & Options page. Use the fourth Titles & Options page to describe titles and the specific appearance of bars and lines in a graph. *Titles* are the names that you give to series, axes, and the overall chart. Using the fourth page, for example, you can change the bars to show a cumulative display, or you can change the line style on line charts. Figure 3.18 shows the fourth Titles & Options page.

Saving the Bar/Line Chart

To save the bar/line chart, press Esc to return to the Main menu, select Get/Save/Remove, and then select Save Chart from the Get/Save/Remove menu.

Complete the Save Chart window just as you did for the bullet chart you created earlier. Use the chart name P&P-2Q and press Enter. You do not need to type the file name's CHT extension because Harvard Graphics does that for you.

```
                    Bar/Line Chart   Titles & Options   Page 4 of 4
▲
          Title:          Pens, Pencils, & Accessories
          Subtitle:

          Footnote:       Company Confidential


        X axis title:
        Y1 axis title: Thousands
        Y2 axis title:
                                  Cum      Y Label   Color   Marker/   Line
  Legend                         Yes  No   Yes  No                     Pattern   Style
  Title:

  1   Mechanical Pencils         No       No        2       1         1
  2   Swirly Pens                No       No        3       2         1
  3   Annihilator Erasers        No       No        4       3         1
  4   Series 4                   No       No        5       4         1
  5   Series 5                   No       No        6       5         1
  6   Series 6                   No       No        7       6         1
  7   Series 7                   No       No        8       7         1
  8   Series 8                   No       No        9       8         1

  F1-Help                  F5-Attributes   F7-Size/Place
  F2-Draw chart            F6-Colors       F8-Data            F10-Continue
```

Fig. 3.18.

The fourth Titles & Options page.

Creating a Pie Chart

The third chart in your presentation will show the projects with the largest effect on the second-quarter's profits. When you assess the sales figures for the second quarter, you are happy to learn that two products new to the Superior Office Supplies line influenced revenues more than any others. These products are the designer pens and pencils and the small, personal appointment notebooks in the stationery division.

Because you were the one to advise introducing these two products, you want to compare the revenues generated by sales of pen and pencil sets with the revenues generated by sales of appointment books. From the computer-generated sales reports that the vice president of sales gave you, you pull the sales figures for the second quarter and jot them on paper. These numbers follow:

	Pen and Pencil Sets	Appointment Books
April	$23,866	$40,676
May	$20,953	$63,800
June	$27,086	$38,539

To compare the sales of these two products, you wisely decide to graph the information as a pie graph chart.

Selecting the Pie Chart Data Screens

Creating a pie chart is much like creating a bar/line chart. First, you type the data into a data screen. Then you alternate between previewing the chart and modifying its appearance by using two Titles & Options pages.

Follow this procedure to reach the Pie Chart 1 Data screen:

1. Select Create New Chart from the Main menu.

2. Select Pie from the Create New Chart menu. The Pie Chart 1 Data screen appears (see fig. 3.19).

Fig. 3.19.

The Pie Chart 1 Data screen.

```
                    Pie Chart 1 Data   Page 1 of 2
         Title:     2nd Quarter Top Performers
         Subtitle:  Superior Office Supplies
         Footnote:  Company Confidential

         Slice|      Label          Value       Cut Slice  Color | Pattern
                     Name            Series 1    Yes  No

           1   Apr                   23866          No       2      1
           2   May                   20953          No       3      2
           3   Jun                   27086          No       4      3
           4                                        No       5      4
           5                                        No       6      5
           6                                        No       7      6
           7                                        No       8      7
           8                                        No       9      8
           9                                        No      10      9
          10                                        No      11     10
          11                                        No      12     11
          12                                        No      13     12

         F1-Help                                           F9-More series
         F2-Draw chart            F6-Colors    F8-Options  F10-Continue
```

Notice the similarity between the Pie Chart 1 Data screen and the Bar/Line Chart Data screen (see fig. 3.10). The Pie Chart 1 Data screen provides the same set of lines for a title, subtitle, and footnote. For a title, enter *2nd Quarter Top Performers*. For a subtitle, enter the name of the company: *Superior Office Supplies*. For a footnote, type *Company Confidential*.

To proceed, you will need to understand one significant difference between the Pie Chart 1 Data screen and the Bar/Line Chart Data screen. Notice that when the Pie Chart 1 Data screen first appears, it provides space for you to enter data for Series 1. To enter a second series of data, you must press F9 (More Series). You can enter up to eight series of data by continuing to press F9.

Notice that the top line of the screen shows Pie Chart 1 Data Page 1 of 2. Two Pie Chart Data screens are available. With pie charts, you can display two pies side by side. The series displayed in the left pie is the series shown on the first screen (page 1), and the series displayed in the right pie is the series shown on the second screen (page 2). To get to the second screen, press the PgDn key while viewing the first screen. To change the series shown on the left or right side of the screen, press PgDn or PgUp to get to the appropriate page and press F9 (More Series) until the correct series appears.

With Harvard Graphics, you can display only two pies at a time, with each graph showing one series. The key to using the Pie Chart Data screens is to match one of the two pies with one of the eight series by pressing PgDn or PgUp to choose the pie (left or right) and F9 (More Series) to select a series for that pie. Figure 3.20 shows the relationship of series and pages with the function keys.

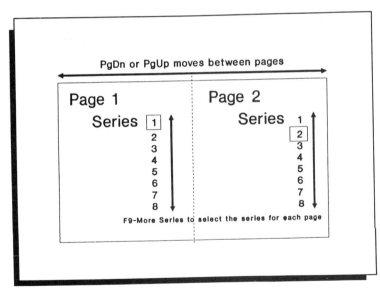

Fig. 3.20.

The relationship of series and pages with their function keys.

Try using the PgDn and PgUp keys to move between the two data screens for pie charts and stop when the first data screen is displayed. Then try pressing F9 (More Series) until you see Series 1 in the Value column. Your screen should appear as shown in figure 3.21.

Next type the labels and data shown in figure 3.22. This is the data for the sales of designer pen and pencil sets.

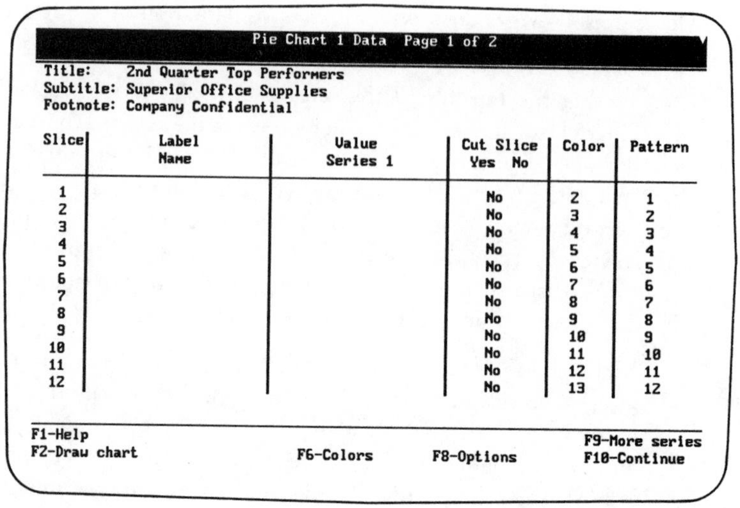

Fig. 3.21.

A blank Pie Chart 1 Data screen.

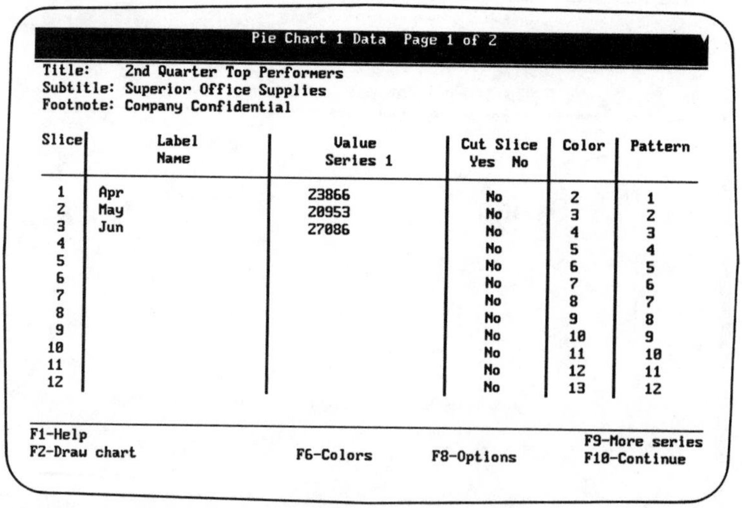

```
                    Pie Chart 1 Data   Page 1 of 2
        Title:    2nd Quarter Top Performers
        Subtitle: Superior Office Supplies
        Footnote: Company Confidential

        Slice   Label              Value        Cut Slice   Color   Pattern
                Name               Series 1     Yes  No

          1                                          No       2        1
          2                                          No       3        2
          3                                          No       4        3
          4                                          No       5        4
          5                                          No       6        5
          6                                          No       7        6
          7                                          No       8        7
          8                                          No       9        8
          9                                          No      10        9
         10                                          No      11       10
         11                                          No      12       11
         12                                          No      13       12

        F1-Help                                              F9-More series
        F2-Draw chart          F6-Colors    F8-Options       F10-Continue
```

Fig. 3.22.

The Pie Chart 1 Data screen with entries.

```
                    Pie Chart 1 Data   Page 1 of 2
        Title:    2nd Quarter Top Performers
        Subtitle: Superior Office Supplies
        Footnote: Company Confidential

        Slice   Label              Value        Cut Slice   Color   Pattern
                Name               Series 1     Yes  No

          1     Apr                23866            No       2        1
          2     May                20953            No       3        2
          3     Jun                27086            No       4        3
          4                                          No       5        4
          5                                          No       6        5
          6                                          No       7        6
          7                                          No       8        7
          8                                          No       9        8
          9                                          No      10        9
         10                                          No      11       10
         11                                          No      12       11
         12                                          No      13       12

        F1-Help                                              F9-More series
        F2-Draw chart          F6-Colors    F8-Options       F10-Continue
```

Before you enter the second product line on the chart, press F2 (Draw Chart) to see the left side of the chart. Figure 3.23 shows how your screen should look.

Press Esc to return to the first data screen and press F9 (More Series) to enter data for Series 2. Enter the data as shown in figure 3.24.

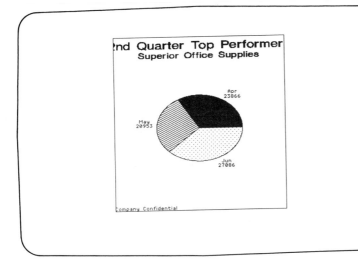

Fig. 3.23.

The pie chart before the second series is added.

Fig. 3.24.

The Pie Chart 2 Data screen.

With both Series 1 and Series 2 data entered, you can specify that the left pie displays Series 1 and the right pie displays Series 2. Press F9 (More Series) enough times to bring the Series 1 data back on-screen. Now press PgDn to display the Pie Chart 2 Data screen. To match this page (for the right pie graph) with Series 2, press F9 (More Series) until the Series 2 data shows up. Now press F2 (Draw Chart) to preview the chart. Figure 3.25 shows the two pie graphs side by side in a chart.

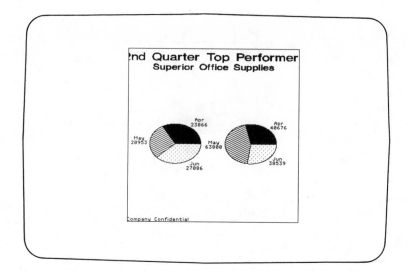

Fig. 3.25.

A pie chart with two series.

Viewing and Changing the Pie Chart Titles & Options Pages

Pie charts have only two simple Titles & Options pages. To see the first page (Page 1 of 2), press F8 (Options) from the Pie Chart 1 Data screen. Figure 3.26 shows the first Titles & Options page. Notice that only one triangular pointer appears at the upper right corner of the screen, pointing down to indicate that one additional Titles & Options page is available.

Move the cursor to Pie 1 title by pressing Enter until your cursor is on the option and enter *Pen & Pencil Sets*. Then press Enter twice more until the cursor is at Pie 2 title and type *Appointment Books*.

You may want to use the F7-Size/Place option at this page to adjust the subtitle's second line size (which has no text) to a setting of 0. Setting the size to 0 reduces the space required for titles and, therefore, increases the size of your pie charts. The Size/Place option also offers you a choice for positioning each pie graph's titles. To position the titles below the pie, leave the down arrows to the left of the titles highlighted. To position the titles above the pie, highlight the up arrows that are to the left of the titles. Figure 3.27 shows the Titles & Options page with titles set to appear below the pie graphs and text set to the correct sizes for this chart. Press F2 (Draw Chart) to see the results of these changes (see fig. 3.28).

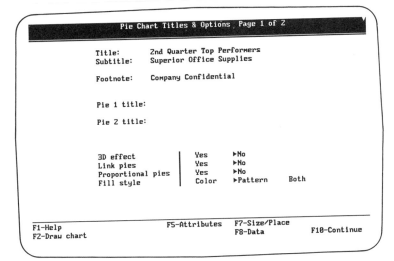

Fig. 3.26.

The first Titles & Options page.

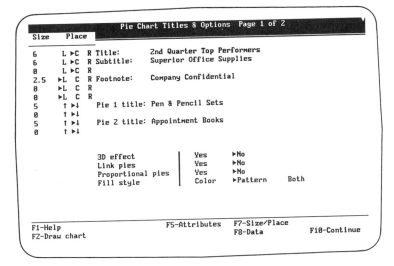

Fig. 3.27.

The first Titles & Options page with the size and place settings.

Press Esc to return to the Titles & Options page and press Tab to move the cursor down to the Proportional pies option. Set this option to Yes to tell Harvard Graphics to calculate the cumulative size of one pie graph in relation to the other pie graph and draw the graphs so their size is proportional to the cumulative amount they represent. Press F2 (Draw Chart) to see how the designer pen and pencil total sales match up proportionally to the appointment book total sales. Figure 3.29 should match your screen.

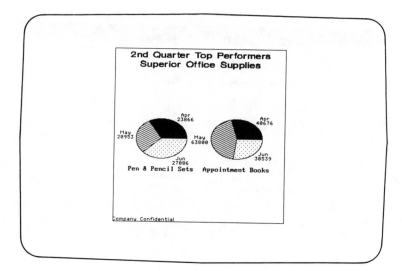

Fig. 3.28.

The pie chart preview.

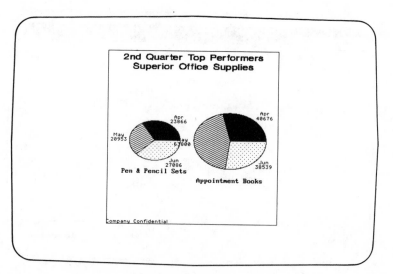

Fig. 3.29.

Proportional pie graphs.

Press Esc to return to the first Titles & Options page and press PgDn to examine the second Titles & Options page. This collection of options is discussed in detail in Chapter 6. For this quick tour, two small changes are in order: you need to remove the actual values from the chart and replace those values with the percentages for each slice of the pie.

Follow these steps to make the changes:

1. Tab to Show value and press the space bar to select No in the Pie 1 column.

2. Also at the Show value line, press the space bar to select No in the Pie 2 column.

3. Tab to Show percent and press the space bar to select Yes for the Pie 1 column.

4. Also at the Show percent line, press the space bar to select Yes for the Pie 2 column.

5. Press F10 (Continue) to confirm your choices. Figure 3.30 shows the second Pie Chart Titles & Options page with these changes completed.

6. Press F2 (Draw Chart) to see the results of your changes (see fig. 3.31).

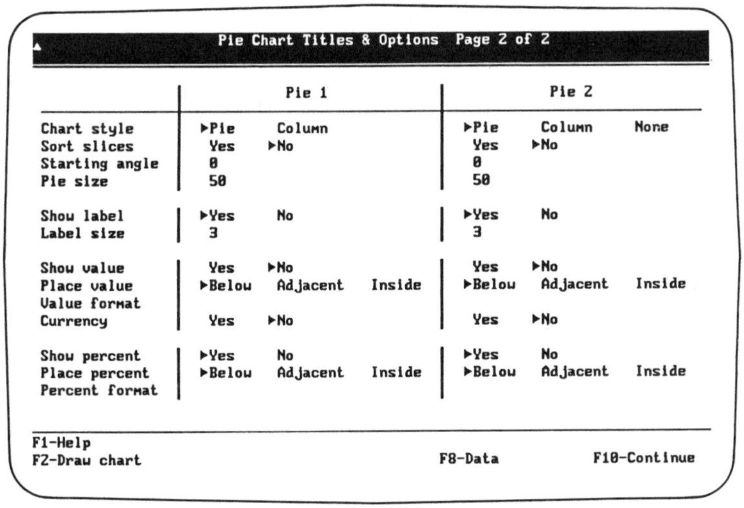

```
Pie Chart Titles & Options  Page 2 of 2

                              Pie 1                        Pie 2

Chart style        ▶Pie     Column           ▶Pie     Column      None
Sort slices        Yes      ▶No              Yes      ▶No
Starting angle     0                         0
Pie size           50                        50

Show label         ▶Yes     No              ▶Yes     No
Label size         3                         3

Show value         Yes      ▶No              Yes      ▶No
Place value        ▶Below   Adjacent  Inside  ▶Below   Adjacent  Inside
Value format
Currency           Yes      ▶No              Yes      ▶No

Show percent       ▶Yes     No              ▶Yes     No
Place percent      ▶Below   Adjacent  Inside  ▶Below   Adjacent  Inside
Percent format

F1-Help
F2-Draw chart                    F8-Data            F10-Continue
```

Fig. 3.30.

The second Titles & Options page with changes.

Saving Your Pie Chart

Now that your chart is complete, save it on disk so you can retrieve it later. To help remind you of the chart's purpose, try to give the chart a mnemonic name, such as PEN-APPT (a chart comparing pen and pencil sets with appointment books).

Fig. 3.31.

The finished pie chart.

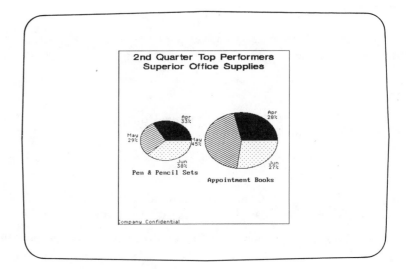

To save your chart, do the following:

1. Select Get/Save/Remove from the Main menu.

2. Select Save Chart from the Get/Save/Remove menu.

3. Type *pen-appt* as the chart name. Harvard Graphics automatically adds a CHT file name extension for you.

Using Draw/Annotate
To Enhance a Chart

As you near the end of the tour, you can proudly look back at your accomplishments. In only a short while, you have created three complete charts: OBJECTVS, a bullet list chart; P&P-2Q, a bar chart; and PEN-APPT, a pie chart. These charts may be perfectly satisfactory as they are, but you can improve their impact dramatically with a special Harvard Graphics feature called Draw/Annotate. Draw/Annotate lets you enhance charts by adding pictures, any of hundreds of symbols from a symbol library, hand-drawn arrows, boxes, circles, and text. For your pie chart, for example, you can use Draw/Annotate to add a graphic of coins next to the smaller pen and pencil set pie graph and a graphic of dollar bills next to the larger appointment book pie graph.

Next, you will retrieve the bullet list chart that you created earlier so that you can use the Draw/Annotate feature to add a box around the last bulleted item for additional emphasis.

Retrieving a Text Chart

To retrieve the bullet chart (OBJECTVS) and switch over to Draw/Annotate mode, follow these steps:

1. Select Get/Save/Remove from the Main menu.

2. Select Get Chart from the Get/Save/Remove menu. Figure 3.32 shows the Select Chart file list, which appears for you to pick one of the charts on disk.

3. Use the down-arrow key to highlight the file named OBJECTVS and press Enter. Highlighting the file automatically places it after the Filename prompt on the screen. The chart appears.

4. Press Esc and then press F10 (Continue) to return to the Main menu.

5. Select Draw/Annotate from the Main menu. The Draw/Annotate screen appears (see fig. 3.33).

```
                          Select Chart

   Directory: C:\GRAPHICS
   Filename:  OBJECTUS.CHT

   Filename Ext |   Date   |  Type   |         Description

    HG      .CHT | 12-01-87 | PIE     | Pie for color palette display
    INTRO   .CHT | 07-01-87 | TITLE   | Sample chart
    OPENING .CHT | 07-01-87 | TITLE   | Sample chart
    PRODS   .CHT | 07-01-87 | LIST    | Sample chart
    REGIONS .CHT | 07-01-87 | BAR/LINE| Sample chart
    SALES   .CHT | 07-01-87 | 2 COLUMN| Sample chart
    TRISALES.CHT | 07-01-87 | BAR/LINE| Sample chart
    TESTMAP .CHT | 08-21-88 | CHART   |
    TESTMAP2.CHT | 08-21-88 | CHART   |
    NECITY  .CHT | 08-21-88 | PIE     |
    UHGQT1  .CHT | 10-23-88 | BULLET  | Fourth Quarter Corporate Goals
    SOSSUCC .CHT | 10-25-88 | FREEFORM|
    SOSTEAC .CHT | 10-25-88 | FREEFORM|
    OBJECTUS.CHT | 11-03-88 | BULLET  | Marketing Objectives
    P&P-2Q  .CHT | 11-03-88 | BAR/LINE| Pens, Pencils, & Accessories

   F1-Help        F3-Change dir
                                                   F10-Continue
```

Fig. 3.32.

The Select Chart screen.

Fig. 3.33.

The Draw/Annotate screen.

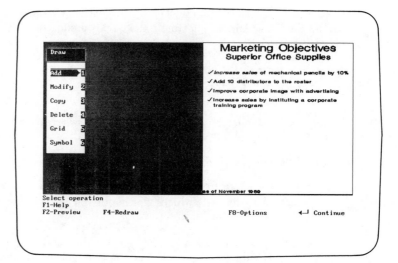

Take a minute to look at the Draw/Annotate screen. On the right, the bullet list chart that you created earlier appears on the *drawing board*, the work area on which you will perform Draw/Annotate chart enhancements.

On the left, the Draw menu appears. Use this menu to choose from among the available Draw/Annotate commands.

Draw/Annotate mode is different from the modes in which you create text and graph charts in two respects:

❑ The options available for modifying the chart appear on the main screen rather than on separate Options pages.

❑ The chart shown on the screen was created in *another* mode (either Text or Graph mode) and brought into Draw/Annotate for embellishment. The only exception occurs when you want to draw with Draw/Annotate on a blank page. In that case, you start a free-form chart (Text mode chart) and bring it into Draw/Annotate without adding any data on the free-form data screen.

When you are in the middle of a Draw/Annotate operation, the left portion of the screen becomes an options panel. When you press F8 (Options), the cursor jumps to the options panel, and the F8 function key choice on the bottom line of the screen changes to F8-Draw. If you press F8 (Draw), the cursor jumps back over to the drawing board. Try this procedure several times to see how it works.

At the lower left corner of the screen, a prompt reminds you of your place in the current operation. Notice that when the screen is at the Draw menu, the instruction line displays Select operation.

Adding Boxes to an Existing Chart

To add the box around the last bulleted item on this chart, follow these steps:

1. Select Add from the Draw menu. (Use the cursor to highlight the choice and press Enter or just press the number 1.)

2. Select Box from the Add menu. The cursor moves to the drawing board. The instruction line displays the message Select first box corner.

3. Position the cursor at the upper left corner of the box you want to draw and press Enter.

4. Press F8 (Options) to move to the options panel.

5. Use the space bar to select No at the Square option. You will draw a rectangle rather than a square.

6. Tab to the Style option and press F6 (Choices) to see the types of boxes available. Figure 3.34 shows the 21 standard box types that are available. Selecting and placing specific box styles is described in detail in Chapter 7. For the purposes of this quick tour, move the cursor to the *rounded* selection (box type 4) and press Enter.

7. Tab to the Fill choice and press the space bar to select No.

8. Press F8 (Draw) to move the cursor back to the drawing board.

9. Use the PgDn and right-arrow keys to position the opposite corner, the lower right corner of the box, and press Enter when the box surrounds the fourth bulleted item (see fig. 3.35).

10. Although you can see the results of your actions on the Draw/Annotate screen, you still can use the F2-Draw chart option to preview the final chart on the full screen before saving and printing it. Press F2 (Draw Chart) to preview the final chart.

11. Press Esc twice to return to the Harvard Graphics Main menu after you finish examining the chart.

12. Select Get/Save/Remove from the Main menu and save the chart with the name OBJEC1. If you use a name that is different from the file's original name, you will end up with two charts on disk—both the original and the new version. You now can return to OBJECTVS if you need to make other changes.

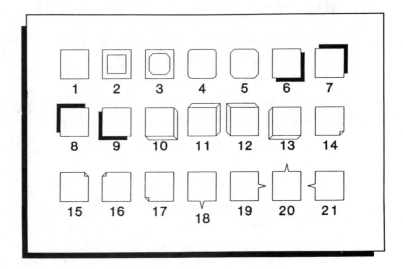

Fig. 3.34.

The Harvard Graphics standard box types.

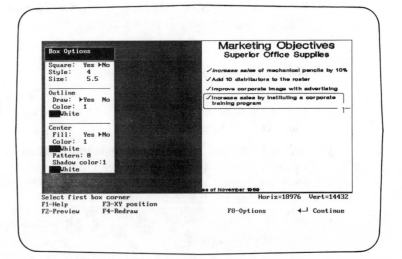

Fig. 3.35.

The rounded box (type 4).

To add other shapes that are in the Harvard Graphics gallery (circles, ovals, squares, rectangles, lines, and arrows), you can follow similar procedures. The methods you use, however, change slightly when you create more sophisticated polygons and polylines. These procedures are explained in detail in Chapter 7.

Including Symbols in an Existing Chart

Not everyone's an artist, so if your drawing skills are less than sublime and you hope to add anything more than simple lines, boxes, circles, and arrows to a chart, you may want to rely on the built-in Harvard Graphics library of predrawn symbols.

To see how symbols work, try adding actual drawings to the pie chart comparing sales of the pen and pencil set with the appointment book (add a drawing of coins for the pen and pencil set and dollar bills for the appointment book).

To bring a chart into Draw/Annotate mode to add drawings, you must retrieve it from disk first. Once you have retrieved the chart, it becomes the current chart, ready for embellishment if you enter Draw/Annotate mode. To retrieve the pie chart you called PEN-APPT, select Get/Save/Remove from the Main menu and select Get Chart from the Get/Save/Remove menu. Use the down-arrow key to highlight PEN-APPT and press Enter. The chart appears. Press Esc to return to the Pie Chart 1 Data screen and press Esc again to return to the Main menu. Now enter Draw/Annotate mode by choosing Draw/Annotate from the Main menu.

The next section explains how you can use the Harvard Graphics symbol libraries to add the drawings to your chart.

Using the Standard Symbol Libraries

A *symbol* in Harvard Graphics is a special kind of picture that has already been drawn for you. Groups of symbols are stored in symbol files provided with Harvard Graphics. Each file follows a theme. The Office symbol file provides images of such standard office implements as staplers, pen and pencil sets, calendars, and filing cabinets. The Computer symbol file includes pictures of computers, computer parts, and so on. Harvard Graphics includes hundreds of symbols for use in your charts and offers you the opportunity to create symbol libraries of your own. Several optional supplementary symbol collections, such as the Business symbol utility library, are available for you to add to your collection. You also can create your own symbol libraries with Harvard Graphics.

For this quick tour, you will adorn the pie graph chart with symbols for coins and dollar bills from the Currency symbol file.

Getting a Symbol

To get a symbol to place on your chart, follow these steps:

1. Select Symbol from the Draw menu.

2. Select Get from the Symbol menu.

3. Select the CURRENCY.SYM file from the list of file names that appears (see fig. 3.36). The Currency symbol library appears on your screen (see fig. 3.37).

4. Position the cursor on the symbol of the coins and press Enter.

5. Press the Backspace key so you can determine where to position the symbol when the Draw/Annotate screen reappears.

6. Position the cursor at the upper left corner of where you want to draw a box to contain the symbol; then press Enter. In this case, position the cursor just under the P of the word Pen and press Enter. Figure 3.38 shows the precise position for the upper left corner of the box.

7. Press the PgDn key and right-arrow key repeatedly to open the box (or press PgUp to make the box smaller) until the box is the proper size for the symbol you will place on the screen. Figure 3.39 shows how the screen looks before you press Enter again.

8. Press Enter to confirm the size and instruct Draw/Annotate to draw the symbol. Figure 3.40 shows how the chart looks with an added symbol.

Now that you have placed the first symbol, finding and placing the second symbol will be a simple procedure. Complete this chart by placing the dollar bills symbol below the words Appointment Books. Then save the chart with the new name 2QPIESYM for "second-quarter pie chart with symbols."

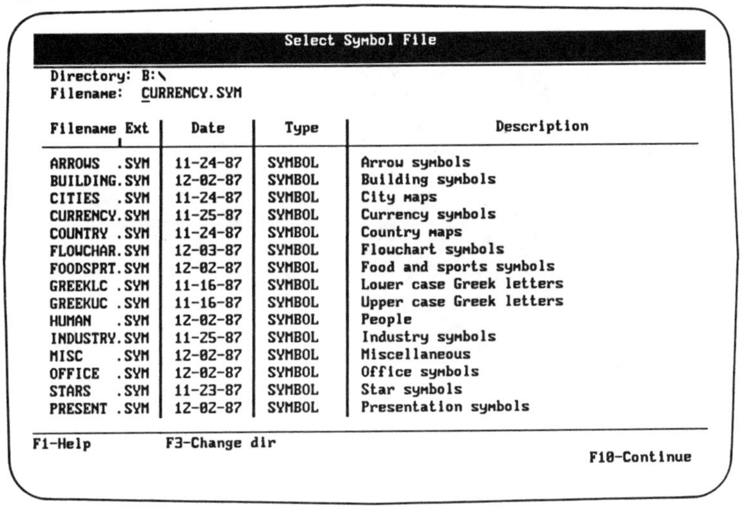

Select Symbol File
Directory: B:\
Filename: CURRENCY.SYM
Filename Ext | Date | Type | Description
ARROWS .SYM | 11-24-87 | SYMBOL | Arrow symbols
BUILDING.SYM | 12-02-87 | SYMBOL | Building symbols
CITIES .SYM | 11-24-87 | SYMBOL | City maps
CURRENCY.SYM | 11-25-87 | SYMBOL | Currency symbols
COUNTRY .SYM | 11-24-87 | SYMBOL | Country maps
FLOWCHAR.SYM | 12-03-87 | SYMBOL | Flowchart symbols
FOODSPRT.SYM | 12-02-87 | SYMBOL | Food and sports symbols
GREEKLC .SYM | 11-16-87 | SYMBOL | Lower case Greek letters
GREEKUC .SYM | 11-16-87 | SYMBOL | Upper case Greek letters
HUMAN .SYM | 12-02-87 | SYMBOL | People
INDUSTRY.SYM | 11-25-87 | SYMBOL | Industry symbols
MISC .SYM | 12-02-87 | SYMBOL | Miscellaneous
OFFICE .SYM | 12-02-87 | SYMBOL | Office symbols
STARS .SYM | 11-23-87 | SYMBOL | Star symbols
PRESENT .SYM | 12-02-87 | SYMBOL | Presentation symbols
F1-Help
F3-Change dir
F10-Continue

Fig. 3.36.

The symbol file name list.

Draw
Add
Modify
Copy
Delete
Grid
Symbol
Symbol
Get 1
Save 2
Group 3
Ungroup 4
Remove 5
Select symbol
F1-Help
F2-Preview
F3-XY position
F4-Redraw
Horiz=10000 Vert=13077
F8-Options
Continue

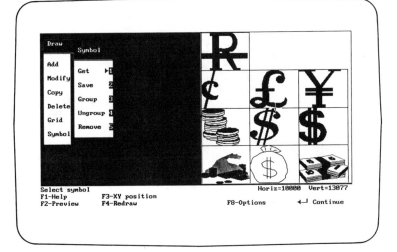

Fig. 3.37.

The Currency symbol file.

Fig. 3.38.

The upper left corner of the box that will hold the symbol.

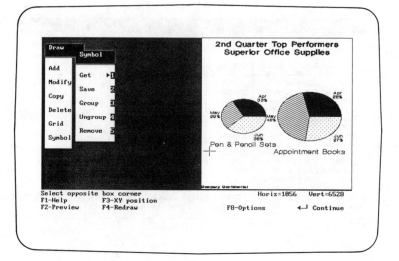

Fig. 3.39.

The box before Enter is pressed again.

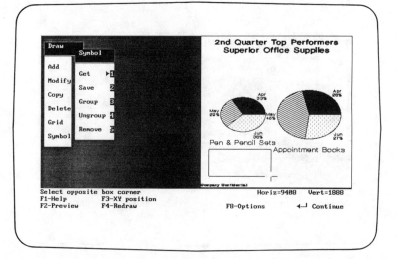

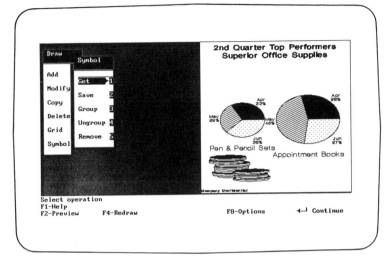

Fig. 3.40.

The pie chart with a symbol added.

Printing Your Charts

The visual accompaniment to your presentation is complete, so now you can accomplish one last detail: creating your final output. Notice that I didn't say "print" your charts. The reason is that Harvard Graphics creates slides and plotted charts as easily as it prints to a standard printer. Because you need to make transparencies for this presentation, though, you will print on a regular printer first and photocopy the completed charts onto transparency film later.

You can start by printing the chart you completed last. 2QPIESYM, the pie chart comparing pen and pencil set sales with appointment book sales is already on-screen. Then you can retrieve the other charts you created and print those.

Before you print for the first time, check to see that Harvard Graphics is set correctly for your printer. Chapter 2 provides important information about setting up Harvard Graphics for your output device. Chapter 9 gives detailed information about creating output.

To print your chart, follow these steps:

1. Select Produce Output from the Main menu.

2. Select Printer from the Produce Output menu. Use the Tab key to move between printing options and use the space bar to highlight the option you want to select.

3. Press F10 (Continue) to send the chart to the printer.

The Print Chart Options overlay choices that you make are saved with each chart. These choices include the following:

❏ Quality. Draft quality prints faster but without the sharpness of standard quality or the extra-fine resolution of high quality. Choose the Draft option the first time you print and check your work, because this option will print the fastest.

❏ Chart size. Harvard Graphics lets you print your chart in one of three sizes to accommodate your final output needs. Usually, on your first try, you should print at full size so you easily can inspect the chart.

❏ Paper size. Choose Letter (8 1/2-by-11-inch) to print on a standard-size page or choose Wide (8 1/2-by-14-inch) to print on a legal-size page.

❏ Printer. With this option, you can pick between two possible printer setups. For detailed information about setting up more than one printer for use with Harvard Graphics, see Chapter 2.

❏ Color. If you have a color printer or another output device that is color, you can select Yes to indicate color and your output will print in color.

❏ Number of copies. After Harvard Graphics constructs a chart to send to the printer, the program can print quickly as many copies as you want.

Chapter Summary

After completing this tour, you have only scratched the surface of the capabilities of Harvard Graphics. In this chapter, you created a text chart bullet list, a bar chart, and a pie chart. You used the F7-Size/Place option to alter the text size and the F5-Attributes option to alter the characteristics of a group of words. Then using the Draw/Annotate mode, you drew a box on a text chart. You also used the Draw/Annotate mode to select symbols and place them on a pie chart. And you saved and printed all the charts you created. In the next chapter, you will learn the details of creating text charts, and you will have the opportunity to create and embellish all the available text chart types.

Part II

Making Charts

Includes

Creating Text Charts

Creating Graph Charts: Bar and Line

Creating Graph Charts:
Area, High/Low/Close, and Pie

4

Creating Text Charts

Text charts are one of the most indispensable tools for business presentations. Overheads, slides, or handouts with bulleted points can distill a speech's central themes into easily understood key phrases. Text charts made into slides or overheads can offer an audience relief from less-than-electrifying orators.

Of all the chart types you will learn about in this book, text charts are the simplest to create. Unlike graph charts, which have many options, text charts require only that you enter and format text. As with any Harvard Graphics chart, however, producing a basic chart is only the start. With Draw/Annotate mode, you can add hand-drawn pictures or hundreds of preexisting symbols to a plain text chart. With Harvard Graphics' slide shows and screenshows, you can string a series of text and graph charts into an automated presentation.

Harvard Graphics offers four predefined text chart types: title, simple, bullet, and column charts. The program also offers a chart type, free-form, that you can use to design a page from scratch.

Creating a Title Chart

Title charts are ideal for the opening slide of a presentation or the first page of a handout. Title charts provide room for a large title, a smaller subtitle, and a second subtitle. These three areas are labeled *top*, *middle*, and *bottom*, and each area can include three lines of text. Figure 4.1 shows a title chart that uses all three text areas.

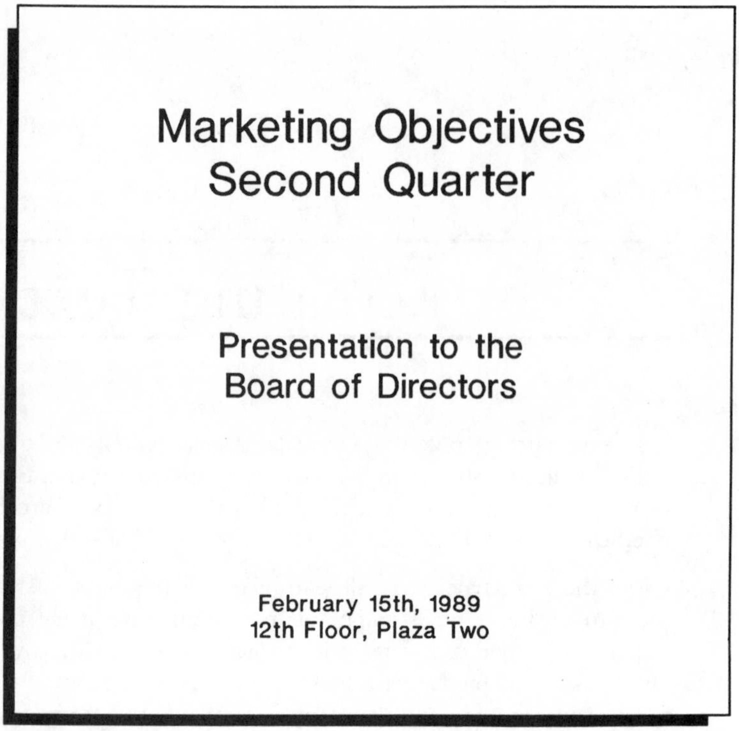

Fig. 4.1.

A sample title chart.

Marketing Objectives
Second Quarter

Presentation to the
Board of Directors

February 15th, 1989
12th Floor, Plaza Two

Starting a Title Chart

Before you create a chart, always press F8 (Options) at the Main menu. The Current Chart Options overlay appears (see fig. 4.2).

When you start Harvard Graphics, the Options settings are the same as the default settings you established when you used Setup on the Main menu. If you set the Orientation option to Portrait by using the Setup command, any chart you create starts in portrait orientation. You may want to modify the settings on the Current Chart Options overlay for this chart. For an explanation of the three options that appear on the Current Chart Options overlay, see the description of the Setup defaults in Chapter 2.

To change any of the current chart options, press the Tab key to move the cursor to the option you want to change and use the space bar to make a selection. To confirm your choice, press Enter. Continue until you have set all three options and returned to the Main menu. You also can set a single option and press Esc to return to the Main menu.

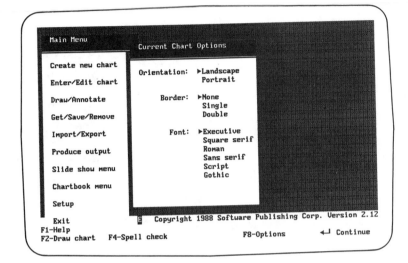

Fig. 4.2.

The Current Chart Options overlay.

To begin creating a title chart, do the following:

1. Select Create New Chart from the Main menu.

2. Select Text from the Create New Chart menu.

3. Select Title Chart from the Text Chart Styles menu.

4. The Title Chart screen appears. (If you have not saved the last chart you created or your latest changes, a warning message appears.)

Figure 4.3 shows the menu path you take to create a title chart.

Entering Title Chart Text

Title charts are the simplest and most easily understood example of how Harvard Graphics requests a few key ingredients and concocts a chart based on built-in chart recipes. You can sample the finished result by pressing F2 (Draw Chart). If the chart looks satisfactory, you need only save and print the chart and continue creating the next part of your presentation. You also can make alterations to customize the chart.

The Title Chart screen that appears after you select Title Chart from the Text Chart Styles menu shows three areas labeled Top, Middle, and Bottom. The top area holds a chart title, the middle area holds a chart subtitle, and the bottom area holds a second subtitle.

Fig. 4.3.

Menu path to the Text Chart Styles menu.

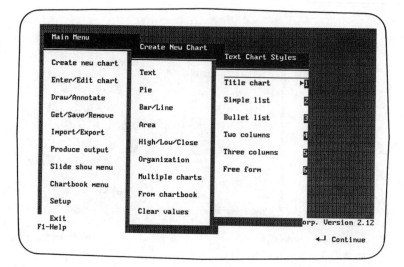

To enter text, position the cursor at one of the three areas by pressing Tab. Type up to three lines of text, pressing Enter at the end of each line to advance to a new line. You may type text into any or all three of the areas. Text entered into the top area appears as a title; text entered into the middle area appears centered vertically on the page, and text entered into the bottom area appears centered across the bottom of the page.

As a demonstration of how to create a title chart, follow this example. Superior Office Supplies needs to deliver a new product presentation to its sales force. The company plans to use a title chart as the first page of a slide presentation and as the first page of a handout distributed after the presentation.

To complete the Title Chart screen for the chart, enter *Superior Office Supplies* and *Marketing Division* into two lines in the top section. Enter *The Annihilator* and *Pencil Eraser* into two lines in the middle section and enter *New Product Presentation* into the bottom area. Figure 4.4 shows the completed Title Chart screen.

Previewing a Title Chart

After you have entered text into the three parts of the Title Chart screen, you can preview the chart by pressing F2 (Draw Chart). You should become accustomed to previewing your charts often as they are developed.

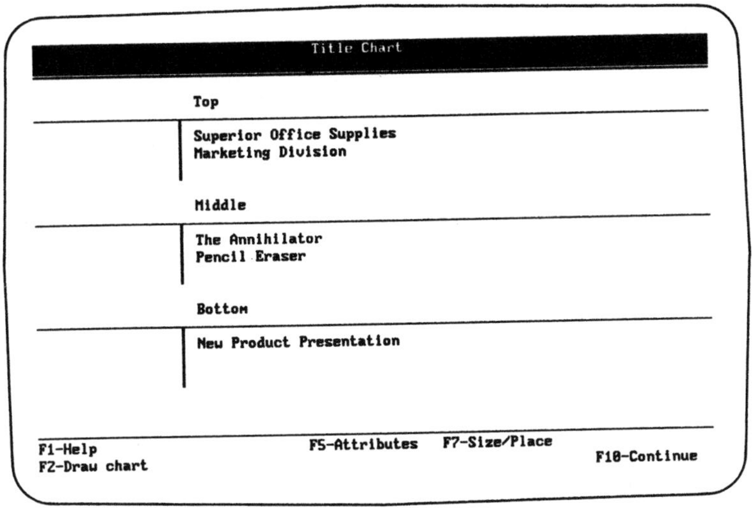

```
                        Title Chart


        Top


        Superior Office Supplies
        Marketing Division


        Middle


        The Annihilator
        Pencil Eraser


        Bottom


        New Product Presentation




F1-Help                    F5-Attributes   F7-Size/Place
F2-Draw chart                                        F10-Continue
```

Fig. 4.4.

The completed Title Chart screen.

Figure 4.5 shows the chart you see when you press F2 (Draw Chart). Harvard Graphics produces the same chart on-screen that the program produces later on paper or film. While previewing a chart, you can make no changes to the content or format.

Superior Office Supplies
Marketing Division

The Annihilator
Pencil Eraser

New Product Presentation

Fig. 4.5.

Previewing the title chart.

Notice that each line on the chart is centered and the top two text lines have the largest text size. The following section discusses how to modify this default. To quit previewing a chart and return to the Title Chart screen, press Esc.

Changing a Title Chart's Text Size and Placement

You can vary the size and placement of a chart's text by pressing F7 (Size/Place) when the Title Chart screen is displayed. When this option is available, it is presented as one of the function key choices at the bottom of the screen. Pressing F7 summons an overlay showing two new columns of information, as shown in figure 4.6.

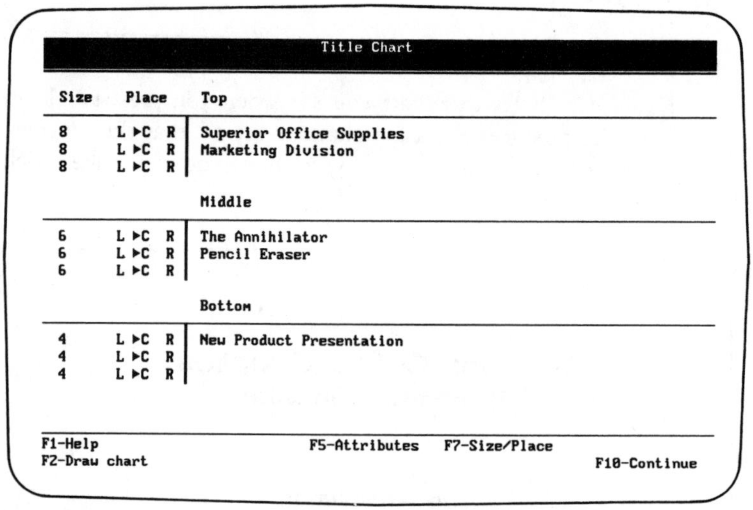

Fig. 4.6.

The Size/Place overlay.

```
                              Title Chart

         Size    Place    Top

          8      L ▸C  R   Superior Office Supplies
          8      L ▸C  R   Marketing Division
          8      L ▸C  R

                           Middle

          6      L ▸C  R   The Annihilator
          6      L ▸C  R   Pencil Eraser
          6      L ▸C  R

                           Bottom

          4      L ▸C  R   New Product Presentation
          4      L ▸C  R
          4      L ▸C  R


  F1-Help                          F5-Attributes   F7-Size/Place
  F2-Draw chart                                          F10-Continue
```

The Size/Place overlay enables you to modify text size and alignment.

Size, the first option you can set on the Size/Place overlay, is a measure of the height of the characters in a line of text. If a line contains no characters, the Size option determines how much space the line occupies. You can use this option to decrease the height of a blank line between two lines of text if you want to move the lines closer together.

The unit of measure may seem arbitrary to users accustomed to working in inches or points, but the simplest way to think of the character size is as a percentage of the largest possible character you can fit on the short side of your page or screen. The largest possible character has a Size of 99.9. All other characters are measured in relation to this hypothetical character, although the largest text size Harvard Graphics will accept is 99.9.

Without a familiar unit of measure, the results of a Size setting can be difficult to imagine. A good approach to using this option is to examine a line's current size and preview the chart. Adjust Size in increments of one or two until text characters look right when you preview the chart.

For example, a title with a Size setting of 11 overwhelms the other text on the chart shown in figure 4.7. A setting of 8, shown in figure 4.8, makes the title stand out but still blend with the rest of the text.

Fig. 4.7.

Overwhelming title (Size setting of 11).

Superior Office Supplies
Marketing Division

The Annihilator
Pencil Eraser

New Product Presentation

A Size setting of 0 removes a line. To delete a line temporarily from a chart, you can set the Size for the line to 0, print the chart, and return the line to its earlier size.

Fig. 4.8.

Title in proportion
(Size *setting of 8*).

Superior Office Supplies
Marketing Division

The Annihilator
Pencil Eraser

New Product Presentation

As you become accustomed to using Harvard Graphics, you will develop a feel for the relationship between the Size and the actual results on the printer, film recorder, or other output device.

Place, the second option you can set on the Size/Place overlay, determines the alignment of text. Text can be left-aligned, right-aligned, or centered.

Try making the Size and Place changes shown in figure 4.9 by following the procedure given here. The chart you preview by pressing F2 (Draw Chart) should match the chart shown in figure 4.10.

To change Size and Place settings, follow these steps:

1. Press F7 (Size/Place) to show the settings of each line of your chart.

2. Press Tab to move from setting to setting or press Shift-Tab to cycle through the settings in reverse order.

3. To enter a new Size, type the new number over the old number and press Enter.

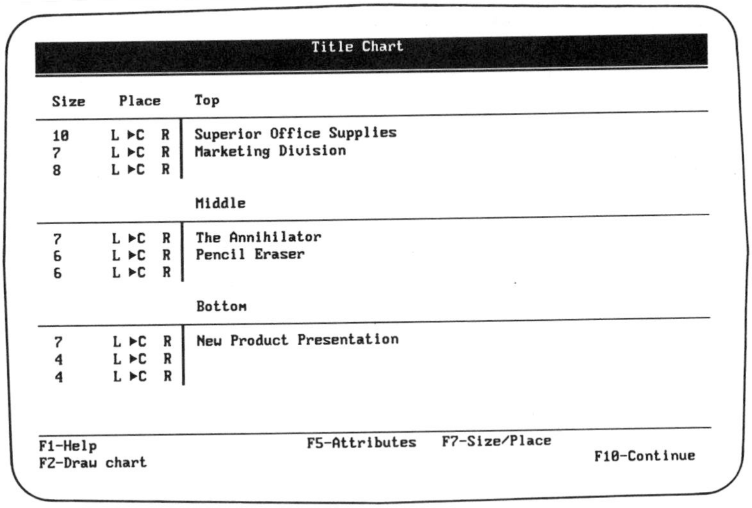
Title Chart
Size Place Top
10 L ▸C R Superior Office Supplies
7 L ▸C R Marketing Division
8 L ▸C R
Middle
7 L ▸C R The Annihilator
6 L ▸C R Pencil Eraser
6 L ▸C R
Bottom
7 L ▸C R New Product Presentation
4 L ▸C R
4 L ▸C R
F1-Help
F2-Draw chart
F5-Attributes
F7-Size/Place
F10-Continue

Fig. 4.9.

The Size *and* Place *selections for the title chart.*

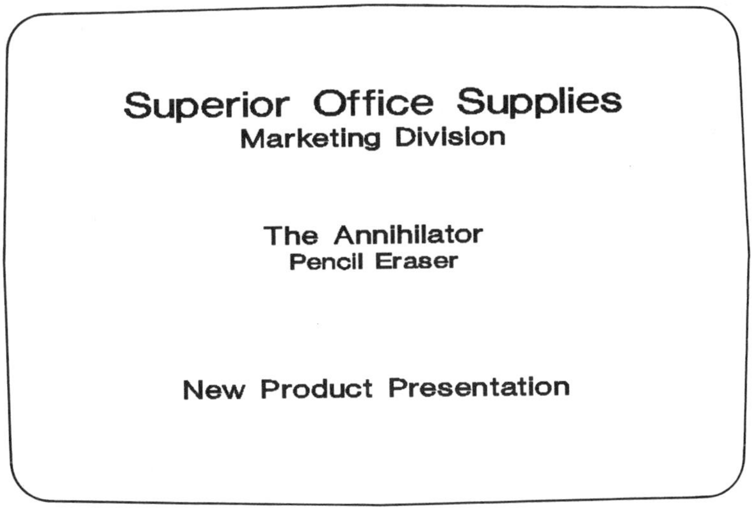
Superior Office Supplies
Marketing Division
The Annihilator
Pencil Eraser
New Product Presentation

Fig. 4.10.

The title chart previewed by pressing F2 (Draw Chart).

To change a line's Place, position the cursor on the setting for the current line (L, C, or R) by using the space bar to move the marker to the new selection and then press Enter. You also can press L, C, or R to make a Place selection.

4. Continue changing the Size and Place selections for all lines.

5. Press F10 (Continue) to return to the Title Chart screen.

6. Press F2 (Draw Chart) to preview the chart.

7. Modify your selections again, if necessary.

Modifying Title Chart Text Appearance

Text size is the first text characteristic you can change after you enter text into a text chart. You also can change text attributes by pressing F5 (Attributes). The Atributes menu bar appears.

The Fill option produces solid text characters. If Fill is off, characters appear as outlines. Figure 4.11 shows the difference between characters with the Fill option toggled on and off.

Fig. 4.11.

Fill on (above) versus Fill off (below).

The Bold, Italic, and Underline options format text as a word processor does. You can use any combination of these attributes.

The Color option modifies the color of text on-screen and as created by devices that produce color output, such as film recorders, color printers, and color plotters.

Modify the title chart you are creating by underlining *Marketing Division* and italicizing and toggling off the Fill option for *New Product Presentation*. To modify the attributes of selected text, follow these steps:

1. Be sure that you are viewing the Title Chart screen.

2. Position the cursor on the first text character you want to modify (the M in Marketing).

3. Press F5 (Attributes).

4. With the Attributes menu bar visible at the bottom of the screen, high-light the text you want to format (*Marketing Division*) by moving the cursor across the text with the arrow keys.

   To highlight an entire line, position your cursor on the first character of the line and press the down arrow. You also can press Shift-F5 to change the attributes for an entire line.

5. Use Tab to move the cursor on the Attributes menu bar from one option to the next. Use the space bar to toggle an option on or off. (An option is on when it is preceded by a small triangular pointer.) Toggle on the Underline option for the highlighted text and press F10 (Continue).

6. Position the cursor anywhere on the line with *New Products Presentation* and press Shift-F5 to highlight the entire line.

7. Press the space bar to turn off Fill and press Tab to move the cursor to Italic.

8. Press the space bar to turn on Italic.

9. Press F10 (Continue) to confirm your choice and F2 (Draw Chart) to pre-view the chart. Figure 4.12 shows the completed title chart.

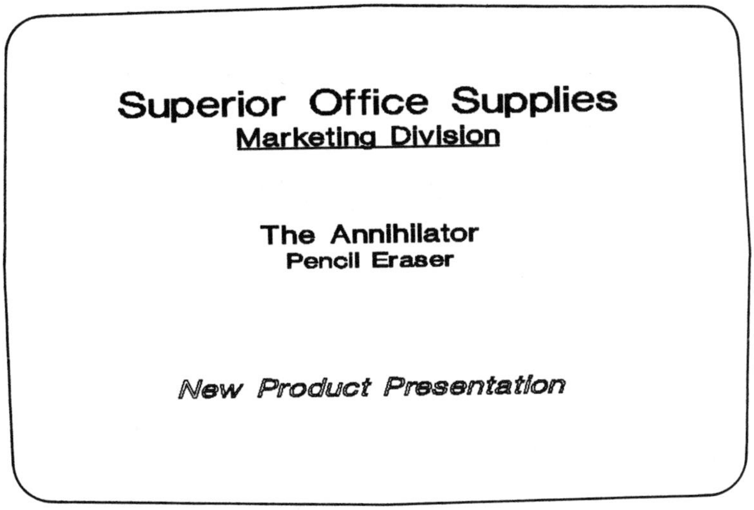

Fig. 4.12.

Preview of the completed title chart.

To set the color of text characters, use Tab to position the cursor on the Color number and press F6 to view a list of available colors. Select a color from the list by moving the cursor and pressing Enter when the correct color is highlighted.

Although you can choose the combination of text attributes you want first and then highlight the text to format, highlighting the text first is easier.

Saving a Title Chart

After you have fine-tuned your first chart to perfection, return to the Title Chart screen by pressing Esc. Press F10 (Continue) to return to the Harvard Graphics Main menu. From the Main menu, you can print the chart or save it on disk. Notice that the screen shows the current chart type near the bottom. When you save the chart, the chart name you choose appears to the right on the same line of the Main menu screen.

To save the chart so that you can modify or print it later, choose Get/Save/ Remove from the Main menu. The Save Chart option is highlighted on the Get/ Save/Remove menu that appears. Harvard Graphics recognizes that you have an unsaved chart in memory and prompts you to save the chart before continuing.

Select Save Chart and the Save Chart overlay appears, as shown in figure 4.13. Notice that Harvard Graphics supplies the disk directory you specified as a default and a description of the chart taken from the first line on the Title Chart screen. Enter *titlecht* as the file name. A file name can have up to eight characters. Press Enter so that you can modify the description, if necessary. As with most Harvard Graphics prompts, you can press Tab to move from one prompt to the next. Leave the current description, *Superior Office Supplies*, by pressing Enter to save the chart on disk. Printing charts is covered in Chapter 9.

Fig. 4.13.

The Save Chart overlay.

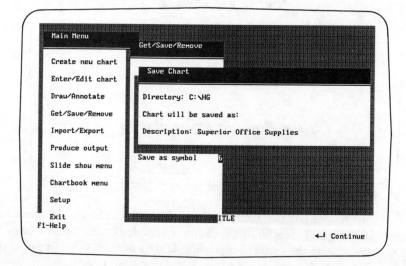

Making a Simple List

A simple list is ideal for presenting items arranged in no particular order and with each item given equal emphasis. The items of a simple list are displayed one under another and centered, unless you specify otherwise.

Use a simple list to identify the central subjects or themes of a presentation. For example, use a simple list as part of the overview of your sales presentation to show the products you will discuss.

By default, simple lists have a title centered at the top of the page, usually in a larger text size, followed by a list of centered items below the title and an optional footnote in the lower left corner. Figure 4.14 shows a simple list.

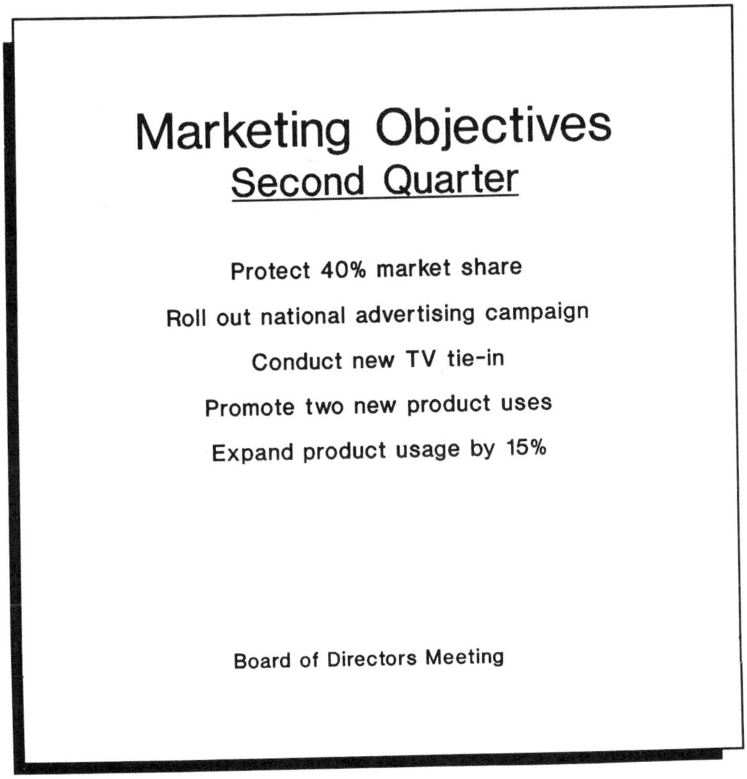

Marketing Objectives
<u>Second Quarter</u>

Protect 40% market share

Roll out national advertising campaign

Conduct new TV tie-in

Promote two new product uses

Expand product usage by 15%

Board of Directors Meeting

Fig. 4.14.

A *sample simple list.*

Unlike bullet lists, simple lists do not provide bullets before items or an automatic means to number items. You can add bullets manually.

Starting a Simple List

Before creating any chart, you should check the settings of the current options from the Main menu by pressing F8 (Options).

To create a simple list, select Simple List from the Text Chart Styles menu. Carry out the following procedure:

1. Select Create New Chart from the Main menu.

2. Select Text from the Create New Chart menu.

3. Select Simple List from the Text Chart Styles menu.

The Simple List screen appears. (If you have not saved the last chart you created or your latest changes, a warning message appears.)

If you have just saved another chart, that chart is still the current chart shown on the Main menu screen. If you select Enter/Edit Chart from the Main menu, the chart reappears. When you start a new chart, therefore, Harvard Graphics asks whether you want to Keep current data. If you select Yes, the program uses the preceding chart's data in the new chart. If you select No, the program presents you with a clear data screen, ready for new text. If you see a warning message, respond by pressing the space bar to change the setting to No and press Enter. The Simple List screen appears, as shown in figure 4.15.

Fig. 4.15.

The Simple List screen.

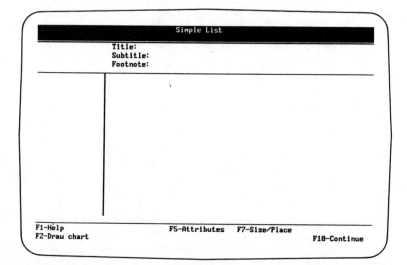

Entering Simple List Text

If you want to label your chart with a title, subtitle, and footnote, type the appropriate text where prompted at the top three lines of the Simple List screen. Use the Tab key to move from one line to another. Press Tab to move the cursor to the body of the page and type the simple list text items.

For the second chart in the Superior Office Supplies presentation, create a simple list by following these steps:

1. Enter *The Annihilator Pencil Eraser* as the title and press Enter.

2. Enter *Identified Customer Needs* as the subtitle and press Enter.

3. Press Enter again to leave the footnote area blank and move the cursor to the main text entry area of the screen.

4. Enter the following five text lines, pressing Enter twice after each line to double-space the lines:

   Total erasure

   Pointed end for precise erasures

   Blunt end for broad erasures

   No eraser flecking--eliminate pesky eraser bits

   Long-lasting

Figure 4.16 shows the completed Simple List screen.

To insert a new line between two items on a text chart screen, position the cursor where you want the new line to appear and press Ctrl-Ins. To delete a line, position the cursor on the line and press Ctrl-Del.

Adding Bullet Points to Simple List Items

If you want to place bullets on simple lists, you must enter the bullets manually. To enter a bullet before an item you are about to type, position the cursor at the beginning of a new line and press Ctrl-B. Select from one of the available bullet styles by using the space bar and press Enter. Leave one space following the bullet and type the item.

You also can add a bullet point to the beginning of a line you already have typed. Position the cursor on the first character of the line and press Ins. The cursor

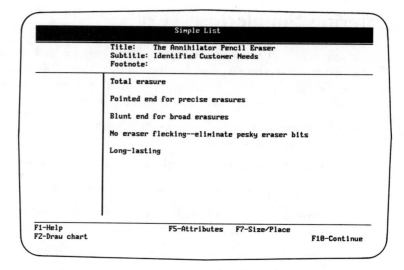

Fig. 4.16.

The completed Simple List screen.

changes from a blinking underline to a blinking block to indicate that anything you add will be inserted in the line. Press Ctrl-B, select a bullet style with the space bar, and press Enter.

Think of a block cursor (Insert on) as an object that can push current text aside to make room for new text. An underline cursor (Insert off) undercuts current text so that anything you add replaces old text.

Previewing a Simple List

To preview your work, press F2 (Draw Chart). Notice that Harvard Graphics has drawn a simple list. You probably can use the list as is, or you can customize the list. To begin making changes, press Esc to return to the Simple List screen.

You can make two changes so that the chart will be more attractive: use a smaller text size for the list of items and underline the chart's subtitle.

Changing a Simple List's Text Size and Placement

Press F7 (Size/Place) to modify the text's size and horizontal positioning. When the Size/Place overlay appears, notice that you can change the Size and Place settings for the title, subtitle, and footnote independently, but you can specify only one setting for all of the list items. You also can choose to indent all the list items by making sure that the items' Place is set to L (left-aligned) and typing over the current indent number with a new number. The number you use should be a percentage of the width of the screen; 50, for example, starts list items half-way across the screen.

Alter the size of your list items from 5.5 to 4, press F10 (Continue) to accept the change, and remove the Size/Place overlay. Press F2 (Draw Chart) to preview the chart and notice the difference in appearance. Figure 4.17 shows the revised simple list. Press Esc to return to the Simple List screen.

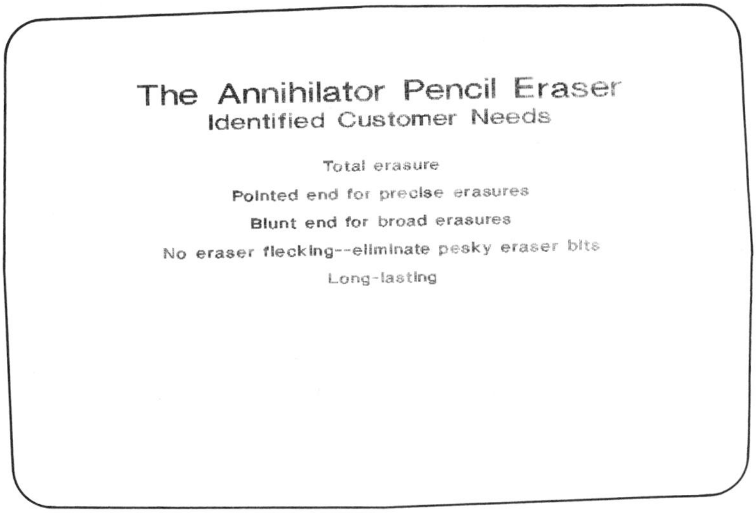

The Annihilator Pencil Eraser
Identified Customer Needs

Total erasure
Pointed end for precise erasures
Blunt end for broad erasures
No eraser flecking--eliminate pesky eraser bits
Long-lasting

Fig. 4.17.

Simple list previewed with items set to Size 4.

Modifying Simple List Text Appearance

With simple lists, you can choose from among the same set of possible text attributes as title charts. For a description of each of these attributes, refer to "Modifying Title Chart Text Appearance" in this chapter.

To perfect this chart, add an underline attribute to the subtitle. To change the attributes of an entire line, you position the cursor and press Shift-F5.

Use the following procedure:

1. Position the cursor on the first character in the subtitle line.

2. Press Shift-F5 to highlight the entire line.

3. Press Tab to move the cursor next to Underline at the bottom of the screen.

4. Press the space bar to turn on the underline attribute and press Enter.

5. Press F2 (Draw Chart) to preview the changes.

Figure 4.18 shows the completed simple list.

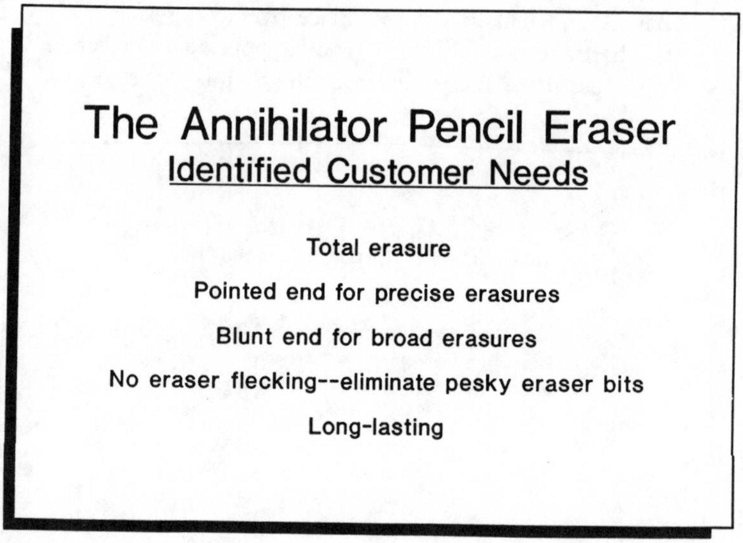

Fig. 4.18.

The completed simple list.

The Annihilator Pencil Eraser
Identified Customer Needs

Total erasure

Pointed end for precise erasures

Blunt end for broad erasures

No eraser flecking--eliminate pesky eraser bits

Long-lasting

Saving a Simple List

To save a simple list, press F10 (Continue) at the Simple List screen to return to the Main menu. Choose Get/Save/Remove from the Main menu and Save Chart from the Get/Save/Remove menu.

At the Chart will be saved as line, type *simplcht* and press Enter. Notice that Harvard Graphics borrows the title of the chart as the description. Alter the description, if you want, by pressing Ctrl-Del to erase the current entry and typing a new entry; or press Enter to save the chart with the name SIMPLCHT.

Preparing a Bullet List

Bullet lists serve the same purpose as simple lists: to communicate a series of ideas or to list a set of items. Bullet lists have several unique characteristics. Unlike simple list items, items in a bullet list are preceded by one of four bullet shapes and aligned so that the bullets line up under one another. A fifth option enables you to number items to designate a sequence.

Bullet lists have a title, subtitle, and footnote, like simple lists. You can add as many lines of text as you want to each bullet point, and you can group logically related items together as subitems under main bullet points, creating an outline format.

Figure 4.19 shows a sample bullet list, and figure 4.20 shows a bullet list with subitems.

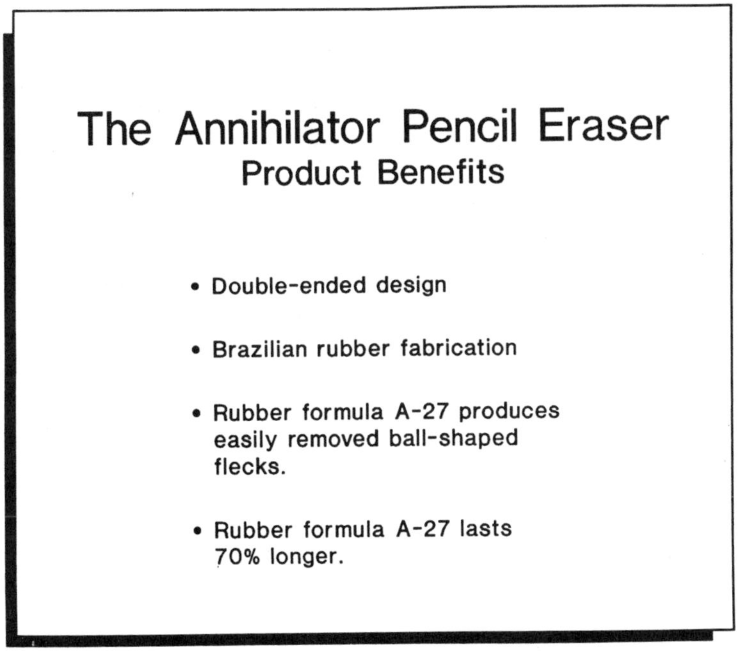

The Annihilator Pencil Eraser
Product Benefits

- Double-ended design

- Brazilian rubber fabrication

- Rubber formula A-27 produces easily removed ball-shaped flecks.

- Rubber formula A-27 lasts 70% longer.

Fig. 4.19.

A sample bullet list.

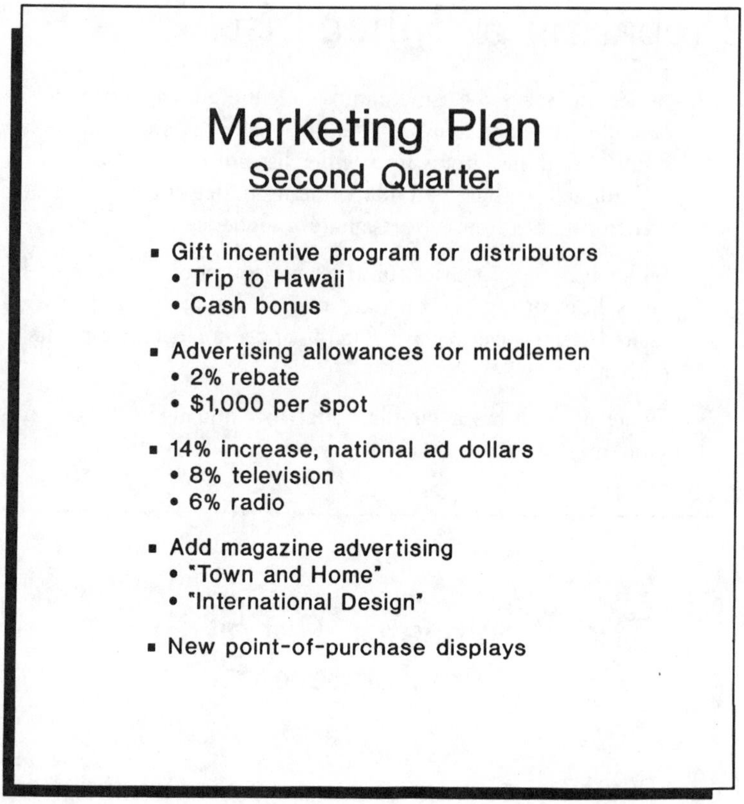

Fig. 4.20.

A bullet list with
subitems.

Marketing Plan
Second Quarter

- ■ Gift incentive program for distributors
  - • Trip to Hawaii
  - • Cash bonus

- ■ Advertising allowances for middlemen
  - • 2% rebate
  - • $1,000 per spot

- ■ 14% increase, national ad dollars
  - • 8% television
  - • 6% radio

- ■ Add magazine advertising
  - • "Town and Home"
  - • "International Design"

- ■ New point-of-purchase displays

Starting a Bullet List

To start a bullet list, follow these steps:

1. Select Create New Chart from the Main menu.

2. Select Text from the Create New Chart menu.

3. Select Bullet List from the Text Chart Styles menu.

The Bullet List screen appears. (If you have not saved the last chart you created or saved your latest changes, a warning message appears.) If the Change Chart Type overlay appears to ask whether to Keep current data, reply No.

Entering Bullet List Text

When the Bullet List screen appears, the cursor is next to the Title prompt. Type a chart title, subtitle, and footnote, pressing Enter after each.

For the third chart in Superior Office Supplies' presentation, enter the title *The Annihilator Pencil Eraser.* For a subtitle, enter *Product Benefits.*

Pressing Enter a third time creates the first bullet point and places the cursor to the right of the bullet.

A new bullet appears each time you leave a blank line by pressing Enter or the down arrow twice. If you press Enter once at the end of a line, any new text you type continues as part of the preceding bullet.

Type the first bullet item, *Double-ended design,* and press Enter once. Notice that the cursor returns to the beginning of the next line, immediately under the first bullet's text. Press Enter again, and a new bullet appears.

Using Subitems To Create Outlines

By inserting a bullet at the beginning of the second line of a bulleted item, you can create the tiered effect shown in figure 4.21. Each new line starts under the first character of text after the bullet in the preceding line.

Notice that the first two levels of the bullet list have consistent bullet styles. The third level is not bulleted. The rule of thumb for creating attractive bullet lists is no more than two bullet types per chart.

To begin a new line with a bullet, press Ctrl-B before entering the line's text, select the square bullet style from the Bullet Shape overlay by using the space bar, and press Enter. After the bullet appears, enter a space and type your text.

To add a bullet to the beginning of an existing line, make sure that you are in Insert mode by pressing Ins. (The cursor should be a flashing block rather than a flashing underline.) Position the cursor at the beginning of the line, press Ctrl-B, select the bullet style you want, and press Enter. Pressing Ctrl-B always adds a bullet at the current cursor position no matter what type of chart you are creating.

Add a second-tier bullet item by pressing the up arrow to move the cursor under the first bullet. Notice that the second bullet disappears. Press Ctrl-B, choose the round bullet from the Bullet Shape overlay by pressing Enter, and enter a space

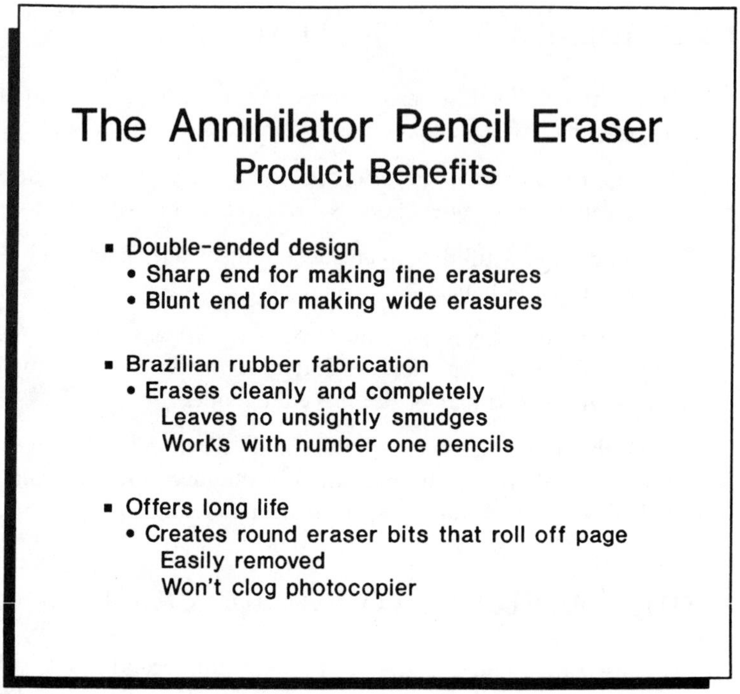

Fig. 4.21.

*Bullet list with
tiered outline effect.*

The Annihilator Pencil Eraser
Product Benefits

- Double-ended design
  - Sharp end for making fine erasures
  - Blunt end for making wide erasures

- Brazilian rubber fabrication
  - Erases cleanly and completely
    Leaves no unsightly smudges
    Works with number one pencils

- Offers long life
  - Creates round eraser bits that roll off page
    Easily removed
    Won't clog photocopier

followed by *Sharp end for making fine erasures*. Press Enter at the end of the line and repeat the procedure to add another second-tier bullet item: *Blunt end for making wide erasures*. Press Enter twice to create a new first-level bullet item. Complete the bullet list to match the items in figure 4.21.

To insert a new blank line between two existing lines, position the cursor anywhere on the second line and press Ctrl-Ins.

To delete a line, position the cursor anywhere on the line and press Ctrl-Del. If the line has a bullet point, the bullet point does not disappear. To remove the bullet point, press the up-arrow key once.

Press F2 (Draw Chart) to preview the appearance of your bullet list. Press Esc to return to the Bullet List screen to make changes.

Changing a Bullet List's Text Size and Placement

Changing the size and placement of lines of bullet lists by pressing F7 (Size/Place) is the same process you used in the section "Making a Simple List." The effect of Place on bullet list items, however, is different from its effect on simple list items.

With simple lists, the left, right, and center options align text lines on the page. The result is shown in figure 4.22.

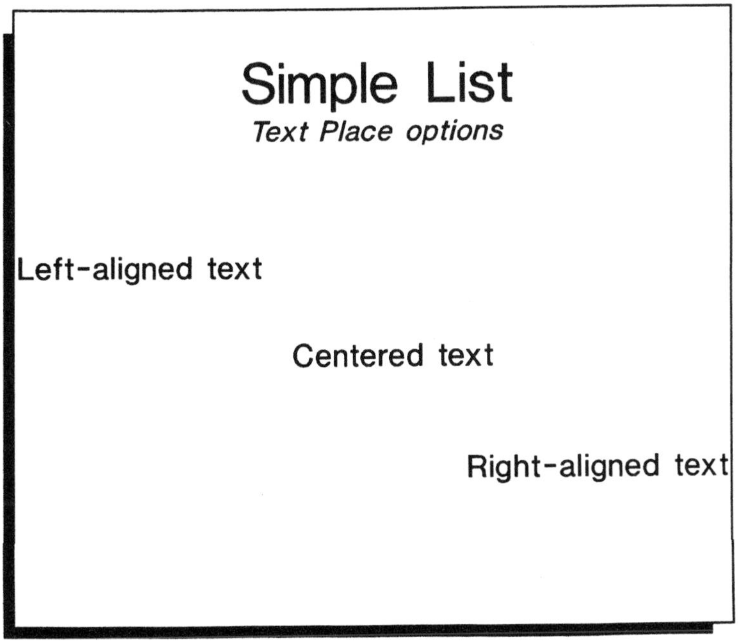

Simple List
Text Place options

Left-aligned text

Centered text

Right-aligned text

Fig. 4.22.

Simple list text alignment.

Bullet list items always line up under one another so that the bullets line up vertically on the page. Choosing left or right alignment moves all bullet list items together so that the left or right edge of the group aligns with the left or right side of the page. The difference between the two actions is evident when bullet items are right-aligned and you have one bullet item longer than the others. The longest item is the only one aligned with the right edge of the page. The results of choosing left, center, and right alignment for bullet items are shown in figure 4.23.

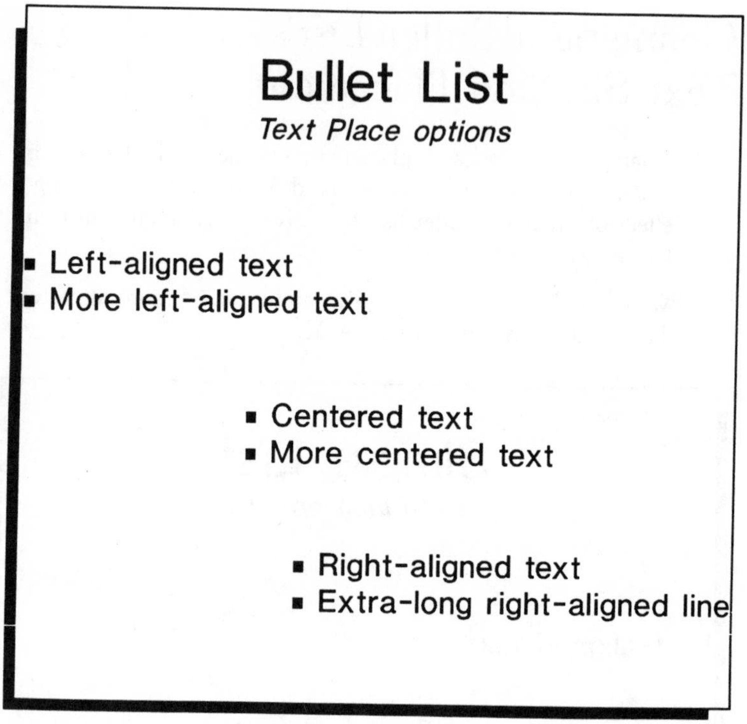

Fig. 4.23.

Bullet list text alignment.

Bullet List
Text Place options

- Left-aligned text
- More left-aligned text

- Centered text
- More centered text

- Right-aligned text
- Extra-long right-aligned line

Changing Bullet Types

The Size/Place command for bullet lists offers a new capability not seen with the charts created earlier in this chapter. With the bullet list Size/Place command, you can change the type of bullet used for main bullet points by selecting from the five bullet shapes shown on the Size/Place overlay. To change the bullet shape used, do the following:

1. Press F7 (Size/Place) with the Bullet List screen displayed.

2. Use Tab to move the cursor to the five bullet shapes.

3. Use the space bar to select a square bullet shape.

4. Press F10 (Continue) to return to the Bullet List screen.

5. Press F2 (Draw Chart) to preview the change.

Numbering Bullets

To number main bullets sequentially, choose the number sign (#) when you select a bullet shape. Subitems created when you press Ctrl-B do not have the # option and can be numbered only manually. Number signs appear on the Bullet List screen to indicate that actual numbers will appear on the final chart.

Modifying Bullet List Text Attributes

To modify text attributes, use F5 (Attributes) as described earlier in this chapter in the section "Making a Simple List." Bullets are the same color as the first character of the text that follows. If you want to alter the color of bullet points without changing the color of the text, follow this procedure:

1. Insert a blank space after the bullet point.

2. Modify the color attribute of only that space.

3. Preview the chart to see that the bullet has changed color.

You also can leave a space when you type the bullet item, so that you can change the bullet's color attribute later.

Saving a Bullet List

To save a bullet list, press F10 (Continue) from the Bullet List screen to return to the Main menu. Choose Get/Save/Remove from the Main menu and Save Chart from the Get/Save/Remove menu.

At the Chart will be saved as line, type *buletcht* as a file name for the chart and press Enter. Notice that Harvard Graphics uses the title of the chart as the description. Alter the description by typing over the current entry and pressing Enter or just press Enter to save the chart.

Making Column Charts

Column charts display related text items side by side in two or three columns. Some ideal uses for two-column charts are comparison lists with benefits and drawbacks. Column charts also are useful in comparing numeric information. Figure 4.24 is a typical three-column chart used to illustrate financial information. This chart compares revenues for the first quarter.

Fig. 4.24.

*Three-column
revenue chart.*

First Quarter Revenues*
Year Two

January	February	March
$246,520	$252,300	$260,170
$230,200	$247,950	$256,469

*Total sales, not including refunds

Starting a Two- or Three-Column Chart

Start a column chart as you do any other text chart but choose Two Columns or Three Columns from the Text Chart Styles menu. Choose Two Columns to create the next chart in the Superior Office Supplies presentation, shown in figure 4.25. If the Keep current data prompt appears, reply No so that you can enter new data. The Two Columns screen appears with spaces to type a title, subtitle, and footnote, and spaces for column headings and column items.

Entering Text into a Column Chart

To enter data into the Two Columns screen, type a title, subtitle, and footnote in the spaces provided. Press Tab or Enter to move to the space for the first column heading. Type a column heading for each column, pressing Tab after

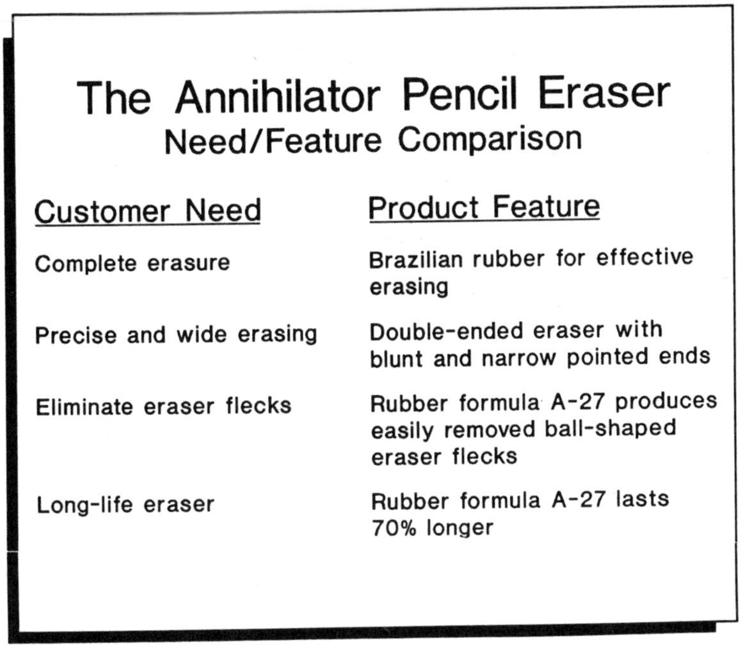

The Annihilator Pencil Eraser
Need/Feature Comparison

Customer Need	Product Feature
Complete erasure	Brazilian rubber for effective erasing
Precise and wide erasing	Double-ended eraser with blunt and narrow pointed ends
Eliminate eraser flecks	Rubber formula A-27 produces easily removed ball-shaped eraser flecks
Long-life eraser	Rubber formula A-27 lasts 70% longer

Fig. 4.25.

Two-column chart.

each one. When all column headings are in place, the cursor jumps to the data area for the first column.

To practice creating a two-column chart, enter *The Annihilator Pencil Eraser* for a title and *Need/Feature Comparison* for a subtitle. Press Enter to leave the footnote area blank and move the cursor to the first column heading. Enter *Customer Need* and press Tab (not Enter) to move the cursor to the second column heading. Enter *Product Feature* and press Enter. Press Shift-Tab to begin entering text items in the first column.

Enter an item and press Tab to jump to the next column. Pressing Enter moves the cursor down one line without moving to the next column. To double-space items, press Tab when you complete the right-hand column item and press Enter to skip a line before typing the next item. Harvard Graphics text chart screens do not have word wrap. You must press Enter at the end of each line to continue typing on the next line.

Enter the items on the Two Columns screen shown in figure 4.26 and press F2 (Draw Chart) to preview your work.

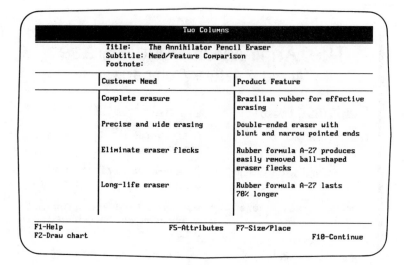

Fig. 4.26.

The Two Columns screen.

Special Size/Place Considerations

Using the F7-Size/Place feature works with text in column charts as it works with text in other text charts. You should be aware of a few special Size/Place uses specific to column charts.

Harvard Graphics presents four options, much like clothes sizes, for column spacing on the Size/Place overlay: S, M, L, and XL. S leaves the smallest spacing between consecutive columns. XL leaves the largest spacing. The best way to select the proper column spacing for your chart is by trying one, previewing the chart, and trying the next setting. You may find that the default column width is the best. In this case, the default is M.

Harvard Graphics places all text items against the left edge of a column and all numeric items against the right edge of a column so that the decimal points align. Numeric items can include dollar signs, commas, and decimal points.

Modifying Text Attributes

The Attributes command used with column charts presents the same formatting commands described earlier. Highlight the text to format and use Tab and the space bar to choose attribute settings. Use Shift-F5 to set attributes for an entire line. When you preview the column chart, notice that the two column headings are underlined automatically.

Saving a Column Chart

After you have created and viewed your column chart, press Esc to return to the Column Chart screen. Press F10 (Continue) to return to the Main menu. Notice that the chart type listed near the bottom of the screen is 2 COLUMN. Choose Get/ Save/Remove from the Main menu and Save Chart from the Get/Save/Remove menu.

Follow the same procedure described earlier for entering the chart's name and revising the description. Name the chart TWOCOL. After the chart is saved, notice that the current chart name appears to the right of the chart type on the Main menu screen.

Adding a Third Column to a Two-Column Chart

You can add a third column to a preexisting two-column chart by using Get Chart to retrieve the two-column chart and then returning to the Main menu.

If you choose Yes when the Keep current data prompt appears, Harvard Graphics uses the two-column chart's existing columns as the left two columns. You need only fill in the third column to complete the chart.

To start a three-column chart, choose Create New Chart from the Main menu, Text from the Create New Chart menu, and Three Columns from the Text Chart Styles menu.

If you have set the two-column chart to portrait orientation, you may need to change the chart to landscape orientation to accommodate a third column. To change the orientation of a chart, return to the Main menu by pressing F10 (Continue) at the Three Columns screen, pressing F8 to call up the Current Chart Options overlay, and choosing Landscape.

Creating Free-Form Charts

Free-form charts let you create a text chart design of your own. Because of this flexibility, free-form charts are ideal for text presentations that do not fit any of the predefined text chart molds. Among charts appropriate for the free-form chart style are charts with unusually wide columns and charts including large areas of text. Free-form charts also are ideal for invitations, directions, and certificates, none of which fall neatly into the predefined text chart categories. Figure 4.27 shows a typical free-form chart.

Fig. 4.27.

A typical free-form chart.

Travel Directions
Smith Wedding

<u>From I–48</u>

Turn right at end of Clovesdale exit ramp. Follow signs to Route 46. Turn right onto Charles St. House is large white Victorian on left. #140 on mailbox.

<u>From Davis Parkway</u>

Exit at Forest Lake Road. Turn left off exit onto Route 117. Go through two intersections to stop light. Turn right onto Woodland Manor. Turn left onto Charles St. Look for large white Victorian on right. #140 on mailbox.

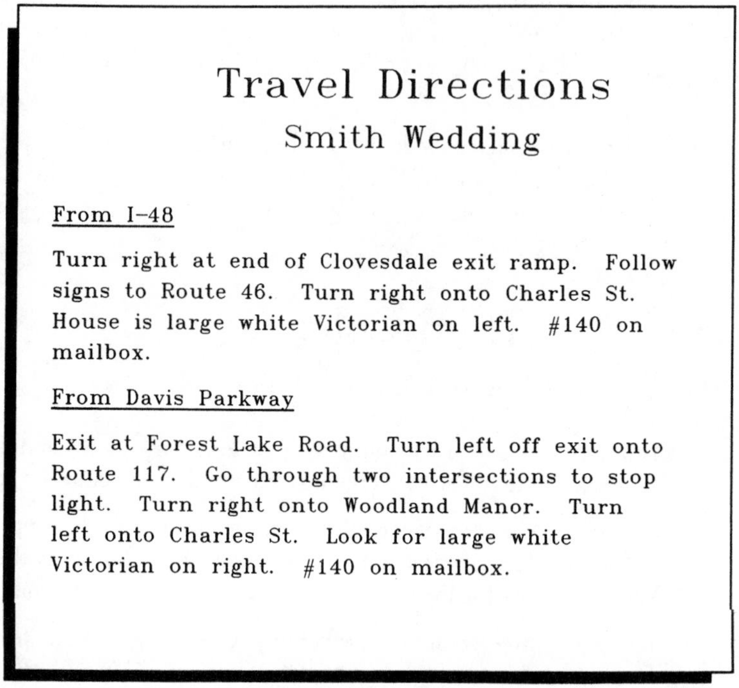

As you create a free-form chart, you can place text anywhere within the text entry area on the Free Form Text screen. Text appears on the page as you place the text on-screen. Figure 4.28 shows the free-form chart Superior Office Supplies uses to introduce promotional plans.

Start a free-form chart by choosing Create New Chart from the Main menu and Text from the Create New Chart menu. When the Text Chart Styles menu appears, choose Free Form. If the Keep current data query appears, reply No to start a new chart.

The Free Form Text screen appearing next shows spaces for a title, subtitle, footnote, and text. You usually type entries into the title, subtitle, and footnote spaces so that Harvard Graphics can position the key elements of your chart on the page.

For the Superior Office Supplies free-form chart, enter *The Annihilator Pencil Eraser* as the title and *Promotion Plan* as the subtitle.

To set up columns in a free-form chart, line up the first characters of items under one another on-screen and be sure to leave at least two spaces between the end of an item in one column and the beginning of an item in the next column.

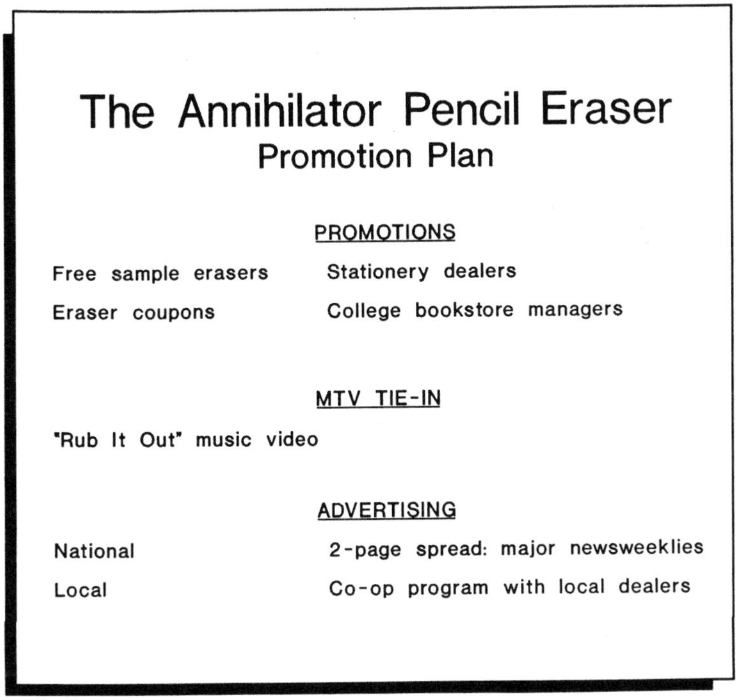

The Annihilator Pencil Eraser
Promotion Plan

PROMOTIONS

Free sample erasers   Stationery dealers

Eraser coupons   College bookstore managers

MTV TIE-IN

"Rub It Out" music video

ADVERTISING

National   2-page spread: major newsweeklies

Local   Co-op program with local dealers

Fig. 4.28.

Superior Office Supplies' free-form chart.

Try creating the free-form chart shown in figure 4.28 by filling out a Free Form Text screen as shown in figure 4.29. Notice that the centered headings on the chart are created from headings centered in the text entry area. The first letters of any items you want to set up in columns line up under one another, and at least two spaces appear before each new column begins. Figure 4.29 does not show the two lines under the ADVERTISING head, but the Free Form Text screen scrolls as you enter text.

Save a free-form chart as you save other charts. Complete the chart and press F10 (Continue) to return to the Main menu. From the Main menu, choose Get/Save/Remove. From the Get/Save/Remove menu, choose Save Chart. Type *free-form* as the name of the sample chart and accept the chart's current description.

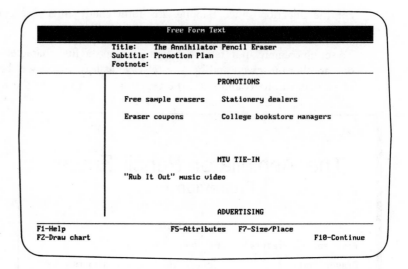

Fig. 4.29.

The Free Form Text screen.

Remember that Harvard Graphics derives the description from the title of the chart.

Setting Up Organization Charts

Because organization charts are so popular for representing the structure of an organization, Harvard Graphics includes a special menu option for constructing the charts.

Organization charts are not on the list of text charts that Harvard Graphics creates, but a discussion of organization charts is in this chapter because of their similarity to text charts and because organization charts concern text information rather than numeric data.

Organization charts diagram the reporting structure of a multilevel organization, such as a corporation, club, or service. Organization charts show the interrelation of managers and subordinates: who reports to whom. Harvard Graphics can create organization charts depicting up to eight levels of hierarchy and showing up to 80 members or components. Rarely, if ever, do you need to create a chart with that much detail. Figure 4.30 shows a typical organization chart produced by Harvard Graphics.

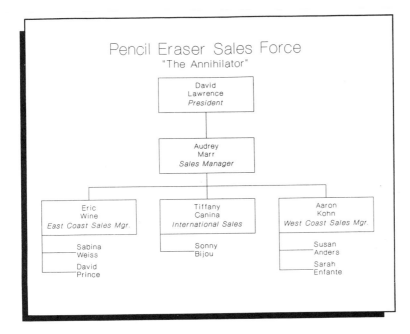

Fig. 4.30.

A typical organization chart.

To help you create an organization chart, Harvard Graphics takes you through a process that involves identifying the members of a hierarchical level and identifying all subordinates to that level.

With Harvard Graphics, you can choose to print the entire organization or pick any one division or section of the organization and print only its members.

Starting an Organization Chart

Before you create any chart, check the current option settings by pressing F8 (Options) at the Main menu. Organization charts are best suited to a landscape orientation with a plain typeface.

To create an organization chart, use the following procedure:

1. Select Create New Chart from the Main menu.

2. Select Organization from the Create New Chart menu.

The Organization Chart screen appears. (If you have not saved the last chart you created or your latest changes, a warning message appears.)

Entering Names, Titles, Comments, and Abbreviations

Before typing the names of the individuals you want to depict in an organization chart, you may want to take a moment to sketch the chart on paper. Although you can preview your chart as you build it, you do not see the chart on-screen as you go. A drawing on paper in front of you, therefore, can serve as a map to the organization chart level by level.

In addition to the standard spaces for title, subtitle, and footnote, the Organization Chart screen has spaces for six items of information about each manager (name, title, comment, and an abbreviation for each) and an area at the right side of the screen for a list of subordinates. Managers are the members of the current level you are creating, and subordinates are members of the level below. When you move down a level, individuals who were subordinates become managers, and you can type a new lower layer of subordinates. The Organization Chart screen provides spaces to fill in full and abbreviated information so that you can choose later which one to display.

To begin creating an organization chart Superior Office Supplies can use to depict the structure of the sales force, enter *Pencil Eraser Sales Force* as the title and *"The Annihilator"* as the subtitle, pressing Enter after each.

Type the manager's information as shown in figure 4.31. You may need to use a combination of the arrow keys, Tab key, and Shift-Tab to move the cursor to the proper location on-screen.

With the manager's information in place, you are ready to enter the subordinates. Position the cursor in the subordinates column and enter *Audrey Marr*. The sales manager is the only subordinate to the president in the sales organization depicted by this chart.

Rearranging the Order of Subordinates

To move a subordinate up or down the list of subordinates, position the cursor on the subordinate's name on the Organization Chart screen and press Ctrl-up arrow or Ctrl-down arrow. Rearranging the order of subordinates also rearranges the order of items on all lower levels.

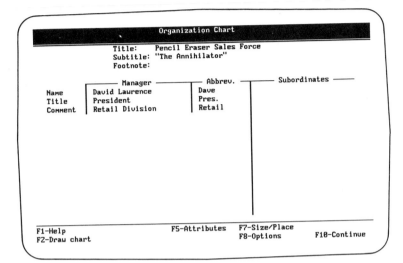

Fig. 4.31.

The manager's information entered on the Organization Chart screen.

Using Ctrl-PgDn To Start a Lower Level

To add subordinates to any of the individuals showing on-screen, position the cursor on a subordinate's name and press Ctrl-PgDn. This instant promotion changes the currently highlighted subordinate to a manager and opens spaces for a lower level of subordinates. You can return to the higher level by pressing Ctrl-PgUp.

As you move about the organization's structure, you can view a single manager and all of that manager's subordinates. To move from one manager to another at the same level, press PgUp or PgDn.

After you have moved down a level in the hierarchy, you can add a title, comment, or abbreviation for the individual in the Manager slot, and you can type a list of that manager's subordinates.

After you press Ctrl-PgDn, enter the list of subordinates under Audrey Marr, who is now the manager. In the subordinates column, enter three names: *Eric Wine, Tiffany Canina,* and *Aaron Kohn.* You also may want to enter a title for Audrey Marr at this point. Position the cursor in the manager column next to Title and type *Sales Manager.* To enter the subordinates for Eric Wine, position the cursor on Eric's name and press Ctrl-PgDn. After subordinates are entered, you may want to press Ctrl-PgUp so that you can enter the subordinates under Tiffany Canina. Continue with this process until the entire organization's structure is depicted, as shown in figure 4.30.

Changing Text Size, Placement, and Attributes

You have seen that pressing F7 (Size/Place) and F5 (Attributes) enables you to modify the appearance of any text in a chart. With organization charts, the function of these two commands is a little different. Size/Place and Attributes operate on the title, subtitle, and footnote only. To change the appearance of text in the body of a chart, use F8 (Options).

Adding a Staff Position

To enter an employee as staff rather than line (outside the hierarchical reporting structure), enter the employee as a subordinate but precede the employee's name with an asterisk. You can have only one staff position in a chart. Staff employees can have no subordinates. If you have already entered subordinates for an employee that you want to make staff, you must delete the subordinates first before inserting an asterisk preceding the staff employee's name.

Fine-Tuning the Chart Layout with Options

With the Organization Chart screen displayed, press F8 (Options) several times. Pressing F8 toggles Harvard Graphics between the screen and the Org Chart Options page shown in figure 4.32. Making changes on the Organization Chart screen changes the *contents* of the current chart. Changing options on the Org Chart Options page modifies the *appearance* of the current chart. The menu at the bottom of the screen shows the result of pressing F8, and the title at the top of the screen indicates whether you are on Options (appearance) or Data (content).

Press F8 to return to the Options page and examine the list of options shown. The options at the top of the page affect the body of the chart and the options at the bottom of the page affect the lowest level.

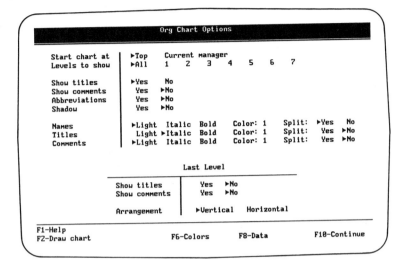

Fig. 4.32.

The Org Chart Options page.

To change options, use the Tab key to move the cursor and the space bar to change the setting. When all options are set as you want, press F8 (Data) to return to the chart or press F10 (Continue) to return to the Main menu.

Organization Chart Options

If you select Top for the Start chart at option on the Org Chart Options screen, Harvard Graphics displays the entire chart. If you choose Current manager, the program displays only the portion of the organization under the current manager. With this option, you can create more than one chart to illustrate your organization's structure. A main chart can show the entire organization, and secondary charts can offer a break-down of employees by manager.

Use Levels to show with Start chart at to display a specific number of organizational levels. To show all levels, select All. To show only the president and vice presidents of an organization, for example, set Levels to show to 2.

Setting the Show titles and Show comments options to Yes displays the titles or comments you supplied for each manager. Titles and comments appear below the manager's name.

Harvard Graphics enables you to display a chart showing only the abbreviations you supplied for each manager. Setting Abbreviations to Yes is helpful when you have many people and a limited amount of space. Unless you show abbreviations, Harvard Graphics produces small boxes with tiny text in an attempt to fit all employees in the chart. If the people you include in your chart have long names, you may see an error message indicating that you should break the names into two lines.

When Shadow is set to Yes, Harvard Graphics creates an appealing shadow effect behind each manager's box. The shadow is the same color as the color set as number 16 on the color palette. Depending on the output device you use, turning Shadow on may slow printing.

With the Names, Titles, and Comments lines on the Org Chart Options page, you can assign most of the text attributes you are accustomed to setting with F5 (Attributes).

Light is normal text. By default, names and comments are light and titles are italicized. To change the color of text, position the cursor on the current color number (the default setting is 1) and press F6 to choose another color from the color palette.

If you set the Split option to Yes, you are telling Harvard Graphics to split names, titles, or comments using two words. These items are split between words so that items appear one under another. Harvard Graphics splits items between the first and second words by default. To indicate where words should be split, place a vertical bar (|) between words as you type.

Last Level Options

You can decide to show titles or comments for items at the last level of the chart. You also can determine a vertical or horizontal arrangement for the last level. Figures 4.33 and 4.34 show the difference between arranging the last line vertically or horizontally.

Saving an Organization Chart

After you complete an organization chart, return to the Main menu by pressing F10 (Continue). Notice that the current chart type is Org and that there is no current chart name. Select the Save Chart option from the Get/Save/Remove menu. Enter the chart name *org* and accept the Harvard Graphics choices for current directory and chart description. Press Enter to save the chart.

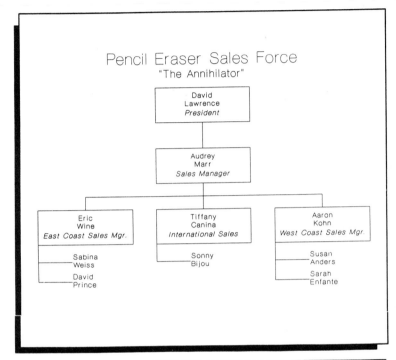

Fig. 4.33.

Last line arranged vertically.

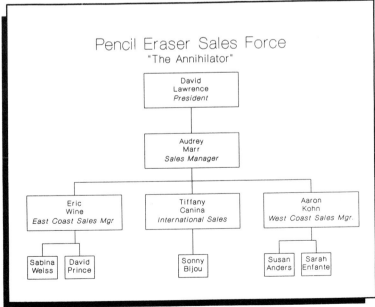

Fig. 4.34.

Last line arranged horizontally.

Importing ASCII Files

If the text you want to use in a text chart exists already in a file in your computer, you can import selected text from the file into a text chart. The file must be in ASCII format, however (plain text). If you created the file with a word processor, you may need to use a special command in the word processor to save the text in ASCII format first.

From an ASCII file, you can import selected text into a Harvard Graphics free-form chart. To use the same text in another text chart type, you can create a new chart after you have imported the text into a free-form chart. Then, when Harvard Graphics asks whether you want to Keep current data, respond with Yes. Figure 4.35 shows a memo that includes data about pencil eraser sales. To try importing text data into a chart, re-create this memo with a word processor and save the resulting file in ASCII format. Your word processor users' manual probably provides specific steps you can follow to save text as an ASCII file. Use spaces or tabs to align the three numbers. Don't worry about positioning the text exactly. Just be sure that you leave at least three spaces between each of the sales figures and between each of their headings.

Fig. 4.35.

An ASCII text file.

```
                    M E M O R A N D U M


To: John Bartlett
From: Marion Clarke
Re: Eraser sales


John, here are the Annihilator sales figures for three regions:

        Annihilator Sales

    East    West    Midwest

    364     256     259


Please pass them on to all concerned.

Best,

Marion
```

Now start Harvard Graphics and create a new text chart of any type. No matter which type you choose, Harvard Graphics imports ASCII text into a free-form chart. Then, before entering any text, return to the Main menu by pressing F10 (Continue) and select Import/Export from the Main menu and Import ASCII Data from the Import/Export menu.

If you have already imported text from an ASCII file during the current Harvard Graphics session, that file appears on the Import ASCII Data screen. To choose a new file, press F3 (Select Files). If you have not yet chosen an ASCII file, select the ASCII memo file you created earlier and press Enter. The file then appears on the Import ASCII Data screen, as shown in figure 4.36.

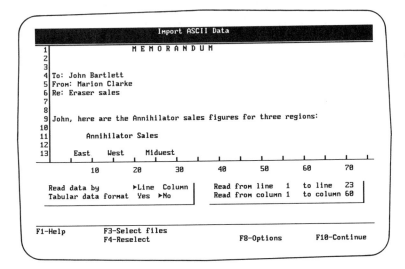

Fig. 4.36.

The Import ASCII Data screen.

Notice that you can press Ctrl-up arrow and Ctrl-down arrow to scroll through the file. Notice also that the Import ASCII Data screen includes four options near the bottom. You must set these options to inform Harvard Graphics which data to import and how to import the data. The options on the Import ASCII Data screen are as follows:

❑ Read data by—Set this prompt to Line to read the selected lines of the file line by line. Set this prompt to Column to read the text column by column.

❑ Read from line and to line—Enter the first and last lines of the text to import. To import one line, enter the same number for both Read from line and to line.

❏ Tabular data format—If the text to be read is tabular (arranged in columns separated by spaces or tabs), set this prompt to Yes. If the text is not tabular (for instance, a paragraph for a free-form chart), set this prompt to No.

❏ Read from column and to column—To read text from only one horizontal position to another, set beginning and ending columns at this prompt.

Follow this procedure to set the options:

1. Press Tab to leave Read data by set at Line. An explanation of these options appears later in this section.

2. At the Read from line prompt, enter the line number of the title "Annihilator Sales" in the memo. In the preceding example, the title is on line 11. By making the title the first line to be read, the title in the file becomes the title on the free-form chart screen.

3. Press Ctrl-down arrow, if necessary, to find the line number of the line containing the sales figure. In the preceding example, that line number is 15.

4. Enter the last line to be read after the to line prompt.

5. Press Tab to move the cursor to the Tabular data format prompt and use the space bar to highlight Yes. The text you want to import is tabular. If the text is not tabular, respond No. Harvard Graphics will display column numbers below the text so that you can fill out the Read from column and to column prompts.

6. Press Tab to move the cursor to the Read from column and to column prompts.

7. If the text is columnar, leave these settings as they are. If the text is not columnar, you can specify a beginning and ending horizontal position for text import at the Read from column and to column prompts. Use the column numbers displayed immediately below the text. The text in this example is columnar, so press Enter to accept each of the default settings and import the text. Figure 4.37 shows the Free Form Text screen with imported ASCII text.

When you import ASCII text, the first line of text imported becomes the text chart title automatically. The next and remaining lines become text items. When you import ASCII text, both the subtitle and footnote lines are left blank. You can enter these titles later if you want.

Modifying Existing Text Charts

You can return to the chart after saving to make minor or major alterations.

To retrieve a chart for editing, perform the following steps:

1. Select Get/Save/Remove from the Main menu.

2. Select Get Chart from the Get/Save/Remove menu.

3. Use the up- and down-arrow keys to highlight the chart from the list of files with a CHT extension and press Enter.

Harvard Graphics uses a three-letter file extension of CHT to mark the files created as chart files. Only files with a CHT extension appear on the list.

As you highlight a file name with the cursor, the name appears at the top of the screen next to the filename prompt. If you know the name of the file you want to retrieve, type the file name at the prompt to avoid searching through the list.

If the file you want to edit is not in the current directory shown at the top of the screen, press F3 to view a list of directories above and below the current directory. The parent directory (signified by two periods) is the directory above the current directory. Subdirectories are below the current directory. Highlight the directory you want to examine, press Enter, and press F3 to view the contents.

When you get a chart from disk, the chart appears on-screen and becomes the current chart. If you have not saved the last chart you were editing, Harvard Graphics prompts you to press Enter to continue without saving the old chart or to press Esc to cancel the Get Chart command.

Changing Chart Orientation from Vertical to Horizontal

Orientation is one of the options you should set before beginning a chart. You can change a completed chart's orientation if you keep in mind that Harvard Graphics uses the same Size/Place settings even after you make the change. You need to update the text size settings to accommodate your new chart layout.

To change a chart's orientation, follow this procedure:

1. Make the chart you want to modify the current chart by using Get Chart from the Get/Save/Remove menu.

2. Press Esc to return to the chart's data screen and press F10 (Continue) from the chart's screen to return to the Main menu.

3. Press F8 (Options), tab to the Orientation option, and select the Orientation setting you want by using the space bar.

4. Press Enter several times until the Current Chart Options overlay disappears.

5. Press F2 (Draw Chart) to see the results of your change or select Enter/Edit Chart from the Main menu to begin editing the chart.

Checking the Spelling of a Chart

The most carefully thought-out and expressive presentation can be undermined by a glaring typographical error or misspelling. To avoid such an embarrassment, you can use the Harvard Graphics spell checking feature, which checks the words in your chart against the words in its dictionary. The spell checker also finds most incorrect punctuation, capitalization, and words that you have inadvertently repeated (*like like* this).

To check the spelling of the chart you just completed, return to the Main menu and press F4 (Spell Check). To check the spelling of a chart on disk, make that chart the current chart by using Get Chart from the Get/Save/Remove menu. Return to the Main menu so that you can choose the F4 (Spell Check) command.

The spell checker scans through your chart, stopping at punctuation errors, repeated words, or words not found in the dictionary. The spell checker displays an overlay showing the error made and recommending possible corrections. If the word is correct, choose Word ok, continue from the overlay. If you want to add the word to your personal dictionary, choose Add to dictionary. Harvard Graphics checks for a match against its dictionary and your personal dictionary so that the word is not flagged as incorrect. To type a correction manually, choose Type correction from the overlay.

Spell checking is finished when you see the message Spelling check complete. At that point, press any key to continue. To stop spell checking a chart, press Esc.

Using Draw/Annotate
To Embellish Text Charts

Without any further changes, the text charts you create with the procedures described in this chapter are satisfactory for most presentations. Using Draw/ Annotate, covered in Chapter 7, you can embellish text charts by adding text, lines, and other graphic shapes, such as arrows, boxes, and circles. You can draw on charts by hand or add symbols chosen from the extensive library provided by Harvard Graphics.

Chapter Summary

Text charts are only one of two types of basic charts you can create with Harvard Graphics. In this chapter, you learned about a variety of text charts and how to set their appearance. You also created and saved on disk a number of charts. You use these charts later when learning about using Draw/Annotate to embellish charts and when you begin creating animated desktop presentations called screenshows.

In the next two chapters, you learn about the second major Harvard Graphics chart type, graph charts.

5

Creating Graph Charts:
Bar and Line

Text charts, which were covered in Chapter 4, are ideal when you need to convey topics, concepts, issues, arguments, or conclusions. But text charts nearly always serve as the accompaniment to a verbal presentation. In contrast, graph charts stand on their own as vivid illustrations of numbers, results, and totals, and as the most dynamic and compelling charts that Harvard Graphics produces.

In this chapter and in Chapter 6, you learn about the varied types of graph charts available with Harvard Graphics and learn how to create and use them. You also learn how to enter data or import data from other programs, such as 1-2-3, into your bar, line, area, or pie charts, how to display your data as a graph, and how to adjust the resulting chart's appearance by using the Titles & Options pages.

Distinguishing the Types of Graph Charts

Harvard Graphics offers a huge variety of graph chart types—nearly two dozen, in fact. The most common are line, bar, and pie charts.

Line charts are especially useful when you want to show trends in data over time. Harvard Graphics can display three different line chart types representing three forms of data analysis: plain line charts, best fit trend charts, and curve charts. The *plain line* chart connects each of the points on the chart with a straight line.

Trend and *curve* lines are based on calculations that analyze the data and depict the line that most closely represents the general trend of the data.

Rather than analyze the progress of data over time, *bar* charts compare discrete data points at intervals. Bar charts are the most common business charts, and they are the starting point for this chapter. Understanding the bar chart options is fundamental to understanding the options for all the available chart types.

You use a *pie* chart to show how each value contributes to the overall "pie" or whole. Then, if you prefer, you can go one step further by analyzing a slice of the pie and showing the component parts with a link to a *column* chart, as shown in figure 5.1. A column chart is a special form of pie chart that shows the whole as a rectangle rather than a circle. The chart in figure 5.1 shows clearly that in the second half of the year the December revenues were greatest and that mechanical pencils were the largest contributor to those revenues.

Fig. 5.1.

A pie chart linked to a column chart.

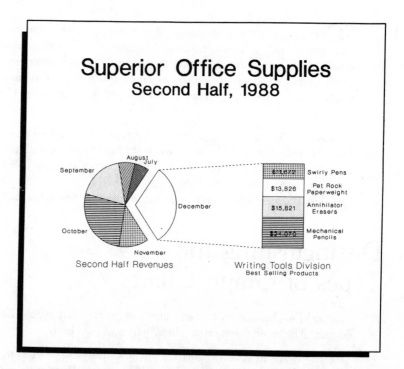

To show the relationship between two totals and analyze each of their components at the same time, you can pair two pie charts to create a set of proportional pies. Proportional pies compare two totals by reflecting the totals in the relative sizes of the two pies.

Harvard Graphics offers a variety of other less common graph charts, too.

100% charts, a variation of bar charts, are similar to column charts in that values are expressed as a percentage of a whole (100 percent). 100% charts are well suited, for example, for examining the relative contribution of each factor in a financial picture.

Bar/line combination charts display changes in data over time while emphasizing a single factor or series.

Area charts highlight volume. Figure 5.2 shows an area chart illustrating the increase in sales volume in the Writing Tools Division of Superior Office Supplies over three years.

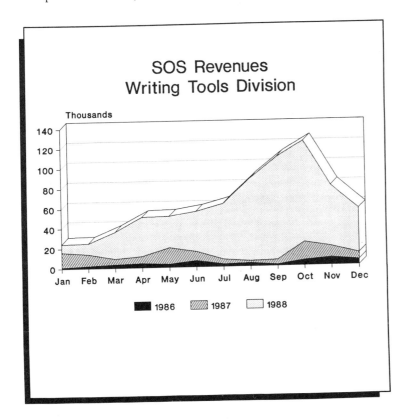

Fig. 5.2.

An area chart.

Point charts, or scattergrams, are composed of a series of points unconnected by a line. Each point represents the intersection of the values of two variables, one on the chart's x-axis and one on the chart's y-axis.

Paired bar charts compare two series that represent independent events. Each series is charted against its own y-axis so that the observer can compare "apples to apples" rather than "apples to oranges."

Dual y-axis charts compare two series that use different units of measure or that differ greatly in magnitude. Each series is measured and charted against its own y-axis.

High/low/close charts are a favorite among stockbrokers and financial professionals. Each item of data is composed of a high point, low point, and closing point, shown in comparison. Figure 5.3 shows the price fluctuations for Swirly pens in the Writing Tools Division for the first half of 1988.

Fig. 5.3.

A *high/low/close*
chart of price
fluctuations.

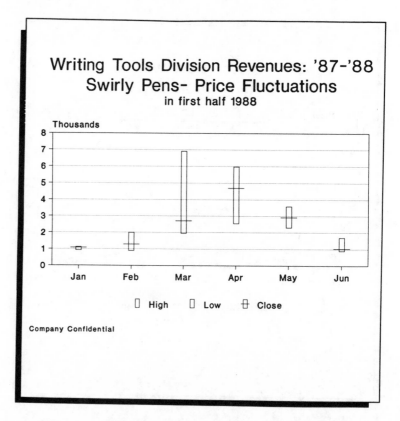

The most basic chart you can create in Harvard Graphics is a bar chart. If you are uncertain about which chart type to make, you always can start with a bar. Then you can try moving the data into other chart types or using the Titles &

Options pages to change the chart's appearance. This chapter covers bar and line charts and their variations. For information on area, high/low/close, and pie charts, see Chapter 6, "Creating Graph Charts: Area, High/Low/Close, and Pie."

Creating a Bar or Line Chart

Before you start a bar chart, you should be sure to check the current orientation setting. The current setting reflects the setup default you established earlier, and the setting may not match what you have in mind for your next chart. Bar charts are best suited to a landscape (horizontal) orientation because these charts convey large amounts of information so that it is easily read. Press F8 (Options) from the Main menu and be sure that Orientation is set to Landscape.

To start a bar or line chart, first choose Create New Chart from the Main menu. Then select Bar/Line from the Create New Chart menu.

Setting the X-Axis

The X Data Type Menu overlay is the first screen to appear after you have chosen Bar/Line (see fig. 5.4). Use this menu to tell Harvard Graphics the range of values that the horizontal axis of your chart (the x-axis) represents and the unit of measure for those values. The program uses this information to create and label the chart's x-axis automatically.

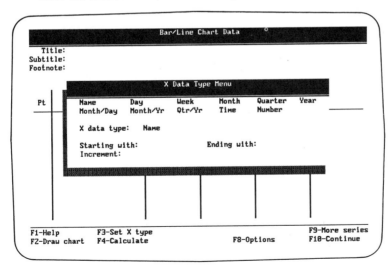

Fig. 5.4.

The X Data Type Menu overlay.

Completing the X Data Type Menu Overlay

To complete the X Data Type Menu overlay for bar/line charts, follow these steps:

1. Use the space bar to highlight one of the X data type selections listed in the top two lines of the menu. Then press Enter. You also can press Tab to select the X data type option currently highlighted and move to the Starting with field. (For descriptions of the 11 data types available, see the next section, "Knowing the Data Types.")

2. Enter a Starting with value and press Enter or Tab to move the cursor to the Ending with option.

3. Enter an Ending with value and press Enter or Tab to move the cursor to the Increment field. You can press Enter at the Increment field if you want to use the default increment of 1.

   The Increment field tells Harvard Graphics how many units to increment each new point on the x-axis. After you select Starting with and Ending with settings, Harvard Graphics automatically supplies the appropriate values in between. If you set the starting and ending values to *Jan* and *Dec* and set the increment to 2, for example, the resulting X values are *Jan, Mar, May, Jul, Sep,* and *Nov* (every other month).

Knowing the Data Types

This section gives you a summary of all the data types available on the X Data Type Menu overlay.

Name lets you name your own x-axis data values. If your media rating company wants to show the popularity of three TV shows in four regions, for example, you can use Name as the X data type option; then, on the next screen that appears, you can enter the name of each show for the chart's x-axis data. Figure 5.5 shows such a chart.

X-axis data that is name-based can include any combination of letters, numbers, and special characters—even a space. You can add up to 60 values for your x-axis when the data type is Name. If you want to split a name into two lines, simply place a vertical bar (|) at the position where the label should split.

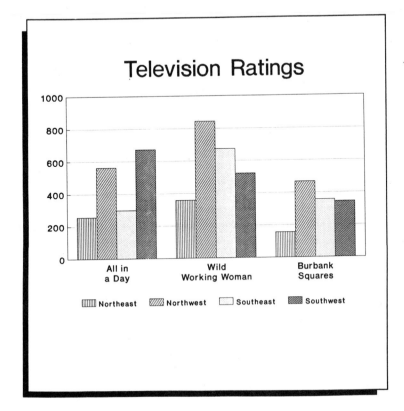

Fig. 5.5.

A TV *ratings chart with* Name *as the* X *data type.*

For example, typing *TV|Sales* produces

TV
Sales

on the chart.

Number is the data type to use when the information you want to represent on the x-axis can be classified numerically. For example, if your graph represents the top 4 television shows for age categories in 5-year increments (15, 20, 25, 30, and so on), you can select Number for the X data type option, press 5 at the Starting with prompt, and press 5 at the Increment option. Harvard Graphics then enters the ages 5, 10, 15, 20, and so forth, on the x-axis automatically.

Numeric X data can be a negative number and can include a decimal. Harvard Graphics also recognizes scientific notation in the Number data type.

Time as an x-axis data type is expressed in hours and minutes. Use a colon in the time, following the format *10:15 AM.* Use the *AM* and *PM* abbreviations if you want to avoid using 24-hour time, which is how your computer keeps track of time (*00:00* is midnight, *23:00* is 11 p.m., and *11:00* is 11 a.m.).

The remainder of the X data types are calendar-based.

When you choose Day, Harvard Graphics enters days of the week on the x-axis. Acceptable options for this field are (of course) Sunday, Monday, Tuesday, Wednesday, Thursday, Friday, and Saturday. If you type a three-letter abbreviation for a day of the week, Harvard Graphics follows your lead and supplies three-letter abbreviations for the other days that are included on your x-axis.

Week is a numeric entry. Its only difference from the Number type is that it labels the x-axis *Week*. This data type is ideal for graphs relating to the management of a project or the weekly sales figures of a product. Acceptable entries for this field are numbers between 1 and 240. If you want to show every other week, press 2 at the Increment field. Note, also, that Harvard Graphics does not roll over to a new year after 52 weeks.

Month, Month/Day, and Month/Yr have similar acceptable entries. You can use the formats *Feb*, *FEB*, or *2* for Month. You can type such entries as *Feb 1*, *FEB 1*, or *2/1* for Month/Day. And you can type *Feb 88*, *Feb 1988*, *FEB 88*, *FEB 1988*, or *2/88* for Month/Yr.

When you use a named date such as *January* or *FEB*, use a space in the date (such as *January 89*) to separate its parts. If the date is numeric, be sure to separate its parts with a slash. You don't have to type a period after abbreviations. Harvard Graphics knows how many days are in each month, so the program supplies the correct number of days in the months that are included when the x-axis spans more than one month.

Quarter and Qtr/Yr are identical; both represent the four business quarters of a year. Harvard Graphics expects entries like *1*, *1/88*, *first*, *First 88*, *Q1*, or *Q1 '88*. When you choose *First*, Harvard Graphics completes the entries with *First*, *Second*, *Third*, and *Fourth*.

Year is a four-digit number, such as *1989*, or a two-digit number, such as *89* or *'89* (with or without the apostrophe).

As mentioned, Harvard Graphics accepts three-letter abbreviations for the calendar-based data types. When you type *Jan* for January, for example, Harvard Graphics accepts it and follows your lead, supplying the abbreviations *Feb* for February, *Mar* for March, and so on. If you type *JAN* in all uppercase letters, Harvard Graphics completes the remaining months in uppercase letters.

When you specify an x-axis data type, the completed chart shows the appropriate data names on the horizontal x-axis. Based on other decisions you make (such as the legend's position), however, Harvard Graphics may abbreviate the x-axis data values later when you modify the appearance of the chart. If you place the legend to the left of the chart, for example, you reduce the horizontal space available for the graph and, therefore, for the labels along the x-axis. Instead of placing x-axis data labels on top of one another, Harvard Graphics abbreviates them to fit the available horizontal space. In an extreme case, for example, x-axis labels showing months might be abbreviated J,F,M,A,M,J,J,A,S,O,N,D. To prevent such abbreviation, you can move the legend under or above the chart. As an alternative, you can change the chart orientation so that its x-axis is vertical and its y-axis is horizontal. You also can alter other aspects on the Titles & Options pages to cause the chart to use the full names or abbreviations you entered originally. For more information, see this chapter's section on "Using the Titles & Options Pages."

Now that you are familiar with X data types, create a graph chart showing a summary of the first six months of expenses at Superior Office Supplies. The X data type option for this chart is Month, the Starting with entry is *Jan*, and the Ending with entry is *Jun*. Leave the Increment entry blank to accept the default of 1.

After you have completed the X Data Type Menu overlay, the Bar/Line Chart Data screen appears. Figure 5.6 shows the Bar/Line Chart Data screen after Month has been chosen as the data type. At this point, Harvard Graphics is ready for you to enter data.

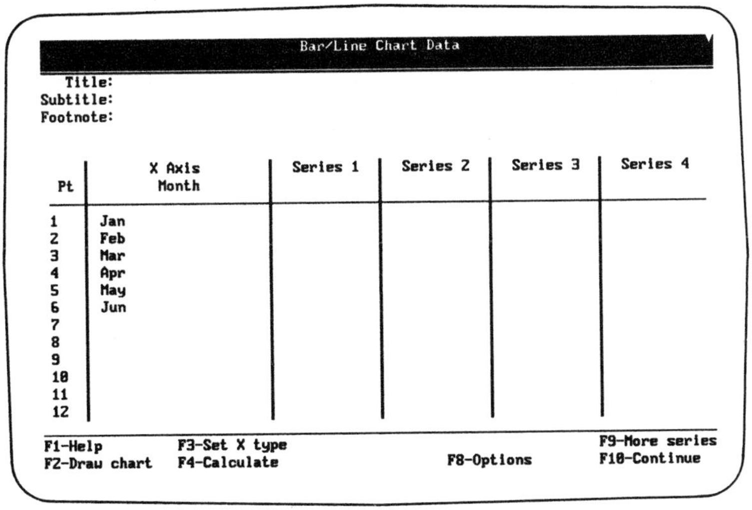

Fig. 5.6.

The Bar/Line Chart Data screen after you have completed the X Data Type Menu overlay.

Entering Data on the Data Page

In the preceding chapter, you entered data onto the data screen of an organization chart and then altered the resulting chart's appearance by using Titles & Options pages. You follow the same procedure with graph charts. You first enter data onto a data page; then you press F8 (Options) to change the appearance of the chart.

In addition to supplying x-axis values automatically when you complete the X Data Type Menu overlay, Harvard Graphics checks to ensure that any x-axis values you manually enter on the Bar/Line Chart Data screen match the data type you selected. If you select Month as the data type, for example, starting with *Jan* and ending with *Jun*, Harvard Graphics enters the months between January and June in the first six lines of the data-entry screen. The program prevents you from entering *Mon* for Monday on the seventh line, because Harvard Graphics recognizes that Monday is not a month (see fig. 5.7).

Fig. 5.7.

The results of entering invalid data.

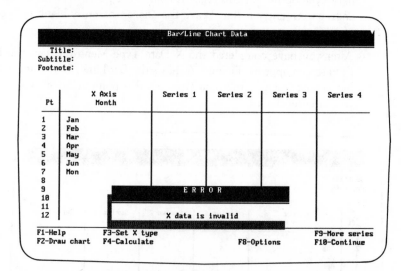

The first three lines on the Bar/Line Chart Data screen are available for you to supply a chart title, subtitle, and footnote. Typically, the title is a description of the chart, the subtitle supplies additional information about the chart, and the footnote appears at the bottom of the chart to provide an extra item of information, such as the date or a confidentiality statement. You can enter text on these three lines now or complete them later, when you are working with the Titles & Options pages. You must be on page 1 of 4 to enter the second line of the subtitle.

To create a bar/line chart, you must type your existing data on the Bar/Line Chart Data screen. You may want to assemble the data on paper first.

In Harvard Graphics, each bar or line on a chart represents one *series*, a set of related data. For example, the bar chart in figure 5.8 showing the expenses of Superior Office Supplies for one year is composed of four series. Series 1 is the administration budget, Series 2 is the manufacturing budget, Series 3 is the sales budget, and Series 4 is the facilities budget.

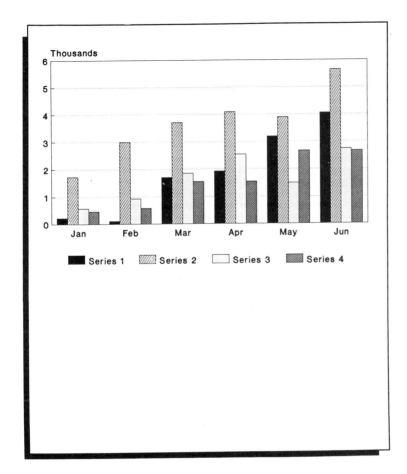

Fig. 5.8.

A bar chart comparing four series of data.

The first six months of expenses in the Superior Office Supplies Writing Tools Division look like this:

	Administrative	Manufacturing	Sales	Facilities
Jan	215	1725	570	465
Feb	102	2993	932	578
Mar	1702	3706	1852	1545
Apr	1926	4096	2532	1545
May	3192	3896	1496	2665
Jun	4050	5653	2741	2665

To enter a chart's numeric data, you use the Tab key to move across the Bar/Line Chart Data screen and use the Enter key to move down line by line. You may find the easiest method to be typing all the values for one series, pressing Enter between each, and then proceeding to the next series.

To enter negative numbers, use a minus sign before the number. To enter decimals, type a period (decimal point) at the decimal place. Of course, Harvard Graphics also accepts extremely large numbers in scientific notation. To enter such a number, use an E and an exponent of 10 (for example, the number 560,000 is expressed as 5.6E5). Figure 5.9 shows a Bar/Line Chart Data screen complete with the four series of data entered. Even if you enter the data in different formats, Harvard Graphics converts the data into a single format after you preview the chart.

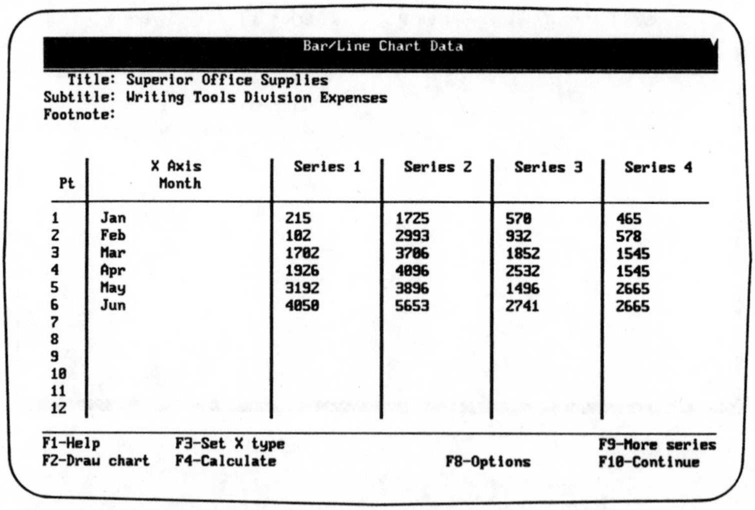

Fig. 5.9.

The Bar/Line Chart Data screen with the data entered.

```
                          Bar/Line Chart Data                              ▼
          Title: Superior Office Supplies
       Subtitle: Writing Tools Division Expenses
       Footnote:

              X Axis       Series 1    Series 2    Series 3    Series 4
       Pt     Month

       1     Jan            215         1725        570         465
       2     Feb            102         2993        932         578
       3     Mar            1702        3706        1852        1545
       4     Apr            1926        4096        2532        1545
       5     May            3192        3896        1496        2665
       6     Jun            4050        5653        2741        2665
       7
       8
       9
       10
       11
       12

       F1-Help        F3-Set X type                          F9-More series
       F2-Draw chart  F4-Calculate              F8-Options    F10-Continue
```

Note: Even after you have finished entering the x-axis data, you can modify it by pressing F3 (Set X Type) to recall the X Data Type Menu overlay. This option is always available as you are entering data.

Previewing the Chart

After entering the title, subtitle, and all the data into the Bar/Line Chart Data screen, you should press F2 (Draw Chart) to preview the chart before you make any adjustments to its appearance. If you haven't done so already, type in the data shown in figure 5.9, and compare your chart preview with the chart preview shown in figure 5.10. Press Esc to return to the Bar/Line Chart Data screen.

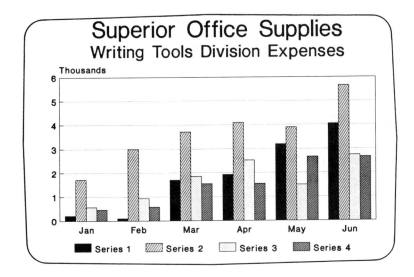

Fig. 5.10.

Preview of an unaltered bar/line chart.

Saving the Chart

Save this first completed bar chart with the name SOSEXPEN. To save the chart, follow this procedure:

1. Press F10 (Continue) to return to the Main menu.

2. Select Get/Save/Remove from the Main menu.

3. Select Save Chart from the Get/Save/Remove menu. The cursor should be at the Chart will be saved as option.

4. Type the chart name, *sosexpen.*

5. Press Enter.

6. The current description is derived from the title line. Press Enter to keep the current description. Or, if you want to change it, type a new description over the current one and press Enter.

7. Press Esc to return to the Main menu and then select Enter/Edit Chart to continue working on the chart.

Editing the Chart

Harvard Graphics allows you to include up to 8 series of data with as many as 240 items in each series, depending on the x-axis data type you select. On the Bar/Line Chart Data screen, you can see only 4 series displayed at one time. To view or enter data into the next 4 series, press F9 (More Series). To return to the first 4 series, press F9 again. Pressing PgDn enables you to see the next 12 lines of data. Pressing PgUp moves the display up a screenful of data. The Home and End keys move the cursor to the first and last values on the screen, respectively.

Changing the order of data on the page in order to show your results in a different sequence is easy with Harvard Graphics. Simply position the cursor on the line you want to move and press Ctrl-up arrow or Ctrl-down arrow. The line of data moves up or down correspondingly. This flexibility is important when you have five years of data entered, for example, and management then decides to change the fiscal year from January through December to April through March. To change fiscal years, you can move the cursor to the line holding January's data and use the Ctrl-down arrow combination to move the line to the bottom of the list. Repeat the same procedure for February's and March's data, and your chart reflects the new fiscal year.

To insert or delete a full line of data, use the Ctrl-Ins and Ctrl-Del key combinations. Move the cursor to the line of data you want to delete and press the Del key while holding down the Ctrl key. Harvard Graphics provides no means to "undelete" a line, though, so be certain of the line you want to delete before proceeding. To insert a blank line at the same position, press the Ins key while holding down the Ctrl key.

Usually, a bar/line chart is more visually appealing if you use four or fewer series. The more series you place in a chart, the more cluttered the chart becomes. You may want to enter multiple series, however, and display only two or three series in each chart. With this approach, you can enter the data only once and show several variations. If your four series are 1985, 1986, 1987, and 1988, for example, you may want to show 1985 as it compared with 1988 and then compare 1987 with 1988 in another chart. In a third chart based on the same data, you can show the full four-year span. To suppress or display series, you can use the Titles & Options pages, described in the next section.

You can use an additional series to perform calculations on existing series. For example, you can use a series to sum all or selected series, calculate an increase in a series over the previous series, or average several series. These calculations work much like the @ functions in 1-2-3. You will find these calculation functions described in detail later in this chapter (see "Calculating Data").

Using the Titles & Options Pages

After you have completed the data screen and previewed your chart in progress, Harvard Graphics generates a standard chart based on the information you entered on the data screen. You will notice that the program has probably already done much of the work in labeling the chart. The y-axis may have a label describing the units of the data in your chart, for example. If you entered numbers in thousands, the y-axis would be labeled Thousands. Harvard Graphics has made other adjustments, too. The bars in your graph probably fit neatly across the width of the x-axis, and a legend appears on the chart.

To refine your chart any further, you need to use the selections on the Titles & Options pages available for your current chart type. Each chart type has its own Titles & Options pages, with entries corresponding to the attributes of the chart. For example, bar charts have Titles & Options page entries that set the width, spacing, and other attributes of a chart's bars. In the next several sections, you learn about the four Titles & Options pages specific to bar and line charts.

Using the First Titles & Options Page

Pressing F8 (Options) at the Bar/Line Chart Data screen calls up the first of the four Titles & Options pages for bar/line charts (see fig. 5.11). You use the first Titles & Options page to tell Harvard Graphics your choices about the overall appearance of the chart. On this page, you can specify whether to represent each series with bars or lines, and you can give the series names that are a little more descriptive than Series 1, Series 2, and so on.

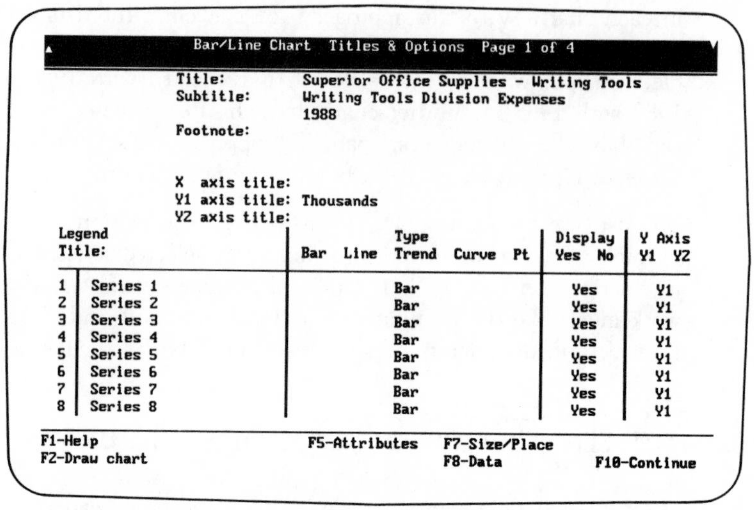

Fig. 5.11.

The first Titles & Options page.

```
┌─────────────────────────────────────────────────────────────────┐
│ ▲          Bar/Line Chart  Titles & Options  Page 1 of 4        ▼│
│            Title:      Superior Office Supplies - Writing Tools   │
│            Subtitle:   Writing Tools Division Expenses            │
│                        1988                                       │
│            Footnote:                                              │
│                                                                   │
│            X  axis title:                                         │
│            Y1 axis title: Thousands                              │
│            Y2 axis title:                                         │
│   Legend                          Type         Display │ Y Axis  │
│   Title:           Bar  Line  Trend Curve  Pt  Yes  No │ Y1  Y2  │
│   1 │ Series 1                   Bar            Yes    │ Y1      │
│   2 │ Series 2                   Bar            Yes    │ Y1      │
│   3 │ Series 3                   Bar            Yes    │ Y1      │
│   4 │ Series 4                   Bar            Yes    │ Y1      │
│   5 │ Series 5                   Bar            Yes    │ Y1      │
│   6 │ Series 6                   Bar            Yes    │ Y1      │
│   7 │ Series 7                   Bar            Yes    │ Y1      │
│   8 │ Series 8                   Bar            Yes    │ Y1      │
│  F1-Help              F5-Attributes    F7-Size/Place             │
│  F2-Draw chart                         F8-Data        F10-Continue│
└─────────────────────────────────────────────────────────────────┘
```

At the top of the first Titles and Options page is a pair of arrows, one pointing up and another pointing down. These arrows indicate that other Titles & Options pages are available both above and below the current page. If you press PgDn, the next Titles and Options page appears (page 2 of 4). If you press PgUp to return to page 1 of 4 and press PgUp again, Harvard Graphics loops back to Titles & Options Page 4 of 4.

If you did not enter a title, subtitle, and footnote on the data screen, these items are blank on the first Titles & Options page. You can now use the Tab key to move the cursor to these lines and enter a title, subtitle, and footnote. In figure 5.11, the title line reads Superior Office Supplies-Writing Tools. If you are practicing by using the procedures in this chapter, add *Writing Tools* to the end of the first title line on the Titles & Options page. Then, add *1988* under the subtitle on the first Titles & Options page. *1988* is the second line of the subtitle.

Using F7 To Change Text Appearance

After the title and subtitle lines are in place, you should preview the chart by pressing F2 (Draw Chart). When you do, notice that the lengthy title you just supplied does not fit within the width of the page (see fig. 5.12). With Harvard Graphics, you can alter the size of the title text, though, by using the F7-Size/Place feature on the first Titles & Options page.

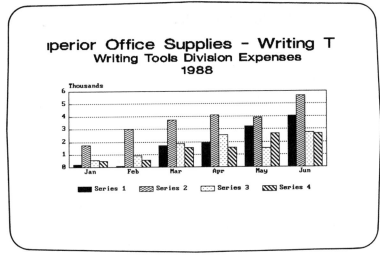

Fig. 5.12.

Preview of the chart with a long title.

In Harvard Graphics, *size* is a measure of the height of the text characters used in a line. You can change a line's size on both the first and fourth Titles & Options pages. The size of a character can be any number from 1 to 99.9, representing a percentage of the length of the shorter side of the page. For example, a character with a size of 99.9 will fill the entire height of the shorter side of the page.

If you set the text in a graph chart's title to a size of 99.9, the title is so big that it overwrites the graph. If you change the size of the title to 0, however, it is removed altogether, and the remaining lines of text and the graph fill the left-over space.

Size determines the height of lines of text. *Place* refers to their positioning. Text can be right-aligned (pushed against the right side of the page), left-aligned (pushed against the left side of the page), or centered.

Standard alignment and text sizes are set by Harvard Graphics when you create a chart. You may find them perfectly satisfactory and choose to make no changes. But if you prefer to adjust text size and place, you can make these changes easily at any time as you build a chart.

To modify the size and place of a line of text, simply press F7 (Size/Place) with the first Titles & Options page on-screen. An overlay appears, as shown in figure 5.13. You can use this overlay to change both the size and placement of the title, subtitle, and footnote.

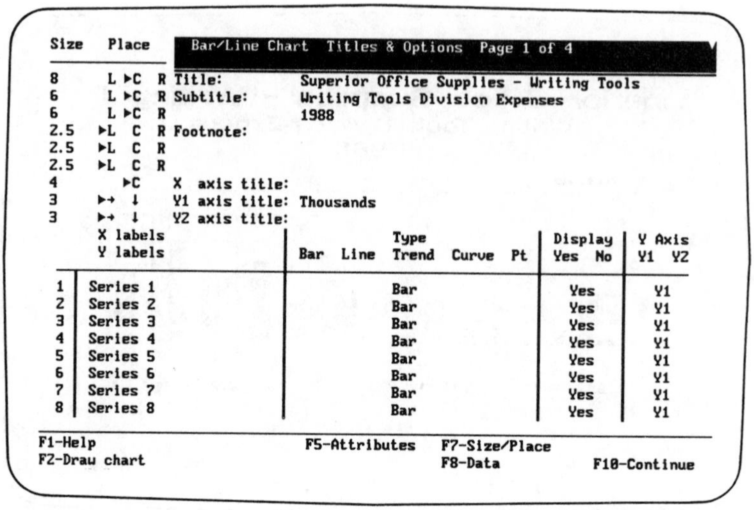

Fig. 5.13.

*The first Titles &
Options page with
the Size/Place
overlay.*

Size	Place				Bar/Line Chart Titles & Options Page 1 of 4						
8	L ►C	R	Title:		Superior Office Supplies – Writing Tools						
6	L ►C	R	Subtitle:		Writing Tools Division Expenses						
6	L ►C	R			1988						
2.5	►L C	R	Footnote:								
2.5	►L C	R									
2.5	►L C	R									
4	►C		X axis title:								
3	►→ ↓		Y1 axis title:		Thousands						
3	►→ ↓		Y2 axis title:								

	X labels						Type			Display	Y Axis
	Y labels				Bar	Line	Trend	Curve	Pt	Yes No	Y1 Y2
1	Series 1						Bar			Yes	Y1
2	Series 2						Bar			Yes	Y1
3	Series 3						Bar			Yes	Y1
4	Series 4						Bar			Yes	Y1
5	Series 5						Bar			Yes	Y1
6	Series 6						Bar			Yes	Y1
7	Series 7						Bar			Yes	Y1
8	Series 8						Bar			Yes	Y1

F1-Help			F5-Attributes	F7-Size/Place	
F2-Draw chart				F8-Data	F10-Continue

To reduce the size and alter the place setting of the title line on your chart,
follow these steps:

1. Type over the Size number next to the title; change the value from
   8 to 5.5.

2. Press the Tab or Enter key to move the cursor to the Size number next to
   the first subtitle line. Change the value from 6 to 4. Reducing the size of a
   line of text increases the available space for the graph.

3. Press the Tab or Enter key to move to the second line of the subtitle and
   replace the number 6 with 4. If you do not have text in the footnote line,
   repeat this procedure for the footnote, making the size of all three lines of
   the footnote 0. To clear the current entry so that you can type a new
   number, position the cursor on the current entry and press Ctrl-Del. You
   are thus assured of having the maximum amount of space for your graph.

   (Two lines are available for the subtitle, and three lines are available for
   the footnote. If you do not have a second line in your subtitle, or second
   and third lines in your footnote, make the values for these lines 0. Your
   graph will be larger as a result.)

4. Press F10 (Continue).

5. Press F2 (Draw Chart) to see the results of your actions. The result is
   shown in figure 5.14.

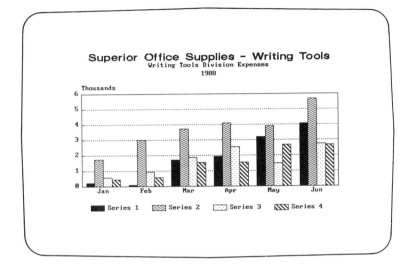

Fig. 5.14.

The bar/line chart after size and place adjustments have been made.

To change a Place setting on the Size/Place overlay, tab to the Place column for the line you want to reposition (left, center, or right) and press the space bar to highlight your choice. Press Enter or Tab to move to the next field and repeat the procedure.

To return to the Titles & Options page, press Esc. If you need to move the cursor back through the Size and Place fields to try other choices, hold down the Shift key and press Tab after pressing F7 to summon the Size/Place overlay.

The Size/Place overlay on the first Titles & Options page also enables you to decide the size and placement of the chart's x-axis and y-axis titles. You will see two arrows next to each axis title in the overlay. Highlighting the arrow pointing to the right causes the axis title to start at the top of the axis and run across the screen to the right. Highlighting the arrow pointing down causes the title to start at the left of the axis and run down the page vertically. Try both of these options and preview the chart to see their effects. Note that you can label both Y1 and Y2 axes. The second axis, Y2, is used for dual y-axis charts, which are discussed later in this chapter (see "Creating Dual Y-Axis Charts").

You can use the last two lines on the Size/Place overlay to set the size of X labels and Y labels. The X and Y labels are the numbers or words that appear in increments on the horizontal and vertical axes of the chart. You can include labels by using a setting on the second Titles & Options page, described later in this chapter (see "Displaying Value Labels"). Harvard Graphics calculates a size for the X and Y labels if you leave these two lines blank. The two settings also affect the size of data shown in a data table. (Data tables are an option on the third Titles

& Options page.) To accept the changes you have made and remove the Size/Place overlay, press F10 (Continue).

Using F5 To Change Text Attributes

Not only can you change the size and placement of text, but you also can change the formatting of text on-screen by changing its attributes. Attributes determine the appearance of text: whether it is italicized, bold, or underlined, or whether the characters are filled or only outlined. If you have a color output device, you also can change the color of text with the F5-Attributes feature.

To italicize "Writing Tools" after the hyphen in the chart's title, for example, follow these steps:

1. Position the cursor on the first letter of the word you want to change (on the W in the word Writing).

2. Press F5 (Attributes) to display the Attributes menu bar on the bottom line of the screen.

3. Use the right arrow to highlight all words that should be changed. You can use the down arrow to highlight an entire line.

4. Tab to the Italic menu option and press the space bar to turn on the italic attribute for those words. You can tab between attributes and press the space bar to turn on or off the small pointers that are to the left of the attribute names. When an attribute's pointer is displayed, the attribute is on.

5. You can tab to the Color option and press F6 (Choices) to see a list of the available colors for the highlighted text. Figure 5.15 shows the Attributes bar with the Color Selection overlay displayed.

   Use the down-arrow key to highlight the color of your choice and then press Enter. Or type the number of the color you want to use.

6. Press F10 (Continue) to confirm your choice.

7. Press F2 (Draw Chart) to see the results of your changes. Figure 5.16 shows how the chart appears on-screen.

Once you have set the title line of your chart, you may want to use other features on the first Titles & Options page to make additional changes to the graph.

```
┌──────────────────────────────────────────────────────────┐
│  Bar/Line Chart  Titles & Options  Page 1 of 4            │
│ ▲                                                          │
│              Title:    Superior Office Supplies - Writing Tools │
│  Color Selection       Writing Tools Division Expenses     │
│                        1988                                │
│  ▶ White        1                                          │
│    Cyan         2                                          │
│    Magenta      3     itle:                                │
│    Green        4     itle: Thousands                      │
│    Blue         5     itle:                                │
│    Red          6                    Type        Display  Y Axis │
│    Yellow       7     Bar Line  Trend Curve  Pt  Yes  No  Y1 Y2 │
│    Orange       8                                          │
│    Royal Blue   9              Bar              Yes      Y1 │
│    Gold        10              Bar              Yes      Y1 │
│    Violet      11              Bar              Yes      Y1 │
│    Pink        12              Bar              Yes      Y1 │
│    Grey        13              Bar              Yes      Y1 │
│    Crimson     14              Bar              Yes      Y1 │
│    Dark Green  15              Bar              Yes      Y1 │
│    Black       16              Bar              Yes      Y1 │
│                        F5-Attributes   F7-Size/Place      │
│  F2-Draw chart ▶Fill  ▶Bold  ▶Italic  Underline  Color ▶  F10-Continue │
└──────────────────────────────────────────────────────────┘
```

Fig. 5.15.

The Attributes bar with the Color Selection overlay.

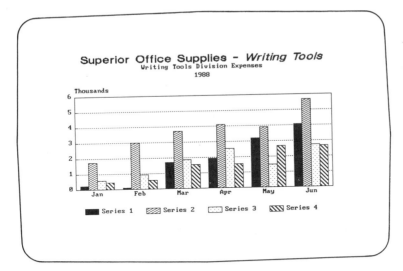

Fig. 5.16.

Preview of the bar/line chart with part of the title italicized.

Adding a Legend Title

The *legend* is the key that correlates series with their bars. You can supply your own description of the series legend by pressing the Tab key until the cursor is at Legend Title on the first Titles & Options page. Then type the title you want to display. To change the placement of the legend, you can use the four legend options that appear on the second Titles & Options page, described in the section on "Using the Second Titles & Options Page."

Naming Series

Another helpful change is to alter the names of the series. The series names appear in the chart's legend. Try typing *Administration* in place of Series 1 in the first column, *Manufacturing* in place of Series 2, *Sales* in place of Series 3, and *Facilities* in place of Series 4. To get there, use the Tab key. You can use the Ctrl-Del key to delete the existing series name and then type in the empty space. To move the cursor to the next line, press Enter.

Remember that the Ins key works as a two-position toggle switch whenever you are entering data. Pressing the Ins key repeatedly toggles it from one position to the other. In one position, the cursor appears as a box, and new text typed on a line pushes existing text to the right. Pressing Ins once more changes the cursor to a small blinking underline that causes new text to be typed over the old.

Selecting a Bar or Line Type for Series

Use the Type column on the first Titles & Options page to tell Harvard Graphics whether to represent each series as a bar, line, trend line, curve, or point. When you first display a chart, Harvard Graphics uses bars for all the series. But you can choose another bar or line type to represent a series.

As mentioned at the beginning of the chapter, bar charts are the most common chart type and are especially effective when your data compares figures relative to one another instead of trends over time. If you want to compare series over a few time periods (division revenues over four quarters, for example), a bar chart is your best choice.

Line charts are best for displaying results over time. Three types of line charts are available in Harvard Graphics: plain, trend, and curve.

Plain line charts are graphs that use straight lines to connect data points in a series. Figure 5.17 shows a plain line chart. To produce this type of chart, choose the Line option in the Type column of the first Titles & Options page.

Trend line charts are useful if your data shows periodic variations but a tendency in one direction over a longer stretch of time. Statistical trends are usually shown as trend charts. When you select Trend as the graph type for a series, Harvard Graphics calculates the line that best fits through the data points. The line itself

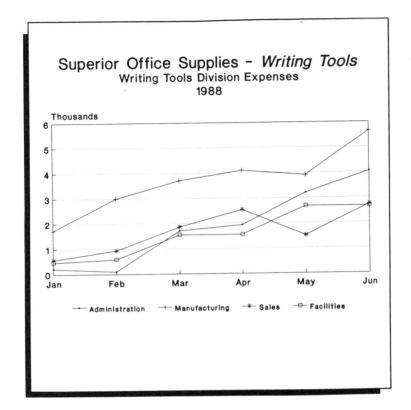

Fig. 5.17.

A plain line chart.

does not connect the data points but rather runs through the chart on a path that is least distant to all points. Figure 5.18 shows an example of a trend line chart in which Trend is chosen as the type for all series.

The *curve* line chart is a variation of the trend chart, but the curve chart uses a line that curves through the chart instead of remaining straight. Curve charts highlight periodic fluctuations as well as the general trend in data. Look at figure 5.19 for an example.

Point charts are not as easily interpreted as line and bar charts. Also called scattergrams and scatterplots, point charts are composed of unconnected dots (see fig. 5.20). Each point on the chart represents the intersection of the values of two variables. Commonly, statisticians use these charts to show correlation between variables. Use point charts with caution because they require an eye trained in statistics for full understanding. In most business environments, point charts are not the most expressive display of data. To create a point type chart, you choose Pt in the Type column.

Fig. 5.18.

Trend *type selected for all series.*

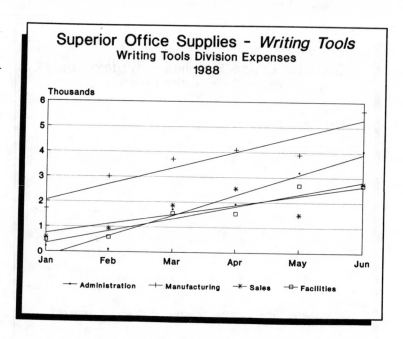

Fig. 5.18.

Trend *type selected for all series.*

Fig. 5.19.

Curve *type selected for all series.*

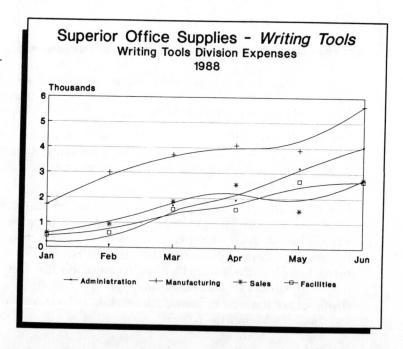

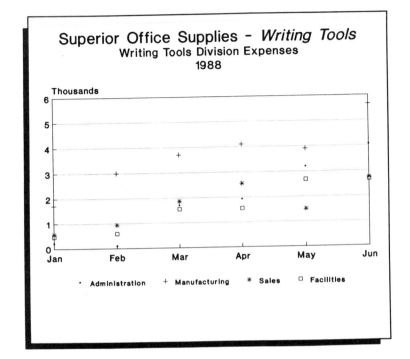

Fig. 5.20.

An example of a point chart.

Select a chart type by following these steps:

1. Press Tab until the cursor is next to the series you want to change and in the Type column of the first Titles & Options page.

2. Press the space bar to highlight the graph type you want to select.

3. Press F2 (Draw Chart) to view the chart with the new graph type.

A mixed bar/line chart, such as the chart shown in figure 5.21, can persuasively demonstrate a large difference among series. In the example in figure 5.21, the manufacturing budget is unusually high compared with other corporate expenses. The chart shows a line for manufacturing expenses well above the highest points of bars representing the other series in the chart.

To Display or Not To Display a Series

The third column on the first Titles & Options page controls the display of series. Use this column to specify whether Harvard Graphics should display or hide a specific series. With this feature, you can create two versions of a chart:

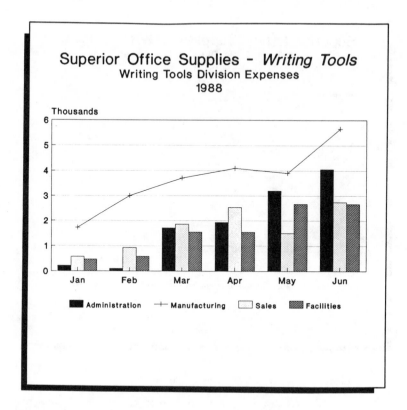

Fig. 5.21.

A mixed bar/line chart.

one for management and one for staff. For the staff, you can choose not to display certain sensitive series data.

To change the display of a series, simply move the cursor to the Display column and press the space bar to change the setting from Yes to No. Once you have set the display, press F2 (Draw Chart) to confirm that the bar is displayed in neither the graph nor the legend.

Try turning off the display for the manufacturing expenses on the SOSEXPEN chart. While you still are looking at the Titles & Options page 1 of 4, tab to the Display column opposite the manufacturing series and press the space bar. Press F10 (Continue) and F2 (Draw Chart) to see the results. Your screen should look like the chart shown in figure 5.22.

Creating Dual Y-Axis Charts

When the range of data in two series is measured based on two different units of measurement, you can use a second Y axis to plot both series on the same chart.

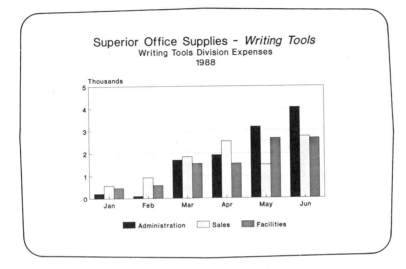

Fig. 5.22.

SOSEXPEN *chart with the manufacturing series display suppressed.*

Figure 5.23 shows a line chart that plots the cost of Annihilator eraser production to the number of cartons shipped. The two products must be compared against their own axes.

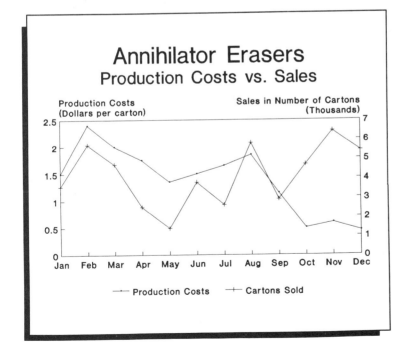

Fig. 5.23.

A dual y-axis chart.

To set up two y-axes, Harvard Graphics enables you to use Y1 at the left side of the chart and Y2 at the right side of the chart. Tab to the Y Axis column in the first Title & Options page, use the down arrow to position the cursor opposite the series you want to change, and press the space bar to toggle that series to Y2. Press F2 (Draw Chart) to see the results. Figure 5.24 shows the Y2 setting.

Fig. 5.24.

The first Titles & Options page with settings for the dual y-axis chart.

```
                    Bar/Line Chart  Titles & Options  Page 1 of 4
  ▲
              Title:          Annihilator Erasers
              Subtitle:       Production Costs vs. Sales

              Footnote:


              X  axis title:
              Y1 axis title: Production Costs|(Dollars per carton)
              Y2 axis title: Sales in Number of Cartons|(Thousands)
       Legend                        Type              Display  Y Axis
       Title:              Bar  Line Trend  Curve  Pt  Yes  No  Y1  Y2

       1   Production Costs          Line                  Yes      Y1
       2   Cartons Sold              Line                  Yes      Y2
       3   Series 3                  Bar                   Yes      Y1
       4   Series 4                  Bar                   Yes      Y1
       5   Series 5                  Bar                   Yes      Y1
       6   Series 6                  Bar                   Yes      Y1
       7   Series 7                  Bar                   Yes      Y1
       8   Series 8                  Bar                   Yes      Y1

       F1-Help                    F5-Attributes   F7-Size/Place
       F2-Draw chart                              F8-Data          F10-Continue
```

Keep these suggestions in mind as you create dual y-axis charts:

❏ When two series have different units of measure, such as cost and volume sold, a dual y-axis chart is most appropriate.

❏ Dual y-axis charts cannot be three-dimensional.

❏ To avoid confusion, be sure to label your y-axes clearly and show which series belongs to which y-axis.

❏ Use line charts for dual y-axis charts that are oriented vertically and bar charts for charts set to a horizontal orientation. (You change orientation on the second Titles & Options page.)

❏ Use the Format option on the third Titles & Options page (described later in this chapter) to format the y-axis scales for the data you are describing.

❏ To show identical left and right y-axes so that the same axis appears on both sides of the graph, select Y2 as the axis on a blank series.

❏ Dual y-axis charts are easier to read if you remove grid lines behind the graph.

Using the Second Titles & Options Page

Once you have completed the first Titles & Options page, you can press PgDn to move to the second Titles & Options page (see fig. 5.25). Use this page to set the characteristics of the elements of the current chart, such as the frame around the graph or the labels placed next to the bars. Also use this page to set the appearance and positioning of the legend.

```
╔══════════════════════════════════════════════════════════════════╗
║           Bar/Line Chart   Titles & Options   Page 2 of 4          ║
║ ▲                                                                  ║
║   Bar style          ▶Cluster   Overlap   Stack    100%   Step  Paired
║   Bar enhancement     3D        Shadow    Link    ▶None
║   Bar fill style     ▶Color     Pattern   Both
║
║   Bar width
║   Bar overlap         50
║   Bar depth           25
║
║   Horizontal chart  │ Yes      ▶No
║   Value labels      │ All       Select   ▶None
║
║   Frame style       │▶Full      Half      Quarter   None
║   Frame color       │ 1
║   Frame background  │ 0
║
║   Legend location   │ Top      ▶Bottom    Left      Right    None
║   Legend justify    │ ← or ↑   ▶Center    ↓ or →
║   Legend placement  │ In       ▶Out
║   Legend frame      │ Single    Shadow   ▶None
║ ─────────────────────────────────────────────────────────────────
║  F1-Help
║  F2-Draw chart                   F6-Colors    F8-Data    F10-Continue
╚══════════════════════════════════════════════════════════════════╝
```

Fig. 5.25.

The second Titles & Options page.

To make adjustments on the second Titles & Options page, simply use the Tab key to move between options and press the space bar to highlight your selection. Always press F2 (Draw Chart) after each change because some of the options on this page interact with options on other pages. If you wait to view the chart until you have made a number of changes, you may have trouble isolating the change that caused a glitch. If you press F2 (Draw Chart) after each change, you can find and resolve problems quickly.

For example, the Horizontal chart option on the second Titles & Options page, which trades x- and y-axes, does not work with three-dimensional graph. You discover this when you press F2. You have to decide between trading the x- and y-axes and displaying the three-dimensional effect.

Changing the Bar Style

You can use the first three options on the second Titles & Options page to give Harvard Graphics specific information about the appearance of the bars or lines in your chart. The Bar style option provides six mutually exclusive types of bars. When combined with Bar enhancement, these types create 16 distinct representations of the same data. With the additional option changes available on this page and other Titles & Options pages, you can produce hundreds of variations on every bar chart. As you become more familiar with these options, you will find ways to make your bar and line charts more creative.

Here are descriptions of the six bar styles:

☐ Cluster: This is the default style when you first set up the bar chart. Selecting this style groups bars into sets of series with one set for each x-axis data value. Figure 5.26 shows the SOSEXPEN chart as a standard cluster style bar chart, with Pattern chosen as the fill style. (Bar fill style is discussed in detail in the section on "Setting the Fill Style.")

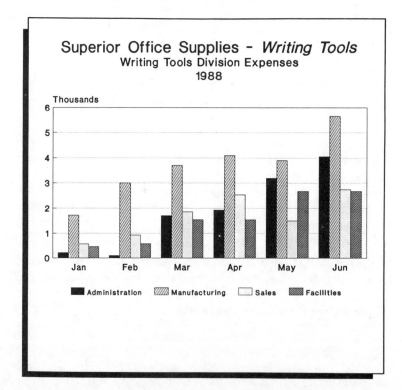

Fig. 5.26.

A cluster style bar chart.

❏ Overlap: When you have two or more series in a bar chart, selecting Overlap can make an interesting visual effect. This style causes the bars at each x-axis data point to overlap each other. Overlap bars are especially expressive when the data values for Series 1 are smaller than the data values for Series 2, and so on. Figure 5.27 shows an overlap style bar chart.

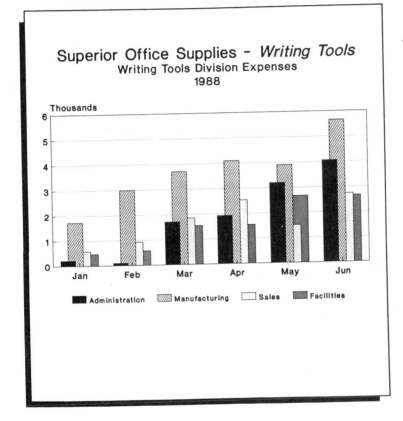

Fig. 5.27.

An overlap style bar chart.

❏ Stack: In a stack style bar chart, series are grouped together for each X value and stacked on top of each other. The values for Series 1 are closest to the x-axis, the values for Series 2 are above that, and so on. Figure 5.28 features a stack style bar chart.

❏ 100%: These bars are similar to stacked bars but do not show the actual values of each series. Instead, the relative percentages of the series in the bars represent their relative percentage contributions to the total. The

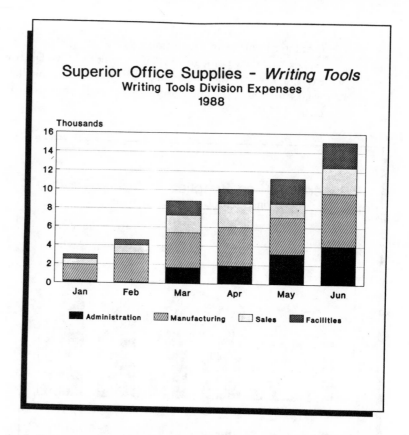

Fig. 5.28.

A stack style bar chart.

total of all series represented by components of this style of bar chart is 100 percent. The bars in this style bar chart are all the same height because each of their totals is 100 percent.

To make a 100% bar chart or any stacked bar communicate with more meaning, use darker colors for the first series and progressively lighter colors for subsequent series. Figure 5.29 shows a 100% style bar chart.

❑ Step: Stepped bar charts are also called histograms or frequency distribution charts. Typically, histograms show the frequency of observations for a given category. For example, a histogram may be appropriate for showing the number of Mechanical pencils sold per district. The y-axis represents sales volume, and the bars show the proportion of the total sales each district contributed. Histograms can be effective particularly when one X value (a single district) accounts for a significantly larger proportion of the whole. Step charts require a trained eye for interpretation, though. Figure 5.30 shows a step style chart.

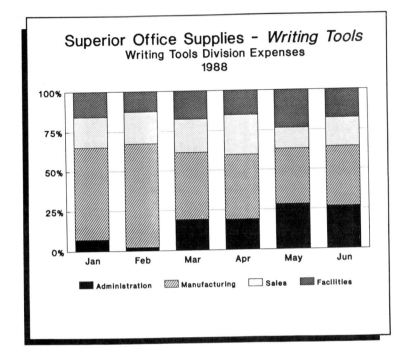

Fig. 5.29.

A sample 100% bar chart.

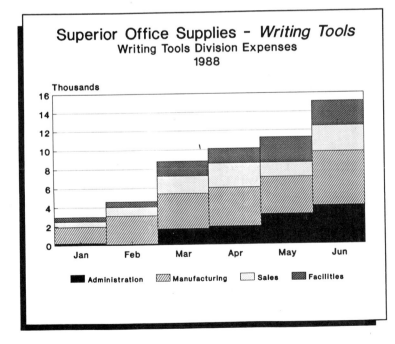

Fig. 5.30.

A step style bar chart (a histogram).

❏ Paired: A paired bar chart is appropriate to show the relationship between two or more series that have the same x-axis data but different y-axis data. Paired bar charts are always horizontal charts so that the x-axis is the vertical axis, and the y-axis is horizontal. The Y1 axis is on the left, and Y2 is on the right. The line down the middle is the y-axis zero point. If your chart has more than two series, Harvard Graphics stacks Series 1 closest to the x-axis zero point, Series 2 further to the right or left, Series 3 even further out, and so on.

Understanding a horizontal chart is easiest when the chart has the fewest series. Figure 5.31 shows a paired bar chart comparing the manufacturing and facilities costs to those of administration and sales. You can see that the chart represents two different measures based on the larger amounts spent on manufacturing and sales.

Fig. 5.31.

A paired style bar chart.

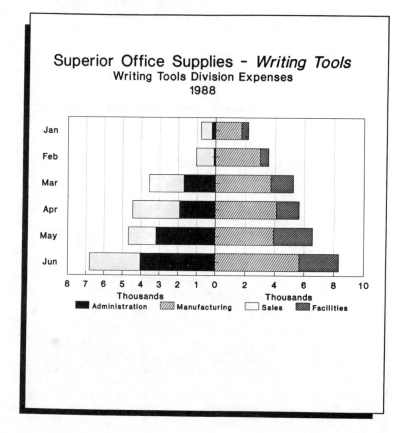

Try making your SOSEXPEN graph into a paired bar chart by following these steps:

1. Press F8 (Options) at the Bar/Line Chart Data screen to call up the first Titles & Options page and check to see that Display is on for all four series.

2. Tab to the Y Axis column opposite Manufacturing and press the space bar to set Manufacturing to Y2.

3. Tab to the Y Axis column opposite Facilities and press the space bar to flip Facilities to Y2.

4. Press PgDn to bring up the second Titles & Options page.

5. Press the space bar to highlight Paired.

6. Press F10 (Continue) and then press F2 (Draw Chart) to see your changes on-screen.

7. Press Esc to return to the Main menu. Save your paired bar chart as SOSEXPR by selecting Get/Save/Remove from the Main menu and then Save Chart from the Get/Save/Remove menu. Press Ctrl-Del to remove the old chart name, SOSEXPEN, and type the name *sosexpr* (for "SOS expenses, paired").

Using Bar Enhancements

You can use the second set of options on the second Titles & Options page to add spunk to your chart by enhancing the appearance of its bars. The four enhancement styles available are 3D, Shadow, Link, and None. Selecting 3D yields a three-dimensional chart. (Remember, this option does not work on a paired chart.) Selecting Shadow produces a shadow effect on cluster, stack, and 100% bars. Choosing Link creates a dotted line linking series across multiple X values in stack and 100% bar charts. To display a plain chart with flat bars and no enhancements, select None for the Bar enhancement option.

Combining the 3D option with an overlap style chart results in an eye-catching display for both bar charts and line charts, as you can see in figure 5.32. This chart works especially well because Series 3 (1988) has the largest figures. This type of chart works best when you order the series from lowest to highest. Try creating the 3-D and overlap bar chart shown in figure 5.32 by entering the data shown in figure 5.33. Follow these steps:

1. Create a new bar chart.

2. Press the space bar to highlight Month for the X data type option; use *Jan* for Starting with and *Dec* for Ending with. Use an increment of 1 or leave Increment blank.

3. Enter the titles and data shown on the Bar/Line Chart Data screen.

4. Change the first three series names on the first Titles & Options page to *1986*, *1987*, and *1988*.

5. Set Bar style to Overlap and Bar enhancement to 3D on the second Titles & Options page.

6. Press F2 (Draw Chart) to preview your choices.

Save this chart as SOSREVS by returning to the Main menu and selecting Get/Save/Remove. Then select Save Chart from the Get/Save/Remove menu and type the name *sosrevs*. You do not need to supply the file name extension (CHT) because Harvard Graphics supplies it for you.

Fig. 5.32.

A bar chart with 3D *enhancement and* Overlap *style.*

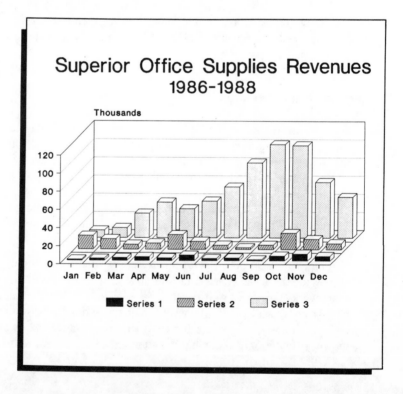

```
┌─────────────────────────────────────────────────────────────┐
│                    Bar/Line Chart Data                      ╲│
│  ▐▀▀▀▀▀▀▀▀▀▀▀▀▀▀▀▀▀▀▀▀▀▀▀▀▀▀▀▀▀▀▀▀▀▀▀▀▀▀▀▀▀▀▀▀▀▀▀▀▀        │
│     Title: Superior Office Supplies Revenues                 │
│  Subtitle: 1986-1988                                         │
│  Footnote:                                                   │
│                                                              │
│           X Axis      1986      1987      1988    Series 4  │
│      Pt   Month                                              │
│                                                              │
│      1    Jan         1356     14953      8215              │
│      2    Feb         2567     11449     11021              │
│      3    Mar         3577      5559     27028              │
│      4    Apr         4588      6978     39268              │
│      5    May         3452     16252     31921              │
│      6    Jun         6544      8938     40507              │
│      7    Jul         2788      4700     56132              │
│      8    Aug         3455      2050     82787              │
│      9    Sep         1517      4880    102834              │
│     10    Oct         5623     17991    101722              │
│     11    Nov         7866     11290     61407              │
│     12    Dec         5345      6745     45000              │
│                                                              │
│  F1-Help       F3-Set X type                F9-More series  │
│  F2-Draw chart F4-Calculate       F8-Options F10-Continue   │
└─────────────────────────────────────────────────────────────┘
```

Fig. 5.33.

The Bar/Line Chart Data screen for the combined three-dimensional and overlap chart.

As you continue to work with bar styles and enhancements, you will develop your own personal favorites. But keep in mind that not all enhancements work with certain bar styles. Using link enhancement with cluster style doesn't make sense, for example, so it doesn't work. When you try to use a conflicting style and enhancement combination, the style takes precedence and Harvard Graphics omits the enhancement.

If you use three-dimensional enhancement with overlap style and your output device is a plotter, the resulting chart will be plotted with overlap but without the three-dimensional enhancement. Standard plotters are incapable of plotting three-dimensional graphics.

Setting the Fill Style

You can fill the bars or lines in a chart with colors, patterns, or both. If you have set Harvard Graphics to use a monochrome monitor only, the program automatically places patterns in the bars even if the Bar fill style option on the second Titles & Options page appears as Color. With monochrome display and a non-color printer, however, you should still select Pattern for your fill style choice. Although Harvard automatically places patterns in the bars, those patterns (which are used for colors) are not as vivid as the patterns that appear when you select Pattern.

Setting Bar Width, Overlap, and Depth

You can set the width, percentage of overlap, and depth of the bars in a chart by using the Bar width, Bar overlap, and Bar depth options on the second Titles & Options page.

When you first create a bar chart, Harvard Graphics automatically determines the optimum width of the bars so that they fit evenly across the page. You can change these options easily, however, by assigning them a number from 1 to 100. The number you use for bar width represents the width of bars measured relative to the overall number of bars in the chart. This option is not valid in step style charts.

The Bar overlap option dictates the percentage amount that one bar overlaps another. When your bar chart is a three-dimensional overlap chart, this field determines the space between each x-axis grouping.

The Bar width and Bar overlap fields interact with each other. If you type a value of 30 in the Bar overlap field, for example, the bars in your chart overlap by 30 percent of their widths. If you type 40 in the Bar width field, the bars are 40 percent of the widest possible bar width in the chart, affected by the bar overlap. Figure 5.34 shows a bar width of 100 with a bar overlap of 20. You can see that the four bars take 100 percent of the available space so that one cluster is right against the next. Each new bar overlaps 20 percent of the bar next to it. Figure 5.35 shows the same chart with the bar width set at 75 percent of the available space for each cluster and the bar overlap set at 35.

To set and observe these changes, follow this procedure:

1. Select Overlap for the Bar style option on the second Titles & Options page by tabbing to the Bar style field and pressing the space bar to highlight your choice.

2. Select a Bar enhancement of None.

3. Select a Bar fill style of Pattern.

4. Tab to Bar width, type *100*, and press Enter to move the cursor to Bar overlap.

5. Type *20* in the Bar overlap field.

6. Press F2 (Draw Chart) to preview your changed chart.

7. Save this chart as SOSREVO (for "SOS revenue chart, overlap").

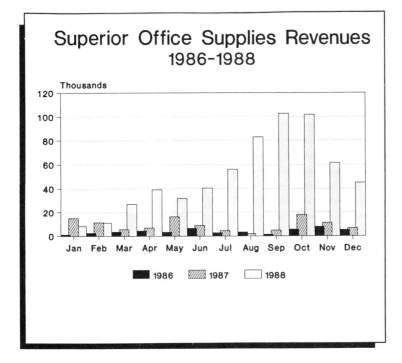

Fig. 5.34.

Overlap bar chart with bar width set at 100 percent and overlap set at 20 percent.

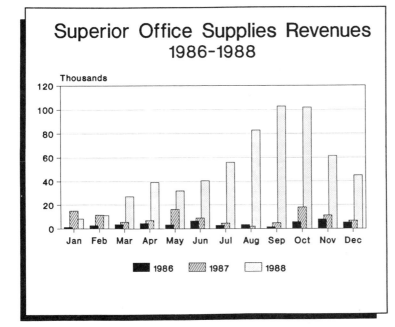

Fig. 5.35.

Overlap bar chart with bar width set at 75 percent and overlap set at 35 percent.

You use the Bar depth option with three-dimensional bars only, to determine the apparent depth of the bars caused by the three-dimensional effect.

Using Horizontally Displayed Bars

While still viewing the second Titles and Options page, toggle the Horizontal chart option to Yes (by pressing the space bar) to switch the x- and y-axes of your chart. Selecting Yes displays the x-axis along the vertical axis and the y-axis along the horizontal plane of the graph. Using a horizontal chart is an effective way to handle a large number of x-axis values. Horizontal charts are most commonly used with bars, but they also work with lines and other chart types. If your x-axis values have a label type of Name, you may want to consider alphabetizing the labels so that the chart is easier to read. Of course, calendar data, such as the data shown in figure 5.36, is best left unalphabetized.

Fig. 5.36.

A horizontal bar/ line chart.

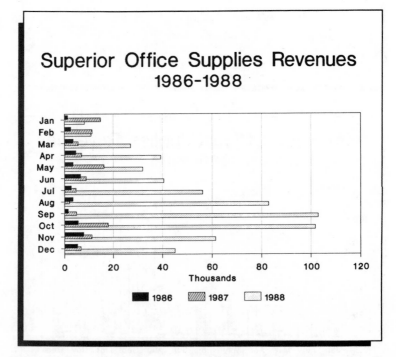

Note that with Horizontal chart set to Yes and Bar enhancement set at 3D, the chart appears as three-dimensional but not horizontal. To create a horizontal chart, you must first set the Bar enhancement style to None because none of the possible bar enhancement types works with horizontal graphs.

Displaying Value Labels

By setting the Value labels option to All, you instruct Harvard Graphics to display on the chart the values represented by each of the bars or by each of the data points joined by line charts. Value labels do not appear in 100% types of charts. Figure 5.37 shows a chart with all value labels displayed. Notice that value labels appear on top of each bar. (If the chart has the Horizontal chart option still set to Yes, the value labels appear to the right of each bar.) The chart looks cluttered because it contains too many series to accommodate all value labels. In the section "Controlling the Interaction of Value Labels," you learn how to select only specific series to display, clearing up the clutter and driving home only those figures you want to emphasize.

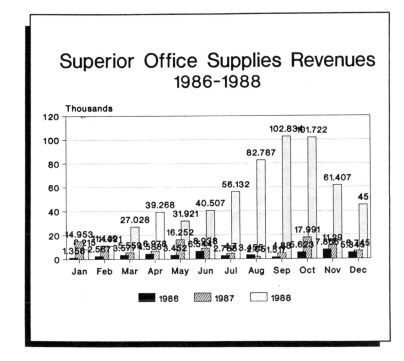

Fig. 5.37.

A bar/line chart with Value labels *set to* All.

Setting the Value labels option to Select enables you to choose later (on the fourth Titles & Options page) which value labels you want to display. Harvard Graphics always sets Value labels to None initially. This choice places no value labels on the points within a chart.

Adding a Chart Frame

You also can change the frame around a graph by using the frame options on the second Titles & Options page. The Frame style field includes these options: Full, Half, Quarter, and None. A full frame is a box surrounding a graph on all four sides. A half frame places a vertical line at the left side of the graph and a horizontal line along the graph's bottom. A quarter frame yields a single line along the bottom of the graph. You also can choose to use no frame at all. Figure 5.38 shows the SOSREVS chart with each of the frame styles.

Fig. 5.38.

*The four frame styles (*Full, Half, Quarter, *and* None).

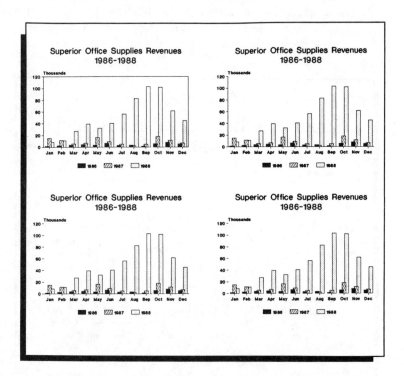

The second and third frame fields refer to the color of the frame and the color of the background. In both cases, you can press F6 (Colors) to see your choices, highlight a color, and press Enter. If you make the frame background the same color as one of your bars, the bar seems to disappear. Selecting a soothing color for a chart background and a contrasting color for a chart's frame can be visually pleasing. For example, select grey for the background, with red as the frame color.

Including and Placing the Legend

Harvard Graphics offers 25 positions for the key to a graph, its legend. Using a combination of Legend location, Legend justify, and Legend placement, you can position the legend or even decide not to display a legend at all. If you prefer, you can use Legend frame to place a single line around the legend, a shadow along the bottom and to the right of the legend, or no line at all around the legend.

Different legend descriptions have an effect on the appearance of your chart. For example, you must decide whether the legend is on the top, bottom, left, or right of the chart by using the Legend location option. Use Legend justify to determine whether the legend is justified to the left or as a line along the top (select the left arrow and up arrow choice) or whether you want to center the legend items. The last choice in Legend justify places the legend along the bottom, or justified right, depending on the decision you made for the location. The third option (Legend placement) tells Harvard Graphics to place the legend inside or outside the graph. A placement inside the graph can be effective only when the legend does not write over the bars. The final legend option determines whether the legend frame is a single line or a shadow. Or you can choose not to use a frame around the legend at all.

Figure 5.39 shows several of the available legend option placements. All these legends have the Shadow option turned on.

Using the Third Titles & Options Page

You use the third Titles & Options page (see fig. 5.40) to change the underlying structure of the chart's appearance. For example, you can use options on this page to set grid lines behind a chart's bars or to scale and format a chart's x- and y-axis values. To set options on the third Titles & Options page, you use the same methods you used on the first two pages. Simply press the Tab key to move from field to field and the space bar to highlight your choice for an option. Then press F2 (Draw Chart) to view the result of your changes.

Adding a Data Table

Data tables, new to Harvard Graphics in Version 2.1, list outside the chart the raw values for each of the points in the chart, by series. By looking at the data table, a viewer of the chart need not depend on his or her judgment to gauge the values of its data points. That information is provided clearly in the data table.

Fig. 5.39.

Legend variations.

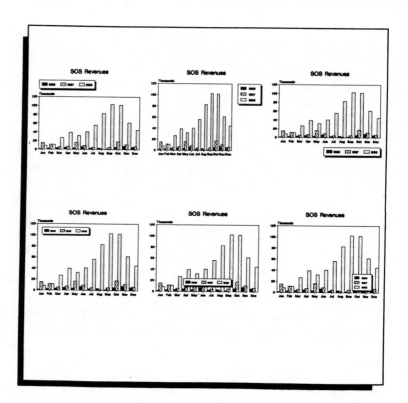

Fig. 5.40.

The third Titles & Options page.

```
▲            Bar/Line Chart   Titles & Options   Page 3 of 4         ▼

   Data Table          | Normal      Framed    ▶None

   X  Axis Labels       | ▶Normal     Vertical   %         None
   Y1 Axis Labels       | Value       ▶$         %         None
   Y2 Axis Labels       | ▶Value      $          %         None

   X  Grid Lines        | ....        ——        ▶None
   Y1 Grid Lines        | ....        ——        ▶None
   Y2 Grid Lines        | ▶....       ——         None

   X Tick Mark Style    | ▶In         Out        Both      None
   Y Tick Mark Style    | ▶In         Out        Both      None

                        |   X Axis     |   Y1 Axis    |    Y2 Axis

   Scale Type           | ▶Linear  Log  | ▶Linear  Log  | ▶Linear  Log
   Format               |
   Minimum Value        |
   Maximum Value        |
   Increment            |

   F1-Help
   F2-Draw chart                         F8-Data        F18-Continue
```

Harvard Graphics does not supply a data table automatically. Instead, you must turn on the data table by using the third Titles & Options page. The first line on that page lists the data table styles: Normal, Framed, and None. A normal data table is a list that appears directly below the graph's x-axis. A framed data table provides the same list but with framing lines surrounding the data. Figure 5.41 shows a framed data table on the SOSREVS chart.

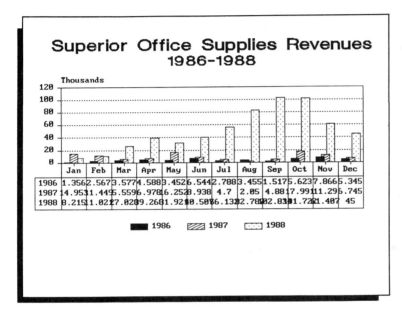

Fig. 5.41.

SOSREVS chart with a framed data table.

Try putting a framed data table on your SOSREVS chart, following this procedure:

1. Select Get/Save/Remove from the Main menu.

2. Use the down arrow to highlight SOSREVS and press Enter.

3. Press Esc to bring up the Bar/Line Chart Data screen.

4. Press F8 (Options) at the Bar/Line Chart Data screen to bring up the Titles & Options pages. Make sure that Horiz. is set to No on the second Titles & Options page.

5. Press PgDn twice to summon the third Titles & Options page.

6. Press the space bar to highlight Framed at the Data Table option.

7. Press F2 (Draw Chart) to preview your chart with a data table.

Previewing Your Data Table

If the raw data in your data table is composed of long numbers, you may find that they do not seem to fit properly in the data table when you preview the chart. Before you worry, check to see how the chart will print out by previewing the printed output on the screen. To preview the output just as it will be sent to your output device, follow these steps:

1. Press Esc to return to the Main menu.

2. Select Produce Output from the Main menu.

3. Press F2 (Draw Chart) to view the chart as it will appear when printed.

Figure 5.42 shows the SOSREVS chart as it is previewed at the Produce Output menu.

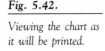

Fig. 5.42.

Viewing the chart as it will be printed.

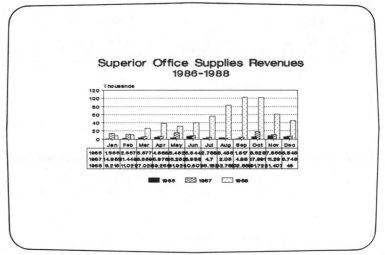

Changing the Size of Data Table and X-Axis Values

If your data doesn't fit when you look at the print view, you need to reduce the size of the numbers in the data table. You can accomplish this task by using the F7-Size/Place feature on the first Titles & Options page. With the Size/Place overlay on-screen (see fig. 5.43), tab to the X labels field and press 1. To complement the X labels, set the Y labels to 1 also. After you press F10 (Continue), press F2 (Draw Chart) and view the data table with its new size (see fig. 5.44).

```
 Size   Place     Bar/Line Chart  Titles & Options  Page 1 of 4

  7      L ►C  R  Title:        Superior Office Supplies Revenues
  6      L ►C  R  Subtitle:     1986-1988
  8      L ►C  R
  8      ►L  C  R  Footnote:
  8      ►L  C  R
  8      ►L  C  R
  4          ►C     X  axis title:
  3      ►→  ↓      Y1 axis title: Thousands
  3      ►→  ↓      Y2 axis title:
  1      X labels                    Type              Display │ Y Axis
  1      Y labels          Bar  Line Trend Curve  Pt  Yes  No │ Y1  Y2

  1  │ 1986                           Bar                  Yes     Y1
  2  │ 1987                           Bar                  Yes     Y1
  3  │ 1988                           Bar                  Yes     Y1
  4  │ Series 4                       Bar                  Yes     Y1
  5  │ Series 5                       Bar                  Yes     Y1
  6  │ Series 6                       Bar                  Yes     Y1
  7  │ Series 7                       Bar                  Yes     Y1
  8  │ Series 8                       Bar                  Yes     Y1

 F1-Help                     F5-Attributes   F7-Size/Place
 F2-Draw chart                               F8-Data          F10-Continue
```

Fig. 5.43.

The Size/Place overlay on the first Titles & Options page.

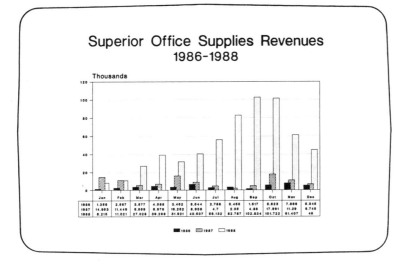

Fig. 5.44.

Preview of SOSREVS with the revised, smaller data table.

Data tables display data for all series, even if you set Display for a series to No on the first Titles & Options page. Eliminating series from a data table is discussed later in this chapter (see "Controlling the Interaction of Value Labels").

To change the size of the numbers in a data table, you change the size of the X labels. Normally, the X labels and Y labels options on the Size/Place overlay allow you to change the sizes of the labels that run along the horizontal and vertical axes of the chart. If you want to leave the Y labels large while changing the X labels, simply press Enter to move past the Y labels line. Harvard Graphics treats each of these labels independently. In figure 5.45, the Y labels have been set to 5.5.

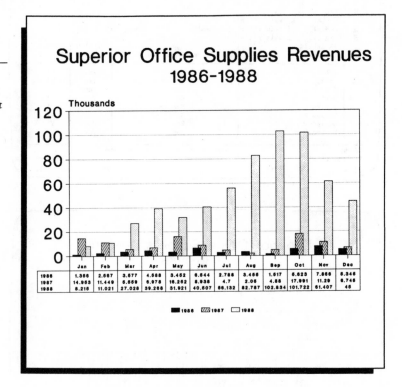

Fig. 5.45.

The bar/line chart with X labels set at 1.0 and Y labels set at 5.5.

Altering X- and Y-Axis Labels

The X Axis Labels, Y1 Axis Labels, and Y2 Axis Labels options on the third Titles & Options page enable you to describe and format the numbers on the x- and y-axes. X-axis labels can appear in three different formats: Normal, Vertical, and %. Normal x-axis labels are displayed horizontally across the page below the axis. Vertical labels are displayed down the page, one letter under another. Figure 5.46 shows an example of vertical x-axis labels. To try this effect, be sure to switch the Data Table option to None first so that you can see the effect.

If you want to keep long x-axis labels horizontal, you can break them into two lines of text by typing a vertical bar (|) at the position at which you want to split the label.

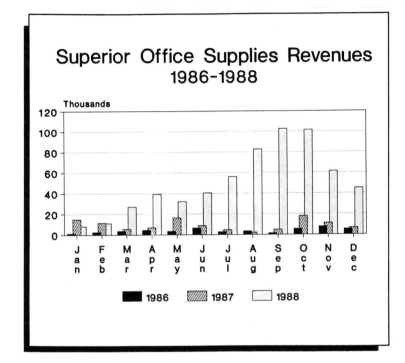

Fig. 5.46.

Vertical x-axis labels.

Selecting the % format for the X Axis Labels option instructs Harvard Graphics to multiply the value by 100 and add a percent sign. Of course this method works only when X data type is Number. If you select None for X Axis Labels, no labels are on the finished chart.

Y1 and Y2 axis labels are normally placed on the left and right vertical sides, respectively, of the graph. Using the Y1 Axis Labels and Y2 Axis Labels options on the third Titles & Options page, you also can format the y-axis label values according to one of three formats: Value, $, and %. In addition, you can choose None to remove the y-axis labels altogether. If you choose None, you may want to include value labels above the bars or lines and eliminate the chart's grid marks. To place the values on top of the bars, read the section in this chapter called "Controlling the Interaction of Value Labels." A clean chart, both informative and specific, is the result.

Altering Grid Lines and Tick Marks

If you have added grid lines behind the bars of the graph, you can change their style with the grid lines options on the third Titles & Options page. Grid lines can be dotted or solid. They can be distracting, so you should use them cautiously. The presence of grid lines on your graph emphasizes values rather than trends. On a three-dimensional overlap chart, adding grid lines can clarify your data substantially.

With the X Tick Mark Style and Y Tick Mark Style options, you can specify whether your graph should include tick marks. Tick marks are notches along the x- and y-axes. You can choose to display tick marks inside the graph by choosing In, outside the graph by choosing Out, or both inside and outside the graph by choosing Both. As an alternative, you can select None to eliminate tick marks altogether.

Scaling X- and Y-Axes

Harvard Graphics provides two methods for scaling the x- and y-axes. *Scaling* an axis sets the distance between its points. Most business graphics use *linear* scaling, in which the distances between axis points are equal. When the change being described by the chart is geometric, a *logarithmic* scale type can better portray the data. A logarithmic scale in base 10 has distances between each unit on the axes that increase logarithmically. Each increment increases further than the preceding increment by a power of 10. For example, the first point is 10 to the first power, or 10; the second point is 10 to the second power, or 100; the third point is 10 to the third power, or 1,000; and so on.

Logarithmic scaling is fairly uncommon, but it can be effective when the data in a chart is diverse, when you have large changes between points, or when the high and low points of data in a series are of a different scope than those in other series in the chart. Large variations within a series are lessened in a logarithmic chart.

When you set the minimum and maximum values for a logarithmic scale axis, the maximum value should be a power of 10 over the minimum value. For example, a typical logarithmic scale may range from 1 to 10,000.

Using the third Titles & Options page, you may choose Log (logarithmic) for one axis and Linear for the other. This setup produces a semilogarithmic chart. Figure 5.47 shows a revenue chart with large variations between series displayed as a linear chart. Figure 5.48 shows the same chart with a logarithmic scale. You can see the visual difference it makes when the scale is based on multiples of 10.

When you set the x-axis on the X Data Type Menu overlay, you tell Harvard Graphics the appropriate starting and ending points for the data you are entering. The x-axis Minimum Value and Maximum Value fields on the third Titles &

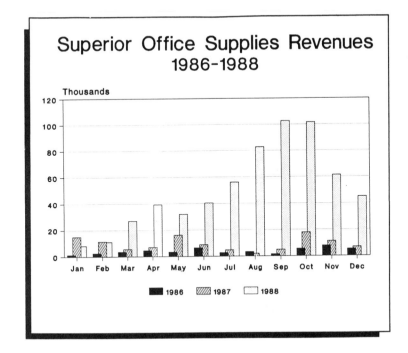

Fig. 5.47.

Chart with large variations between series displayed as a linear chart.

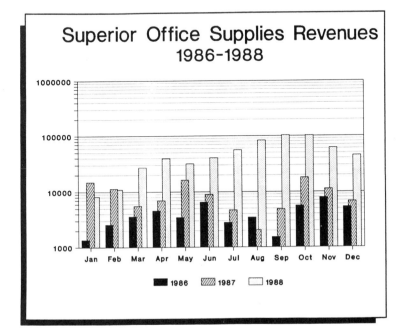

Fig. 5.48.

The same chart with a logarithmic scale.

Options page affect the final Starting with and Ending with points you see when you preview the chart.

Formatting the Axis Labels

You can use the features on the bottom of the third Titles & Options page to add meaning to the x- and y-axis labels. Figure 5.49 shows the third Titles & Options page with scaling and formatting commands added. Use this figure and the format commands in table 5.1 to determine the appropriate scaling for your chart. You can include commas and measurement characters such as $, *ft.*, and ". In addition, you can set the number of decimal places for chart labels or display them in scientific notation. The scaling options interact with the Format option near the top of the third Titles & Options page. When you select $ or % in the Format option at the top of the page, Harvard Graphics formats the label on the x- or y-axis in your chart but not on the Bar/Line Chart Data screen.

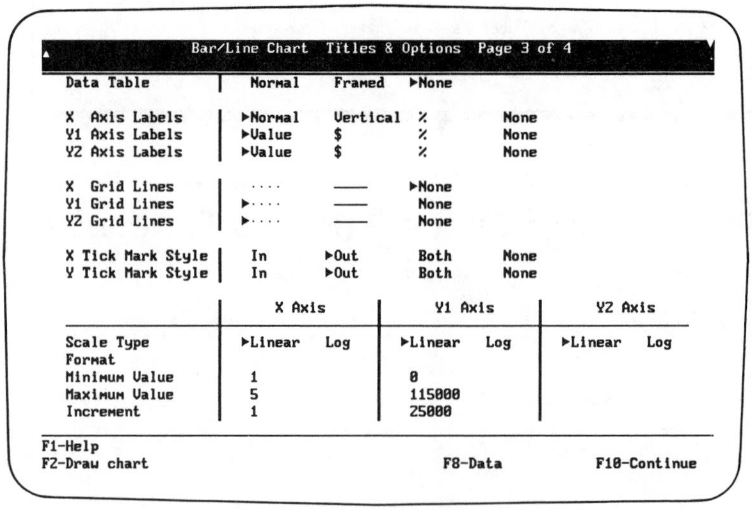

Fig. 5.49.

The third Titles & Options page with scaling and formatting commands included.

Bar/Line Chart Titles & Options Page 3 of 4			
Data Table	Normal	Framed	▶None
X Axis Labels	▶Normal	Vertical	% None
Y1 Axis Labels	▶Value	$	% None
Y2 Axis Labels	▶Value	$	% None
X Grid Lines	· · · ·	——	▶None
Y1 Grid Lines	▶· · · ·	——	None
Y2 Grid Lines	▶· · · ·	——	None
X Tick Mark Style	In	▶Out	Both None
Y Tick Mark Style	In	▶Out	Both None

	X Axis	Y1 Axis	Y2 Axis
Scale Type	▶Linear Log	▶Linear Log	▶Linear Log
Format			
Minimum Value	1	0	
Maximum Value	5	115000	
Increment	1	25000	

```
F1-Help
F2-Draw chart                          F8-Data          F10-Continue
```

Formatting the y-axis labels also formats the y-data values shown on your chart in Harvard Graphics. The four special Harvard Graphics axis-formatting commands are simple to use. You need only type the format instruction on the Format line after you have selected the scale type for the x- and y-axes. Table 5.1 provides a summary, some examples, and descriptions of the formatting commands.

Table 5.1
Format Commands for the X- and Y-Axes

To display:	Enter on the Format line:	Description:
4,000	,	Inserts a comma in the number, if necessary
19.68	2	Displays two decimal places
2,590.6	,1	Displays both a comma and a specific number of decimal places
12.2 mm	l1 mm	Vertical bar (l) adds preceding or trailing text (like mm) to the formatted value and 1 tells Harvard Graphics to include one decimal place after the decimal point
Yen 9,899.50	Yenl,2	Precedes number with Yen, places a comma in the number, and displays the number to two decimal places
£456.25	£,2	Displays a UK pound sign (£). To create a pound sign, type 156 on the keypad while holding down the Alt key
9.55E+02	!	Displays numbers in scientific notation

If all the numbers in your data are large, you can use the Format field to reduce the number of digits in the values by dividing all the numbers in your data by a constant. The result is fewer digits and numbers that are more easy to read. Scaling formats are identical to standard formats. Figure 5.49 shows the third Titles

& Options page with scaling formats. Figure 5.50 shows a preview of the chart with the new scale.

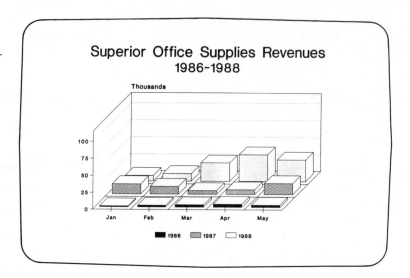

Fig. 5.50.

Three years of revenues with no scaling adjustments on the x-axis.

Here's how to use scale formats:

To display 2 cartons, use this command:

15|cartons

If you have the numbers of actual Mechanical pencil sets sold (30 in this example), but you want to list the values in the chart by the number of cartons sold, you can use this scaling format to specify that each carton contains 15 sets of pencils.

To display 40 thousand, use this command:

1000|thousand

This formatting instruction divides the entered value by 1,000 and places the word thousand after the number.

Setting Minimum and Maximum Values

Use the Minimum Value, Maximum Value, and Increment fields on the third Titles & Options page to override the scale that Harvard Graphics automatically uses for the axes of your chart. By specifying minimum and maximum values and increments in the X Axis column, you can limit the number of data points in a chart. If your chart includes data for the last 20 years of growth, for example, you can show data at 5-year intervals by using 1 as the minimum value, 20 as the maximum value, and 5 as the increment. To show only the first 5 years, you can use 1 as the minimum value and 5 as the maximum value and leave increment blank. If you omit an increment, Harvard Graphics assumes that you want an increment of 1.

Figure 5.50 shows three years of revenues for the Superior Office Supplies Writing Division. Figure 5.51 shows the third Titles & Options page set to show only the first five months of data, and figure 5.52 shows the same bar chart with the adjusted scaling. Note that if the X data type option is set to Number, you cannot reduce the number of X values by using this technique.

You can scale the Y1 and Y2 axes in a similar fashion. When you change minimum and maximum Y values, though, be sure that the minimum is smaller than the smallest value on the data screen and the maximum is larger than the largest value on the data screen. If you don't, Harvard Graphics overrides your values so that it can chart every value in your data.

Sometimes the smallest value in your chart is considerably larger than 0. But Harvard Graphics still starts the y-axis at 0. Suppose, for example, that your smallest value is 45 and your largest value is 200. To magnify the results shown on this chart, make its minimum Y value 30 and its maximum Y value 225. You may want to use a larger increment to reduce the chart clutter, too. If you decide that you want to return to the Harvard Graphics defaults, simply remove the minimum, maximum, and increment values you entered.

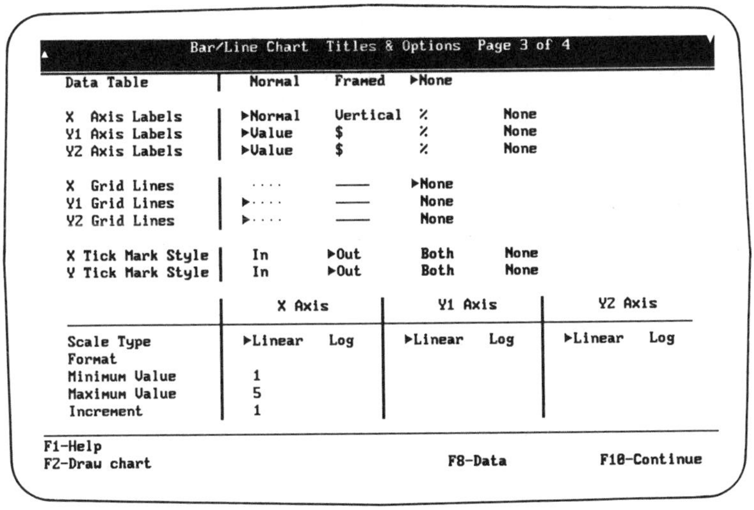

Fig. 5.51.

The third Titles & Options page with x-axis scaling.

```
               Bar/Line Chart  Titles & Options  Page 3 of 4
  ▲
  Data Table          | Normal    Framed    ▶None

  X  Axis Labels      | ▶Normal   Vertical  %         None
  Y1 Axis Labels      | ▶Value    $         %         None
  Y2 Axis Labels      | ▶Value    $         %         None

  X  Grid Lines       | . . . .             ▶None
  Y1 Grid Lines       | ▶. . . .    ———      None
  Y2 Grid Lines       | ▶. . . .    ———      None

  X Tick Mark Style   | In        ▶Out      Both      None
  Y Tick Mark Style   | In        ▶Out      Both      None

                      |   X Axis        |   Y1 Axis      |   Y2 Axis

  Scale Type          | ▶Linear   Log   | ▶Linear  Log  | ▶Linear   Log
  Format
  Minimum Value       | 1
  Maximum Value       | 5
  Increment           | 1

  F1-Help
  F2-Draw chart                          F8-Data          F10-Continue
```

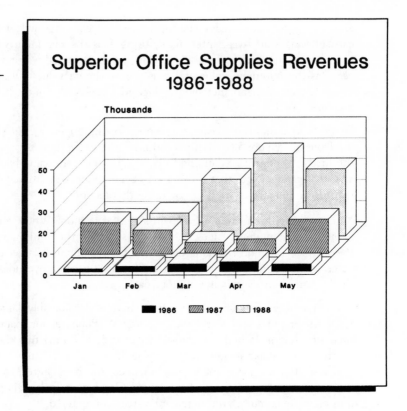

Fig. 5.52.

The x-axis adjusted to show only the first five months.

Using the Fourth Titles & Options Page

Press PgDn at the third Titles & Options page to summon the fourth Titles & Options page (see fig. 5.53). The fourth page is the last of the Titles & Options pages for bar/line charts. Use this page to place the finishing touches on the appearance of your chart's titles and bars or lines. (*Titles* are the names you give to series, axes, and the overall chart.)

For example, you can use the fourth Titles & Options page to set any series to display as a cumulative set of values, with each successive value representing its own value added to the sum total of all values before it. Or you can change the style of marker used to indicate each point on a line chart. On the fourth Titles & Options page, you also can type in x- and y-axes titles, alter their size/place characteristics and their attributes, and change the line style of a line chart series. The fourth Titles & Options page also lets you select which Y labels to display on the completed graph. This feature interacts with the third Titles &

```
┌─────────────────────────────────────────────────────────────────┐
│  ▲  ┃    Bar/Line Chart  Titles & Options  Page 4 of 4    ┃  ▼   │
│                                                                   │
│           Title:      Superior Office Supplies Revenues           │
│           Subtitle:   1986-1988                                   │
│                                                                   │
│           Footnote:                                               │
│                                                                   │
│           X  axis title:                                          │
│           Y1 axis title: Thousands                                │
│           Y2 axis title:                                          │
│     Legend             Cum     Y Label   Color   Marker/   Line   │
│     Title:           Yes  No  Yes  No                     Style   │
│                                                                   │
│     1 │ 1986           No      No        2       1         1      │
│     2 │ 1987           No      No        3       2         1      │
│     3 │ 1988           No      No        4       3         1      │
│     4 │ Series 4       No      No        5       4         1      │
│     5 │ Series 5       No      No        6       5         1      │
│     6 │ Series 6       No      No        7       6         1      │
│     7 │ Series 7       No      No        8       7         1      │
│     8 │ Series 8       No      No        9       8         1      │
│                                                                   │
│   F1-Help              F5-Attributes   F7-Size/Place              │
│   F2-Draw chart        F6-Colors       F8-Data       F10-Continue │
└─────────────────────────────────────────────────────────────────┘
```

Fig. 5.53.

*The fourth Titles &
Options page.*

Options page when you tell Harvard Graphics to display only select Y values, described in this chapter section.

You are already familiar with the first several lines on this screen, and you have almost certainly entered a title, subtitle, and footnote before you get to this page. But Harvard Graphics gives you yet another opportunity to make changes and alterations, using the F7-Size/Place and F5-Attributes options.

Building a Cumulative Chart

The second column of the fourth Titles & Options page, Cum, enables you to set a series to be calculated and displayed as a *cumulative* set of values. In a cumulative series, the data from the first Y value in the first bar is added to the data of the second Y value in the second bar. The data from the first and second Y values are then added to the third Y value in the third bar, and so on. A cumulative chart, with Cum set to Yes for all series, is shown in figure 5.54.

Setting the Cum column to No results in a display of actual values rather than cumulative totals. Cumulative charts are effective for showing running totals but can be deceiving if not properly labeled. These charts can make a series of equal data values look like phenomenal growth.

A dual y-axis cumulative chart with a horizontal orientation can be particularly impressive. To see this effect, recall the dual y-axis chart (SOSEXPR) you made

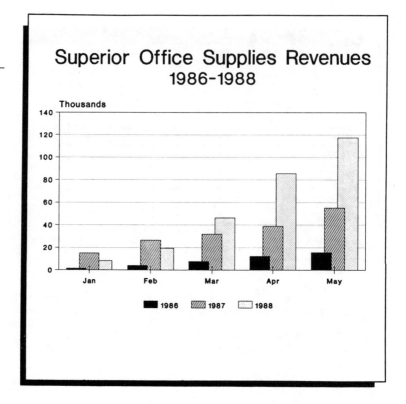

Fig. 5.54.

A cumulative chart.

previously in this chapter and set all the series to cumulative. Figure 5.55 shows the resulting chart.

Displaying Y Labels

The Y Label column on the fourth Titles & Options page is tied directly to the Value labels option on the second Titles & Options page. When you choose Select at the Value labels option on page 2, Harvard Graphics displays only the Y values set to Yes in the Y Label column on page 4. You can use these two options to label only the single most significant series in a chart with four series, for example. Figure 5.56 shows a bar chart with just one series labeled. This figure uses the SOSREVS chart, emphasizing only the last year. Its Y values were formatted with the third Titles & Options page (a 0 in the Y1 Axis Format line). If you try to reproduce this chart, be sure that you set Value labels to Select on the second Titles & Options page.

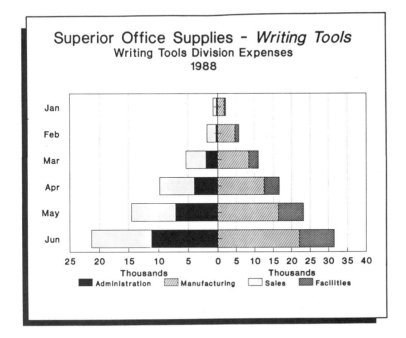

Fig. 5.55.

A dual y-axis chart with Cum *selected for all series.*

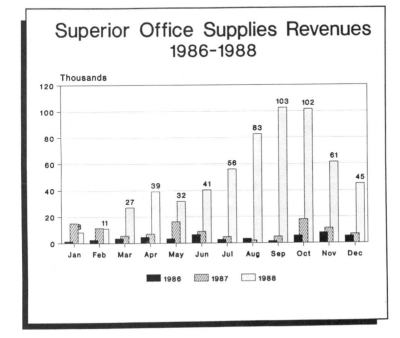

Fig. 5.56.

A bar chart with just one series labeled.

Controlling the Interaction of Value Labels

When you display a value label, it appears on the chart above the point for that value. But when a value is displayed on the graph, that value does not appear in a data table. Therefore, you must choose whether to display Y labels in the data table or on the graph itself.

Harvard Graphics leaves no option for omitting specific series values from both the graph and the data table if you are using a data table. If you suppress the display of a bar on the graph, you will not want the data to show on the table. To keep the data from showing on the table, you must take advantage of a complex interaction between options on all four Titles & Options pages.

You begin by following this procedure:

1. On the first Titles & Options page, choose the series to display.

2. Set the Value labels option on the second Titles & Options page to Select.

3. Set Data Table to Normal or Framed on the third Titles & Options page.

4. On the fourth Titles & Options page, choose the series that should get Y labels, using the Y Label column.

Then, to turn off the display of the values of a specific series both in the data table and on the graph, follow this procedure:

1. Set Display to No on the first Titles & Options page for the series you want to affect.

2. For that same series, set Y Label to Yes on the fourth Titles & Options page.

Controlling Color, Markers, Patterns, and Line Styles

The remaining columns on the fourth Titles & Options page describe the physical attributes of the markers, bars, and lines available for a chart. (*Markers* are the dots, circles, asterisks, and other figures used to mark each point in a line chart.) Harvard Graphics automatically selects a different line style, color, and marker style for each series when you create a graph. The program provides four line styles and eight marker styles. Line style 1 produces a thin, solid line; line style 2, a thick, solid line; line style 3, a dotted line; and line style 4, a dashed line. Markers are varied: asterisks, plus signs, x's, circles, and other markers are available. Figure 5.57 shows the full range of line styles and all 12 marker styles available to you. (Unfortunately, in these black-and-white illustrations, you cannot see the phenomenal rainbow of colors chosen.)

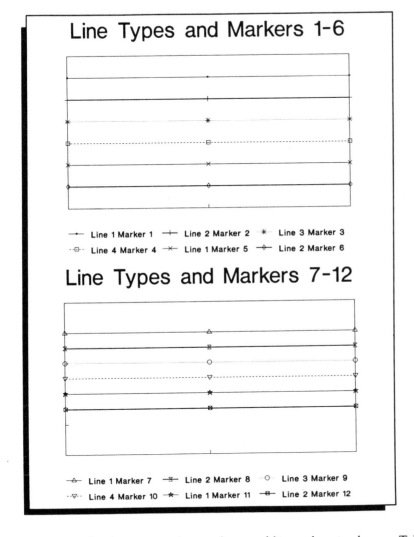

Fig. 5.57.

The available line and marker styles.

To make changes in color, markers, and line styles, simply press Tab to move the cursor to the appropriate column and line on the fourth Titles & Options page. Press the space bar to highlight your choice. When the cursor is in the Color column, you can press F6 (Colors) to see your choices. If you want your lines to have no markers, press 0 in the Marker/Pattern column.

Now that you are familiar with the four Bar/Line Chart Titles & Options pages, you are ready to learn about another important feature of the program: automatic calculation.

Calculating Data

A helpful Harvard Graphics feature is the program's capacity to calculate new data based on the data you supply and then graphically display those results. If you supply sets of sales data for different items over six months, for example, Harvard Graphics can calculate and graph six-month sales totals.

The calculation features resemble the calculation functions in 1-2-3. You type a calculation referring to a group of values, and Harvard Graphics performs the calculation and creates a new series of data based on that calculation. To specify the calculations to perform, you use keywords that instruct Harvard Graphics to average, sum, divide, calculate a moving average, or execute a host of statistical functions on your data.

To work with the calculation features in Harvard Graphics, you must have the current graph's data screen displayed. You can return to this screen from any of the Titles & Options pages by pressing F8 (Data). Press F4 (Calculate) with the cursor on an unused series. The Calculate overlay then appears.

To practice some simple calculations, use the chart called SOSREVS to project the growth of Superior Office Supplies during the following year. Try a calculation that shows a 1.6 percent growth in the preceding year and start with the Calculate overlay shown in figure 5.58:

Follow this procedure to perform the calculation:

1. Retrieve SOSREVS and press Esc to view the Bar/Line Chart Data screen.

2. Position the cursor at the top data line of the Series 4 column and press F4 (Calculate). Harvard Graphics overwrites any existing values in a column when filling the column with calculated data, so you must be certain that the cursor is in a blank column.

3. Press Ctrl-Del to delete Series 4.

4. Type *1989* over the words Series 4, which appear after the Legend prompt. Press Enter.

5. Type the calculation *#3*1.6* (see fig. 5.59). This calculation multiplies the data in Series 3 by 1.6.

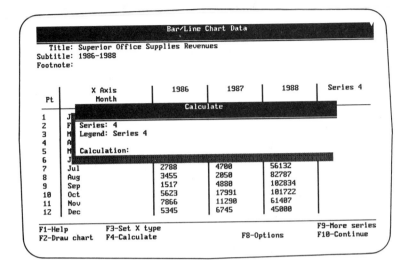

Fig. 5.58.

Blank Calculation overlay.

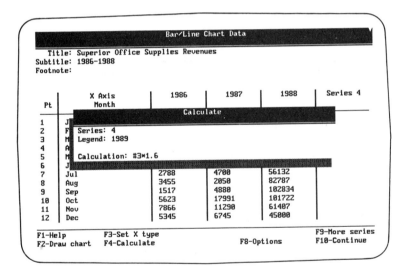

Fig. 5.59.

The completed overlay.

6. Press F10 (Continue) to calculate the series. Harvard Graphics displays calculated series with a diamond in front of the series name on the Bar/Line Chart Data screen.

7. Press F2 (Draw Chart) to view the calculated series. See figure 5.60 for the results.

Fig. 5.60.

Preview of the completed chart.

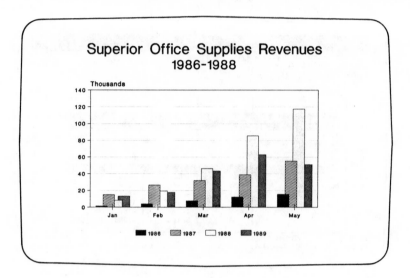

Save the new revenue chart as SOSRPROJ (for "SOS revenues, projected"). To save the chart, select Get/Save/Remove from the Main menu and select Save Chart from the Get/Save/Remove menu. Type the new name of the chart, *sosrproj*. Press Enter to move the cursor to the Description line. Delete the current description by pressing Ctrl-Del and enter the new description, *Revenue projections*. Press Enter to save the chart.

Following Calculation Syntax Rules

Straightforward arithmetic, such as adding two sets of data, is the most simple Harvard Graphics calculation. Suppose that you want to add the total of all manufacturing expenses to the total of all equipment expenses and then display only that result. You can instruct Harvard Graphics to perform the summation and then display only the sum line on your line chart, suppressing both the equipment and manufacturing lines. If equipment is Series 1 and manufacturing is Series 2, the syntax for the calculation is

$\#1 + \#2$

The pound sign (#) represents the word *Series* in Harvard Graphics. Even though you may have renamed each of the series, Harvard Graphics remembers their original numeric names: Series 1, Series 2, Series 3, and so on. In this example, Harvard Graphics adds all the numbers in Series 1 to those in Series 2 and produces a third series with the results.

The four primary arithmetic calculations that you can instruct Harvard Graphics to perform are addition ($+$), subtraction ($-$), multiplication ($*$), and division (/). In addition to using series values in simple arithmetic calculations, you can include actual numeric values. Here are some sample arithmetic calculations with both series names and numeric values:

#4*#1/2   (Multiply Series 4 by Series 1 and divide by 2)

#3*6.7   (Multiply Series 3 by the number 6.7)

Caution: In Harvard Graphics, the order of precedence for arithmetic calculations is left to right. In the preceding example, Series 4 is multiplied by Series 1 before the result is divided by 2. Although you usually can change the order of calculation in a standard formula by enclosing certain parts of it in parentheses, you cannot use this method to change the order of precedence in Harvard Graphics. Instead, you must carefully arrange the order.

When calculations include series that have been calculated from other series, you can press F10 at the Calculate overlay to update all the calculations in a chart. Calculations are always performed from left to right on the data screen, so Harvard Graphics starts by updating Series 1, then Series 2, and so on.

Using Keywords To Perform Calculations

You can type a calculation that includes data from several series by referring to all the series in a formula. For example, #1 + #2 + #3 adds data in Series 1, 2, and 3. As an alternative, you can use one of the four Harvard Graphics row keywords listed in table 5.2.

Table 5.2
Row Keywords

Keyword	Result
@AVG	Calculates the average of a row of values
@MAX	Extracts the maximum value from a row of numbers
@MIN	Extracts the minimum value from a row of numbers
@SUM	Sums or totals a row of numbers

Row keywords can calculate up to seven series. You always must type an @ sign in front of a keyword, precede a series name by a pound sign (#), and enclose the series references in parentheses. To list several series, separate them with commas. An example of a valid row keyword formula is

@SUM(#1,#2,#3)

Figure 5.61 shows an @AVG calculation used to average 1986, 1987, and 1988 values in the chart. Notice that no spaces are included between the series numbers and the commas.

Fig. 5.61.

A sample @AVG calculation.

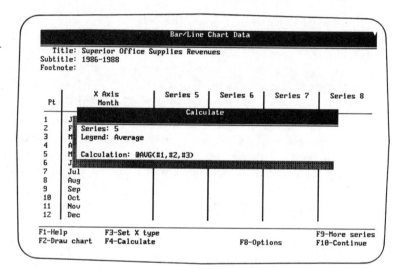

All the calculations described so far calculate series across rows. With one of these calculations, for example, you can add data from Series 1, Series 2, and Series 3 for a particular month. A second form of calculation, series calculation, calculates all the data in a single series column. With a series calculation, for example, you can total all the data in Series 3.

When you calculate across rows, you can use specific numbers in your calculation formulas. For example, you can multiply Series 3 by 1.6 by using #3*1.6. When you calculate down a series column, however, the calculation can include only the actual series data. The pound sign (#) represents the word *Series* in series calculations just as it does in row calculations.

Harvard Graphics provides 15 keywords for calculations on series. Each keyword performs a different statistical calculation. Table 5.3 lists the available series keywords and provides an example of each.

Table 5.3
Series Keywords

Keyword	Example	Results
@CLR	@CLR	Clears the contents of a series. Use this keyword only when you want to erase a series. A series erasure cannot be undone. (**Note:** The program erases the @CLR keyword after clearing the series.)
@COPY	@COPY(#3)	Copies the contents of Series 3 to the current series. The program then erases the keyword.
@CUM	@CUM(#2)	Creates a cumulative series in which each value is added to the total of all previous values in the series. Using the @CUM keyword is the same as selecting Cum on the fourth Titles & Options page.
@DIFF	@DIFF(#4)	Subtracts the value of each value in the series from its predecessor and calculates the net change in each new value.
@DUP	@DUP(#2)	Series 2 is duplicated in the current series. Each time you press F10 at the Calculate overlay, @DUP updates values again. The @DUP keyword is different from the @COPY keyword because of the continual updating of values that @DUP performs. Use @DUP when you want to look at the behavior of a calculated series in another series column.
@EXCH	@EXCH(#5)	Trades series or exchanges the values and series legend between Series 5 and the series in which you called up the Calculate overlay. The program erases the @EXCH keyword after performing the calculation.

Table 5.3—*Continued*

Keyword	Example	Results
@MAVG	@MAVG(#5,3,5)	Calculates the statistical moving average of Series 5 with 3 points before and 5 points after each value. Valid "points before" and "points after" values are between 1 and 120. If you omit the points before and points after values, Harvard Graphics assumes that you want 1 for each value.
@MOVE	@MOVE(#2)	Moves the values from the series in which the cursor rests to Series 2 and clears the series in which the cursor is located.
@PCT	@PCT(#4)	Calculates the percentage of the total of Series 4 that each value in Series 4 represents and places the results in the current series.
@REDUC	@REDUC	Reorders all series and X data on the Bar/Line Chart Data screen. This calculation is described in detail in the next section. The program erases the @REDUC keyword after performing the calculation.
@RECALC	@RECALC	Recalculates all the calculated values in the current chart. You can invoke the @RECALC keyword from any series column or even from the X Axis column. Your cursor can be almost anywhere in the data screen when you perform this function. After the calculations are performed, the @RECALC keyword disappears.
@REXP	@REXP(#4)	Calculates the exponential regression curve for Series 4. Don't use this calculation with a trend type of line series. The results of an exponential

Table 5.3—*Continued*

Keyword	Example	Results
		regression curve are not linear. The trend line in Harvard Graphics is the result of another internal calculation, which is linear.
@RLIN	@RLIN(#2)	Calculates the linear regression for Series 2. Linear regression can be calculated for any bar/line style series.
@RLOG	@RLOG(#1)	Calculates the logarithmic regression curve for Series 1 and places the results in the current series. Do not use a trend line with this keyword calculation.
@RPWR	@RPWR(#5)	Calculates the power regression curve for Series 5. Don't use this calculation with a trend line.

Be careful to position the cursor where you want the series to appear before you summon the Calculate overlay. If you position the cursor on the wrong series when you perform a calculation, the calculated results could overwrite the existing data in a series.

Using the @REDUC Keyword

Data reduction is a method of consolidating and reordering the data in a chart. When you instruct Harvard Graphics to perform an @REDUC calculation, the program eliminates any duplicate x-axis labels or values, reorders imported data, removes spaces in the X data that cause gaps in the graph, and sorts x-axis labels or values. The x-axis data is set in sequence from smallest to largest or earliest to latest for all x-axis types except Name.

Normally, you check data as you enter it, so you do not need to perform data reduction. When you import data from 1-2-3, however, the layout of the data in the spreadsheet may not be appropriate for Harvard Graphics. For example, the data in your 1-2-3 spreadsheet may have blank lines between lines of data. You can remove those blank lines with the @REDUC keyword. When you use @REDUC, Harvard Graphics performs the following processes:

❏ *An X and Y value check:* The program checks all X and Y values to ensure that they are valid entries. If the selected X data type is Month, for example, every X data point in the chart is checked against valid month entries. If an entry is invalid, Harvard Graphics displays the message Invalid X data type.

❏ *Value consolidation:* The program checks each X value to make sure that you don't have duplicate entries with the same X value. If it finds two Y values for the same X value, Harvard Graphics adds the Y values to produce only one entry for each X value. If the X data type is Number, however, Harvard Graphics does not sum the Y values.

❏ *Data sort:* Harvard Graphics sorts the data. When the X data type is Name, the program does not sort the data but removes blank lines that do not contain X data. Harvard Graphics places Y values that do not have corresponding X values after the sorted data. Blank lines are moved to the end of the chart.

Importing Lotus Data into Charts

Many Harvard Graphics users maintain data in 1-2-3 or a program that generates 1-2-3 worksheets. Harvard Graphics, therefore, provides a smoothly integrated mechanism for pulling data from a 1-2-3 spreadsheet directly into a chart data screen. Users no longer have to manually duplicate numbers in a spreadsheet on a chart data screen.

Combining 1-2-3 number crunching and Harvard Graphics chart building is a financial analyst's dream come true. With a few keystrokes, you can create a detailed pictorial view of the data you need to analyze. Figure 5.62 shows the SOSREVS spreadsheet.

Before you begin importing spreadsheet data, select Setup from the Main menu and Defaults from the Setup menu so that you can enter the default import directory. By specifying an import directory, you can instruct Harvard Graphics to look in a specific directory on your hard disk for 1-2-3 spreadsheets. If you keep your spreadsheets in C:\LOTUS, for example, you can specify C:\LOTUS as the default import directory. You also can specify a default import file. Harvard Graphics imports from the default file unless you specify otherwise.

To try the Lotus data-import process, copy the spreadsheet data shown in figure 5.62 into a 1-2-3 spreadsheet. Use the Range Name Create command to name the data ranges for each year in the spreadsheet. Give the data in the 1986 col-

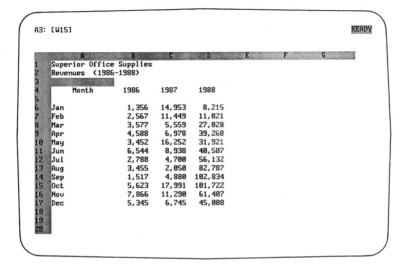

Fig. 5.62.

The SOSREVS spreadsheet.

umn the range name 1986. Give the data in the 1987 column the range name 1987, and so on. Name the range that contains the x-axis titles, as well. Try naming the range with the month names Jan through Dec as XAXIS. Importing Lotus data is easiest when you name the ranges in your spreadsheet. When you instruct Harvard Graphics which spreadsheet data to import, you can use range names such as 1987 rather than range addresses such as C6..C17.

Save the spreadsheet as SOSREVS.WK1. Harvard Graphics accepts files from 1-2-3 versions 1A or 2 (WKS or WK1 files) and Symphony spreadsheet data (WRK or WK1 files). After you save the spreadsheet, start Harvard Graphics and create a new graph chart (bar/line, area, high/low/close, or pie). Select an appropriate X data type to match the spreadsheet data and press Enter to reach a blank data screen.

After you see the blank data screen, return to the Main menu and follow this procedure:

1. Select Import/Export from the Main menu.

2. Select Import Lotus Data from the Import/Export menu.

3. Select the file SOSREVS.WK1.

4. At the Import Lotus Data screen, if you want to import the title in the spreadsheet, type a backslash (\) followed by the Lotus cell address of the title. In this case, type \A1.

5. If you want to import the subtitle in the spreadsheet, type a backslash followed by the Lotus cell address of the subtitle. In this case, type \A2.

   Follow the same procedure if you want to import a spreadsheet's footnote.

6. Position the cursor at the entry for Data Range for the x-axis data and type the range name *XAXIS*.

7. Position the cursor on Series 1 and press Ctrl-Del to erase Series 1. Type the series name *1986* and tab to the Data Range column. Type the range name *1986* and press Enter to move the cursor to the next line.

8. Continue filling in the second and third series lines as you did in step 7.

9. Press Enter to move the cursor to Append data and select No. Press F10 to continue. If you select Yes for Append data, Harvard Graphics adds the spreadsheet data to the end of any data already present on the Bar/Line Chart Data screen. Selecting No instructs Harvard Graphics to write over any existing data with the newly imported Lotus data. Figure 5.63 shows the completed Import Lotus Data screen.

10. Press F2 (Draw Chart) to view the chart with imported data.

Fig. 5.63.

The Import Lotus Data screen.

```
                          Import Lotus Data
         Worksheet name: SOSREUS .WK1

                  Title: \A1
               Subtitle: \A2
               Footnote:

                      Legend              Data Range

                 X | X axis data          XAXIS

                 1 | 1986                  1986
                 2 | 1987                  1987
                 3 | 1988                  1988
                 4 | Series 4
                 5 | Series 5
                 6 | Series 6
                 7 | Series 7
                 8 | Series 8

                 Append data:    Yes   ▶No

  F1-Help        F3-Select files
                 F4-Clear ranges                      F10-Continue
```

After you import titles from a spreadsheet, you can format the files using the Size/Place overlay as you would any chart title.

If you have not named the ranges in your spreadsheet, you can type cell addresses when Harvard Graphics asks for data ranges on the Import Lotus Data screen. In the preceding spreadsheet, for example, you could have specified the 1986 data as B6..B17.

When you import Lotus data into a pie chart, do not type pie slice names because Harvard Graphics automatically imports pie labels.

After you import Lotus spreadsheet data into a Harvard Graphics chart, you can save the chart as a template to create a data link that imports Lotus data into a new chart. Instructions for creating a template are in Chapter 8.

Importing ASCII Data into a Graph Chart

1-2-3 spreadsheets are not the only data files you can import with Harvard Graphics. You also can import data arranged in columns in standard ASCII files.

Figure 5.64 shows the SOSREVS data as it appears in an ASCII file. To follow along with this example, type the data shown in the figure into an ASCII file with any word processor capable of creating ASCII files. Make sure that you use three or more spaces between columns of data so that Harvard Graphics recognizes each column as a series. Follow this procedure:

1. Create a new bar/line chart and complete the X Data Type Menu overlay by pressing Enter to accept Name at the X data type prompt and leave Starting with, Ending with, and Increment blank. You must use Name at X data type when importing ASCII data.

2. Press F10 (Continue) to return to the Main menu.

3. Select Import/Export from the Main menu and Import ASCII Data from the Import/Export menu.

4. Select the ASCII file on the Select File screen that appears and press Enter.

5. Press Enter to accept all the selections at the bottom of the screen. These selections are described following this procedure. The Import Titles and Legends overlay appears as shown in figure 5.65.

6. Press Enter twice to select Yes in answer to both prompts on the Titles and Legends overlay. Your Bar/Line Chart Data screen should look like the one in figure 5.66.

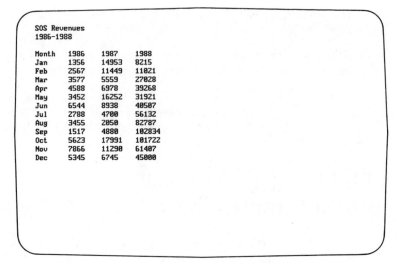

Fig. 5.64.

ASCII data ready for importing.

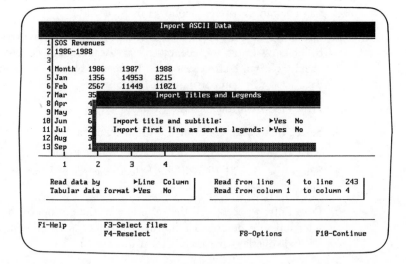

Fig. 5.65.

The Import Titles and Legends overlay.

```
┌─────────────────────────────────────────────────────────────┐
│                    Bar/Line Chart Data                       ▼│
│       Title: SOS Revenues                                     │
│    Subtitle: 1986-1988                                        │
│    Footnote:                                                  │
│                                                              │
│              X Axis        1986      1987      1988   Series 4│
│      Pt       Name                                           │
│      1    │ Jan          1356      14953     8215           │
│      2    │ Feb          2567      11449     11021          │
│      3    │ Mar          3577      5559      27028          │
│      4    │ Apr          4588      6978      39268          │
│      5    │ May          3452      16252     31921          │
│      6    │ Jun          6544      8938      40507          │
│      7    │ Jul          2788      4700      56132          │
│      8    │ Aug          3455      2050      82787          │
│      9    │ Sep          1517      4880      102834         │
│      10   │ Oct          5623      17991     101722         │
│      11   │ Nov          7866      11290     61407          │
│      12   │ Dec          5345      6745      45000          │
│                                                              │
│   F1-Help        F3-Set X type              F9-More series   │
│   F2-Draw chart  F4-Calculate       F8-Options  F10-Continue │
└─────────────────────────────────────────────────────────────┘
```

Fig. 5.66.

The imported ASCII data on the Bar/Line Chart Data screen.

The four selections near the bottom of the Import ASCII Data screen perform the following functions:

Read data by — Select Column if the first value in each column is the X data or pie slice label.

Select Line if the first value of each line is the X data or pie slice label.

Read from line — Type the number of the first line of the file to include in the chart as data. If you want to include only one line of data, enter the same number for the prompt as you enter for the to line prompt.

Tabular data format — Select Yes for this prompt if your ASCII data is in columns or set by tabs, such as the data shown in figure 5.66. If your data is not tabular, select No. Harvard Graphics displays column numbers underneath the data on-screen so that you can judge the position of the characters in the file to fill out the field labeled Read from line.

Read from column — Use this prompt and the to column prompt to enter the starting and ending column numbers that mark the limits of the data you want to include.

When you read data from an ASCII file by line, the data in the first column becomes the x-axis labels on the Bar/Line Chart Data screen or the pie slice labels on the pie chart screen (covered in the next chapter). The second column fills Series 1. The third column fills Series 2, and so on. However, when you read data from an ASCII file by column, the data in the first line becomes the x-axis labels (or the pie slice labels). The second line fills the first series of data, the third line fills the second series of data, and so on.

The Import Titles and Legends overlay enables you to import the first three lines with any data in an ASCII file as the title and subtitle by setting Import title and subtitle to Yes. If you set this prompt to No, Harvard Graphics uses the title and subtitle you enter. The Import first line as series legend prompt instructs Harvard Graphics to use the first line included at the Read from line setting as series legends. If you set Read data by to Column, Harvard Graphics displays Import first column as series legend, instead.

Importing Mixed ASCII Data

Suppose that you receive from a colleague a report with mixed ASCII text and columnar information, and you want to take selective portions of the file to analyze. You can use a special feature when importing this ASCII file to a graph chart. In figure 5.67, the same ASCII file used in the preceding section is shown, but some text is added to the file. You can extract just the columnar data from this memo.

Fig. 5.67.

The ASCII file with mixed text and data.

```
TO:   Linda Morgan
FROM:  Chris Verbanic
RE:   SOS Revenues      1986-1988

As you can see from these figures 1988 was a winning year.  I think our success
this year can be attributed to:
         -The addition of the Annihilator Eraser to our line.
         -The increase of sales of Mechanical Pencils.
         -The addition of Swirly Pens to our line of products.

Month    1986     1987     1988
Jan      1356    14953     8215
Feb      2567    11449    11021
Mar      3577     5559    27028
Apr      4588     6978    39268
May      3452    16252    31921
Jun      6544     8938    40507
Jul      2788     4700    56132
Aug      3455     2050    82787
Sep      1517     4880   102834
Oct      5623    17991   101722
Nov      7866    11290    61407
Dec      5345     6745    45800
```

To display and import the columnar data from the memo, do the following:

1. Create a new bar/line chart. At the X Data Type Menu overlay, select Name at the X data type prompt. Press Enter to move through the rest of the options and to return to the Bar/Line Chart Data screen. Then press Esc at the Bar/Line Chart Data screen to return to the Main menu.

2. Select Import/Export from the Main menu and select Import ASCII Data from the Import/Export menu.

3. From the Select File screen that appears, choose the ASCII file that you are importing. Press Enter and the Import ASCII Data screen appears. Notice that you can see only the text portion of the memo; the columnar data is not in view.

4. Press Ctrl-PgDn to position and view the columnar data on the screen.

5. Tab to the Read from line prompt and type *17* if you are following the example presented at the beginning of this section.

6. Tab to the to line field and type *29*.

7. Press Enter and then select Yes at the Tabular data format prompt.

8. Press F4 (Reselect) to view the available columns. Harvard Graphics displays column numbers under each column of data. Press F10 to confirm that you want four columns imported.

9. The Import Titles and Legends overlay appears. Select No at the Import title and subtitle option. Select Yes at the Import first line as series legend option.

10. Press Enter to import your data.

Selecting ASCII Data Columns To Include in Your Chart

You can customize your data to select only specific columns rather than all the columns in an ASCII file. Using the same ASCII data shown in figure 5.67, you can show just the 1986 and 1988 columns by following this procedure:

1. Create a new bar/line chart. At the X Data Type Menu overlay, select Name at the X data type prompt. Press Enter to move through the rest of the options and to return to the Bar/Line Chart Data screen. Press Esc to return to the Main menu.

2. Select Import/Export from the Main menu and select Import ASCII Data from the Import/Export menu.

3. Select the file to import and press Enter. When you are viewing the memo at the Import ASCII Data screen, press Ctrl-PgDn to view the columnar data.

4. Position the cursor at the Tabular data format option and select Yes. Press F4 (Reselect) to display the data column numbers on the bottom of the columns.

5. Press F8 (Options) to select and adjust your columns. The first column should be highlighted.

6. Press the right-arrow key twice to expand the width of the column by two spaces and include the entire word Month. Press Enter.

7. Press Tab to highlight the second column, 1986, and press Enter to include Column 2 in your chart data.

8. Press Tab to highlight the third column, 1987. This column will be omitted from your chart data, so press Ctrl-Del to remove it from the highlighted columnar data. The fourth ASCII column is now highlighted. Notice that its label is now 3. Figure 5.68 shows the ASCII file with the first, second, and fourth columns highlighted. Just as you press Ctrl-Del to omit a column of data, you can press Ctrl-Ins to add a column or series between two other series.

9. Press Enter to confirm your choices and press F10 to continue.

10. The Import Titles and Legends overlay appears as shown in figure 5.69. Select No at Import title and subtitle and select Yes at Import first line as series legends. Press Enter to accept your data and return to the Bar/Line Chart Data screen.

When you complete the preceding procedure, your Bar/Line Chart Data screen should look like the one shown in figure 5.70.

Chapter Summary

In this chapter, you learned how to make bar and line charts and how to use the Titles & Options pages to change the appearance of those charts. This chapter also covers how to import data from 1-2-3 and tabular ASCII files. In the next chapter, you learn how to create and alter the other types of graph charts available in Harvard Graphics.

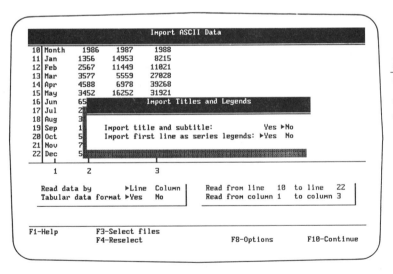

```
                    Import ASCII Data
10 Month      1986     1987     1988
11 Jan        1356    14953     8215
12 Feb        2567    11449    11021
13 Mar        3577     5559    27028
14 Apr        4588     6978    39268
15 May        3452    16252    31921
16 Jun        6544     8938    40507
17 Jul        2788     4700    56132
18 Aug        3455     2050    82787
19 Sep        1517     4880   102834
20 Oct        5623    17991   101722
21 Nov        7866    11290    61407
22 Dec        5345     6745    45000

      1         2              3

   Read data by          ►Line Column    Read from line    10  to line    22
   Tabular data format ►Yes    No        Read from column 1   to column 3


F1-Help        F3-Select files
               F4-Reselect                  F8-Options      F10-Continue
```

Fig. 5.68.

The ASCII file with three columns showing.

```
                    Import ASCII Data
10 Month      1986     1987     1988
11 Jan        1356    14953     8215
12 Feb        2567    11449    11021
13 Mar        3577     5559    27028
14 Apr        4588     6978    39268
15 May        3452    16252    31921
16 Jun        65          Import Titles and Legends
17 Jul        2
18 Aug        3
19 Sep        1       Import title and subtitle:         Yes ►No
20 Oct        5       Import first line as series legends: ►Yes  No
21 Nov        7
22 Dec        5

      1         2              3

   Read data by          ►Line Column    Read from line    10  to line    22
   Tabular data format ►Yes    No        Read from column 1   to column 3


F1-Help        F3-Select files
               F4-Reselect                  F8-Options      F10-Continue
```

Fig. 5.69.

The Import Titles and Legends overlay.

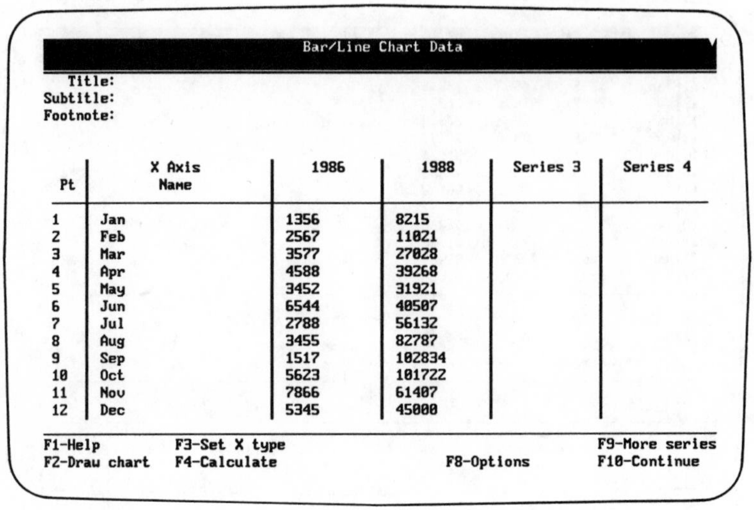

Fig. 5.70.

The completed Bar/ Line Chart Data screen.

```
┌──────────────────────────────────────────────────────────────────┐
│                         Bar/Line Chart Data                      ▼ │
│    Title:                                                          │
│ Subtitle:                                                          │
│ Footnote:                                                          │
│                                                                    │
│        │ X Axis    │  1986  │  1988  │ Series 3 │ Series 4         │
│     Pt │ Name      │        │        │          │                  │
│                                                                    │
│     1  │ Jan       │  1356  │  8215  │          │                  │
│     2  │ Feb       │  2567  │ 11021  │          │                  │
│     3  │ Mar       │  3577  │ 27028  │          │                  │
│     4  │ Apr       │  4588  │ 39268  │          │                  │
│     5  │ May       │  3452  │ 31921  │          │                  │
│     6  │ Jun       │  6544  │ 40507  │          │                  │
│     7  │ Jul       │  2788  │ 56132  │          │                  │
│     8  │ Aug       │  3455  │ 82787  │          │                  │
│     9  │ Sep       │  1517  │ 102834 │          │                  │
│    10  │ Oct       │  5623  │ 101722 │          │                  │
│    11  │ Nov       │  7866  │ 61407  │          │                  │
│    12  │ Dec       │  5345  │ 45000  │          │                  │
│                                                                    │
│ F1-Help          F3-Set X type                        F9-More series│
│ F2-Draw chart    F4-Calculate            F8-Options   F10-Continue │
└──────────────────────────────────────────────────────────────────┘
```

6

Creating Graph Charts: Area, High/Low/Close, and Pie

This chapter takes up where Chapter 5 left off and continues the discussion of Harvard Graphics graph charts. In this chapter, you learn how to create and modify area, high/low/close, and pie charts.

Creating Area Charts

Area charts dramatically illustrate large increases in volume. The SOSREVS bar chart shown in figure 6.1, for example, displays a minor increase in revenues in 1986 and 1987, and a major increase in 1988. The area chart shown in figure 6.2 shows the magnitude of this significant increase far more effectively than the SOSREVS bar chart does.

An area chart is a variation of one type of bar/line chart (the trend chart). Not surprisingly, the procedure for creating an area chart is nearly identical to the procedure used to create a standard bar/line chart (see Chapter 5). In addition, the four Titles & Options pages for area charts are almost identical to the four Titles & Options pages for bar and line charts.

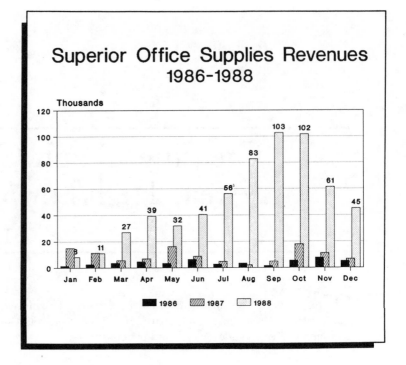

Fig. 6.1.

The SOSREVS bar chart.

Changing from a Bar/Line to an Area Chart Type

You may find that you want to try different chart types with the same data, to determine which chart best suits your purposes. For example, you may want to convert the data from the SOSREVS bar chart into area chart data. By converting the data, you avoid having to reenter it in an Area Chart Data screen. To use the data from SOSREVS for your area chart, follow this procedure:

1. Select Get/Save/Remove from the Main menu.

2. Select Get Chart from the Get/Save/Remove menu.

3. Use the down-arrow key to highlight the file SOSREVS and press Enter.

4. When SOSREVS is displayed, press Esc twice—once to return to the Bar/Line Chart Data screen and a second time to return to the Main menu.

5. Select Create New Chart from the Main menu.

6. Select Area from the Create New Chart menu and press Enter.

7. Press Enter to select Yes in the Change Chart Type overlay (see fig. 6.3).

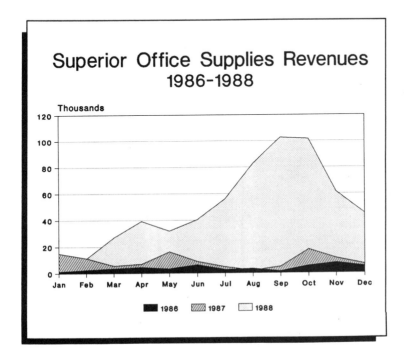

Fig. 6.2.

An area chart showing the SOSREVS data.

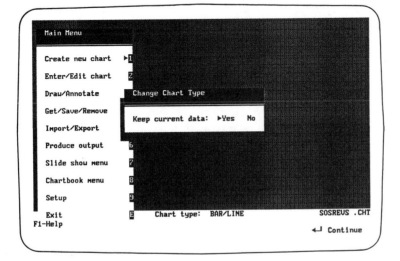

Fig. 6.3.

The Change Chart Type overlay.

If you borrow data directly from another chart type, the first screen you see is the Area Chart Data screen. If you answer No to the Keep current data prompt in the Change Chart Type overlay, however, Harvard Graphics displays the X Data Type Menu overlay first, in the customary procedure for starting a new chart. You must choose a setting for the X data type option, as usual, if that overlay appears. (For more information, see "Setting the X-Axis" in Chapter 5.)

Review the area chart you converted from a bar style and save it with the name SOSREVA (for "SOS revenues, area chart").

Entering Data in an Area Chart

When you start a new chart, the procedure for entering data on an Area Chart Data screen is the same as entering data on a Bar/Line Chart Data screen. As you enter data, you should be aware that Harvard Graphics will arrange it in the chart in series order. Series 1 is shown at the bottom, Series 2 is above that, and so on. After entering your data and previewing the default area chart, Press F8 (Options) at the Area Chart Data screen to summon the first Titles & Options page.

Using the Titles & Options Pages

The four Titles & Options pages for area charts are so similar to the Titles & Options pages for bar/line charts, which are described in detail in Chapter 5, that this section highlights only the differences between the two sets of pages. To learn about options not described in this chapter, refer to "Using the Titles & Options Pages" in Chapter 5.

When you convert from a bar or line chart to an area chart, the area chart acquires the option settings of the bar or line chart. All series are converted initially to area style representations. To make changes to options on the Titles & Options pages, follow the same procedures you're accustomed to using with bar/line charts. Use the Tab key to move from option to option, the space bar to highlight a choice, and the Enter key to move to the next option. Press F2 (Draw Chart) after you have changed a graph option so that you can see each incremental change.

Using the First Titles & Options Page

Use the first Area Chart Titles & Options page, shown in figure 6.4, to inform Harvard Graphics about your choices for the overall appearance of an area chart. On this page, you can specify whether to represent each series as an area, line, bar, or trend type, and you can give the series names that are more descriptive than Series 1, Series 2, and so on. You can mix these different area types on a chart to emphasize a specific series. The bar, trend, and line chart types are the same in area charts as they in bar/line charts (described in Chapter 5). The resulting mixed chart can be useful when there are large differences among series values. In figure 6.4, the first three series have been renamed 1986, 1987, and 1988. By pressing F7 (Size/Place) and F5 (Attributes) on the first Titles & Options page, you can change the appearance of the text in the titles and series names. You also can choose whether to display the series or whether to use dual y-axes.

```
         Area Chart  Titles & Options  Page 1 of 4

        Title:        Superior Office Supplies Revenues
        Subtitle:     1986-1988

        Footnote:

    X  axis title:
    Y1 axis title: Thousands
    Y2 axis title:
                                  Type          Display  Y Axis
  Legend
  Title:                  Area  Line  Trend  Bar  Yes  No  Y1  Y2

  1  1986                        Area               Yes      Y1
  2  1987                        Area               Yes      Y1
  3  1988                        Area               Yes      Y1
  4  Series 4                    Area               Yes      Y1
  5  Series 5                    Area               Yes      Y1
  6  Series 6                    Area               Yes      Y1
  7  Series 7                    Area               Yes      Y1
  8  Series 8                    Area               Yes      Y1

  F1-Help                  F5-Attributes   F7-Size/Place
  F2-Draw chart                            F8-Data          F10-Continue
```

Fig. 6.4.

The first Area Chart Titles & Options page.

Press PgDn to view the second Titles & Options page.

Using the Second Titles & Options Page

Use the second Area Chart Titles & Options page, shown in figure 6.5, to set the characteristics of the elements of the current chart, such as the location and appearance of the legend or the style of the frame around the graph. As with the first Titles & Options page, this Titles & Options page is identical to the second Titles & Options page for bar/line charts, with the following exceptions:

❑ Area charts provide only six combinations of styles and enhancements.

❑ Overlap at the Chart style field refers to the overlap of one area on another.

❑ If you select Stack at the Chart style field, Harvard Graphics displays the series one on top of another.

❑ Harvard Graphics displays a 100% chart as an area chart, regardless of the choice made on the first Titles & Options page in the Type column.

❑ If you mix series types (bar with area), Harvard Graphics does not display a three-dimensional enhancement.

❑ The 3D option (for Chart enhancement) does not work with Horizontal chart set to Yes or with dual y-axis charts.

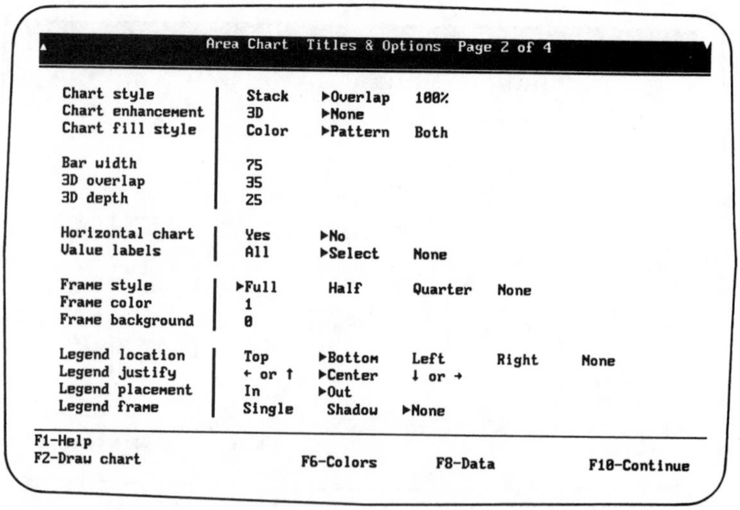

Fig. 6.5.

The second Area Chart Titles & Options page.

```
▲              Area Chart  Titles & Options  Page 2 of 4              ▼

        Chart style         Stack    ►Overlap   100%
        Chart enhancement   3D       ►None
        Chart fill style    Color    ►Pattern   Both

        Bar width           75
        3D overlap          35
        3D depth            25

        Horizontal chart    Yes      ►No
        Value labels        All      ►Select    None

        Frame style         ►Full    Half       Quarter   None
        Frame color         1
        Frame background    0

        Legend location     Top      ►Bottom    Left      Right   None
        Legend justify      ← or ↑   ►Center    ↓ or →
        Legend placement    In       ►Out
        Legend frame        Single   Shadow     ►None

    F1-Help
    F2-Draw chart              F6-Colors      F8-Data         F10-Continue
```

Press PgDn to move to the third Titles & Options page.

Using the Third Titles & Options Page

Use the third Area Chart Titles & Options page, shown in figure 6.6, to change the underlying structure of the chart's appearance. This Titles & Options page, like the same page for bar/line charts, lets you include grid lines and tick marks and revise the scaling and formatting provided by Harvard Graphics.

```
┌─────────────────────────────────────────────────────────────┐
│ ▲    Area Chart  Titles & Options  Page 3 of 4           ▼   │
│    Data Table      │ Normal    Framed   ▶None                │
│                    │                                          │
│    X  Axis Labels  │ ▶Normal   Vertical  %        None        │
│    Y1 Axis Labels  │ ▶Value    $         %        None        │
│    Y2 Axis Labels  │ ▶Value    $         %        None        │
│                    │                                          │
│    X  Grid Lines   │ · · · ·   ──────   ▶None                 │
│    Y1 Grid Lines   │ ▶· · · ·  ──────    None                 │
│    Y2 Grid Lines   │ ▶· · · ·  ──────    None                 │
│                    │                                          │
│    X Tick Mark Style │ In   ▶Out   Both   None                │
│    Y Tick Mark Style │ In   ▶Out   Both   None                │
│                    │                                          │
│              X Axis │        Y1 Axis  │    Y2 Axis            │
│    Scale Type      │ ▶Linear   Log  │ ▶Linear  Log │ ▶Linear  Log │
│    Format          │                │ ,0            │              │
│    Minimum Value   │                │              │              │
│    Maximum Value   │                │              │              │
│    Increment       │                │              │              │
│ ────────────────────────────────────────────────────────────│
│ F1-Help                                                      │
│ F2-Draw chart                F8-Data        F10-Continue     │
└─────────────────────────────────────────────────────────────┘
```

Fig. 6.6.

The third Area Chart Titles & Options page.

If you set the x- or y-axis Scale Type to Log (logarithmic), you cannot use the 3D option on the second Titles & Options page. This limitation applies also to bar/line charts. Three-dimensional and logarithmic are conflicting options.

Press PgDn to work on the fourth Titles & Options page.

Using the Fourth Titles & Options Page

On the last Area Chart Titles & Options page, shown in figure 6.7, you can place the finishing touches on the appearance of your chart's titles, areas, bars, or lines. To make your chart easy to understand, select colors or patterns so that the layers of the graph vary from dark to light, with the darkest pattern in the back.

You can use the calculation features in Harvard Graphics to re-sort the data and change the order of the series, if necessary. For more information, see "Calculating Data" in Chapter 5.

In area charts (unlike bar/line charts) when you use calendar-based data and a gap exists between dates, you cannot set a single series to Cum on the fourth Titles & Options page. Either all of the series or none of them should be set to Cum.

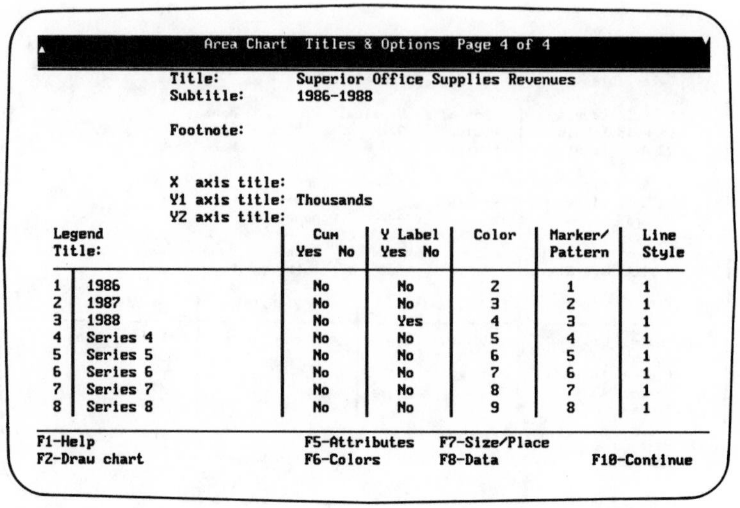

Fig. 6.7.

The fourth Area
Chart Titles &
Options page.

```
┌─────────────────────────────────────────────────────────────┐
│ ▲        Area Chart  Titles & Options  Page 4 of 4          ▼ │
├─────────────────────────────────────────────────────────────┤
│              Title:       Superior Office Supplies Revenues   │
│              Subtitle:    1986-1988                           │
│                                                               │
│           Footnote:                                           │
│                                                               │
│           X  axis title:                                      │
│           Y1 axis title: Thousands                            │
│           Y2 axis title:                                      │
│  Legend              Cum    │ Y Label │ Color │ Marker/ │ Line│
│  Title:             Yes No  │ Yes No  │       │ Pattern │Style│
│  1 │ 1986            No     │ No      │   2   │   1     │  1  │
│  2 │ 1987            No     │ No      │   3   │   2     │  1  │
│  3 │ 1988            No     │ Yes     │   4   │   3     │  1  │
│  4 │ Series 4        No     │ No      │   5   │   4     │  1  │
│  5 │ Series 5        No     │ No      │   6   │   5     │  1  │
│  6 │ Series 6        No     │ No      │   7   │   6     │  1  │
│  7 │ Series 7        No     │ No      │   8   │   7     │  1  │
│  8 │ Series 8        No     │ No      │   9   │   8     │  1  │
├─────────────────────────────────────────────────────────────┤
│  F1-Help              F5-Attributes   F7-Size/Place           │
│  F2-Draw chart        F6-Colors       F8-Data      F10-Continue│
└─────────────────────────────────────────────────────────────┘
```

Creating High/Low/Close Charts

Another variation of the bar/line chart format is the high/low/close chart. Typically, high/low/close charts show the opening, closing, high, and low values at specific intervals for a single stock, bond, or other financial instrument.

To see how high/low/close charts work, try creating a chart that shows the stock prices for Superior Office Supplies during the month of December. Suppose that the stock prices during the month varied as follows:

Week	High	Low	Close	Open
1	19.0	17.5	18.5	17.75
2	18.75	17.75	18.5	18.5
3	18.5	17.5	17.75	18.0
4	18.75	17.25	17.75	17.5

Entering Data in a High/Low/Close Chart

To create and enter data in a high/low/close chart, follow this procedure:

1. Select Create New Chart from the Main menu.

2. Select High/Low/Close from the Create New Chart menu.

3. Press the space bar to highlight Week on the X Data Type Menu overlay and press Enter.

4. Press 1 at the Starting with field and press Enter to move to the Ending with field.

5. Press 4 at the Ending with field and press Enter to move to Increment. Press Enter again because the default increment of 1 is correct. Figure 6.8 shows how the X Data Type Menu overlay should appear at this point.

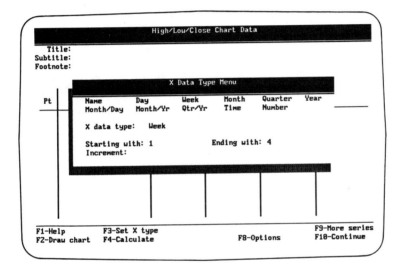

Fig. 6.8.

The X Data Type Menu overlay.

6. Type the following chart title at the Title option on the High/Low/Close Chart Data screen:

   SOS December Stock Prices

   Press Enter three times to move the cursor to the X Axis column at point 1.

7. Press Tab to move the cursor to the High column and type the high value for week 1. Then press Tab to move from column to column and Enter to move from line to line, typing the remainder of the data. Figure 6.9 shows the completed data screen.

8. Press F2 (Draw Chart) to view the chart with the data entered.

You also can use the High/Low/Close Chart Data screen to calculate other series. For example, try this procedure with the stock data you just entered:

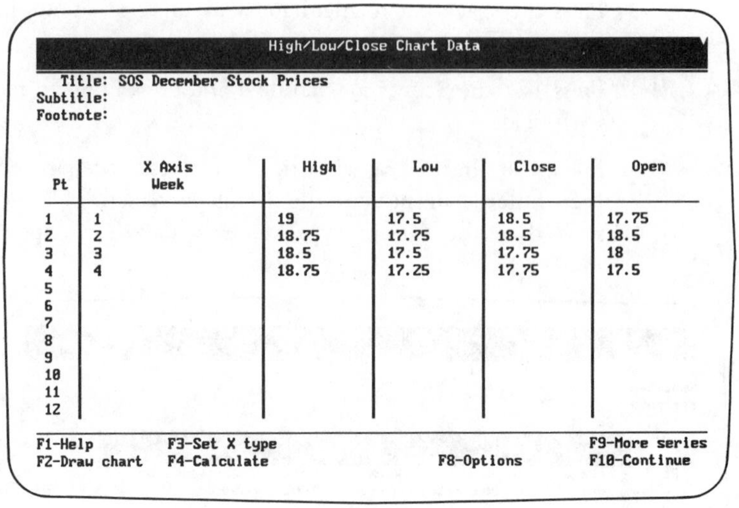

Fig. 6.9.

*The High/Low/
Close Chart Data
screen.*

```
                              High/Low/Close Chart Data
        Title: SOS December Stock Prices
     Subtitle:
     Footnote:


               X Axis         High        Low        Close        Open
     Pt        Week

     1    1                   19         17.5        18.5        17.75
     2    2                   18.75      17.75       18.5        18.5
     3    3                   18.5       17.5        17.75       18
     4    4                   18.75      17.25       17.75       17.5
     5
     6
     7
     8
     9
     10
     11
     12

     F1-Help          F3-Set X type                          F9-More series
     F2-Draw chart    F4-Calculate              F8-Options   F10-Continue
```

1. Return to the data screen by pressing Esc.

2. Press F9 (More Series) to display Series 5 through 8.

3. Tab to any line on Series 5 and press F4 (Calculate).

4. At the Legend prompt, type *High/Low/Close Avg.* over the words Series 5. Press Enter to move to the Calculation prompt.

5. Type the calculation *@AVG(#1,#2)*. Then press F10 (Continue).

6. Press F8 (Options) to bring up the first Titles & Options page.

7. Tab to line 5, High/Low/Close Avg., and then press Tab to move to the Type column. Press the space bar to highlight Line if it is not already highlighted.

8. Press F2 (Draw Chart) to preview the chart (see fig. 6.10).

Save this chart by selecting Get/Save/Remove from the Main menu and Save Chart from the Get/Save/Remove menu. Type *sosstock* for the chart name and press Enter twice.

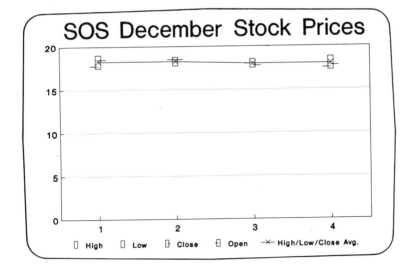

Fig. 6.10.

Preview of the high/low/close chart with the high/low average calculated.

Using the Titles & Options Pages

To modify the appearance of a high/low/close chart, press F8 (Options) at the data screen. You will notice that the information in the Type column on the first High/Low/Close Chart Titles & Options page has been set automatically by Harvard Graphics (see fig. 6.11).

Using the First Titles & Options Page

If you use the Tab key to move the cursor to Type, Harvard Graphics prevents you from changing the type of the first four series, which are set as High, Low, Close, and Open, respectively. You can change the legend entries, though, and the size, placement, and attributes of the titles by using F7 (Size/Place) and F5 (Attributes).

Connecting a second y-axis (Y2) with one of the first four series in a high/low/ close chart is effective if you want to make the chart more clear by showing the

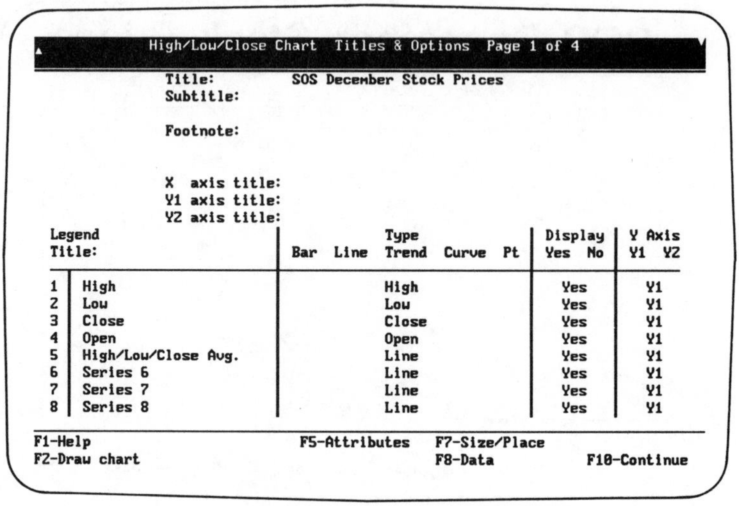
High/Low/Close Chart Titles & Options Page 1 of 4
Title: SOS December Stock Prices
Subtitle:
Footnote:
X axis title:
Y1 axis title:
Y2 axis title:
Legend Title:
Type
Bar Line Trend Curve Pt
Display Yes No
Y Axis Y1 Y2
1 High High Yes Y1
2 Low Low Yes Y1
3 Close Close Yes Y1
4 Open Open Yes Y1
5 High/Low/Close Avg. Line Yes Y1
6 Series 6 Line Yes Y1
7 Series 7 Line Yes Y1
8 Series 8 Line Yes Y1
F1-Help
F2-Draw chart
F5-Attributes
F7-Size/Place
F8-Data
F10-Continue

Fig. 6.11.

The first High/Low/Close Chart Titles & Options page.

same y-axis measure on both sides of the chart. The Y2 axis has no effect on the actual chart, however, unless you apply the axis to additional data added to the chart in Series 5 through 8.

Press PgDn to see the second Titles & Options page.

Using the Second Titles & Options Page

Use the second High/Low/Close Chart Titles & Options page, shown in figure 6.12, to change the style and width of any bars in the chart. These style options (`Cluster`, `Overlap`, and `Stack`) apply only to series that are not part of the high/low/close series.

The three available high/low/close styles are `Bar`, `Area`, and `Error bar`. An *error bar* is a straight line that connects the high and low points of each value. Figure 6.13 shows a high/low/close chart that uses error bars to show clearly which bar correlates to which date.

Figure 6.14 shows a high/low/close chart with `Area` selected as the `High/Low style` option. This type of chart, when shown with both x- and y-axis grid lines, can be an informative display of stock data.

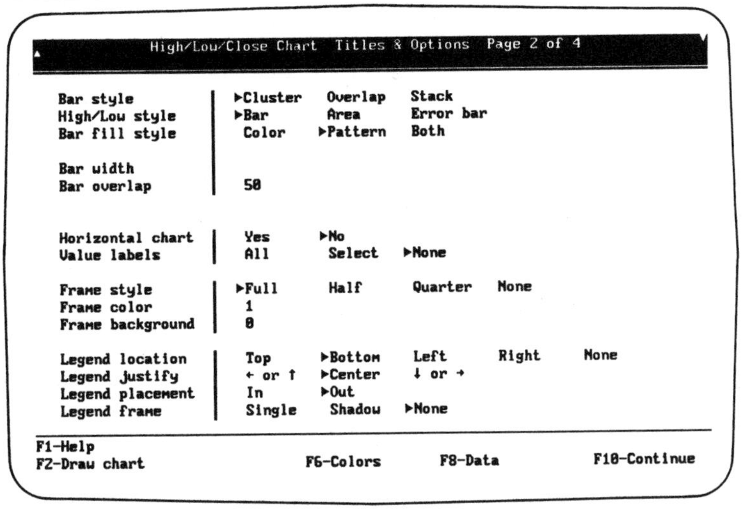

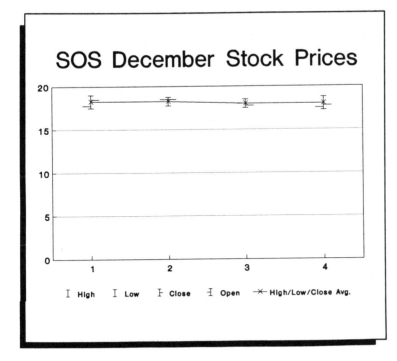

High/Low/Close Chart Titles & Options Page 2 of 4
Bar style ▶Cluster Overlap Stack
High/Low style ▶Bar Area Error bar
Bar fill style Color ▶Pattern Both
Bar width
Bar overlap 50
Horizontal chart Yes ▶No
Value labels All Select ▶None
Frame style ▶Full Half Quarter None
Frame color 1
Frame background 0
Legend location Top ▶Bottom Left Right None
Legend justify ← or ↑ ▶Center ↓ or →
Legend placement In ▶Out
Legend frame Single Shadow ▶None
F1-Help
F2-Draw chart
F6-Colors
F8-Data
F10-Continue

Fig. 6.12.

The second High/Low/Close Chart Titles & Options page.

SOS December Stock Prices
20
15
10
5
0
1
2
3
4
High
Low
Close
Open
High/Low/Close Avg.

Fig. 6.13.

High/low/close chart with `Error bar` *chosen for the* `High/Low style`.

Fig. 6.14.

A high/low/close chart in Area *style.*

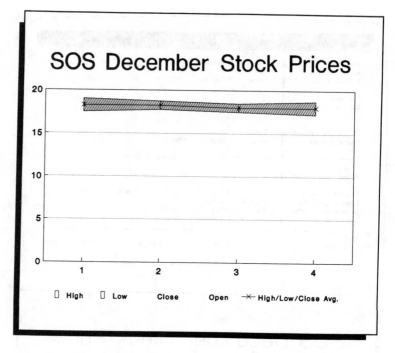

You also can use the second Titles & Options page to specify bar widths for the bars in Series 5 through 8 for the high and low series. Setting the SOSSTOCK Bar width option to *100* (when High/Low style is set to Bar) yields the chart shown in figure 6.15. If you chart only the high/low/close and open series, the default bar width is usually best. Harvard Graphics automatically sets the optimum default for you if you leave the Bar width option blank.

Clear the Bar width option to return to the Harvard Graphics default and set Horizontal chart to Yes. Figure 6.16 shows SOSSTOCK with this setting.

Now change the chart back to vertical by moving the cursor to Horizontal chart and highlighting No. Then press PgDn to work on the third Titles & Options page.

Using the Third Titles & Options Page

You can use this High/Low/Close Chart Titles & Options page to zoom in on the active portion of your high/low/close chart by modifying the minimum and maximum numbers on the y-axis. You also can clarify the chart with grid lines and tick marks by using this page.

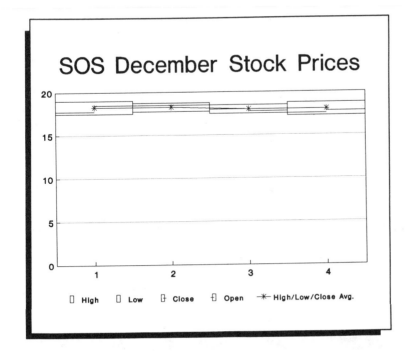

Fig. 6.15.

SOSSTOCK *with the bar width set to 100.*

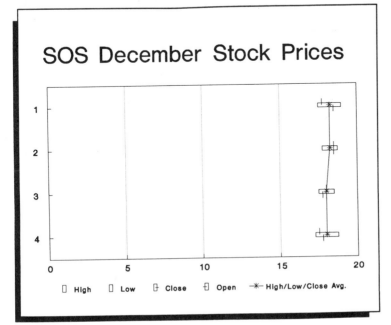

Fig. 6.16.

SOSSTOCK *with* Horizontal chart *set to* Yes.

Try following this procedure to modify the y-axis range of SOSSTOCK and make the chart more readable:

1. On the third Titles & Options page, tab to the Y1 Axis Labels option. Press the space bar to highlight the $ sign.

2. Tab to the Y1 Axis column near the bottom of the page.

3. Type 2 (for two digits after the decimal) opposite the Format field and press Enter.

4. Type 17 for the Minimum Value option.

5. Type 19 for the Maximum Value option. Figure 6.17 shows the completed Titles & Options page 3.

6. Press PgUp to return to the second Titles & Options page and tab to the Bar width option.

7. Type 25 for the bar width.

8. Press F2 (Draw Chart) to view the chart. Figure 6.18 shows the results.

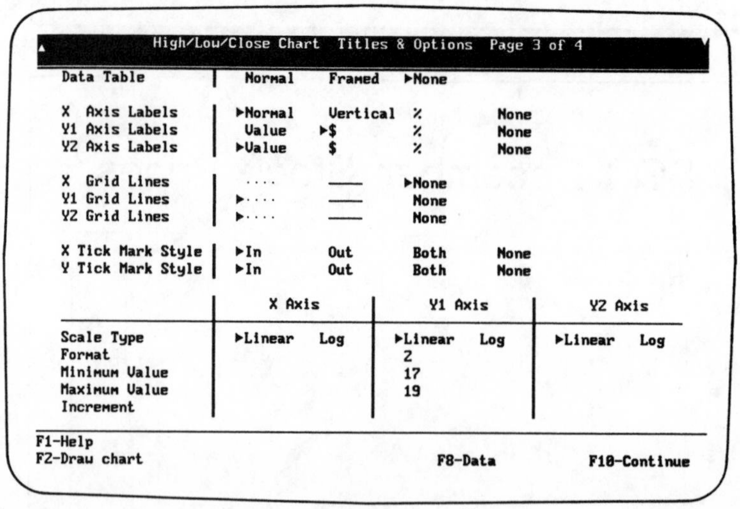

Fig. 6.17.

The completed High/Low/Close Chart Titles & Options page 3.

High/Low/Close Chart Titles & Options Page 3 of 4				
Data Table	Normal	Framed	▶None	
X Axis Labels	▶Normal	Vertical	%	None
Y1 Axis Labels	Value	▶$	%	None
Y2 Axis Labels	▶Value	$	%	None
X Grid Lines	....	———	▶None	
Y1 Grid Lines	▶....	———	None	
Y2 Grid Lines	▶....	———	None	
X Tick Mark Style	▶In	Out	Both	None
Y Tick Mark Style	▶In	Out	Both	None

	X Axis	Y1 Axis	Y2 Axis
Scale Type	▶Linear Log	▶Linear Log	▶Linear Log
Format		2	
Minimum Value		17	
Maximum Value		19	
Increment			

F1-Help
F2-Draw chart   F8-Data   F10-Continue

Press Esc to return to the second Titles & Options page and press PgDn twice to use the options on the fourth Titles & Options page.

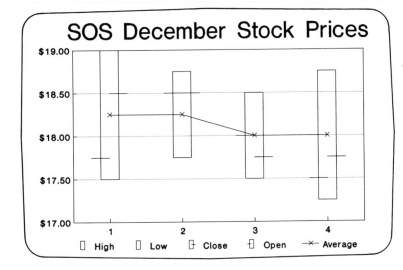

Fig. 6.18.

Preview of the high/ low/close chart with a modified y-axis.

Using the Fourth Titles & Options Page

The fourth High/Low/Close Titles & Options page, shown in figure 6.19, lets you modify the physical qualities of the bars: their fill patterns, labels, colors, and attributes. With this page, you also can make the chart cumulative and choose which Y labels to display.

To see the effect of the Cum option, try setting the option to Yes for all five series. The resulting chart shows stock fluctuations adding each successive stock price to the total of the previous prices (see fig. 6.20). Obviously, the resulting graph is highly misleading. This stuff is what gets good people like you thrown into jail.

Creating Pie Charts

Pie charts are the ideal Harvard Graphics graph chart type for representing the relative contributions of parts to a whole. To illustrate the month-by-month

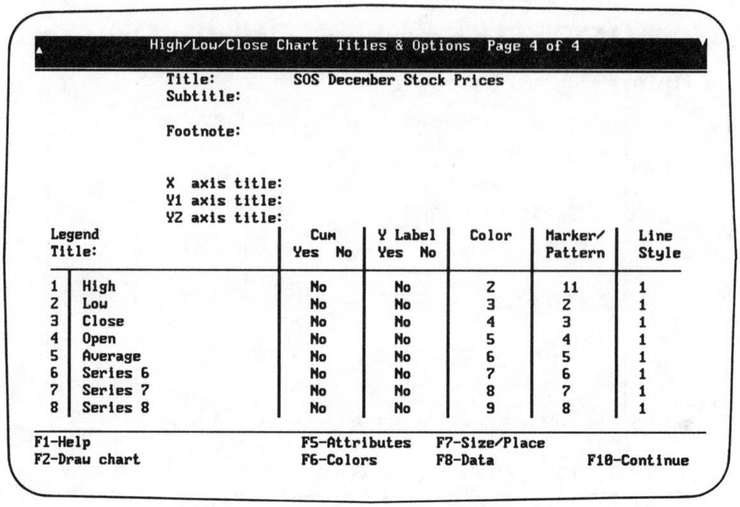

Fig. 6.19.

The fourth High/Low/Close Chart Titles & Options page.

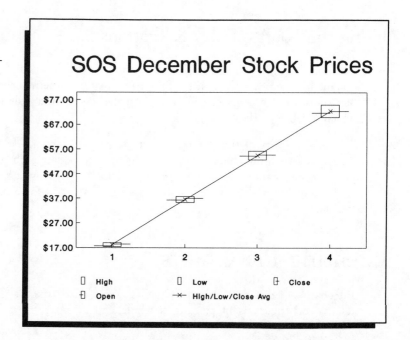

```
┌─────────────────────────────────────────────────────────────────────┐
│  ▲    High/Low/Close Chart   Titles & Options   Page 4 of 4        ▼  │
│                                                                       │
│                    Title:        SOS December Stock Prices            │
│                    Subtitle:                                          │
│                                                                       │
│                    Footnote:                                          │
│                                                                       │
│                                                                       │
│                X  axis title:                                         │
│                Y1 axis title:                                         │
│                Y2 axis title:                                         │
│  Legend                        Cum     Y Label    Color   Marker/  Line│
│  Title:                        Yes No   Yes No             Pattern  Style│
│  1 │ High                       No       No         2       11       1 │
│  2 │ Low                        No       No         3        2       1 │
│  3 │ Close                      No       No         4        3       1 │
│  4 │ Open                       No       No         5        4       1 │
│  5 │ Average                    No       No         6        5       1 │
│  6 │ Series 6                   No       No         7        6       1 │
│  7 │ Series 7                   No       No         8        7       1 │
│  8 │ Series 8                   No       No         9        8       1 │
│                                                                       │
│  F1-Help                   F5-Attributes   F7-Size/Place              │
│  F2-Draw chart             F6-Colors       F8-Data          F10-Continue│
└─────────────────────────────────────────────────────────────────────┘
```

Fig. 6.20.

Setting all series to Cum.

SOS December Stock Prices

☐ High   ☐ Low   ☐ Close
☐ Open   ✕ High/Low/Close Avg

breakdown of a year's revenues, for example, you can represent each month with one pie slice. By adding a second special pie chart format, called a *column* chart, you also can show the breakdown of one month's revenues.

To begin a pie chart, select Create New Chart from the Main menu and Pie from the Create New Chart menu. Harvard Graphics displays the Pie Chart 1 Data screen shown in figure 6.21.

```
╭──────────────────────────────────────────────────────────────╮
│              Pie Chart 1 Data    Page 1 of 2                   ⟩
│  Title:                                                        │
│  Subtitle:                                                     │
│  Footnote:                                                     │
│                                                                │
│  Slice│    Label      │    Value    │ Cut Slice │ Color │ Pattern │
│       │    Name       │   Series 1  │  Yes  No  │       │         │
│                                                                │
│    1  │               │             │    No     │   2   │    1    │
│    2  │               │             │    No     │   3   │    2    │
│    3  │               │             │    No     │   4   │    3    │
│    4  │               │             │    No     │   5   │    4    │
│    5  │               │             │    No     │   6   │    5    │
│    6  │               │             │    No     │   7   │    6    │
│    7  │               │             │    No     │   8   │    7    │
│    8  │               │             │    No     │   9   │    8    │
│    9  │               │             │    No     │  10   │    9    │
│   10  │               │             │    No     │  11   │   10    │
│   11  │               │             │    No     │  12   │   11    │
│   12  │               │             │    No     │  13   │   12    │
│                                                                │
│  F1-Help                                        F9-More series │
│  F2-Draw chart          F6-Colors    F8-Options F10-Continue   │
╰──────────────────────────────────────────────────────────────╯
```

Fig. 6.21.

The Pie Chart 1 Data screen.

Entering Data on the Pie Chart Data Screens

Entering pie chart data is a little different from entering data in a bar/line, area, or high/low/close chart. Because Harvard Graphics can display two pies side by side, you enter pie chart data onto two "pages" corresponding to the sides of the chart. The pie on the left side represents data you enter on the Pie Chart 1 Data screen, and the right-side pie represents data you enter on the Pie Chart 2 Data screen. If you enter data on the first data page only, Harvard Graphics displays only one chart. To move between pages, press the PgDn or PgUp key. The top line of the screen indicates the current page.

You can enter up to eight series of data on the data pages and decide later which pie (right or left) should represent which series. To enter more than two series, press F9 (More Series) from either page 1 or page 2. Notice that the series number increments in the Value column. Unless you specify otherwise, the left pie (page 1) corresponds to Series 1 and the right pie (page 2) corresponds to

Series 2. To change the series attached to the right or left pie, press PgDn or PgUp until the correct page is in view. Then press F9 (More Series) until the correct series appears. (Pressing F9 repeatedly cycles the eight available series onto the page.)

Confusing pages in pie charts with series is an easy thing to do. Figure 6.22 clarifies the distinction by showing the relationship between series and pages in pie charts.

Fig. 6.22.

The relationship between series and pages in pie charts.

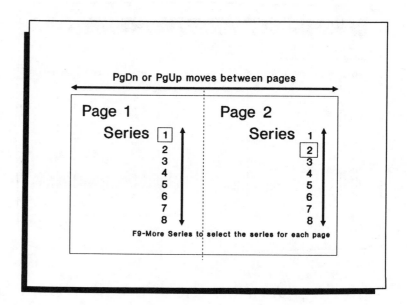

Many of the features available in bar/line charts are also available in pie charts. To reorder the data, for example, you can press and hold down Ctrl while pressing the up- or down-arrow key. To insert or delete a line, you can use the Ctrl key with Ins or Del.

Using the Tab and Enter keys to move through the chart, enter the Superior Office Supplies Writing Tools Division revenues for the second half of the year. Enter the month names in the Label column and the revenue figures in the Value column. Use the Tab key to move the cursor from column to column, and press Enter to move the cursor down one line at a time. The figures line up like this:

Month	Revenue
July	12,098
August	13,663
September	37,994
October	56,323
November	24,557
December	65,389

Unlike bar charts, which use an X Data Type Menu overlay to set label data, pie charts have no x-axis. Series labels can be of mixed types. When you originate data on a bar chart and set an X data type option, that data type remains the same when you bring the data into a pie chart; you cannot change the X data type option for a different series in the pie.

See figure 6.23 to see how to complete the remainder of the columns on the page. The patterns selected in figure 6.23 contrast clearly when adjacent to each other, highlighting the differences among slices on a printed illustration.

```
          Pie Chart 1 Data   Page 1 of 2

Title:     Superior Office Supplies
Subtitle:  Second Half, 1988
Footnote:

Slice|     Label       |   Value    | Cut Slice | Color | Pattern
     |     Name        |  Series 1  |  Yes  No  |       |

  1     July              12098         No         2       1
  2     August            13663         No         3       2
  3     September         37994         No         4       3
  4     October           56323         No         5       4
  5     November          24557         No         6       5
  6     December          65389         No         7       6
  7                                     No         8       7
  8                                     No         9       8
  9                                     No        10       9
 10                                     No        11      10
 11                                     No        12      11
 12                                     No        13      12


F1-Help                                        F9-More series
F2-Draw chart            F6-Colors   F8-Options F10-Continue
```

Fig. 6.23.

The completed Pie Chart 1 Data screen.

Press F2 (Draw Chart) to see how the pie chart looks before you add the data for the second pie. Figure 6.24 shows the results.

The second page of data on this chart will be the components of December's revenue, the Writing Tools Division's biggest month. Here's how the revenue breakdown looks:

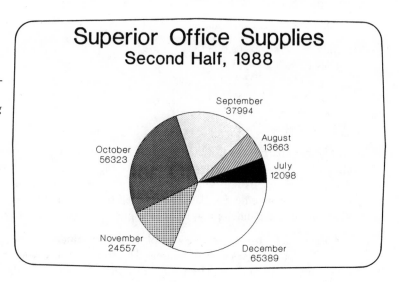

Fig. 6.24.

Previewing the pie chart before entering data for the second pie.

Swirly Pens	11,672
Mechanical Pencils	24,070
Annihilator Erasers	15,821
White Mountain Pens	13,826

With the Pie Chart 2 Data screen (and Series 2) on-screen, enter the data for the right pie. Press Tab to move to the first line and press Enter to move down line by line. Typing a vertical bar (|) between words in the label splits the label onto two lines at the location of the vertical bar. Figure 6.25 shows the completed second data screen. Be sure to enter vertical bars where shown.

Press F2 (Draw Chart) to preview the chart with two pies. Figure 6.26 shows the chart as it appears with two pies, unaltered.

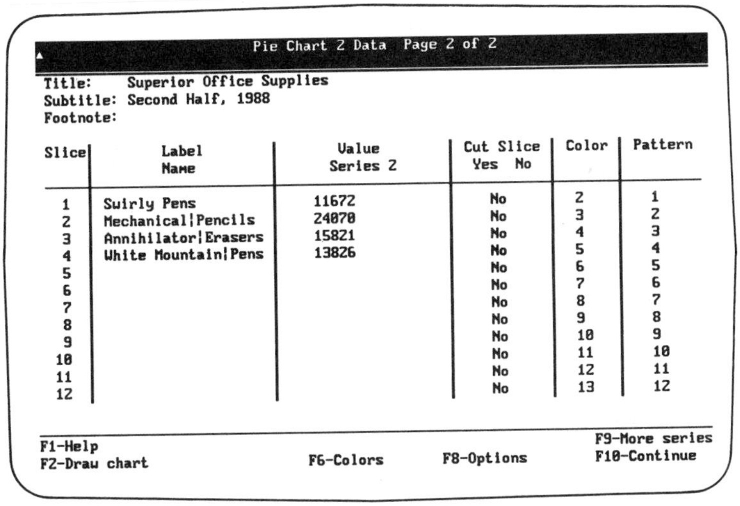

```
┌─────────────────────────────────────────────────┐
│ ▲           Pie Chart 2 Data   Page 2 of 2        │
│ Title:    Superior Office Supplies                │
│ Subtitle: Second Half, 1988                       │
│ Footnote:                                         │
│                                                   │
│ Slice│    Label      │   Value  │Cut Slice │Color │Pattern │
│      │    Name       │ Series 2 │Yes   No  │      │        │
│                                                   │
│   1  │ Swirly Pens        │ 11672  │    No  │  2  │   1   │
│   2  │ Mechanical│Pencils  │ 24070  │    No  │  3  │   2   │
│   3  │ Annihilator│Erasers │ 15821  │    No  │  4  │   3   │
│   4  │ White Mountain│Pens  │ 13826  │    No  │  5  │   4   │
│   5  │                    │        │    No  │  6  │   5   │
│   6  │                    │        │    No  │  7  │   6   │
│   7  │                    │        │    No  │  8  │   7   │
│   8  │                    │        │    No  │  9  │   8   │
│   9  │                    │        │    No  │ 10  │   9   │
│  10  │                    │        │    No  │ 11  │  10   │
│  11  │                    │        │    No  │ 12  │  11   │
│  12  │                    │        │    No  │ 13  │  12   │
│                                                   │
│ F1-Help                              F9-More series│
│ F2-Draw chart        F6-Colors   F8-Options  F10-Continue │
└─────────────────────────────────────────────────┘
```

Fig. 6.25.

The Pie Chart 2 Data screen with Series 2 data.

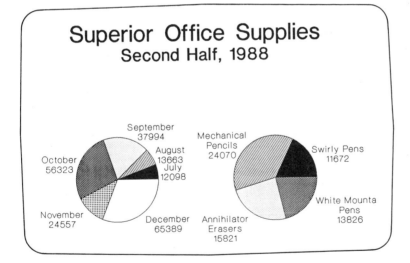

Fig. 6.26.

Preview of the two pies, unaltered.

Cutting Slices and Changing Colors and Patterns

Press PgUp to return to the Pie Chart 1 Data screen so that you can modify the left pie. Move the cursor to December, tab to the Cut Slice column, and press the space bar to highlight Yes. Selecting Yes cuts the selected slice out of the pie. Use the Color and Pattern columns on page 1 to change the patterns and colors of individual slices of the pie. Press F2 (Draw Chart) to see the results, which are shown in figure 6.27.

Fig. 6.27.

Preview of the pie chart with the December slice cut out.

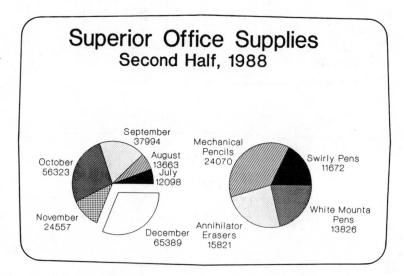

Creating Effects with Titles & Options Pages

Press F8 (Options) to use the two Titles & Options pages Harvard Graphics provides for pie charts. The options on these pages are much like those in bar/line, area, and high/low/close charts.

Using the First Titles & Options Page

Figure 6.28 shows the first Pie Chart Titles & Options page. Use this page to set the titles and effects of the chart. Enter the titles for the two pies as shown in the figure. To change an option, simply tab to that option and press the space bar to highlight a new choice. Press Enter to move to the next line.

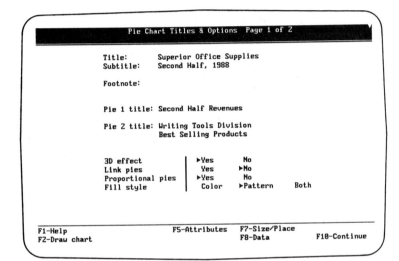

Fig. 6.28.

The first Pie Chart Titles & Options page.

Notice that F7-Size/Place and F5-Attributes are available on the function key menu at the bottom of the screen. You can use these features to adjust the titles in your chart.

Making Three-Dimensional Pies

You can make any pie three-dimensional by setting the 3D effect option to Yes. When the three-dimensional effect is turned on, however, no slices are cut. If you cut a slice and set 3D effect to Yes, the three-dimensional effect overrides the option to cut a slice. Try turning on the three-dimensional effect in the current chart (see fig. 6.29).

Save this pie chart with the name SOS2HP3D (for "SOS second-half pie, three-dimensional").

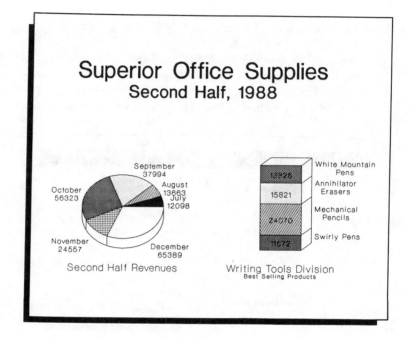

Fig. 6.29.

*Three-dimensional
pie charts.*

Linking Pies

Now set 3D effect to No and turn on the Link pies option by highlighting Yes in that line. Harvard Graphics links the cutout slice to the second pie. When used in combination with a column chart (which is set on the second Titles & Options page), the Link pies option can be especially effective. Figure 6.30 shows a pie linked to a column chart. You set Chart style for the right pie to Column on the second Pie Chart Titles & Options page.

Making Proportional Pies

Selecting Yes for the Proportional pies option tells Harvard Graphics to display the right and left pies so that their relative sizes reflect their relative totals. Selecting No for this option bases the size of each pie on the Pie size option on the second Titles & Options page. When you select No for Proportional pies, Harvard Graphics makes each pie 50 percent of the page.

Turn on the Proportional pies option for the current chart. The results should look like figure 6.31.

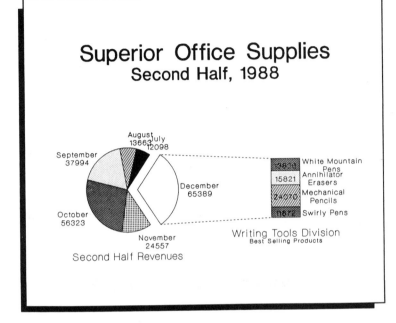

Fig. 6.30.

Linked pie and column charts.

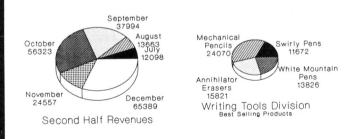

Fig. 6.31.

The Proportional pies *option set to* Yes.

Selecting a Fill Style

As you can see by the Fill style option, you can choose to fill the slices of pies with colors, patterns, or both colors and patterns. You select the patterns used to fill the slices on the data pages. Try different combinations of patterns for the clearest marking of pie slices.

Using the Second Titles & Options Page

The second Pie Chart Titles & Options page includes options that let you change the style of the chart, control the labels, and format and scale the chart (see fig. 6.32). The settings you establish on this page control the overall appearance and readability of the chart. On the left side of the second Titles & Options page are the options that control the left pie (Pie 1). The options on the right side of this Titles & Options page control the right pie (Pie 2).

Fig. 6.32.

The second Pie Chart Titles & Options page.

```
▲                Pie Chart Titles & Options   Page 2 of 2

                              Pie 1                          Pie 2

         Chart style     ▶Pie      Column          ▶Pie      Column     None
         Sort slices     Yes       ▶No             ▶Yes      No
         Starting angle  0                         0
         Pie size        50                        50

         Show label      ▶Yes      No              ▶Yes      No
         Label size      2                         2

         Show value      Yes       ▶No             ▶Yes      No
         Place value     ▶Below    Adjacent  Inside    Below  Adjacent  ▶Inside
         Value format                                    ,
         Currency        Yes       ▶No             ▶Yes      No

         Show percent    Yes       ▶No             Yes       ▶No
         Place percent   ▶Below    Adjacent  Inside    ▶Below  Adjacent  Inside
         Percent format

         F1-Help
         F2-Draw chart                      F8-Data        F10-Continue
```

Selecting a Chart Style

Harvard Graphics provides two pie chart styles: columns and pies. A column chart displays percentages of a whole just as the pie chart does, but the column chart is rectangular rather than circular. To set a pie to column style, position the cursor at the Chart style field on the second Titles & Options page and press the space bar to highlight Column. You can opt to suppress the display of the right pie altogether by selecting None for Chart style on that side of the page. For this example, change the right pie on the current chart to Column style. Figure 6.33 shows the results of this change. (To change the month that is selected, simply cut a different slice on the Pie Chart 1 Data screen.)

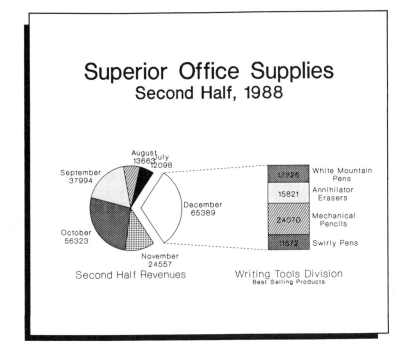

Save this chart as SOS2HLK (for "SOS second-half, linked pie").

Sorting Pie Chart Slices

The second option on the second Titles & Options page is Sort slices. If you turn Sort slices on by selecting Yes for that option, Harvard Graphics sorts the slices in the pie in the order of their individual contributions to the whole. The largest slice appears on the right side of the pie or on the top of a column-style pie. The remaining slices run clockwise around the pie (or down a column chart) from largest to smallest.

Selecting No for Sort slices leaves the pie slices in the order in which they appear on the data page. The Sort slices option works dependably unless you have Link pies set to Yes on the first Titles & Options page. In that case, the cutout slice is the slice at the right side of the left pie, and that slice is the one that links to the second pie. Because this slice must be on the right side, the slices cannot be sorted.

Changing the Starting Angle

To rotate a pie that is not linked to another pie, use the Starting angle option on the second Titles & Options page. Setting a starting angle of 180 degrees, for example, rotates the pie exactly one half of the circle. Slices previously on the right side of the pie appear on the left. The pie rotates counterclockwise. Rotating a pie can help fix overlapping labels and titles.

Changing the Pie Size

The Pie size option enables you to modify the pie size to make the chart more visually appealing. You can supply a number from 1 to 100. This option conflicts with the Proportional pies option on the first Titles & Options page. If Proportional pies is set to Yes, Harvard Graphics does not acknowledge a specified pie size for the second pie. The default pie size is 50. Try increasing or decreasing the Pie size option until you are pleased with the result.

Adjusting Labels

You can control the appearance of labels on the chart with the Show label and Label size options. Set Show label to No to suppress the display of labels or series names on the finished chart.

Type a number from 0 to 20 at the Label size option to modify the size of the labels in your chart. As with size in text charts, Harvard Graphics increases or decreases the size of the letters in your chart based on the number you enter. Try experimenting with different sizes to find the best size for your chart. You will notice that the values and percentages described in the next section will be the same size as the labels you set.

Setting Value and Percentage Placement and Formats

Use the Show value, Place value, Value format, and Currency options to alter the appearance of the values that display in your chart. As in bar/line charts, showing values places the actual data numbers on-screen. Showing percentages (with the Show percent option) places percentage numbers on-screen instead. To emphasize dramatic contributions to the whole, use percentages rather than values. Although you can use both, your chart will look cluttered.

Formatting pie chart percentages and values is identical to formatting bar/line chart values. Do so to show less data or to modify the appearance of the values shown in your chart. For example, you may want to show data up to two decimals, or you may want to reduce the slice of the numbers used by dividing them by 10. The scaling and formatting options enable you to modify your chart's values manually. Refer to "Using the Third Titles & Options Page" in Chapter 5 for complete information.

Chapter Summary

This chapter explained how you create various types of charts with Harvard Graphics: bar, line, area, high/low/close, and pie. Many of the screens for these different charts are similar, so you can use the same general procedures to create many charts.

Part III introduces the Harvard Graphics "pizzazz" features, which enable you to enhance your chart-creating abilities and print your completed charts. In Chapter 7, the first chapter in Part III, you learn about the Draw/Annotate feature, which allows you to draw charts and annotate charts in Harvard Graphics.

Part III

Adding Pizzazz

Includes

Drawing with Harvard Graphics:
Draw/Annotate

Using Step-savers:
Templates and Macros

Producing Stellar Output

7

Drawing with Harvard Graphics: Draw/Annotate

In Chapter 4, you learned how to create text charts to express concepts and relate information. In Chapters 5 and 6, you learned how to create graph charts that make numeric data clear and easily understood. This chapter introduces Draw/Annotate, a feature you can use to greatly enhance and embellish both the text and graph charts you have created.

What Is Draw/Annotate?

Even without Draw/Annotate, you can be confident that the text and graph charts that emerge from Harvard Graphics are colorful, clear, and attractive. The program's built-in chart designs help ensure that. But you may want to add elements to charts that Harvard Graphics does not add on its own, such as boxes, lines, arrows, and circles. In addition, you may want to add freehand drawings, symbols, and an assortment of other effects to spice up your charts and make them even more presentable.

With Draw/Annotate, Harvard Graphics provides a special drawing board that you can use to add distinctive adornments to either text or graph charts once they are otherwise complete. If you're a good artist, you can draw freehand on the drawing board. If your imagination is better than your drawing hand, you can select from Draw/Annotate's symbol libraries and add predrawn figures to your charts. Just as the possibilities with a standard drawing program are unlimited, the possibilities with Draw/Annotate, Harvard Graphics' drawing program within a program, are endless.

When you are ready to work with Draw/Annotate, you can start with a current chart made in Graph or Text mode or you can begin with a blank drawing board. If you have just finished a chart or have retrieved a chart from disk, Harvard Graphics displays that chart in the drawing board when you enter Draw/Annotate. If no chart is in memory, the drawing board is empty when you start Draw/Annotate.

Understanding the Draw/Annotate Main Menu

To start Draw/Annotate, simply select Draw/Annotate from the Harvard Graphics Main menu. The Draw/Annotate screen, shown in figure 7.1, looks very different from other screens in Harvard Graphics. Usually, the Harvard Graphics menus disappear after you begin working with a chart. The Draw/Annotate menus on the left, however, share the screen with the drawing board and provide quick access to Draw/Annotate commands.

Fig. 7.1.

The blank Draw/Annotate screen.

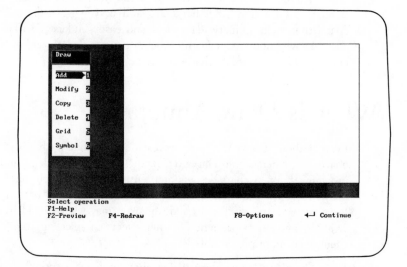

Examine the Draw menu. Choosing from its options, you can do the following:

❏ Add boxes, text, lines, circles, polygons, and a special type of line (called a *polyline*) used to make curved figures.

❏ Modify the objects you add in Draw/Annotate by moving them, resizing them, changing their characteristics, or placing objects in front of or behind other objects.

❑ Copy objects to other parts of the drawing board.

❑ Delete one or several of the objects added to your chart with Draw/Anno-
tate.

❑ Set a grid to align objects easily with others or with specific locations on
the drawing board.

❑ Use the Harvard Graphics symbol libraries to add predrawn pictures to a
chart or save your own drawn objects as symbols for use again and again.

The process of enhancing with Draw/Annotate is similar for both graph and text
charts. First, select a Draw/Annotate command, such as Draw. Then begin drawing an object by positioning the small crosshair cursor on the drawing board and
pressing Enter to anchor the first point on-screen. With one point of an object
drawn, you can press F8 (Options) to alter the options for the object.

F8 works differently in Draw/Annotate from the way it works elsewhere in Harvard Graphics. Usually, pressing F8 calls up a series of Options pages that let you
set formatting characteristics for the current chart. In Draw/Annotate, pressing
F8 displays the options for the current command. To move the cursor back to the
drawing board, press F8 again. When an options panel is visible at the left of the
screen, F8 is labeled F8-Draw on the bottom of the screen to indicate that pressing F8 moves the cursor back to the drawing board. To return to the Draw/
Annotate menus from the drawing board, press F8 once again. Now the bottom
of the screen shows F8-Options.

When the options for the current object are set and the cursor is back on the
drawing board, you can draw the remainder of the object. Press Enter one final
time to complete the drawing. Once you set the options for an object, they
remain in effect for any other objects you draw of the same type. If you set a
circle's color to red, for example, all new circles you draw are red too until you
stop drawing circles.

Using the Draw/Annotate Screen

The Draw/Annotate screen has several other features worth noting. The bottom
two lines of the screen display the function key commands available. These lines
change as you work with different Draw/Annotate features. F2-Preview in Draw/
Annotate works just like F2-Draw chart from the Main menu.

As you work with Draw/Annotate, Harvard Graphics prompts you every step of
the way by describing the current action or the next step you should perform.
The prompts appear in a special prompt line under the Draw/Annotate menus.

Each operation in Draw/Annotate involves a sequence of prompted steps. By reading the prompts and checking the menu at the left of the screen, you can always determine your next step.

Understanding Symbols and Symbol Libraries

Symbols are collections of individual objects that form predrawn images. Typical symbols are pictures of buildings, people, cities, and figures such as arrows, stars, and currency signs. These images are stored in special Harvard Graphics files called symbol files. Each symbol file, distinguished by the SYM extension, has as many as 20 different symbols from which you can choose to place on the current chart.

You can assemble your own symbol libraries by saving the objects you draw in existing symbol libraries. You can continue collecting new symbols to build a customized set of symbol libraries ready for use in new charts. You can even save an entire chart as a symbol and then modify it as a whole just as you modify a single symbol. You can change the size of a symbol, stretch its shape, or make any of a variety of other alterations. Later, you can separate or *ungroup* the elements in the chart saved as a symbol and change the appearance of any element individually. This feature, described later in this chapter, is one of the most powerful and unique features in Harvard Graphics.

Sizing and Placing a Chart at the Main Menu

Before starting Draw/Annotate, you should be familiar with F7-Size/Place on the Main menu. This selection allows you to reduce the size of an entire chart proportionally. Once the chart is made smaller on the page, you can add drawings and annotations with Draw/Annotate in the remaining white space around the chart. Reducing the size of an entire chart first may be necessary because Harvard Graphics fills as much of the page as possible when it creates a chart. You may need to add some space around the chart for your graphics.

To try using Draw/Annotate, imagine that you are the marketing manager of the Superior Office Supplies Writing Tools Division. You have just attended a presentation given by the company vice president in which a Harvard Graphics bar chart was used to depict the company's phenomenal recent growth. Now, you want to share this news with your staff by adapting the chart for your own presentation. For your purposes, you decide to reduce the size of the bar chart and add text describing some of the division's successes. The vice president used the bar chart SOSREVS for the presentation, so you borrow a copy of the file, copy it into your data directory, and use it for your chart. As you recall, you created SOSREVS in Chapter 5.

If the Draw menu is on the screen now, press Esc to return to the Harvard Graphics Main menu. Retrieve SOSREVS with the Get Chart command. After the SOSREVS chart is displayed, press Esc twice to return to the Main menu and then press F7 (Size/Place). The chart appears on a screen that looks like the Draw/Annotate screen. Near the bottom of the screen is the prompt Select first box corner. Harvard Graphics expects you to draw a box on the screen and will fit a smaller version of the bar chart in the box you draw.

To draw the box, press and hold down the Home key to position the cursor at the top left corner of the drawing board area. Press Enter to set the top left corner of the box. The prompt now reads, Select opposite box corner. Press the PgDn key several times to enlarge the box diagonally. When the Horiz= indicator shows approximately 19450 and the Vert= indicator shows approximately 7680, press Enter again to set the bottom right corner of the box. The chart is redrawn in the confines of the box. Figure 7.2 shows the reduced chart. Now press F10 (Continue) to return to the Main menu. Select Draw/Annotate from the Main menu.

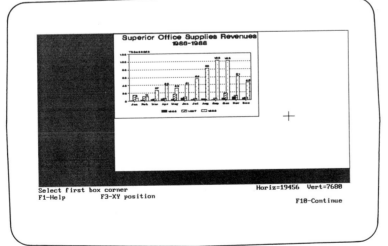

Fig. 7.2.

The reduced chart after using F7- Size/Place *from the Main menu.*

The F7-Size/Place selection from the Main menu has one inconsistency worth noting: It does not reduce the size of objects added to a chart with Draw/Annotate. Be sure to use the Size/Place command to reduce charts before you enhance them with Draw/Annotate.

Adding Elements to a Chart

In the next sections, you learn how to add text, boxes, lines, polygons, and polylines to enhance the base graphs you have already created.

Adding Text

To explain the dramatic growth in the company's revenues, you can add a few lines of text to the SOSREVS revenue chart. Try adding the following bullet items:

✔ White Mountain Pens - introduced in August
✔ Swirly Pens - a huge success in October
✔ Annihilator Erasers - a winner in September
✔ Mechanical Pencils - doubled in December

Press F10 (Continue) to return to the Main menu and then select Draw/Annotate. To add the text, select Add from the Draw menu; then select Text from the Add menu. Figure 7.3 shows the Draw/Annotate screen as it appears when it is ready for you to add text.

Follow this procedure to add the lines of text:

1. Press Ctrl-B to enter a bullet on the Text line under the drawing board. Press the space bar to select the checkmark bullet type from the Bullet Shapes overlay superimposed over the menu. Press Enter when the correct bullet type is highlighted.

2. Enter a space after the bullet character and then type *White Mountain Pens - introduced in August*. Press Enter. A long horizontal box representing the line of text you typed appears on the drawing board.

3. Before positioning the text properly, press F8 (Options) to move the cursor to the Text Options menu.

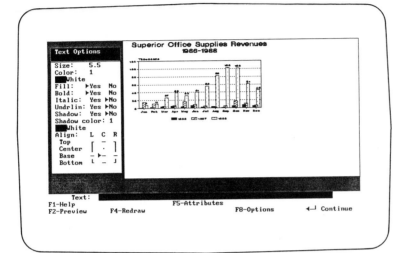

Fig. 7.3.

The Draw/Annotate screen ready for you to add text.

4. Press Enter to move the cursor past the Size option to Color. Size in Draw/Annotate is equivalent to the Size option used with text and graph charts on the Size/Place overlay. The Harvard Graphics default text size is 5.5.

5. Press F6 (Choices) to view the available color choices. Select any color for the text by highlighting it and pressing Enter.

6. Press Enter again to move the cursor to Fill; leave the selection at Yes by pressing Enter. Detailed descriptions of Fill and the remaining options on the Text Options menu follow this procedure.

7. Press Enter to move the cursor past Bold to Italic; set Italic to No.

8. Press Enter to move the cursor to Undrlin.

9. Press Enter to leave the Undrlin choice No.

10. Press Enter three more times to move the cursor past Shadow and Shadow color to Align.

11. At Align, press the space bar repeatedly until the bottom left corner of the Align box is highlighted.

12. Press F8 (Draw) to move the cursor back to the drawing board. Notice that the horizontal box representing the line of text reappears in the color you have chosen. (Because Align is the last option on the Text Options

menu, you also can press Enter after setting the alignment to return the cursor to the drawing board.)

13. Use the arrow keys to position the box under the graph where you want the text to appear. Press Enter. The text replaces the horizontal box. Figure 7.4 shows the screen before you press Enter.

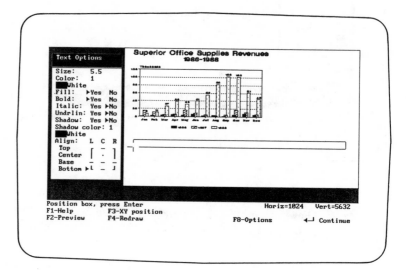

Fig. 7.4.

Adding text to the chart.

14. Press Ctrl-B to make a bullet for the second line of text. Press Enter to select another checkmark bullet. Leave a space after the bullet and then type the next line of text: *Swirly Pens - a huge success in October.* Press Enter twice to position the line on the page, directly under the first line of text. Notice that the text options have not changed, so the new text takes on the same characteristics as the first line of text.

15. Press Ctrl-B again and select the bullet type for the third line of text. Enter a space and type the third line of text: *Annihilator Erasers - a winner in September.* Press Enter twice to position this line under the first two lines of text.

16. Make another bullet and type the final line of text: *Mechanical Pencils - doubled in December.* Press Enter twice to position this line of text under the first three lines. Press Esc three times to return to the Main menu. Figure 7.5 shows the chart as it appears with the text added.

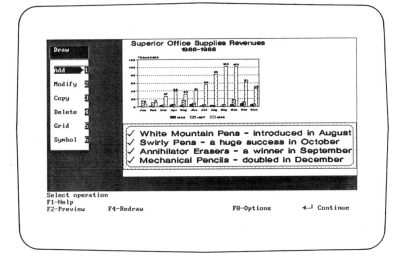

Fig. 7.5.

The SOSREVS chart with new lines of text.

When you used the Text Options menu to set the characteristics of the text you added, you noticed several options that were not explained in the preceding steps. Following is a list of the options available on the Text Options menu with explanations about the options.

Size in Draw/Annotate is identical to the Size option used with the F7-Size/ Place feature on text or graph charts. Size can be a number from 1 to 99.9 and represents a percentage of the shorter of the two sides of the page.

Color colors the current object with the selected color. Press F6 (Choices) to see the available colors. Use the space bar to move the highlight from color to color; press Enter to choose the highlighted color.

Fill tells Harvard Graphics whether to color in letters or draw outlines.

Bold, Italic, and Undrlin change the characteristics of the text you are adding to boldface, italic, or underline. These options affect an entire line when it is entered. To format selected words, you must add those individually formatted words separately. To add the italicized word *new!* at the end of any phrase in this chart, you must add the word as a second italicized text addition.

Shadow allows you to add a shadow effect to text characters. Shadow is a text attribute available only in Draw/Annotate. If you set Shadow to Yes, you can select a color for the shadow at the Shadow color option.

Align determines the placement of the text in relation to the position of the cursor. The Align option shows a picture of the text box and allows you to pick one of eight cursor positions around the edge of the box or one of three cursor positions called Base. Harvard Graphics places the text box on the drawing board in the selected position relative to the cursor. If you select one of the three Base positions, Harvard Graphics aligns the baseline of the text (the line on which most characters rest) with the cursor position. The Align option stays constant when you type multiple lines of text so they align under one another.

Adding Boxes

To highlight an aspect of a chart, you can add a box to enclose and call attention to it. Placing a box around a group of objects can show that they are related or that together they form a set.

Try placing a box around the text you just added by following this procedure:

1. Press Esc twice to return to the Draw menu and then select Add from the Draw menu.

2. Select Box from the Add menu. The cursor appears on the drawing board.

3. Position the cursor at the upper left corner of the lines of bullet text as shown in figure 7.6 and press Enter.

Fig. 7.6.

The upper left corner of the box.

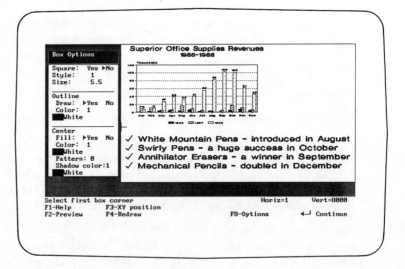

4. Use the PgDn and right-arrow keys to open the box until it surrounds the text completely. Do not press Enter yet. You can press the gray minus key (−) on the numeric keypad to make cursor-movement increments smaller, or you can press the gray plus key (+) to make them larger. Pressing an asterisk resets the movement increment to the default.

5. Press F8 (Options) to move the cursor to the Box Options panel and make selections regarding the box you are drawing. A description of the options available for the box follows this procedure.

6. Set the Square option to No, if necessary.

7. With the cursor on the Style option, press F6 (Choices) to view the available box types. Select Oct Frame (octagonal frame) by pressing the space bar twice and pressing Enter. Box types are described in detail later in this chapter.

8. Press Enter again to move the cursor to Size. Type 7.5.

   Notice that the next several options on the Box Options menu are divided into two groups. The first group sets the attributes of the Outline of the box you are drawing; the second group defines the Center of the box.

9. Press Enter to move the cursor to Draw. Select Yes to indicate that you want to draw the outline of the box.

10. Press Enter to move the cursor to Color. Press F6 (Choices) so you can select a color for the outline of the box. Highlight a color and press Enter to move to the Center options.

11. With the cursor at the Fill option, press the space bar to select Yes and fill the box. Press Enter to move the cursor to Color.

12. Press F6 (Choices) to select a color for the inside of the box you are drawing. Press Enter to move to Pattern.

13. Press F6 (Choices) to select a pattern for the center of the box. Select pattern 3. Figure 7.7 shows the screen with the patterns available.

14. Press Enter twice to return the cursor to the drawing board. Position the cursor below and to the right of the last line of text and press Enter to draw the box.

Figure 7.8 shows the completed chart with the new box. In octagonal boxes, the fill pattern or color fills in the frame between the inside and outside box.

Fig. 7.7.

The box Pattern *choices.*

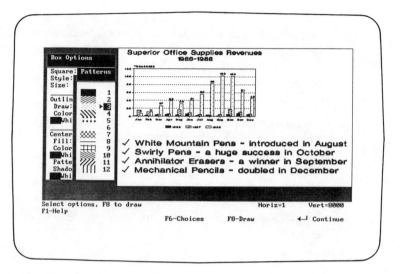

Fig. 7.8.

The chart with a box around bulleted items.

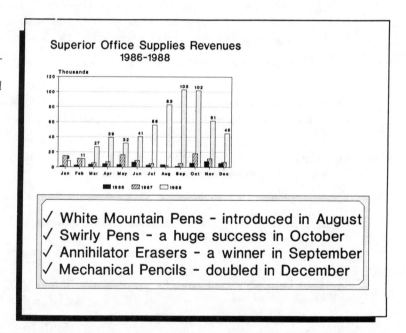

Press Esc several times to return to the Main menu. Save the finished chart with the name SOSRVBX (for "SOSREVS with a box around the text").

The options available for boxes on the Box Options menu are described in the following sections.

Square

Set Square to Yes if you want the box to be a perfect square with four equal sides. Even if you set Square to No, you can hold down the Shift key as you draw a box to make it square.

Style

Harvard Graphics has 21 different box styles. Figure 7.9 shows these styles. When the cursor is on the Style option, you can press F6 (Choices) to see the different box options. Press the space bar to cycle through all 21 box types. Press Enter when you have highlighted the desired box style to select that style.

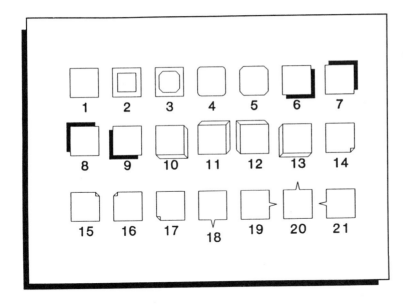

Fig. 7.9.

The 21 available box types in Draw/ Annotate.

Size

The Size of a box interacts with the Style setting for the box. If you draw a box in style 1, Size has no effect. If you draw a box in style 2 or 3, Size dictates the width of the space between the inner box and the outer box. If you draw a box in style 4, Size determines how round the corners of the box are. Size on box style 5 specifies how deep Draw/Annotate is to cut the diagonals into the sides of the box. A Size of 100 with a square box of style 5 creates a diamond. The Size option affects the depth of the shadow or of the third dimension in box styles 6 through 13. Box styles 14 through 17 have a turned corner, much like a dog-eared page corner. Size with these styles determines how wide the page corner is. Size on box styles 18 through 21 sets the size of the caption box in relation to the pointer. A Size of 100 with box type 18 makes the caption arrow very large with a small caption box.

Outline Options

A box in Draw/Annotate is composed of two parts: its outline and its center. You can choose whether or not to draw the outline and fill the center. If the center of the box is filled, you may want to omit the box outline for a varied effect. Pressing F6 (Choices) when the cursor is on the Color option displays the available options for the outline color.

Center Options

To draw a box outline only, set Fill to No. To fill a box with a color or pattern, set Fill to Yes. Fill with a box type of 2 or 3 fills only the space between the two boxes; it does not fill the inside of the box.

Once you set Fill to Yes, you can select the color or pattern for the fill by positioning the cursor next to each option and pressing F6 to see the choices available. You can choose both color and pattern if you choose.

Adding Lines

To experiment with adding lines to a chart, try annotating some of the facts in the chart called SIMPLCHT, which you created in Chapter 4. Use Get Chart to retrieve SIMPLCHT. Figure 7.10 shows the chart on the drawing board ready for enhancements.

In this example, you can highlight the most important entries on the list of customer needs with arrows. Then you can use an annotation to remind your viewers that the A-27 formula for eraser rubber was a major breakthrough for Superior Office Supplies in satisfying customer needs. Figure 7.11 shows the chart as it will look when completed.

Draw
Add 1
Modify 2
Copy 3
Delete 4
Grid 5
Symbol 6
The Annihilator Pencil Eraser
Identified Customer Needs
Total erasure
Pointed end for precise erasures
Blunt end for broad erasures
No eraser flecking--eliminate pesky eraser bits
Long-lasting
Select operation
F1-Help
F2-Preview
F4-Redraw
F8-Options
Continue

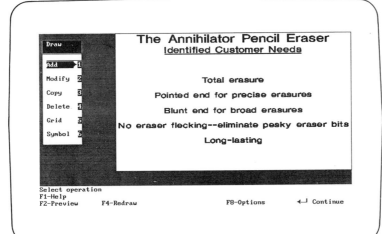

Fig. 7.10.

The SIMPLCHT list ready for enhancement in Draw/Annotate.

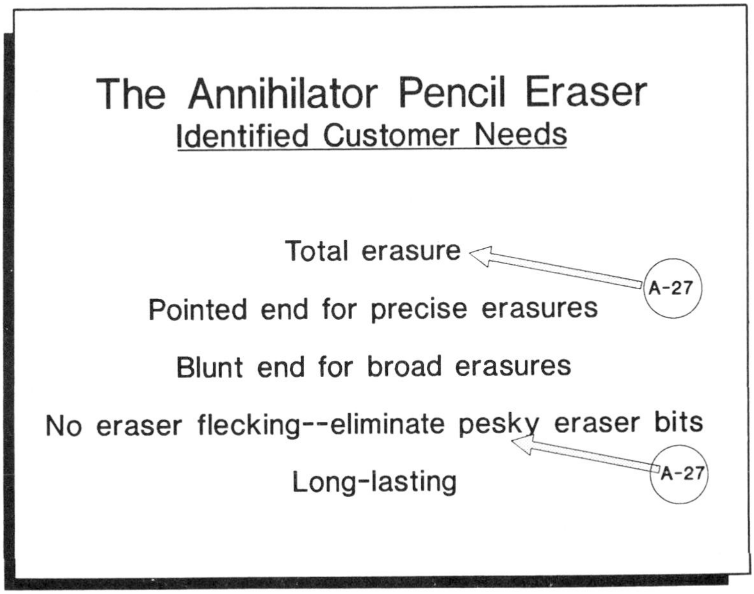

The Annihilator Pencil Eraser
Identified Customer Needs
Total erasure
A-27
Pointed end for precise erasures
Blunt end for broad erasures
No eraser flecking--eliminate pesky eraser bits
Long-lasting
A-27

Fig. 7.11.

The SIMPLCHT list with arrows, circles, and text added.

To add the arrows, follow this procedure:

1. Retrieve SIMPLCHT if you have not already done so and return to the Main menu. Select Draw/Annotate from the Main menu.

2. Select Add from the Draw menu; select Line from the Add menu. The cursor appears on the drawing board.

3. Position the cursor just to the right of the last e in the word erasure in the first line and press Enter to set the first point of your line.

4. Use the PgDn and right-arrow keys to move the line diagonally out and away from the starting point.

5. Press F8 (Options) to move the cursor to the Line Options panel.

6. Select the arrow with the arrowhead on the left at the Arrows option. Press Enter to move to the Width option.

7. Press Enter to leave the width at 5.5 and move the cursor to Outline.

8. At the Draw option, select Yes. Press Enter to move to Color.

9. Press F6 (Choices) to view the available colors for the outline of the arrow. Use the down-arrow key to highlight red, 6, and press Enter.

10. Press Enter again to move to the Center option.

11. Set Fill to Yes and press Enter to move the cursor to Color.

12. Press F6 (Choices) to view the colors available for the center of the arrow. Use the down-arrow key to highlight gray, 13, and press Enter.

13. Press Enter once more to move the cursor to Pattern.

14. Press F6 (Choices) to view the pattern choices. Use the down-arrow key to highlight pattern 3 and press Enter (see fig. 7.12).

15. Press Enter again to return the cursor to the drawing board. Press Enter again to anchor the other end of the arrow.

16. With the cursor still on the drawing board, position the crosshair under the word pesky in the fourth line of text and press Enter to anchor a new arrow.

17. Use the PgDn and arrow keys to draw the arrow. Press Enter when the arrow is positioned properly.

18. Press Esc twice to return to the Draw menu. Press F2 (Preview) to view the chart. Figure 7.13 shows the chart with arrows.

Save this chart as SLARRO (for "simple list with arrows").

When you used the Line Options menu to set the characteristics for the arrows, you noticed several options on the menu that may have been unfamiliar. The following sections describe the options available on the Line Options menu.

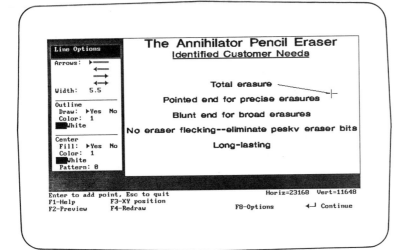

Fig. 7.12.

Adding an arrow.

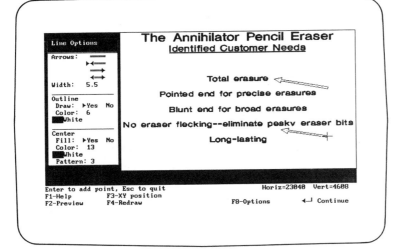

Fig. 7.13.

Previewing the chart with arrows.

Arrows

You may draw four types of lines, depicted by the four lines shown next to the Arrows prompt on the Line Options menu. To draw a line, position the cursor at one end of the line you want to draw and press Enter. Use the arrow keys to move the cursor to the other end of the line and press Enter again. Press F8

(Options) to move the cursor to the Line Options panel. To draw a plain line, select the first line at the Arrows prompt. To draw a line with the arrowhead at the beginning of the line, select the second line. To draw a line with the arrowhead at the end of the line, pick the third line. The fourth line draws an arrowhead at both ends of the line.

Width

Width determines the width of the line and arrowhead. Line width can be a number from 1 to 100. To determine the best width, experiment with several different settings.

Outline and Center Options

The Outline and Center options for lines are identical to the Outline and Center options for boxes. To select colors or patterns, press F6 (Choices) to view your choices.

Adding Circles

Now that you have pointed to the principal product benefits in the list with arrows, try adding text annotations to the other end of the arrows. For these annotations, use the characters A-27, the name of the formula referred to in an earlier chart as the cause for these product benefits. Then you can add two circles to the ends of the arrows to contain the text.

Using the add text procedure you just learned, add the text A-27 to the end of the arrows. Use a text size of 3.5. Figure 7.14 shows the chart with the A-27 text added.

The process of adding circles is similar to the process of adding boxes. The first point you locate on the screen is the center of the circle; the second point is a corner of a box surrounding the circle. Once you set an anchor by locating the first point for the circle on the screen, use the PgUp, PgDn, Home, and End keys to open the box. If necessary, you can use the Backspace key to break the anchor and move the cursor freely to a new position and try again.

Follow this procedure to add a pair of circles to contain the text annotations:

1. Select Add from the Draw menu; select Circle from the Add menu.

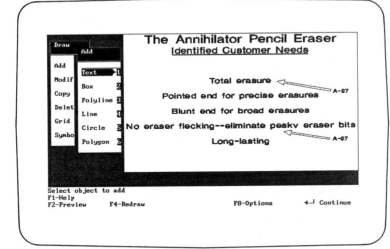

Fig. 7.14.

The chart with added text ready for circles.

2. Position the crosshairs at the middle of the circle you want to draw. In this example, position the crosshair directly over the hyphen in A-27. Press Enter to set the anchor. Figure 7.15 shows the middle of the first circle on SLARRO.CHT.

3. Use PgUp and PgDn to open the circle box until it surrounds the text. Do not press Enter yet.

4. Press F8 (Options) to view and change the Circle Options menu. The cursor is on Shape: Circle.

5. Press Enter to leave Shape set to Circle and move to Draw in the set of options for the circle's outline.

6. Set Draw to Yes to draw the outline of the circle and press Enter to move to Color for the outline.

7. Enter a color number for the outline of the circle or press F6 (Choices) to view the available colors, highlight your choice, and press Enter. (For this example, select red, 6.)

8. Press Enter to move the cursor to the Center options.

9. Set Fill to No and press Enter three times to return the cursor to the drawing board.

10. Press Enter once again to draw the circle.

11. Position the cursor at the exact position of the center of the second circle. Figure 7.16 shows the proper positioning for the second circle center on SLARRO.

12. Use the PgDn, PgUp, Home, and End keys to open up the box around the text.

13. Press Enter when the box is the correct size. Notice that the second circle has the same characteristics as the first.

Fig. 7.15.

The first circle center.

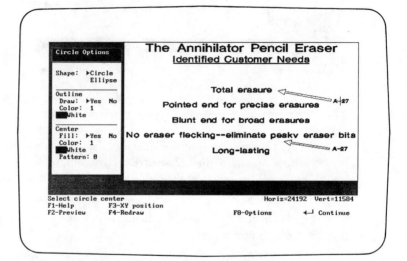

Fig. 7.16.

The center of the second circle on SLARRO.

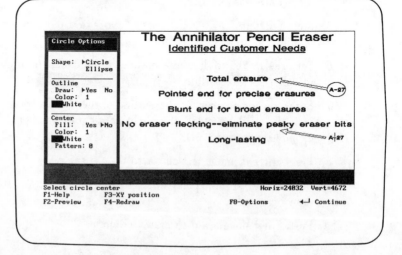

Save the revised chart as SLDRAW (for "simple list with drawing") by returning to the Main menu and using Save Chart.

The options for circles are virtually identical to those for boxes and arrows. Only the Shape option is different. Setting Shape to Ellipse as opposed to Circle produces an elongated circle.

Adding Polygons

A *polygon* is a figure with multiple sides. To draw a polygon, you must position the cursor at each of the polygon's corners and press Enter. Each time you press Enter, Draw/Annotate adds another polygon segment. Press Backspace to remove segments in reverse order. Press Esc at any point to complete the polygon.

Figure 7.17 shows the Polygon Options panel and a star drawn using Add Polygon. After you have created a star once, you can save it and use it on charts later. The section of this chapter describing symbols teaches you how to save a figure for use with other charts later.

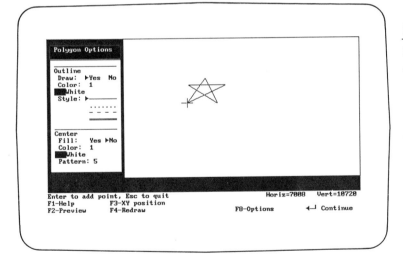

Fig. 7.17.

Making a star using Add Polygon.

To draw a star, start with a clean drawing board by creating any type of new chart, using the Create New Chart command from the Main menu. Then press Esc to return to the Main menu and select Draw/Annotate.

From the Draw menu, select Add. Then select Polygon (not Polyline) from the Add menu. Draw the star, pressing Enter at each corner of the figure. Try pressing Backspace to erase segments of the polygon. Before you press Esc to complete the star, press F8 (Options) to adjust the polygon's characteristics. When you have set the options for the shape on the Polygon Options menu, press F8 (Draw) to return the cursor to the drawing board and press Esc to complete the star.

When you press F8 (Options) to open the Polygon Options menu, you notice that the options are split into two groups: those for the outline of the polygon, and those for its center. The following sections describe these options.

Outline Options

To draw the outline of the polygon, set Draw to Yes. If the polygon has fill, you may want to consider omitting the outline.

You can use four line styles when drawing polylines: solid, dotted, dashed, and bold. To select a line style, highlight the representation of the line style you want to use at the Style option and press Enter.

Center Options

You can fill the center of a polygon with a color, a pattern, or both. Position the cursor on the Color or Pattern option and press F6 (Choices) to reveal the roster of available choices. Select the desired color or pattern and press Enter to return to the Polygon Options menu.

Adding Polylines

Polylines are lines composed of multiple straight or curved segments. To draw a polyline, follow the same procedure used to draw a polygon. Simply press Enter for each segment end point and press Esc to complete the polyline. If you chose a curved shape for the segments from the Polyline Options menu, you may notice that the segments of the polyline curve between the starting and ending points may not touch all the points you set. To cause the polyline to follow your points more closely, press Enter more often as you draw the segments. To force the polyline to touch a point, press Enter three times when you position the point. Figure 7.18 shows two versions of the same star made with curved polylines. The left star was made by pressing Enter multiple times; the right star was made by pressing Enter a single time. Figure 7.19 shows several curves and indicates the number of times Enter was pressed at each point.

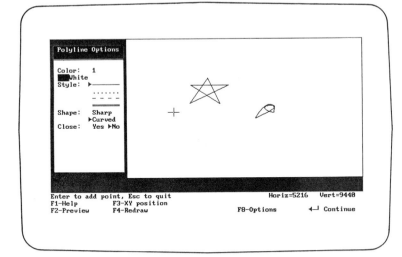

Fig. 7.18.

The star figure as a polyline instead of a polygon.

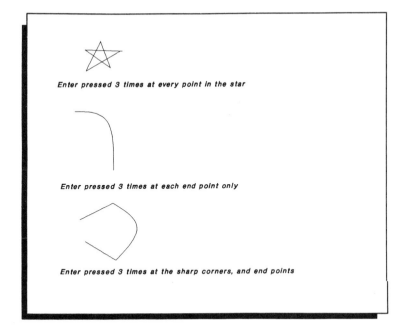

Fig. 7.19.

Polylines in Draw/Annotate.

The options in the Polyline Options menu are similar to the polygon options with two additions: Shape and Close. These options are described in the following sections.

Shape

Shape tells Harvard Graphics whether you want the segments of the line to be sharp or curved. Selecting Sharp draws straight lines between points. Selecting Curved draws curved lines between points.

Close

Setting Close to Yes instructs Harvard Graphics to connect the first and last points on the polyline when you press Esc. Creating a polyline with Close to Yes and Shape to Sharp is the same as creating a polygon. If you set Close to No, the polyline remains open-ended when you press Esc to complete the figure. A polygon is always closed.

Deleting, Copying, and Moving Elements

If you inadvertently pressed Enter before pressing F8 (Options) as you drew any of the preceding objects, the results on the screen may not be exactly as you wanted. Fortunately, Draw/Annotate lets you easily delete, copy, or move any object or text created in Draw/Annotate.

To modify, copy, or delete an object, you must follow this general sequence:

1. Tell Harvard Graphics which function to perform: Delete, Copy, or Modify.

2. Select the object to delete or modify.

3. Confirm your selection by pressing Enter.

The following sections explain each step of these Modify commands more fully.

Selecting and Deleting an Object

To practice modifying an object, retrieve the chart you saved earlier with the name SLDRAW. This chart has three different types of objects: text, circles, and arrows. Suppose that you want to remove the circles and leave the text only. Follow this procedure after entering Draw/Annotate:

1. Select Delete from the Draw menu; select Choose from the Delete menu. You see this prompt at the bottom of the screen:

   Choose this   Select next   Retry

2. Highlight the object you want to modify by placing the cursor on it and pressing Enter.

3. Harvard Graphics surrounds the object with four small circles. If the correct object is highlighted, press Enter to confirm your choice. If the small circles surround the wrong object, use the right-arrow key to highlight Select next at the bottom of the screen and press Enter. Figure 7.20 shows SLDRAW with the first circle selected.

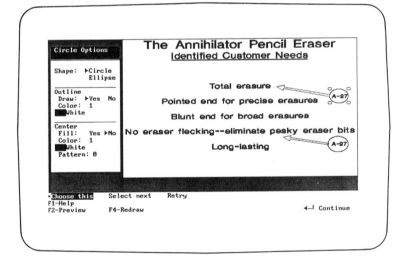

Fig. 7.20.

SLDRAW *with the first circle selected for deletion.*

If you want to delete both the circle and the text it encloses, you can select both for deletion simultaneously by enclosing them in a box. To do this, first select Delete from the Draw menu and Choose from the Delete menu. Then position the cursor above and to the left of the objects you want to delete. Notice the prompt at the bottom of the screen: Select first box corner. Press Enter and PgDn to anchor and open the box to enclose the entire circle. Press Enter again and notice the prompt at the bottom of the screen:

   Choose this   Select next   Retry

Leave the cursor on Choose this and press Enter to tell Harvard Graphics that the correct object is selected. The object will be deleted.

Once you have deleted an object, you can change your mind immediately by selecting Undo from the Delete menu. Undo "undeletes" the last object you deleted. If you choose All from the Delete menu to delete all the Draw/Annotate additions to your chart, selecting Undo doesn't work.

Copying an Object

If you regret having removed the first circle from SLDRAW, you can easily copy the remaining circle to the first circle's place. To copy the second symbol, follow these steps:

1. Select Copy from the Draw menu. The prompt at the bottom of the screen reads, `Select Object`.

2. Position the cursor on the circle you want to copy and press Enter. Harvard Graphics places four small circles around the circle to indicate that the circle is the chosen object. Notice the prompt now:

   `Choose this   Select next   Retry`

   Figure 7.21 shows SLDRAW with the remaining circle selected.

3. Use the arrow keys to position the box for the destination of the duplicate and press Enter.

Fig. 7.21.

SLDRAW with the second circle selected for copying.

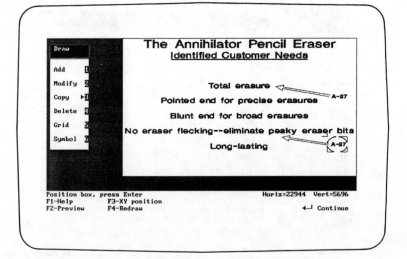

Once you successfully copy an object once, you can continue pressing Enter to copy the object again and again. The second time you press Enter, a duplicate of the object appears the same distance from the first copy as the first copy was from the original. Each time you press Enter, the object is copied at the same distance. With this technique, you can make evenly spaced, repetitive patterns on a page.

Modifying Objects

You can use the Draw/Annotate Modify command to move and resize an object or group of objects. You also can use it to change the option settings of an object. You can change an object's color, for example, or change the attributes of text. The Modify command also enables you to place one object in back or in front of another.

Moving and Resizing Objects

To move an object, select Modify from the Draw menu; select Move from the Modify menu. Choose the object you want to move by pointing to it with the cursor and pressing Enter. Check to see that you have selected the correct object and then position the box that appears where you want to move the object. Complete the move by pressing Enter to confirm your positioning choice.

When you use the Move command and select an object to move, it appears as though you are moving a box around the screen and not the object. After you press Enter to confirm the Move command, the object moves to the new position and may even appear to take pieces of surrounding objects with it. Press F4 (Redraw) to refresh the screen and gain an accurate view of the chart.

To change the size of an object but leave it at the same place, select Size from the Modify menu. Select the object to resize; Harvard Graphics draws a box around the object you selected. You see the prompt Select opposite box corner. Reposition the bottom right corner of the box with the cursor to resize the box and the object in the box. Then press Enter.

You can change both the size and position of an object or group of objects simultaneously with the Size command. Select the object or group of objects as described in the preceding paragraph. Press the Backspace key to release the cursor and allow it to move freely around the screen. Position the cursor at the upper left corner of the new location of the object. Press Enter to anchor this corner. Use PgDn, PgUp, Home, or End to open and size the box to its new proportions. When the lower right corner of the box is in the correct position, press Enter. Then press F4 (Redraw) to see the true appearance of your changes.

Modifying the Options of a Group

Normally, you modify the options of objects one at a time. With Draw/Annotate, you can modify the options of a group of objects simultaneously.

To try modifying the options of a group of objects, retrieve SOSRVBX, the chart you made earlier in this chapter. Select Modify from the Main menu; select Options from the Modify menu. For this exercise, you will change all the text in the chart, adding the italic attribute and making the text smaller. Follow this procedure to make the changes:

1. Position the cursor just above and to the left of the first line of text and press Enter.

2. Press PgDn and the right-arrow key several times until all the lines of text are enclosed in the box and press Enter.

3. Select Choose this from the bottom of the screen by pressing Enter.

4. Harvard Graphics recognizes that the currently selected object is text. When the Text Options menu appears, change Size to 3.5 and select Italic: Yes. Then press F8 (Draw) to return the cursor to the drawing board.

5. Press F4 (Redraw) to clear and redraw the chart. Figure 7.22 shows SOSRVBX with the modified text.

Using Harvard Graphics Symbols

Harvard Graphics offers a host of predrawn graphics called symbols. A *symbol* is a group of objects joined together to form a recognizable image. A symbol can include circles, boxes, lines, polylines, and text—all grouped together as a single image. A symbol may also be a group of objects of one type, such as a series of names.

To understand symbols, try creating a useful monthly calendar symbol by drawing boxes and entering the days of the week as text. Once the calendar outline is completed and saved on disk, you can insert new dates once a month, publish the current month's calendar, and save the new calendar as a chart. At the end of the year, when you want to show the activities of the entire year, you can save the monthly calendar charts as symbols and place them all on one page.

As another example of how useful symbols can be, you can convert your company logo into a symbol and save it for use again and again in a variety of charts

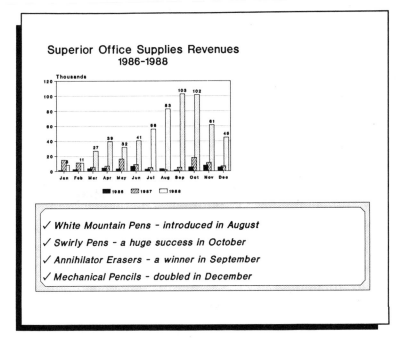

Fig. 7.22.

SOSRVBX *with smaller, italicized text after modifying the options.*

at a variety of sizes. Although you can save virtually anything you create as a symbol and use it in charts in the future, you may want to start with the pre-drawn symbols provided by Harvard Graphics in its symbol libraries.

To spruce up the Superior Office Supplies Writing Tools Division presentation you have been creating throughout this book, you can create the company logo with Draw/Annotate and save it as a symbol. Then you can add the symbol to all the charts in your presentation.

To make a simple logo, start by creating a new free-form text chart. (Free-form charts are described in Chapter 4.) Then press Esc to return to the Main menu and press F8 (Options) to change the current font to Roman. Select Draw/Annotate from the Main menu and add the words *Superior Office Supplies* so that each word begins under the first letter of the preceding word. Remember: to align successive lines of text, set the Align option to left-justified. Figure 7.23 shows a new free-form chart with the words *Superior Office Supplies* added. Refer to the "Adding Text" section earlier in this chapter for specific instructions.

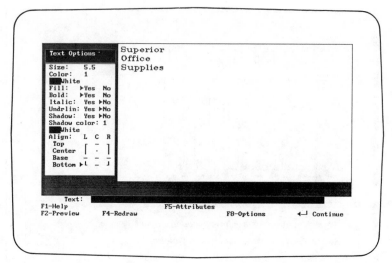

Fig. 7.23.

The beginning of the logo.

Getting and Placing Symbols

Follow this procedure to add symbols and customize the chart for the Writing Tools Division:

1. Select Symbol from the Draw menu.

2. Select Get from the Symbol menu. Harvard Graphics displays a list of the available symbol files.

3. Use the down arrow to highlight OFFICE.SYM and press Enter. Figure 7.24 shows the Office symbol library as it appears on-screen.

4. Position the cursor on the envelope, paintbrush, and pen symbol on the right side of the second line of symbols and press Enter.

5. Press the Backspace key to release the cursor to move about the screen freely.

6. Position the cursor under the first letters of Superior Office Supplies and press Enter to anchor the first corner of the symbol.

7. Use the PgDn key to position the opposite corner of the box under the last letters of the company name.

8. Press Enter to draw the symbol.

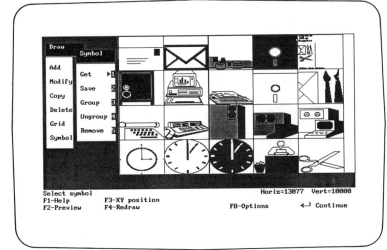

Fig. 7.24.

The Office symbol library.

The symbol would look better when printed if it was not colored. The following procedure modifies the symbol to make its fill color black:

1. Press Esc to return to the Draw menu and select Modify.

2. Select Options from the Modify menu. Select Choose from the Modify menu and position the cursor over the envelope, paintbrush, and pen symbol. Press Enter to select the symbol as the one you want to modify.

3. Set the Outline color to 1 (white) and press Enter to move to the Fill color option.

4. Set Fill color to 16 (black). Press Enter twice to pass Shadow color and redraw the symbol with black fill.

Next, get another symbol for your logo by following this procedure:

1. Select Get from the Symbol menu and choose the OFFICE.SYM library again.

2. Select the scissors symbol and place it under the envelope, paintbrush, and pen symbol. Follow steps 5 through 8 of the preceding procedure to place the second symbol.

Figure 7.25 shows the logo with the two symbols placed as described.

Fig. 7.25.

The SOS logo with two symbols.

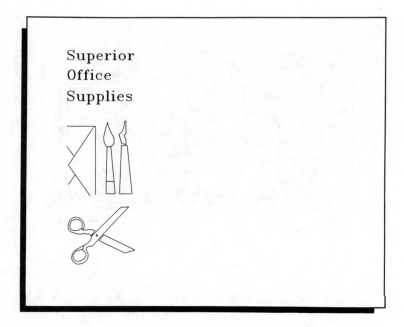

To complete the logo, add a line and the name of the division. Use the following procedure:

1. Press Esc twice to return to the Draw menu. Add a vertical line just to the right of the symbols to enclose the logo visually. If you use a mouse, hold down the Shift key as you draw the line to keep it straight. Before you press Enter the second time to complete the line, use F8 (Options) to set Width to a thin 1.5.

2. Add the words *Writing Tools Division* under the vertical line, as shown in figure 7.26. Set the text with italics and a size of 4.5.

Grouping and Ungrouping Symbols

Using the Group command, you can gather together all the individual objects composing a drawing so that you can save the whole image as a symbol in one of the symbol libraries. Follow this procedure to group the objects in your logo and save them as a symbol in the OFFICE.SYM file.

1. Select Symbol from the Draw menu.

2. Select Group from the Symbol menu.

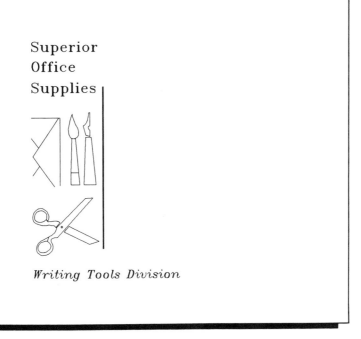

Fig. 7.26.

The completed logo.

3. Move the cursor above and to the left of the logo and press Enter to anchor the first corner of the selection box.

4. Press PgDn to position the box around all the items in the logo and press Enter. Harvard Graphics places four small circles around each object.

5. Press Enter to select Choose this from the bottom of the screen. Press Esc to group all the selected objects. When you press Esc, all the small surrounding circles disappear. Harvard Graphics now treats all the items as one object.

To test that the objects are in one group, select Modify Options, position the cursor in the middle of the logo, and press Enter. Notice that small circles surround the entire group of objects as shown in figure 7.27.

If you want to change only one object in the group, you must ungroup the objects before you can modify it. To ungroup the objects, select Symbol from the Draw menu; select Ungroup from the Symbol menu. Highlight the group you want to separate and press Enter. Each object in the group is treated as an individual object once again.

Fig. 7.27.

All the objects in the logo treated as one.

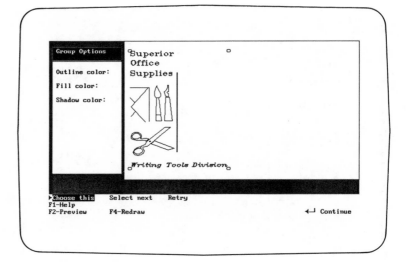

Saving a Group of Objects as a Symbol

To save the logo as a symbol in an existing library, follow this procedure:

1. Select Symbol from the Draw menu.

2. Select Save from the Symbol library.

3. Highlight the group so that the four small circles surround it.

4. Press Enter to select Choose this.

5. Use the down-arrow key to highlight a symbol library file name, in this case OFFICE.SYM, and press Enter to save the object in the symbol library.

Next, check to see that the symbol was saved in OFFICE.SYM by selecting Get from the Symbol menu and then selecting the OFFICE.SYM library. When the library is drawn on the screen, you should see the symbol in the upper right corner of the symbol library.

Saving and Modifying a Chart as a Symbol

You can save an entire chart as a symbol. When you save a chart as a symbol, each element in that chart is treated as an object that could be made in Draw/Annotate. For example, in a bar chart, the bars are treated as boxes when the chart is converted to a symbol. In a pie chart, the slices of a pie become poly-lines. The text of the chart—the title, subtitle, footnote, and labels—is inter-preted in Draw/Annotate as text, and so on.

Retrieve the pie chart named SOS2HLK, the linked pie chart of the second-half revenues that you created in Chapter 6. To save this chart as a symbol, follow these steps:

1. Press Esc at the chart display and Esc again at the Pie Chart 1 Data screen to return to the Main menu.

2. Select Get/Save/Remove from the Main menu and Save as Symbol from the Get/Save/Remove menu.

3. The cursor is on Symbol will be saved as on the Save Chart as Symbol overlay. Type the name *sos2hpic* for "second-half picture" and press Enter to move the cursor to For device.

4. Select the output device you want to use (printer or plotter), press the space bar to highlight it, and press Enter to confirm your choice.

5. Because you typed a new symbol library name, another overlay appears for you to type a description. If you typed the name of an existing symbol library, the chart would be added to it.

Once you have saved a chart as a symbol, you can retrieve the symbol and ungroup it as described elsewhere in this chapter. Then, using Modify from the Draw menu, you can change the appearance of the bar chart by moving individ-ual bars or changing the size or placement of text. Follow this procedure to try changing the pie chart symbol:

1. Create a new, free-form text chart and press Esc to return to the Main menu.

2. Select Draw/Annotate from the Main menu.

3. Select Symbol from the Draw menu and Get from the Symbol menu. Retrieve the symbol library you just made: SOS2HPIC.

4. Position the cursor on the pie chart symbol and press Enter. The Draw/Annotate screen appears again. Notice that a symbol does not appear to be in memory. Because the pie chart is the size of the entire screen, the box surrounding the symbol also fills the entire screen, so you cannot see that a symbol is in memory.

5. Press Backspace to break the symbol anchor. Press F3 (XY Position), type *1000* at the Horiz= space, type *19000* at Vert=, and press Enter. Press Enter again to set the first corner of the box surrounding the symbol.

6. Press PgDn several times to open the box that surrounds your symbol and press Enter when Vert=20000 and Horiz=3000. Press Enter again. The symbol is drawn on the screen.

7. Select Ungroup from the Symbol menu and press Enter with the cursor on the symbol. The four small circles surround the symbol. Press Enter again to ungroup the symbol.

8. Press Esc to return to the Draw menu and select Modify.

9. Select Move from the Modify menu and choose the September slice.

10. Move the September slice to cut it artificially from the pie.

You can see that when the pie chart is a symbol that has been ungrouped, you can change its appearance by altering its components individually.

Importing CGM Files

You can add symbols to your collection with clip-art files you purchase from third-party vendors. Harvard Graphics provides a utility for converting Computer Graphics Metafiles (CGM files) to symbol files. One company that produces excellent CGM files is Marketing Graphics Inc., of Richmond, Virginia. You can purchase a variety of predrawn files, convert them into symbols, and incorporate them in Harvard Graphics symbol libraries. In addition, if you have saved as CGM files graphics in other packages such as Freelance Plus, you can import those graphics as well.

A special utility on the Harvard Graphics Utility disk, META2HG.EXE, performs the conversion. To use it, you must copy the utility from the Harvard Graphics Utility disk to the directory in which you have installed Harvard Graphics. Then copy the CGM file you want to convert into the directory holding the Harvard Graphics symbol files.

From your Harvard Graphics program directory, type the command

META2HG *filename1*.cgm *filename2*.sym.

Filename1 is the name of the CGM file you want to convert, and *filename2* is the name of the symbol library in which you want to place the symbol. Do not use the name of an existing symbol library, because the metafile symbol will write over and replace the existing library.

Using Special Drawing Tools

Harvard Graphics offers two helpful drawing tools you can use to "line up" and position the objects you are drawing. You can turn these tools on and off as you are drawing in Draw/Annotate and reduce your chance of producing a crooked chart.

Using the Grid Feature

With the Grid feature in Harvard Graphics, you can display a grid made up of dots arranged in a grid pattern behind any objects or text you place on the page. When Snap is turned on, each dot on the grid acts like a magnet, pulling objects to it and automatically aligning them with the horizontal and vertical grid lines.

To use a grid, select Grid from the Draw menu and complete the Grid Options panel:

Size	The size of the intervals between grid points is a number between 1 and 25 that is a percentage of the shorter side of the drawing board. A good grid size to work with is 4, the default grid setting. With a setting of 4, the grid has 25 rows of dots.
Show	If you want to show the grid, select Yes. If you prefer not to look at the grid, select No. When you remove a grid by turning off Show, you should press F4 (Redraw) to clean up the screen.
Snap	Use Snap to turn on the magnet effect for each dot in the grid. Use Snap with Show set to Yes. Turning on Snap doesn't affect the objects you have already drawn.

Using Cursor Position Indicators

As you have seen in the previous procedures in this chapter, you can use Draw/Annotate's cursor position indicators to set the points of your objects with precision. Simply press F3 to set manually the position of the cursor in any Draw/Annotate operation. When the cursor is at the lower left corner of the screen, both Horiz= and Vert= should be at 1. As you move the cursor up the screen, the Vert= number increases. As you move the cursor to the right, the Horiz= number increases.

Setting Draw/Annotate's Defaults

If you are accustomed to adding text with a size of 3 and box type 4 when you use Draw/Annotate, you will appreciate the default settings feature in Draw/Annotate. When you set Draw/Annotate defaults, Harvard Graphics uses those settings when it first displays each options panel. To summon the Draw/Annotate Default Options menu, press F8 (Options) at the main Draw menu (see fig. 7.28).

Fig. 7.28.

The Draw/Annotate Default Options menu.

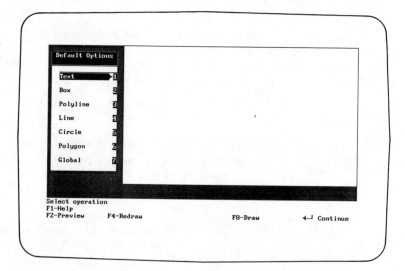

When you choose to set defaults for one of the options types, the options panel shown is exactly the same as the options panel you use when adding or modifying that object. Of course you can always change the setting for an object as you are drawing it by pressing F8 before pressing Enter the second time to confirm your choice.

To set defaults, simply tab through the options, highlight the default you want to set, and press Enter to make your choice and move to the next option. Press F10 to return to the Draw menu and continue with your drawing.

The exceptions to this rule are the global options, which are unique in Draw/Annotate. When you select Global from the Default Options menu, the options panel shown in figure 7.29 appears.

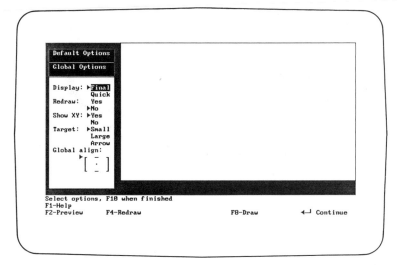

Fig. 7.29.

The Global Options panel.

The Global Options panel includes the following options:

Display   Set Display to Final to view the most accurate picture of
               the finished work, including all the details in your graphic.
               Setting Display to Quick displays the chart faster, but bold
               text does not display.

Redraw   Selecting Yes at this prompt directs Harvard Graphics to
               redraw the graphic each time you make a change. If you
               select No at Redraw, the chart is redrawn only when you
               press F4. As a result, you may see blank spaces when you
               move, resize, or delete objects, and when you use the Back
               or Front feature, the results do not appear until you
               press F4.

Show XY   Select Yes at this prompt to display the Vert= and Horiz=
               numbers under the right side of the drawing board. As you
               have seen, these numbers are useful when you are lining up
               objects.

Target   The crosshairs on the drawing board are called a *target*. If
               you select Small, the target is the plus sign that you are
               accustomed to. If you select Large at this option, the
               crosshairs extend to the edges of the screen, making a large
               cross the entire size of the screen. If you select Arrow, the
               target appears as a diagonal arrow like the one shown in
               figure 7.30.

Global align   You can set the alignment point of the rectangle you used to position an object. The *alignment point* is the corner of the rectangle referred to by the XY position indicators. You can always reset the alignment of the target while you are drawing an individual object.

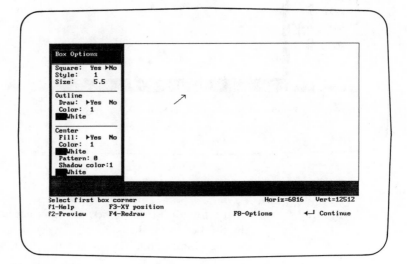

Fig. 7.30.

The target as an arrow.

Chapter Summary

In this chapter, you learned how to enhance charts by using Draw/Annotate. In this mode you can add lines, circles, boxes, polylines, polygons, and symbols. You also learned how to create symbols from a group of objects and how to create a new symbol library from a graph or text chart. This chapter also covered how you can resize an entire chart by pressing F7 (Size/Place) at the Main menu. In the next chapter, you will read about using step-saving templates and macros.

8

Using Step-Savers: Templates and Macros

If you need to create charts and graphs regularly, the information in this chapter will help you quite a bit. Especially if you update the same charts over and over, you will find that templates and macros are invaluable.

Templates are remarkable time- and effort-savers that store the basic blueprints for Harvard Graphics charts. With templates, you need to create a chart of a certain type from scratch only once. After that, you can load its template and let Harvard Graphics do all the work. The only embellishments you may want to add are annotations unique to that particular chart.

This chapter explains how to create and use templates, and it addresses both their benefits and their limitations. This chapter also covers how to manage groups of templates by storing them in a separate Harvard Graphics feature called a *chartbook*.

Macros, another step-saver covered here, can reduce your work still further. After you have stored the keystrokes used to create a chart in a special macro file, you can replay them any time later with a single command. Harvard Graphics then imitates the exact same actions, producing a new chart with all the same characteristics almost instantaneously. Using macros, you can automate virtually anything you find yourself doing repetitively in Harvard Graphics.

By combining templates and macros, you can reduce to almost nothing the amount of work required to create certain charts. After you have updated the information in a 1-2-3 worksheet, for example, you can run the macro you created earlier to import that data into a bar chart template. The template formats the chart, and then the macro saves the chart and prints it automatically.

Those of you who need to graph data daily, or even more often, will delight in the ability to use templates and macros in combination.

Templates

Templates are special Harvard Graphics files that store predefined charts. Templates provide a number of benefits:

- ❏ Eliminate creating frequently prepared charts from scratch
- ❏ Eliminate typing errors in recurring charts by including constant information
- ❏ Ensure that the formatting of all charts in a presentation is consistent
- ❏ Set the default features for new charts of each Harvard Graphics chart type
- ❏ Set up prefabricated charts for Harvard Graphics beginners

If you chart the same type of data regularly, you can use a template to store the characteristics that reappear time and time again in each subsequent chart. For example, a template for a bar chart can include your company's name as an underlined subtitle. Each week the company name appears automatically as an underlined subtitle in the new bar chart. You need only to fill in the updated data.

If you need to prepare a presentation with a sequence of similar charts, you can create a single chart and then save it as a template. For the sales volume of identical products at six regional sales offices, for example, you can create a single sales chart and then save it as a template. To create similar charts for the other sales offices, recall the same template for each office in succession, supply that office's data, and save the new chart.

Sometimes, the task of creating complex charts falls to people who are newcomers to computers and business graphics software. You can predefine charts for computer neophytes so they can create full-fledged presentations with only minimal training.

Templates also come in handy as you prepare slide shows and screenshows (both covered in detail in Chapter 9). You can use templates to ensure that successive slides share certain characteristics, such as color choices.

To create a template, you simply save a completed chart as a template file. To create a new chart with the same features later, you call up the template instead of starting a chart from scratch.

By using special reserved names when you save templates, you can even have Harvard Graphics use template information when beginning any of its basic pre-defined chart types, such as line graphs. A special template for creating bullet lists, for example, might set all main bullets as checkmarks and their text sizes to 6. Any time you choose to create a bullet list in the future, the new chart will use checkmarks and 6 automatically as a text size. Another ideal use for templates is setting all charts created in a division so they automatically include the division's name as an italicized footnote.

Templates store the following characteristics of charts:

- ❏ Actual text and data
- ❏ Text size and placement
- ❏ Text attributes
- ❏ All Titles & Options page settings
- ❏ Draw/Annotate embellishments
- ❏ Import data links
- ❏ Titles and subtitles

Templates do not store the following:

- ❏ Print settings
- ❏ Setup Defaults settings

Creating a Template

To create a template, create a chart first with all its characteristics set. So that you can preview the chart and be sure that its settings are proper, use data similar to the data you will be using when you employ the template. Either real or dummy information will do the trick. Return to the Main menu, choose Get/Save/Remove, and then choose Save Template from the Get/Save/Remove menu. When Harvard Graphics prompts you for a name, enter up to eight characters. The program automatically supplies the template's TPL file extension, and it provides a description based on the title you supplied for the chart. To retrieve a template, choose Get Template from the Get/Save/Remove menu.

To learn how templates are made, create a template that Superior Office Supplies can use weekly to track sales of its two most popular products, pens and pencils, over the course of each week. To display the sales results vividly, use a graph chart that combines both bars (for pencils) and a line (for pens).

To create the chart, follow these steps:

1. Start a new bar chart by choosing Create New Chart from the Harvard Graphics Main menu and then Bar/Line from the Create New Chart menu.

2. On the X Data Type Menu overlay, set the X data type option to Day and then type *Mon* at the Starting with option and *Fri* at the Ending with option. Leave the Increment option blank.

3. On the Bar/Line Chart Data screen, enter *Pen/Pencil Sales* as a title and *Stationery Division* as a subtitle. Leave the footnote section blank.

4. Use the following two sets of sales results for Series 1 and Series 2:

Series 1	Series 2
21,000	32,000
26,300	21,700
27,500	29,800
28,200	21,700
34,000	20,000

5. Once you have entered the data, pull up the Titles & Options pages by pressing F8 (Options). On the first Titles & Options page, set the X axis title to *Day* and the Y1 axis title to *Units*.

6. For the first Legend Title option, type *Pens*, and for the Type option, select Line. For the second Legend Title option, type *Pencils*, and for the Type option, select Bar.

7. Press PgDn to view the second Titles & Options page. On this page, set Bar style to Overlap and Bar enhancement to 3D.

8. Press PgDn to view the third Titles & Options page. On this page, include a data table by setting Data Table to Framed.

9. Press F2 to preview the chart. Figure 8.1 shows the completed pen/pencil weekly sales chart.

Because this chart is exactly what you have in mind for a weekly report, save it as a template to reuse from week to week. To save the chart as a template, press Esc several times until you have returned to the Main menu. Choose Get/Save/Remove from the Main menu and then select Save Template from the Get/Save/Remove menu. Figure 8.2 shows the Save Template overlay that appears. When Harvard Graphics asks for a template name, enter *pen-pncl*, for "pen/pencil chart template." Harvard Graphics derives the template description it provides from the title of the chart. To accept the description already present, simply press Enter. To change it, type a new description over the present description and press Enter.

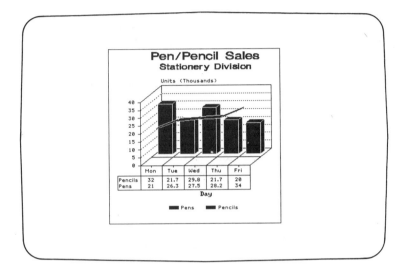

Fig. 8.1.

The Pen/Pencil Sales chart.

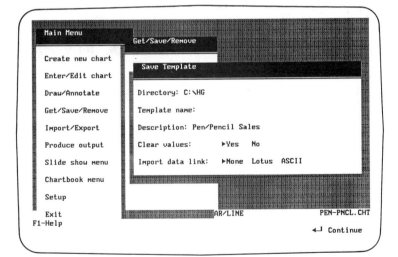

Fig. 8.2.

The Save Template overlay.

On the Save Template overlay, still visible on your screen, Harvard Graphics asks whether you want to clear values. When you create a chart that will become a template, you will need to use actual data so you can format the chart properly.

If you set Clear values to Yes, Harvard Graphics deletes the chart's data before saving it as a template. To retain the current data so it is included the next time the template is retrieved, set Clear values to No. For this template, set Clear values to Yes so Superior Office Supplies can start with a new, clear chart each week. That way, the company needs only enter new data and the chart is complete.

The last option on the overlay asks whether your chart includes a Lotus or ASCII data link. (Using templates with data links is covered in the following section.) For now, select None and press Enter. You see a warning message that reads Chart values are about to be cleared. Press Enter to continue and then press Esc once to return to the Main menu.

To use the template the following week, choose Get Template from the Get/ Save/Remove menu (which you access from the Main menu). Harvard Graphics displays a list of available templates and allows you to pick PEN-PNCL from the list.

When the template appears (see fig. 8.3), notice that it has retained its title and subtitle. In fact, all the settings on the Titles & Options pages are preset as well. Notice also that the X data type is already set to Day and that Series 1 and Series 2 are properly renamed Pens and Pencils.

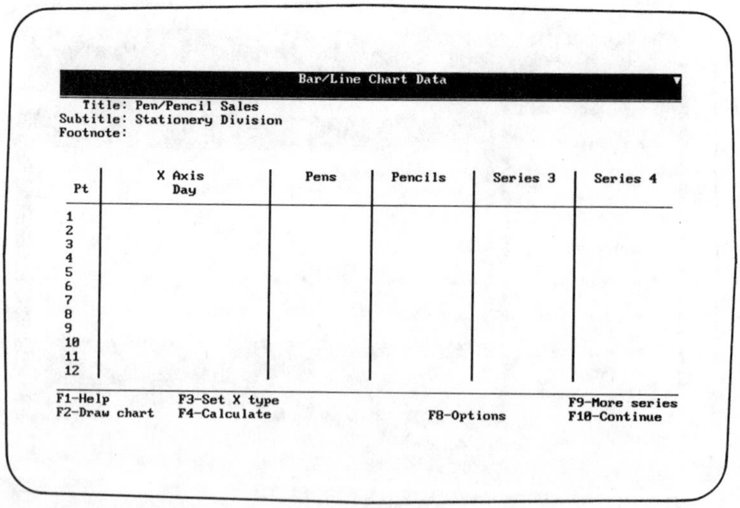

Fig. 8.3.

The PEN-PNCL template.

To use the template, you will need to reset the x-axis Starting with and Ending with settings, but that will take only a moment. Press F3 (Set X Type) and reenter *Mon* and *Fri* as the Starting with and Ending with options, respectively. Now try typing imaginary data for the chart's values and then pressing F2 to preview the chart. Notice that all the chart's formatting is in place. Save the chart as PEN-PCL1 so you can retrieve it later in this chapter as you learn how to create a chartbook.

Using Templates To Set Default Chart Styles

Using templates, you can predefine the default formatting for each of the charts in the Harvard Graphics repertoire. When you choose Create New Chart from the Main menu, Harvard Graphics scans the files on disk to see whether you have created a template for that chart type. If you have, the program uses that template to set whatever characteristics of the chart that you have predefined.

By using templates to set default chart styles, you can ensure consistency in the charts produced within a company, department, or division. For example, you can determine that all pie charts created will display a graphic of the company logo in the top right corner, use the Roman font, and include the company name italicized with a text size of 8 in the subtitle.

To create a default template for a chart type, simply create one representative chart that includes all the characteristics you want to include in all future charts of that type and save the chart with the proper reserved template names. To create the default template for all future area charts, for example, name the template AREA when you save it. Here are the reserved names for default chart style templates:

Chart Style	Name
Title charts	TITLE
Simple lists	LIST
Bullet lists	BULLET
Two-column charts	2_COLUMN
Three-column charts	3_COLUMN
Free-form charts	FREEFORM
Pie charts	PIE
Bar or line charts	BARLINE
Area charts	AREA
High/low/close charts	HLC
Organization charts	ORG
Multiple charts	MULTIPLE

Importing Data into a Template-Based Chart

If you have established a data link with a Lotus worksheet or an ASCII data file, you can instruct Harvard Graphics to use the same data link when it creates a new chart from a template. That way, you can simply update the data in the Lotus or ASCII data file, for example, by changing your figures in a Lotus worksheet. When you retrieve the template, Harvard Graphics will automatically pull in the revised data from the worksheet or data file and use the template settings to format the chart. With just one step in Harvard Graphics, your chart is complete.

To create a template with a data link to an external data file, create a chart that uses a data link and save it as a template. When you save the template, the Import data link option on the Save Template overlay will reflect that you used a Lotus or ASCII data link. Simply leave the Import data link setting as is and save the chart. Setting Import data link to None breaks the data link so you can create a new and different data link.

Using Chartbooks To Manage Templates

Templates are so useful that you probably will create dozens of them as you use Harvard Graphics more and more. For you to manage groups of templates, Harvard Graphics provides a special type of file called a *chartbook*.

A chartbook contains a catalog of templates you assemble to manage related charting needs. A typical chartbook may hold, for example, all templates you have fashioned for bulleted lists. Another chartbook may hold all the charts you create as part of a quarterly presentation to the division vice president.

Creating a Chartbook

You can practice creating a chartbook with more than one template by using the chart you created earlier in this chapter to create a second template that is slightly altered in several respects.

Follow this procedure to create a second template:

1. Get the chart entitled PEN-PCL1 by selecting Get Chart from the Get/ Save/Remove menu.

2. On the second Titles & Options page, set Bar style to 100% so that you can compare the relative percentages of sales of pens and pencils.

3. Save the new chart as a template with the name PP-PRCNT. Set Clear values to Yes and Import data link to None.

4. Press Esc to return to the Main menu.

Now you have two related templates that you can store in a chartbook. To create the chartbook, follow these four steps:

1. Select the Chartbook Menu option from the Main menu.

2. Select Create Chartbook from the Chartbook menu. The Create Chartbook overlay appears (see fig. 8.4).

3. Enter *pen-pncl* as the name of the chartbook. There's no problem in using the same name as one of the templates because Harvard Graphics automatically supplies the chartbook file with an extension reserved for chartbooks, CBK.

4. Enter *Pen and Pencil Sales Comparison Charts* as a description for the chartbook and press Enter. The Create/Edit Chartbook screen appears (see fig. 8.5).

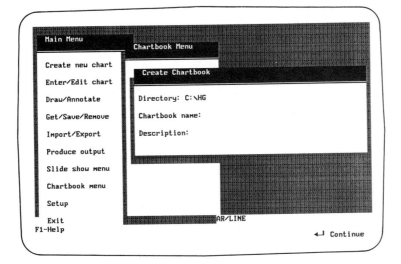

Fig. 8.4.

The Create Chartbook overlay.

At the top of the Create/Edit Chartbook screen is a list of templates in the current directory on your disk. Below that is the contents of the new chartbook you are about to create. The chartbook is empty, but the currently highlighted template name on the list above appears to be the first entry. To choose a different template, use the up- and down-arrow keys to highlight another template name

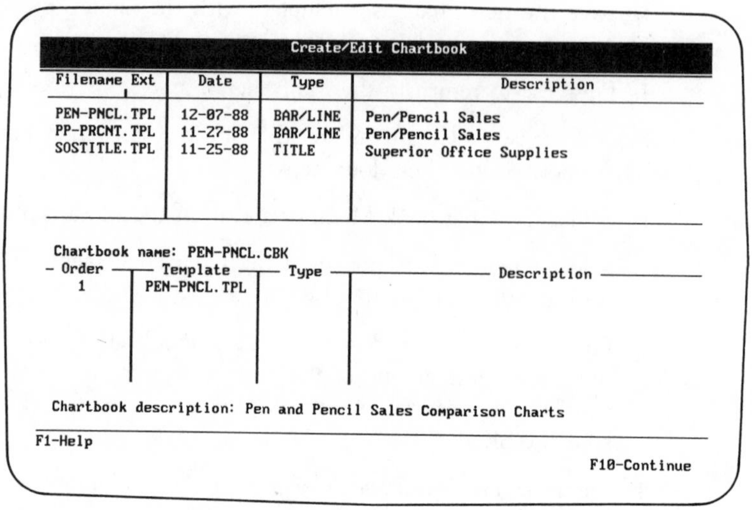

Fig. 8.5.

The Create/Edit Chartbook screen.

```
┌──────────────────────────────────────────────────────────────┐
│                     Create/Edit Chartbook                      │
├─────────────┬──────────┬──────────┬───────────────────────────┤
│Filename Ext │   Date   │   Type   │        Description         │
├─────────────┼──────────┼──────────┼───────────────────────────┤
│PEN-PNCL.TPL │ 12-07-88 │ BAR/LINE │ Pen/Pencil Sales          │
│PP-PRCNT.TPL │ 11-27-88 │ BAR/LINE │ Pen/Pencil Sales          │
│SOSTITLE.TPL │ 11-25-88 │ TITLE    │ Superior Office Supplies  │
│             │          │          │                           │
├─────────────┴──────────┴──────────┴───────────────────────────┤
│ Chartbook name: PEN-PNCL.CBK                                   │
│ - Order ─────┬─ Template ──┬─ Type ──────── Description ────── │
│     1        │ PEN-PNCL.TPL │                                  │
│                                                                │
│ Chartbook description: Pen and Pencil Sales Comparison Charts  │
├────────────────────────────────────────────────────────────── │
│ F1-Help                                                        │
│                                              F10-Continue       │
└────────────────────────────────────────────────────────────────┘
```

and press Enter. To include the template called PEN-PNCL.TPL, highlight its name and press Enter. To add a second related template, PP-PRCNT.TPL, use the up- and down-arrow keys to highlight its name and press Enter. Figure 8.6 shows the Create/Edit Chartbook screen with both templates added to the PEN-PNCL chartbook.

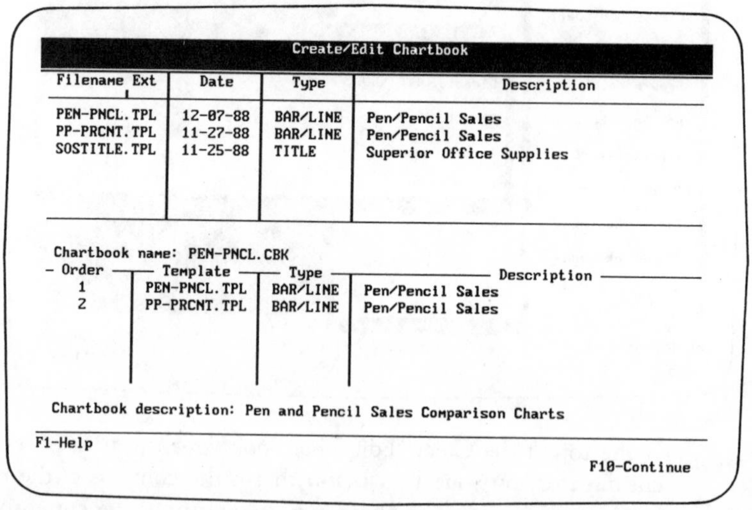

Fig. 8.6.

The PEN-PNCL chartbook.

```
┌──────────────────────────────────────────────────────────────┐
│                     Create/Edit Chartbook                      │
├─────────────┬──────────┬──────────┬───────────────────────────┤
│Filename Ext │   Date   │   Type   │        Description         │
├─────────────┼──────────┼──────────┼───────────────────────────┤
│PEN-PNCL.TPL │ 12-07-88 │ BAR/LINE │ Pen/Pencil Sales          │
│PP-PRCNT.TPL │ 11-27-88 │ BAR/LINE │ Pen/Pencil Sales          │
│SOSTITLE.TPL │ 11-25-88 │ TITLE    │ Superior Office Supplies  │
│             │          │          │                           │
├─────────────┴──────────┴──────────┴───────────────────────────┤
│ Chartbook name: PEN-PNCL.CBK                                   │
│ - Order ─────┬─ Template ──┬─ Type ──────── Description ────── │
│     1        │ PEN-PNCL.TPL │ BAR/LINE │ Pen/Pencil Sales      │
│     2        │ PP-PRCNT.TPL │ BAR/LINE │ Pen/Pencil Sales      │
│                                                                │
│ Chartbook description: Pen and Pencil Sales Comparison Charts  │
├────────────────────────────────────────────────────────────── │
│ F1-Help                                                        │
│                                              F10-Continue       │
└────────────────────────────────────────────────────────────────┘
```

Now press Tab several times and notice three different results in the bottom half of the screen. Your three possible courses of action (other than saving the chartbook and continuing on) are

❏ Edit the description of the chartbook

❏ Add another template to the chartbook's contents

❏ Change the order of the templates in the chartbook

When the cursor moves to the chartbook description, stop pressing the Tab key. Now you can change the chartbook's description by editing it or typing in a new description. Press Tab once and notice that you can now add another template to the chartbook by highlighting a template name with the up- and down-arrow keys and pressing Enter. Press Tab once again. Now one of the templates in the chartbook is highlighted. You can change the order of templates in the chartbook to suit your own personal preference by positioning the highlight on a template name and pressing Ctrl-up arrow or Ctrl-down arrow. The highlighted template will move up or down in the list. When you are satisfied with the new template order, press F10 (Continue) to save the chartbook on disk and return to the Chartbook menu.

To delete a template from a chartbook, press Tab so that any one of the template names on the chartbook contents list is highlighted, move the highlight to the template you want to delete by using the up and down arrows, and press Ctrl-Del. The chartbook no longer includes the template in its catalog, but the template remains available on disk.

Choosing a Template from a Chartbook

To open a chartbook so you can select from among its templates, follow these steps:

1. Select the Chartbook Menu option from the Harvard Graphics Main menu.

2. Choose Select Chartbook from the Chartbook menu.

3. Highlight the chartbook you want to select and press Enter to open the chartbook and return to the Chartbook menu.

If you choose From Chartbook after selecting Create New Chart from the Main menu, Harvard Graphics will let you choose from among the templates in the currently open chartbook.

If you have specified a default chartbook on the Default Settings screen, you need only select a chartbook to open if it is different from the default chartbook. Otherwise, the default chartbook is open at all times. The From Chartbook option on the Create New Chart menu will automatically show you the contents of the default chartbook.

Modifying an Existing Chartbook

You can modify the contents or order of templates in an existing chartbook easily. If the chartbook you want to modify is the default chartbook, simply choose Edit Chartbook from the Chartbook menu. If the chartbook you want to modify is not the default chartbook, you must first use Select Chartbook from the Chartbook menu and then select Edit Chartbook.

Macros

Of all the work computers do, repetitive chores are the tasks for which they are probably the most adored. Even though their human counterparts perform tasks more than once only begrudgingly, computers obey repetitive commands unquestioningly. Of course, you're no different from most humans. You dislike performing the same job over and over, too. So, if you need to perform a charting task regularly, such as creating a weekly pie chart for your office, why not put your computer on the case?

To automate repetitive procedures, you can use a feature common to most popular software programs called a *macro*. Harvard Graphics provides its own version of macros with a special add-on utility called MACRO. With macros, you can record all the keystrokes that go into performing a specific Harvard Graphics function. Later, when you need to carry out the exact same task, you can run the macro and watch as Harvard Graphics performs an instant replay of the same routine, step by step, just as you recorded it. Using a special feature of the Harvard Graphics MACRO utility, you can even have a macro depart from its script, pausing temporarily to allow whoever is sitting at the computer to enter revised data or make additional changes to the chart.

By using macros in combination with templates, you can speed your work even further. With a macro, you can load a preformatted chart, pull revised data from an external data file, save the file, and even print the chart with as little as a single keystroke combination. As the ultimate example of the power of macros, imagine a hypothetical 1-2-3 user employing a 1-2-3 macro to update automatically the figures in a 1-2-3 worksheet by importing sales results from a Point-of-Sale system. Combined with that, our user takes advantage of a Harvard Graphics macro that automatically retrieves a template including a data link to the Lotus worksheet and prints the chart. With just a few keystrokes, our hypothetical chart maker has fashioned a complete Harvard Graphics chart, with all the bells and whistles.

Recording a Macro

To record macros, you must run a separate utility first before actually starting Harvard Graphics. This utility, called MACRO, resides in the same DOS directory as Harvard Graphics. It was installed there automatically when you installed Harvard Graphics.

To run MACRO, follow these steps:

1. Change to the directory in which Harvard Graphics is installed.

2. Before typing *hg* to start Harvard Graphics, type *macro* and press Enter.

You will see an overlay indicating that the MACRO utility is now ready for action (see fig. 8.7).

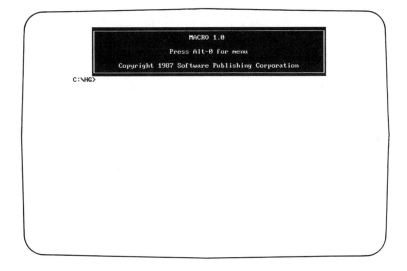

Fig. 8.7.

MACRO *loaded and ready.*

Once MACRO is loaded, do the following:

1. Start Harvard Graphics by typing *hg* and pressing Enter.

2. Press Alt-0 (zero) when the Harvard Graphics Main menu appears.

The main MACRO overlay appears (see fig. 8.8).

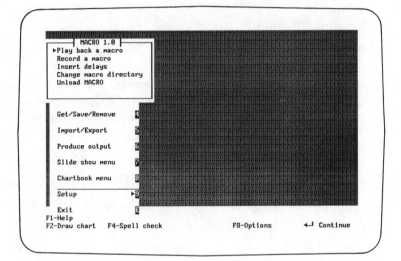

Fig. 8.8.

The main MACRO overlay.

Pressing Alt-0 any time you are viewing one of the Harvard Graphics menus summons the MACRO overlay, which offers a number of choices. To play back an existing prerecorded macro, choose Play back a macro. To create a new macro, choose Record a macro. The other choices on the MACRO menu provide additional commands covered later in this chapter.

To record a macro, choose Record a macro on the MACRO overlay, carry out the exact same steps you want to have the computer repeat later, and then press Alt-0 and choose Stop recording macro from the MACRO overlay. Stop recording macro is a new choice that appears after you start recording a macro. As an example, imagine that you want to create a macro to retrieve and print PEN-PCL1, the chart you created earlier in this chapter. To start such a macro, select Record a macro from the MACRO overlay (press R—the first letter of the option's name—or move the cursor key to highlight the choice and press Enter). A second, smaller overlay appears to request a standard DOS file name of up to eight characters for the macro you want to record. Notice that the cursor is positioned next to a prompt showing the current directory. If you type the macro name at the current cursor position, Harvard Graphics saves the macro in your main Harvard Graphics directory.

Storing macros in the same directory as the Harvard Graphics program or data files works fine, but you also may want to keep all macros together in a separate directory so that they do not clog your main Harvard Graphics directory with too many additional files. To make this step easy, type the following at the DOS prompt before starting the MACRO utility:

set macros = *path name*

(You may want to include this step in a batch file that starts Harvard Graphics.) The *path name* is the full name of a directory you have created especially for storing macros—C:\HG\MACROS, for example. Then, when Harvard Graphics prompts for a macro name, the program will automatically supply the correct directory location for saving the macro.

For now, type *pp-print* (for "print the pen-pencil chart") at the Macro name prompt and press Enter. Figure 8.9 shows how the Macro Name overlay looks before you type the macro name. Then the MACRO overlay disappears and Harvard Graphics looks ready for business as usual. Record these steps by simply running through them once (be sure to use numbers rather than the space bar at this stage to select from Harvard Graphics menus):

1. Press 4 to select Get/Save/Remove from the Main menu.

2. Press 1 to select Get Chart from the Get/Save/Remove menu.

3. Type *pen-pncl* and press Enter to select the chart named PEN-PNCL from the file list.

4. Press Esc to return to the Bar/Line Chart Data screen.

5. Press F10 (Continue) to return to the Main menu.

6. Press 6 to select Produce Output from the Main menu.

7. Press 1 to choose Printer from the Produce Output menu.

8. On the Print Chart Options overlay, choose the following:

   ```
   Quality: High
   Chart size: 1/4
   Paper size: Letter
   Printer: Printer 1
   Color: No
   Number of copies: 1
   ```

9. Press Enter and watch as your output device produces the chart.

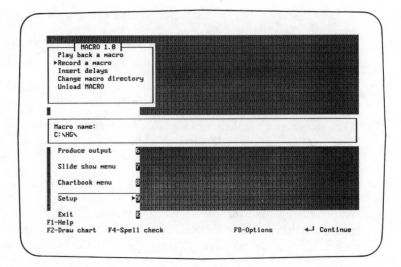

Fig. 8.9.

The Macro Name overlay.

When you successfully have run through all the steps you want to record, press Alt-0 to call up the MACRO overlay once again. Now select Stop recording macro from among the options by pressing S, the first letter of the command name, or by moving the highlight to the choice and pressing Enter. Figure 8.10 shows the MACRO overlay as it appears when you press Alt-0 while recording a macro. Notice three new choices on the overlay: Stop recording macro, Insert delays, and Type macro commands. The macro menus change as necessary to offer you the proper options for the current step in working with macros.

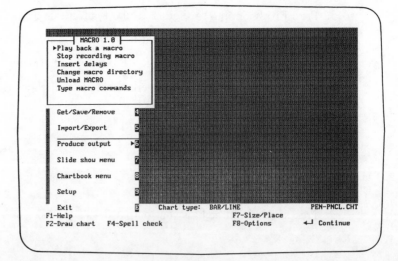

Fig. 8.10.

The MACRO overlay with three new choices.

Recording any macro always works the same way:

1. Summon the MACRO overlay by pressing Alt-0.

2. Select Record a macro from the overlay.

3. Execute the procedures to be recorded.

4. Summon the MACRO overlay again by pressing Alt-0.

5. Select Stop recording macro from the overlay.

Here is one suggestion for recording macros: Always start recording a macro from the Harvard Graphics Main menu and return to the Main menu before stopping the macro recording. That way, you can be sure that the macro will start properly at the Harvard Graphics Main menu.

By naming a macro with a single letter or number, you can instruct MACRO that you want to be able to play back the macro by pressing Alt and that key. To create a macro that will run when you press Alt-S, for example, name the macro S.

Playing Back a Macro

To play back a prerecorded macro, you must have the MACRO utility loaded in memory before you start Harvard Graphics. To load the MACRO utility, type *macro* before starting Harvard Graphics. You will see an overlay indicating that MACRO is ready for business. Once you start Harvard Graphics and its Main menu appears, press Alt-0 to summon the MACRO overlay and select Play back a macro from the overlay options. You will see a prompt for the name of the macro. Type in the correct macro name and press Enter. Harvard Graphics runs through its paces automatically. If you ever need to interrupt a macro as it executes, press Alt-End.

To play back the macro you recorded earlier in this chapter, press Alt-0 at the Harvard Graphics Main menu to call up the MACRO overlay. Select Play back a macro by pressing P, type the file name *pp-print* when Harvard Graphics requests the name of the macro to play back, and press Enter. Unless you have taken special care when recording the macro to have it return to the Main menu before proceeding, make a habit of starting macros from the Main menu. That way, you can be sure that they always will start at the same place you started when you recorded them.

Editing a Macro File

If you make a mistake while recording a macro, you can do one of two things: stop recording the macro and start over or edit the macro file to make your corrections. In fact, editing a macro file is the only way for you to change the operation of a macro after it is recorded without creating a new macro from scratch.

As you record a macro, you actually are writing abbreviations for each of the keystrokes you carry out into a standard DOS file. To change the macro, you can simply delete some abbreviations and add others with any word processor capable of reading and writing ASCII computer files (plain text file format). And, while you're at it, you can add comments to the macro so it is easier to understand or you can include messages the user will see as the macro runs.

To edit a macro file, call it up with any standard word processor and make additions and deletions just as you would to any text document. If you were to edit the macro file that prints the PEN-PNCL chart you recorded earlier, PP-PRINT.MAC, the macro would appear as shown in figure 8.11. Notice that special macro commands are surrounded by ‹CMD›. If you pressed the space bar to choose from among menu options as you recorded the macro, actual spaces appear in the macro file. Special keys other than the alphanumeric set are enclosed in greater-than and less-than symbols, and any alphanumeric characters you typed appear exactly as entered. Appendix H in the Harvard Graphics manual provides a list of actual keystroke combinations and their macro file representations. If you need to add keystrokes, you should know that the letters C, A, and S can replace Ctrl, Alt, and Shift in the macro keystroke representations. For example, you can type <CtrlM> as <CM>.

Notice that the PP-PRINT.MAC macro shown in figure 8.11 begins with two special commands (T0 and P40). These two commands, which start every macro, set an initial timing delay and polling delay. A *timing delay* slows down the execution rate of a macro by adding additional time between each macro step. A *polling delay* also slows macro execution to prevent Harvard Graphics from dropping keystrokes as it runs macros. The MACRO program automatically records both a default timing and polling delay in each macro file that you create. The next section of this chapter describes these two commands and a number of others that you will encounter and use in Harvard Graphics macros.

Harvard Graphics macros have a variety of special features that you can set by calling up the MACRO overlay again as you record a macro. These features, discussed later in this chapter, carry out such tasks as waiting until a specific time before continuing the macro. Each of these features adds a special command to

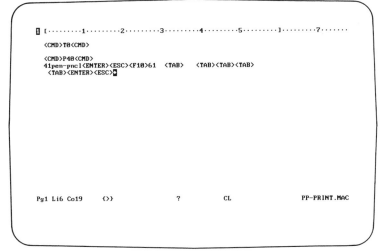

```
▌[·········1·········2·········3·········4·········5·········]·········7······
  <CMD>T8<CMD>

  <CMD>P48<CMD>
  41pen-pnc1<ENTER><ESC><F18>61  <TAB>   <TAB><TAB><TAB>
  <TAB><ENTER><ESC>▐
```

```
Pg1 Li6 Co19    <>}           ?        CL              PP-PRINT.MAC
```

Fig. 8.11.

The PP-PRINT macro as it appears in a word processor.

the macro file you are recording. When you examine such a file, therefore, you are likely to encounter these special entries:

<*comment>

You can embed comments in macro files as a reminder to you of how they work or to communicate that information to someone else examining the macro file later. Comments start with <* and end with>. Comments are completely transparent to the operation of the macro. They do not affect how it works at all. An example is <*This next section prints the file>.

<AUTO>

If you want to send a macro into a repeating loop that returns to the beginning of the current macro, place <AUTO> at the end of the macro to be repeated. The MACRO utility will repeat the current macro even if it is embedded within another macro. You can cancel a repeating macro by pressing Alt-End as the macro is playing back.

<CMD><*Message to be displayed on-screen><CMD>

When Harvard Graphics encounters the preceding command in a macro file, the program displays the message following the asterisk. This message can be up to 22 lines long. An example is <CMD><*Please enter a chart file name><CMD>.

<CMD>Pnnnn<CMD>

To introduce a polling delay in a macro, type a polling delay number from 1 to 9,999. Polling delays slow the execution of the macro so that it does not drop any of your keystrokes as it plays back (for technical reasons). If you find that your macros are skipping steps, try increasing the polling delay by 50 and try again. You may have to try increasing the delay several times until the macro works dependably. An example is <CMD>P1500<CMD>.

<CMD>F*macro file name*<CMD>

The preceding entry temporarily pauses the current macro and runs the second macro specified after the F by *macro file name*. The macro allows you to nest a second macro, such as a macro to print the current chart, within a macro. An example is <CMD>Fprntr2.mac<CMD>. You must be sure to include the extension of the macro file name (MAC).

<CMD>R*hh:mm:ss:nn*<CMD>

The preceding entry pauses the execution of a macro for the time specified in hours (hh), minutes (mm), seconds (ss), and milliseconds (nn). You must specify each time unit, even if it is zero, but you can drop leading zeros. To enter a minute-and-a-half pause in the execution of a macro, enter <CMD>R0:1:30:0<CMD>.

<CMD>T*nnn*<CMD>

The preceding entry enters a timing delay into a macro. The time unit *nnn* is a number from 0 to 999. A timing delay of 18 is equal to 1 second. So divide the timing delay by 18 to calculate the current delay between each macro step. An example is <CMD>T35<CMD> (35 divided by 18 is nearly 2 seconds).

<CMD>W*hh:mm*<CMD>

The preceding entry pauses the macro until a time specified in hours (hh) and minutes (mm). Be sure to use 24-hour time. As an example, to continue a macro that will print charts late in the evening when the printer is free, enter <CMD>W23:00<CMD>. Of course, if you forget to leave on the printer before leaving for the night, Harvard Graphics will stop and display the same message it always displays when the printer is not ready (Output device is not ready) until you arrive the next morning.

<STOP>

The preceding entry stops the execution of a macro and unloads MACRO from memory if you have exited Harvard Graphics and returned to DOS.

<VFLD><VFLD>

This entry inserts a variable field in a macro. Variable fields are described in detail later in this chapter.

Using Special MACRO Features

The MACRO program provides a host of special commands for fine-tuning the execution of macros. You can use these features by selecting from the MACRO program's menu, summoned with Alt-0, or by entering commands manually as you edit a macro in a word processor.

Nesting Macros

When programmers write computer programs, they make their work easier by writing and then joining separate modules, each designed to accomplish a specific task. You can emulate this method by writing individual macros to accomplish specific tasks, such as retrieving a chart from disk or printing the current chart. This approach also provides you with a set of macros you can use to automate specific Harvard Graphics steps as well as larger macros that carry out full procedures. Once each macro that accomplishes a specific step is recorded and saved on disk, you can call it from within another macro as you record the macro by using one of two approaches.

First, as you create a macro and reach the point where a second macro should run, press Alt-0 and select Play back a macro from the MACRO overlay. Enter the second macro name and press Enter. When the second macro finishes running, continue recording the first macro.

A second approach is to edit the macro file and enter the special command described earlier:

<CMD>F*macro file name*<CMD>

Figure 8.12 shows how several lines of a macro may look with a second macro embedded. Notice that the embedded macro is named C:\HG\PP-PRINT.MAC.

When you run a second macro within a macro, you need to employ the same care as when you record a single macro alone. You should play back every macro from the same place you started recording it. To ensure that you do, return to the Main menu during a macro before calling up a second macro. In fact, because you are always returning to the Main menu before starting a new macro, you can think of nesting macros as stringing a chain of macros together.

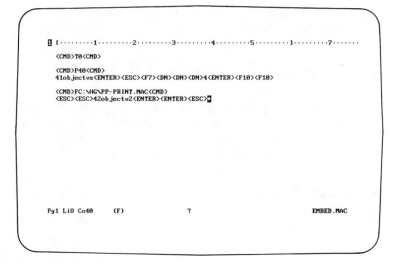

Fig. 8.12.

*The PP-PRINT
macro embedded
within another
macro.*

Pausing a Chart Display

Whenever a macro includes the command to preview a chart with the F2-Draw chart selection, the macro pauses for 30 seconds while the chart is displayed. To cut short this pause as you record the macro, press the Ctrl key and the right Shift key at the same time (Ctrl-Right Shift).

You also can set a specific delay by pressing Alt-0 just before pressing F2 (Draw Chart) as you record a macro. Select Insert delays from the MACRO overlay and Real-time delay from the Delays overlay that appears (see fig. 8.13). Type the number of seconds for the delay and press Enter. Then press Esc twice to return to recording the macro.

You also can change a playback delay by editing the macro file and entering a <CMD>R*hh:mm:ss:nn*<CMD> command just before F2 in the macro file.

Including Variable Fields

By including a *variable field*, you can let whoever is playing back the macro supply certain information as the macro proceeds. If your macro prints a chart, for example, you can let the user enter the chart name to print. The macro will pause for your input during playback. Another good use for variable fields is to request that the user enter a new name for a saved chart so the new chart's information does not overwrite the original.

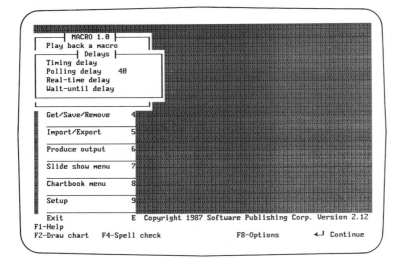

Fig. 8.13.

The Delays overlay.

To include a variable field in a macro, press Ctrl-[hyphen] as you record the macro. Nothing will appear any different, but the macro recording will pause and allow you to enter anything you want without recording it. To continue recording actual macro commands, press Alt-0.

When the macro with the variable field plays back, it stops at the variable field for your input, telling you to press F10 to begin typing whatever you want. Figure 8.14 shows this prompt on-screen during macro playback. When you are finished, press Alt-0 to continue playing back the macro.

Starting a Macro at a Specific Time

To continue a macro's execution at a specific hour, you can enter a *wait-until delay*. As an example of the value of wait-until delays, suppose that the data in your 1-2-3 spreadsheet is automatically updated with information from the company's mainframe at 2 a.m. each morning. You can have Harvard Graphics run a macro at 3 a.m. to create and print a new chart that will be ready for your arrival later that morning based on the new data.

To enter a wait-until delay at the beginning of a macro, press Alt-0 after starting a macro recording, choose Insert delays from the MACRO overlay, and choose Wait-until delay from the Delays overlay. Specify the time for the macro to continue in hours and minutes using 24-hour time. To enter 1:15 p.m., for example, type *13:15*. After you enter the delay, press Esc twice to continue recording the macro that will execute at the specified time.

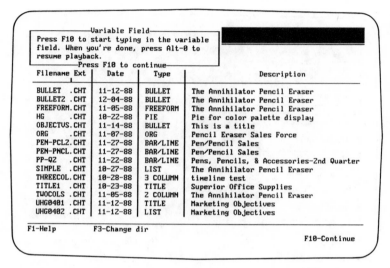

Fig. 8.14.

A variable field during macro playback.

You also can manually enter a wait-until delay in a macro by using the <CMD>W*hh:mm*<CMD> command described earlier in this chapter.

Including On-Screen Messages to Users

As a macro proceeds, you may want to have it display messages to the user about its progress or to request the user's input at a variable field. To include an on-screen message to a user, press Ctrl-F10 at the point during recording a macro that you want to include a message. Type a message of up to 78 characters on the overlay that appears (see fig. 8.15) and press Enter to continue recording the macro.

To include a longer message of up to 22 lines, you must use the <CMD><*Message to appear on-screen*><CMD> command, described earlier in this chapter, when you edit the macro file in your word processor.

Debugging Macros

On the odd chance that your macro does not perform as you expected or you need to examine someone else's macro to determine what steps it carries out, you can have a macro advance only one step at a time so you can examine it carefully. To play back a macro one keystroke at a time, press Ctrl-Alt to pause a macro you are playing back as it begins and change Single-step playback on the Pause menu from No to Yes. Then press Esc to return to playing back the macro and press any key to advance the macro one step.

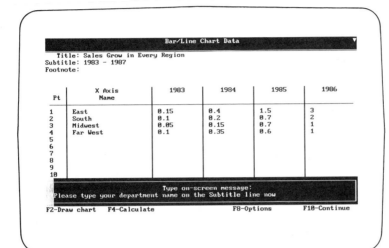

Fig. 8.15.

Entering an on-screen message in your macro.

Unloading MACRO from Memory

If you loaded MACRO before starting Harvard Graphics, MACRO will remain in your computer's memory even after you exit Harvard Graphics normally. To remove MACRO from memory to free that memory for the use of other programs, exit Harvard Graphics and then press Alt-0 at the DOS prompt and select Unload MACRO from the MACRO overlay. Press Enter to confirm your choice or any other key to leave MACRO in memory.

Examining Useful Macros

The macros you decide to create will depend on the nature of the work that you do. As you work, try to remember that any procedure you find yourself doing repetitively deserves a macro. In the sections that follow, you will examine three useful suggestions for taking advantage of the power of macros.

A Macro To Print a Draft of the Current Chart

As you work, you may want to see how your chart is shaping up so far on paper. Normally, you would leave your work, return to the Harvard Graphics Main menu, and print a 1/4-page copy of the chart in draft quality. The following macro, called DRAFT, automatically prints a 1/4-page draft of the current chart for you.

To create the macro, follow these steps:

1. Load MACRO and then start Harvard Graphics.

2. Make sure that you are at the Harvard Graphics Main menu.

3. Press Alt-0 to bring up the MACRO overlay.

4. Press R to select Record a macro.

5. For a macro file name, enter *draft*.

6. Press Esc seven or eight times so Harvard Graphics will be sure to return to the Main menu from wherever you are in the program.

7. Press 6 to select Produce Output from the Main menu.

8. Press 1 to select Printer from the Produce Output menu.

9. Press D when the Print Chart Options overlay appears.

10. Press Tab once and press the space bar three times to set Chart size to 1/4.

11. Press Tab three times to move the cursor past Paper size and Printer to the Color option.

12. Press N to set Color to the No option.

13. Press Tab to move to Number of copies and press Enter to print one copy of the chart. (Make sure that your printer is connected when you send the chart to the printer; otherwise, the machine will hang up when you are in the middle of recording a macro.)

14. After the chart finishes printing, press Alt-0 to bring up the MACRO overlay again.

15. Press S to select Stop recording macro.

To test the macro, try retrieving any of the charts you have on disk and viewing its data screen or bringing it into Draw/Annotate mode. Press Alt-0 and then press P to select Play back a macro. When MACRO prompts you for a macro name, type *draft* and press Enter. The current chart should be printed as a draft-quality, 1/4-page chart.

Figure 8.16 shows how the DRAFT macro looks when displayed in a word processor. Notice that the actual numbers you typed at the Harvard Graphics menus while you were recording the macro appear in the file. A different way to select from among Harvard Graphics menu choices is to use the space bar, but doing so places enigmatic spaces in the macro file instead of more easily understood numbers. Perhaps more importantly, if you select from among Harvard Graphics menus by using numbers when you record a macro, you can be sure that the macro will play back the same selections again later, even if the macro is started with the cursor highlighting a different command on the menu.

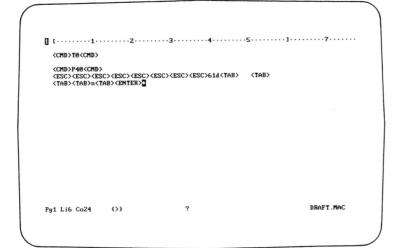

Fig. 8.16.

The DRAFT macro file in a word processor.

A Macro To Save Your Work in Progress

Another useful macro is one that will save your work in progress to a temporary file on the disk with a single keystroke combination: Alt-S (for Save). Regardless of the name or type of the current chart, this macro will save it to a temporary file named TEMP. By naming the macro S when asked for a macro file name, you can specify that you want to begin the macro by pressing Alt-S in the future.

Before you create this macro, you will need to call up any chart on the disk and save it as TEMP. Because you will be saving every chart as TEMP, you always will see a warning message reminding you that TEMP already exists on disk. By saving a file as TEMP before you create the macro, you can cause this circumstance to occur the first time as you create the macro so you record the proper steps for dealing with it.

To record the temporary save macro, follow these steps:

1. Load MACRO before starting Harvard Graphics.

2. Retrieve any chart in Harvard Graphics and save it as TEMP.

3. Return to the Harvard Graphics Main menu and press Alt-0 to summon the MACRO overlay.

4. Press R to select Record a macro.

5. Name the macro S and press Enter.

6. Press Esc seven or eight times to be sure that Harvard Graphics will return to the Main menu from wherever you are in the program when you start the macro.

7. Press 4 to select Get/Save/Remove from the Main menu.

8. Press 2 to select Save Chart from the Get/Save/Remove menu.

9. Press Del seven or eight times so that any file name that is already present at the Chart name prompt will be deleted.

10. Type *temp* and press Enter, leave the description as is, and press Enter twice to save the chart.

11. Press Esc to return to the Main menu. Press Alt-0 to bring up the MACRO overlay.

12. Press S to select Stop recording macro.

Figure 8.17 shows the resulting macro file called S.MAC.

Fig. 8.17.

The S.MAC macro file.

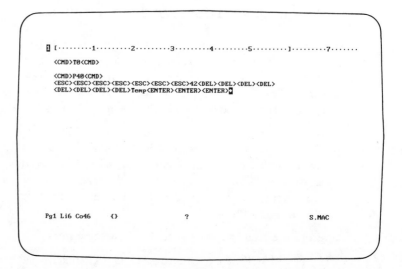

Test the macro by retrieving any file and viewing its data screen or bringing it into Draw/Annotate mode. Press Alt-S and watch as the file is automatically saved on disk as TEMP. Now, if you need to leave your desk suddenly, you can press Alt-S quickly to save your work temporarily.

A Macro To Print a User-Specified Chart

So that a macro will print a specific chart determined by whoever is operating the program, the macro must give the user the chance to enter the chart name and the macro should contain a message to the user with instructions about how to proceed. To accomplish these objectives, you should use a variable field and an on-screen message. This macro will print using the options Chart size: 1/2 and Quality: High. You may want to replace these two print settings for others, though, or create a set of macros to print at varying qualities and sizes.

To record the macro to print a user-specified chart, follow these steps:

1. Load MACRO before starting Harvard Graphics.

2. At the Harvard Graphics Main menu, press Alt-0 to call up the MACRO overlay.

3. Press R to select Record a macro.

4. Type *printhq* (*hq* for "high quality") as the macro file name and press Enter.

5. At the Main menu, press 4 to select Get/Save/Remove.

6. Press 1 to select Get Chart from the Get/Save/Remove menu.

7. Press Ctrl-F10 after the Select Chart menu appears so that you can enter a message to the user.

8. Type *Type the name of a chart in the following variable field* in the overlay that appears and press Enter.

9. Press Ctrl-[hyphen] to insert a variable field.

10. Type the file name *pen-pcl1* to be sure that the macro works but do not press Enter. The macro will not record PEN-PCL1 as the specific file name but will stop for user input at this point.

11. Press Alt-0 to continue recording the macro.

12. Press Enter, press Esc, and then press F10 to return to the Main menu.

13. Press 6 to select Produce Output from the Main menu.

14. Press 1 to select Printer from the Produce Output menu.

15. Press H to select High at the Quality prompt on the Print Chart Options overlay.

16. Press Tab once to move to Chart size and press the space bar once to select 1/2.

17. Press Tab several times to move the cursor past Paper size and Printer to the Color option.

18. Press N to set Color to the No option.

19. Press Tab once and press Enter to set Number of copies to 1 and print the chart.

20. When the printing is complete, press Alt-0 to call up the MACRO overlay again.

21. Press S to select Stop recording macro.

To test this macro, start Harvard Graphics with the MACRO program already loaded, press Alt-0, and choose P for Play back a macro from the MACRO overlay. Supply *printhq* as the name. Notice that a window appears during the macro's execution to remind the user how to fill out the variable field that follows.

Figure 8.18 shows how the PRINTHQ macro file appears in a word processor. Notice the embedded message to the user and the two <VFLD> references that cause a variable field.

Using Macros with Chartbook Templates

The ultimate in automated chart building is to set up a one-keystroke macro that first loads a template that automatically pulls its data from an external data file and then prints the resulting chart. For example, a hypothetical macro named D lets you press Alt-D to load a template with a data link to a 1-2-3 worksheet, pause because of a variable field to allow you to make any minor adjustments to the chart you want, and then pause again to let you modify the print settings if desired before printing the chart.

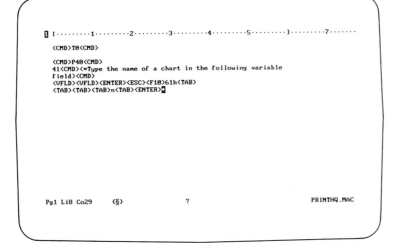

Fig. 8.18.

The PRINTHQ macro file.

Chapter Summary

This chapter described how to use two of the most powerful tools of Harvard Graphics: templates and macros. With templates and macros, you can automate the task of creating graphs and make repetitive chores easy. In the next chapter, you will learn how to produce output and how to set up slide shows and screen-shows, methods for printing batches of charts and making dazzling animated presentations.

9

Producing Stellar Output

Harvard Graphics, part of the newest generation of easy-to-use software, makes getting output one of the smoothest steps in the process of creating graphics. In this chapter, you learn about how Harvard Graphics can send charts to a variety of output devices, accommodating just about any printer, plotter, or slide maker you have on hand. You also learn about several other forms of output, some of which have little to do with traditional printed pages or slides. A Harvard Graphics output feature called a screenshow reproduces charts on-screen rather than on paper or film. Slide shows, used to create screenshows, can display slides, create practice cards, and print a succession of charts automatically.

Printing, Plotting, and Making Slides

Before graphics software surged into popularity, getting printouts from word processors, spreadsheets, and other common business packages was a snap one moment and a struggle the next. Printing a page was easy, usually just a matter of choosing Print from the menu. But finding a compatible software-printer combination could be maddening unless you stuck with one of just a few market leaders.

To compound the difficulty, a wide array of printers, plotters, and slide makers has appeared on the market as a result of the popularity of graphics software. Each new piece of hardware promises to reproduce faithfully graphs and charts on paper, transparencies, or film, and in black and white or color.

Printing Versus Plotting

Harvard Graphics provides full support for a broad range of dot-matrix, ink-jet, and laser printers. Unlike Harvard Graphics, some computer programs demand that you have one of the most popular printers, such as an Epson dot-matrix printer or a Hewlett-Packard LaserJet™, or they expect you to use a printer that emulates one of these models. Harvard Graphics provides a host of printer drivers, special software that serves as an interpreter between Harvard Graphics and your printer. By using a printer driver written expressly for a certain model printer, Harvard Graphics can send the printer the proper commands to control its capabilities.

Harvard Graphics also supports a variety of plotters, devices that draw graphs on paper using pens. Plotters provide sharp, crisp drawings that can be very large. Plotters used in architectural and engineering firms routinely produce pages that are 36 inches by 48 inches and larger.

The advantage to using a plotter is its precision and capacity to draw graphs that look carefully hand-drawn. Formerly, plotters provided perhaps the only way to get charts with multiple colors. But new ink-jet and thermal printers can create graphs in unlimited colors, as opposed to a set number of colors determined by the pens used in a plotter.

A clear disadvantage to using a plotter with Harvard Graphics is the inability of plotters to produce three-dimensional images. Plotters are incapable of drawing objects that overlap, the prime means of achieving a three-dimensional effect in a chart.

If you use a printer with Harvard Graphics, you almost certainly are limited to a standard page size, but you enjoy relatively fast output speed. When you use a color printer, you can produce full-color charts. Laser printers offer high-resolution black-and-white charts that look professional.

Printing Sideways: Landscape Printing

Printing sideways used to be easy—nothing more than putting the paper in sideways. However, with some new printers, all laser printers, and plotters, you can feed paper only one way. To print sideways on a page, you must tell Harvard Graphics to rotate a graph 90 degrees. Sideways printing is called printing in *landscape orientation*. Standard printing, with the paper vertical, is called printing in *portrait orientation*. With Harvard Graphics, you can mix landscape orientation with a portrait chart only by printing in a slide show at half size.

By choosing landscape as the default for a chart, you inform Harvard Graphics that the paper or film area available is horizontal rather than vertical. Harvard Graphics displays a horizontal page on-screen and creates a chart to fill a space wider than it is long.

Landscape charts are best for slides and charts that show data measured over extended time periods. They also are best for organization charts, two- and three-column charts, and bar/line charts.

You can set landscape orientation as the default for all future charts, overriding the default only when necessary by setting a particular chart's orientation to portrait.

To set landscape as the default orientation, follow these steps:

1. Select Setup from the Harvard Graphics Main menu.

2. Choose Defaults on the Setup menu.

3. Use the Tab key to move the cursor to the Orientation field. Portrait or Landscape is already chosen.

4. Press the space bar to change the current selection to Landscape, if necessary.

5. Press F10 (Continue) to return to the Setup menu.

6. Press Esc to return to the Main menu.

All future charts are in landscape orientation unless you override landscape by following this procedure before or while creating a chart:

1. Press F8 (Options) at the Main menu. The cursor is positioned next to the Orientation prompt on the Current Chart Options overlay.

2. Use the space bar to select Portrait.

3. Press Enter three times to pass the Border and Font fields and return to the Main menu.

Sending a Chart to an Output Device

You can send a chart you have just completed to a printer, plotter, or slide maker, or you can retrieve a chart from disk and then send it to an output device. In either case, the chart you print must be the current chart. The current chart is the one whose file name appears near the bottom right side of the Main menu screen. The current chart is the chart you are presently working on or the chart you have just retrieved from disk with Get Chart. When you save a chart on disk, it remains the current chart until you exit Harvard Graphics, start a new chart, or retrieve a different chart from disk.

To send the current chart to an output device, follow these steps:

1. Select Produce Output from the Main menu.

2. Choose Printer, Plotter, or Film Recorder (slide maker) from the Produce Output menu depending on the output device you are using. The other options on this menu are discussed later in this chapter.

3. Complete the Print Chart Options, Plot Chart Options, or Record Chart Option overlay that appears.

Figure 9.1 shows the Produce Output menu.

Fig. 9.1.

The Produce Output menu.

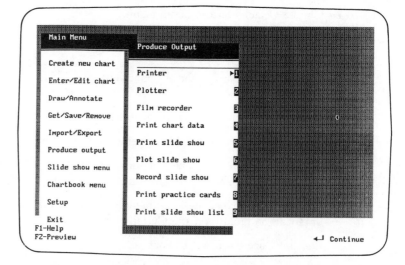

If your output device is a printer, you see the Print Chart Options overlay (see fig. 9.2) when you select Printer from the Produce Output menu. The Print Chart Options overlay presents several options, discussed next.

Quality is a measure of the resolution and clarity of your chart printing. You can choose from among Draft, Standard, or High quality output. The higher the quality, the sharper a graph looks. But the higher the quality, the longer charts take to print. Figures 9.3, 9.4, and 9.5 show the same chart printed in draft, standard, and high quality. The difference in appearance you see with your charts depends on the type of printer you use.

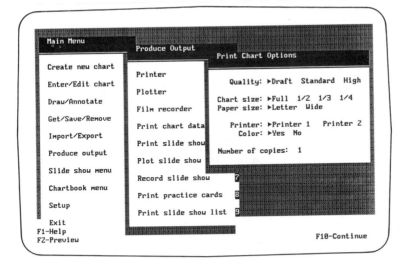

Fig. 9.2.

The Print Chart Options overlay.

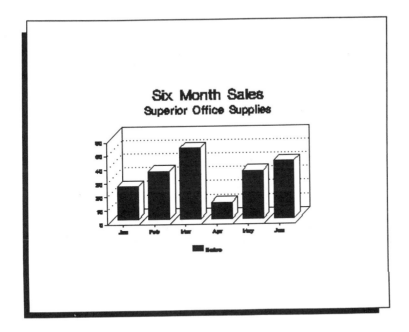

Fig. 9.3.

Draft quality.

Fig. 9.4.

Standard quality.

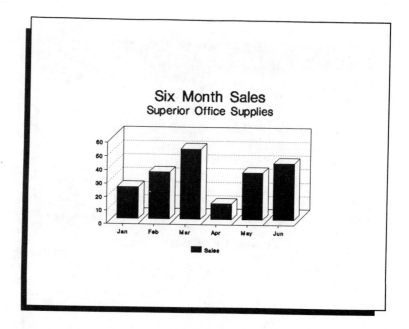

Fig. 9.5.

High quality.

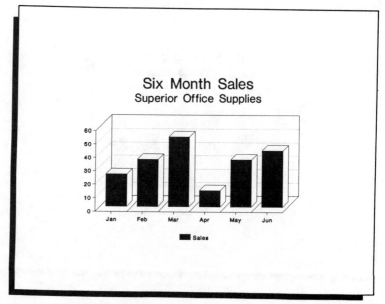

Generally, you should print draft-quality charts to check a chart's appearance quickly. You should print standard-quality charts to show others your charts, perhaps for their approval. And, finally, you should take the time to print high-quality charts only when you are certain your charts are ready for presentation.

If you have a laser printer with less than 1.5 megabytes of memory (such as the Hewlett-Packard LaserJet or LaserJet Series II without a memory expansion card), you may not be able to print a full page of high-quality graphics when the chart is complex, like a 3-D bar chart. Unless you supplement the memory in your printer, you can get around this problem by printing a smaller chart size (discussed next) or using standard resolution rather than high-quality resolution.

You can print charts in one of four sizes. To fill a page with a chart, choose Chart size: Full. The other options, 1/2, 1/3, and 1/4, print charts at the left of the page or, in the case of 1/4, at the top left of the page.

You can choose between two paper sizes, Letter or Wide. Letter size is 8 1/2 inches by 11 inches and wide is 11 inches by 14 inches.

When you set Harvard Graphics defaults, you can set up two printers, Printer 1 and Printer 2. By selecting one of the printers in the Print Chart Options overlay, you tell the program which of the two printers you have connected.

Set Color to Yes if you have a color printer. Set Color to No if you have a color printer but you want to print the current chart in black and white. When you print a chart with Color set to No, Harvard Graphics uses patterns to fill colored series bars, pie slices, or areas in a graph chart. If your printer is black and white only, Harvard Graphics ignores the color setting.

For the Number of copies option, the standard default is 1. To print more than one copy, your printer or plotter must have the capacity to feed sheets of paper automatically or use continuous form paper. Unlike most other graphics packages, Harvard Graphics constructs a chart only once before sending multiple copies to a printer. Other packages use valuable time to reconstruct the chart for each copy.

If your output device is a plotter, you see the Plot Chart Options overlay (see fig. 9.6) when you select Plotter from the Produce Output menu. The Plot Chart Options overlay options are discussed next.

Much like the Quality setting when you print, the three possible Quality settings when you plot cause the plotter to operate at one of three levels, from quick-and-dirty to slower, final presentation form. Unlike printer resolution,

Fig. 9.6.

The Plot Chart Options overlay.

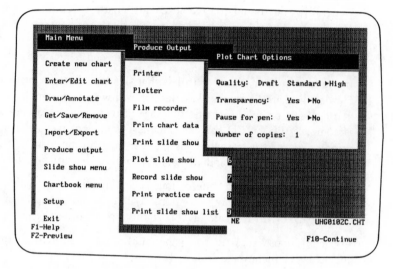

though, plotting resolution remains constant. What differs is the level of detail, the attention to your color and text attribute selections, and the fonts used.

Use table 9.1 to anticipate the results of the Quality setting when plotting.

Table 9.1
Quality Settings

	Draft Quality	*Standard Quality*	*High Quality*
Fonts:	Built-in plotter fonts only	Built-in plotter fonts proportionally spaced	Harvard Graphics fonts
Fill	Bars and pie slices filled with patterns	Bars and pie slices filled in	Characters, bars, and pie slices filled in
Color	Line of text color determined by color of first character	Each character can be colored individually	Each character can be colored
Text Attributes	Do not appear	Do not appear	All appear

When you use transparency paper, Harvard Graphics plots more slowly and separates the slices of a pie to prevent colors from running together. Check your plotter's instructions regarding special considerations when using transparencies rather than paper.

Harvard Graphics matches the pen it uses for a bar or pie slice to the color number you chose when you created the chart. For example, Harvard Graphics draws a color 4 bar with pen 4.

When your plotter accommodates fewer pens than your chart has colors, you can set Pause for pen to Yes. If the color your chart uses is not one of the current pens in the plotter, Harvard Graphics pauses and enables you to replace the pen in the pen 2 holder with another color. To continue plotting with the new pen, press Enter. If you set Pause for pen to No, Harvard Graphics uses the pens available in your plotter to draw the chart without pausing.

As with printing, you can plot more than one copy of a chart. Harvard Graphics pauses between each copy so that you can insert another page, except when the plotter supports continuous feed paper or has a paper bin.

If your output device is a film recorder, you see the Record Chart Option overlay (see fig. 9.7) when you select Film Recorder from the Produce Output menu. The only setting on the Record Chart Option overlay is Number of copies. Harvard Graphics automatically advances the film between each of the copies (exposures) you request. When you use a Polaroid Palette or PalettePlus with 669 film, Harvard Graphics prompts you to remove the film after each exposure. When you are ready to record the next chart, press Enter.

Printing Chart Data

Harvard Graphics can print a table of only a chart's data when the current chart is a graph chart rather than a text chart, whether the data is displayed in the chart or not. To print a chart's data, select Print Chart Data from the Produce Output menu. In the Chart Data Option overlay that appears, Harvard Graphics enables you to send the output to Printer 1 or Printer 2.

Printing a Series of Charts

Normally, you can print, plot, or record only one chart at a time. To send a series of charts to an output device, you should create a slide show that incorporates the charts and then choose Print Slide Show, Plot Slide Show, or Record Slide Show at the Produce Output menu. Complete information about creating slide shows is provided later in this chapter.

Fig. 9.7.

The Record Chart Option overlay.

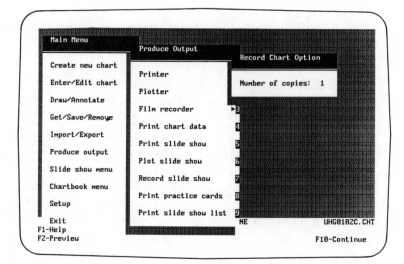

When you send a series of charts to an output device using this method, the Print Slide Show Options overlay appears. This overlay is much like the Print Chart Options, Plot Chart Options, or Record Chart Option overlay. The two following options on this overlay are new, however:

From slide/To slide — To print only part of the slide show of charts you have created, enter the beginning slide show chart number and the ending slide show chart number at these two prompts. To check the numbers of slides in a slide show, you can print a slide show list by choosing Print Slide Show List from the Produce Output menu.

Collate — By setting Collate to Yes when you have chosen to print more than one copy, you can produce the full set of charts and then a second full set of charts. Setting Collate to No produces more than one copy of each chart in succession. By not collating charts, producing multiple copies of slide show charts is much faster.

Multiple Charts

Harvard Graphics enables you to reproduce more than one chart on a page or screen. By displaying up to six charts side by side in a multiple chart, you can facilitate comparisons among charts or, perhaps, pair a text chart describing information with a graph chart showing it. Figure 9.8 shows a typical multiple chart.

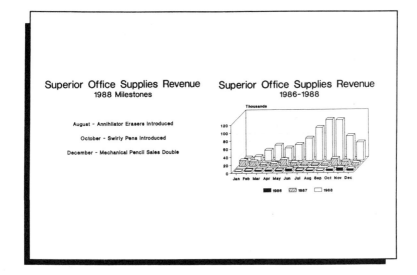

Fig. 9.8.

A typical multiple chart.

A multiple chart depends on the charts you have already created and saved on disk. You do not create a new text or graphic chart as you work with a multiple chart. Instead, you combine preexisting charts into a multiple chart. After you have created a multiple chart, though, you can bring it into Draw/Annotate mode and give it a life of its own by adding annotations and symbols. After you decide which charts to display together, you can arrange up to four charts by selecting from among three preset layouts, or you can create a custom layout according to your needs and arrange up to six charts.

After you complete a multiple chart, you can save or print the chart as a standard Harvard Graphics chart. You can even bring a multiple chart into Draw/Annotate to add annotations, which point out the differences among the charts on a page or screen.

Each time you recall a multiple chart from disk, the multiple chart gathers its component charts from disk, as well. If you change one of the individual charts that constitute a multiple chart, the multiple chart also changes.

Making a Multiple Chart

Making a multiple chart requires only a few simple steps. First, you must select the charts you want to display together. Then, when you know how many charts you need to arrange, you may accept a standard layout or custom-design your own. Figure 9.9. shows the three Harvard Graphics standard layouts. If you have chosen a standard arrangement, the charts appear in their allotted positions. If you have chosen custom-design, you must position the charts manually.

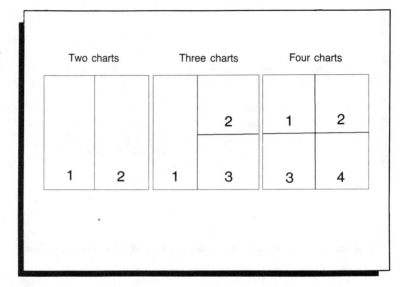

Fig. 9.9.

The three standard multiple chart layouts.

To try creating a standard multiple chart, combine three of the charts you created in earlier chapters, OBJECTVS, SOSREVS, and SOSEXPEN, onto a single page. Follow these steps:

1. Select Create New Chart from the Main menu.

2. Select Multiple Charts from the Create New Chart menu.

3. Select Three from the Multiple Charts Styles menu that appears.

The Edit Multiple Chart screen appears, as shown in figure 9.10.

The Edit Multiple Chart screen shows a list of the charts in your data directory and, below that, a list of the charts in the current multiple chart. At the bottom

```
                        Edit Multiple Chart
 ┌─────────────────────────────────────────────────────────────────────┐
  Filename Ext    Date      Type              Description
 ─────────────────────────────────────────────────────────────────────
  HG      .CHT  01-06-89  PIE       Pie for color palette display
  BULLET  .CHT  01-09-89  BULLET    Bullet chart without colors
  BULLET2 .CHT  01-09-89  BULLET    Tiered bullet chart
  FREEFORM.CHT  01-09-89  FREEFORM  The Annihilator Pencil Eraser
  OBJECTUS.CHT  01-16-89  BULLET    Marketing Objectives
  ORG     .CHT  01-09-89  ORG       Pencil Eraser Sales Force
  PEN-PCL2.CHT  11-27-88  CHART
  PEN-PNCL.CHT  11-27-88  CHART
 ─────────────────────────────────────────────────────────────────────

  ─ Order ──┬── Chart ──┬── Type ──┬────── Description ──────
      1     │ HG  .CHT  │          │
      2     │           │          │
      3     │           │          │

          ┌──────┐ 2
       1  │  ├───┤
          └──────┘ 3

 F1-Help          F3-Change dir
 F2-Draw chart                               F10-Continue
```

Fig. 9.10.

The Edit Multiple Chart screen.

left of the screen is a small diagram representing the arrangement of the charts. If you choose a custom layout, the word custom appears.

All the charts included in a multiple chart must come from the same directory on your hard disk. Harvard Graphics keeps track of the names of the charts in a multiple chart but not the directory from which they come.

Use the Edit Multiple Chart screen to select the three charts for the multiple chart by following these steps:

1. Use the up or down arrows or the PgUp or PgDn keys to position the highlight on the chart name OBJECTVS in the list at the top of the screen and press Enter, or type the file name *objectvs*, press Enter, and press Tab to continue highlighting chart names.

2. Use the same method to pick the remaining two charts for the multiple chart (SOSREVS and SOSEXPEN). Figure 9.11 shows the completed Edit Multiple Chart screen.

3. Press F10 (Continue) to return to the Main menu.

4. Save the multiple charts just as you would save any other chart. Harvard Graphics automatically gives the multiple chart a standard CHT file name extension. Press Esc to return to the Main menu.

5. Press F2 (Draw Chart) to see the multiple chart, as shown in figure 9.12.

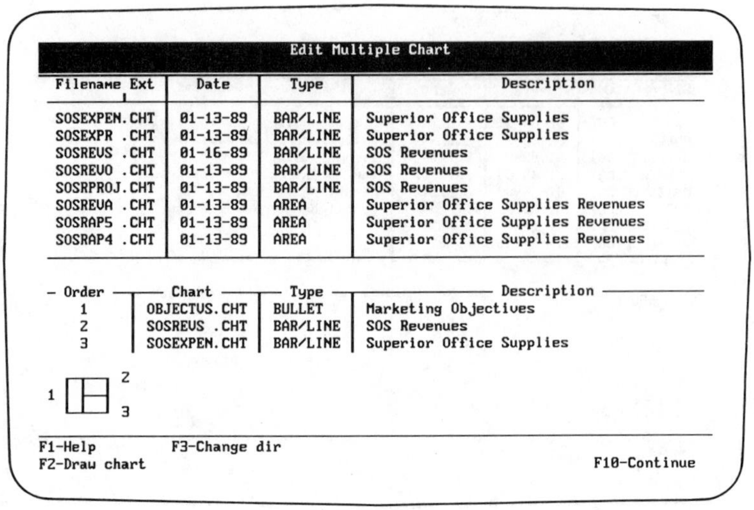

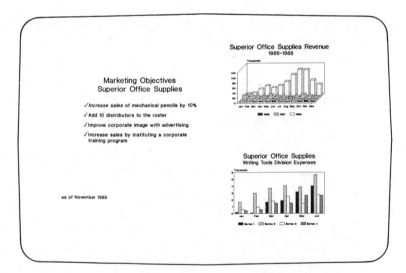

Edit Multiple Chart
Filename Ext | Date | Type | Description
SOSEXPEN.CHT 01-13-89 BAR/LINE Superior Office Supplies
SOSEXPR .CHT 01-13-89 BAR/LINE Superior Office Supplies
SOSREVS .CHT 01-16-89 BAR/LINE SOS Revenues
SOSREVO .CHT 01-13-89 BAR/LINE SOS Revenues
SOSRPROJ.CHT 01-13-89 BAR/LINE SOS Revenues
SOSREVA .CHT 01-13-89 AREA Superior Office Supplies Revenues
SOSRAP5 .CHT 01-13-89 AREA Superior Office Supplies Revenues
SOSRAP4 .CHT 01-13-89 AREA Superior Office Supplies Revenues
Order Chart Type Description
1 OBJECTVS.CHT BULLET Marketing Objectives
2 SOSREVS .CHT BAR/LINE SOS Revenues
3 SOSEXPEN.CHT BAR/LINE Superior Office Supplies
1 2 3
F1-Help F3-Change dir
F2-Draw chart
F10-Continue

Fig. 9.11.

The completed Edit Multiple Chart screen.

Marketing Objectives
Superior Office Supplies
✓Increase sales of mechanical pencils by 10%
✓Add 10 distributors to the roster
✓Improve corporate image with advertising
✓Increase sales by instituting a corporate training program
as of November 1989
Superior Office Supplies Revenue
1986-1988
Superior Office Supplies
Writing Tools Division Expenses

Fig. 9.12.

Preview of the completed multiple chart.

Creating a custom chart layout is slightly more involved. To create a custom chart arrangement with the same three charts, follow these steps:

1. Select Create New Chart from the Main menu.
2. Select Multiple Charts from the Create New Chart menu.
3. Select Custom from the Multiple Charts Styles menu.

If you are trying this procedure immediately after creating the preceding multiple chart, a Change Chart Type overlay appears with the query Keep current data: Yes No. To use the same three charts in the same order, press Enter to accept Yes as the response. To create a multiple chart composed of different charts, highlight No and press Enter. If you are beginning a new custom multiple chart from scratch, you must select the three charts to include in the custom chart by following the same procedure described previously.

When all three charts for the custom multiple chart are listed on the Edit Multiple Chart screen, press F2 (Draw Chart) to preview the multiple chart. Figure 9.13. shows how the multiple chart preview appears. Notice that the three charts are displayed left to right across the bottom of the screen. Above the three charts is space for an additional three charts. Remember that a custom multiple chart can hold up to six charts.

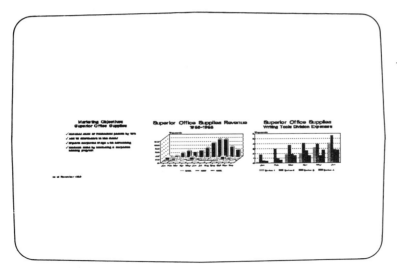

Fig. 9.13.

The custom multiple chart as previewed.

To vary the size and positioning of the charts in the custom multiple chart, use the F7-Size/Place feature at the Edit Multiple Chart screen. To try F7-Size/Place, follow these steps:

1. Press Esc to return to the Multiple Chart Edit screen.

2. Press F7 (Size/Place) to view the Custom Layout screen, as shown in figure 9.14.

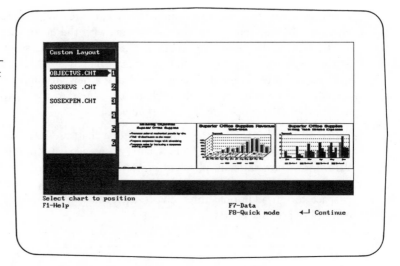

Fig. 9.14.

The Custom Layout screen.

The panel on the left lists the charts included in the multiple chart. The area to the right, which resembles the Draw/Annotate drawing board, displays the current size and positioning of the charts. You may find working in Quick mode faster than in Final mode. Press F8 (Quick Mode) to see its effect. Quick mode displays only the frame holding the chart and the chart's name. It operates much faster because it does not need to draw each chart on-screen. Figure 9.15 shows how the same custom layout shown in figure 9.14 is displayed in Quick mode.

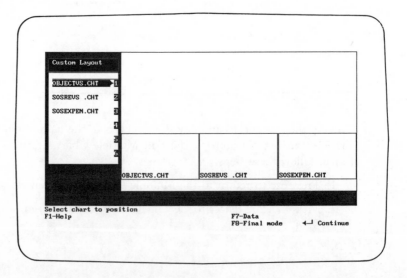

Fig. 9.15.

Custom layout displayed in Quick mode.

To vary the size and positioning of a chart, pick the chart to modify from the menu at the left and draw a new frame to contain the chart. Try it by following these steps:

1. Position the cursor on the first chart name in the list, OBJECTVS, and press Enter. A small crosshair cursor appears in the drawing board area to the right.

2. Position the cursor at the top left of the rectangle that will contain the chart and press Enter to anchor the first point.

3. Press PgDn repeatedly and use the arrow keys to position the bottom right corner of the rectangle and press Enter. The chart frame appears at the new position.

When you define the custom layout for a multiple chart, you can place one chart on top of another or superimpose an area of one chart on another chart. When you display the actual charts on the screen by pressing F8 (Final Mode), you may notice that the chart maintains its original proportion of length to width even though the rectangle containing the chart may have different proportions. Harvard Graphics maintains every chart's width to height ratio (aspect ratio) so that it does not become distorted. To see this, trying creating a tall, narrow rectangle for chart number 2 (SOSREVS).

If you want to alter the ratio of a chart's width to its height, you can save it as a symbol and then modify the symbol's shape. You find complete information about saving a chart as a symbol in Chapter 7.

To save the multiple chart or change which charts are included in the multiple chart, press F7 (Data) at the Custom Layout screen to return to the Edit Multiple Chart screen. To edit the multiple chart, follow the procedures in the next section. To save the chart, press F10 (Continue) to return to the Main menu.

Editing a Multiple Chart

To change the charts in a multiple chart, you must either return to the Edit Multiple Chart screen from the Custom Layout screen or select Enter/Edit Chart from the Main menu. When the Edit Multiple Chart screen appears, notice that one of the three charts in the lower portion of the screen is highlighted. You may delete any of the charts and replace it with another chart from the list by following these steps:

1. Position the highlight on the chart to be replaced.

2. Press Tab to delete the chart name and replace it with the currently high-lighted chart on the list above.

3. Position the cursor on a new chart name to replace the old and press Enter.

From the Harvard Graphics Main menu, you also can change the current multiple chart's orientation and border by pressing F8 (Options) to summon the Current Chart Options overlay. These changes affect the multiple chart, not the individual charts constituting the multiple chart. The font setting on the Current Chart Options overlay has no effect on the individual charts in a multiple chart. If you change the chart's orientation, be sure to preview the chart immediately after. You almost certainly need to modify the positioning of the charts in the multiple chart using the F7-Size/Place feature.

Slide Shows

For most of the output you need, sending individual charts one by one to a printer, plotter, or film recorder is perfectly satisfactory. Occasionally, a presentation requires an entire set of charts, and, from time to time, printed pages or projected slides are not enough. With slide shows, Harvard Graphics provides an answer to both of these needs.

What Is a Slide Show?

A slide show is a collection of charts that you can instruct Harvard Graphics to display on-screen one after another, much like an actual slide presentation. A slide show also can send a series of charts to an output device rather than to the screen, saving you the tedium of manually printing, plotting, or recording charts one by one.

After you have assembled charts into a slide show in a specific sequence, you can print a list of the show's contents or create practice cards with notes for your speech about each of the show's charts. You also can add special transition effects between each of the charts in a slide show to create an animated presentation called a screenshow.

Assembling a Slide Show

To assemble a slide show, you must pick from among the charts you created earlier that now reside in your data directory and add them to the slide list one by one. After you have completed the list, save the slide show in the same data directory with your charts.

To begin assembling a slide show, follow these steps:

1. Select the Slide Show Menu option from the Main menu and press Enter. The Slide Show menu appears, as shown in figure 9.16.

2. Select Create Slide Show from the Slide Show menu and press Enter.

3. At the Slide show name prompt, type a name of up to eight characters for the slide show and press Enter. Usually, when you create a Harvard Graphics file, you create the file first and save it with a name. Here, you name the file first and then create its contents. As you add charts to the slide show, the revised show is saved on disk.

4. Type a description for the slide show after the Description prompt on the Create Slide Show overlay and press Enter. (Harvard Graphics automatically supplies the SHW file name extension.) The Create/Edit Slide Show screen appears, as shown in figure 9.17.

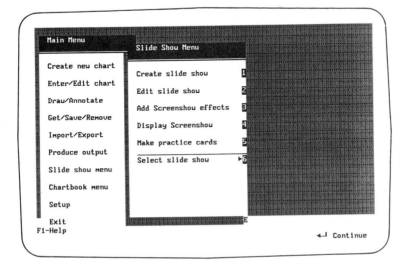

Fig. 9.16.

The Slide Show menu.

Fig. 9.17.

*The Create/Edit
Slide Show screen.*

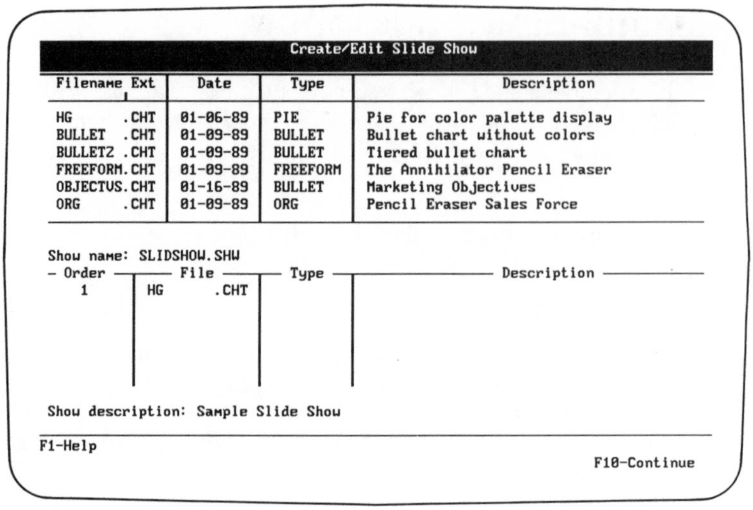

```
                            Create/Edit Slide Show

 Filename Ext      Date        Type              Description

   HG     .CHT   01-06-89    PIE        Pie for color palette display
   BULLET .CHT   01-09-89    BULLET     Bullet chart without colors
   BULLET2 .CHT  01-09-89    BULLET     Tiered bullet chart
   FREEFORM.CHT  01-09-89    FREEFORM   The Annihilator Pencil Eraser
   OBJECTUS.CHT  01-16-89    BULLET     Marketing Objectives
   ORG    .CHT   01-09-89    ORG        Pencil Eraser Sales Force


 Show name: SLIDSHOW.SHW
 — Order ——— File ——— Type ——————— Description ———————
     1        HG     .CHT






 Show description: Sample Slide Show

 F1-Help
                                                          F10-Continue
```

The Create/Edit Slide Show screen is much like the Create/Edit Chartbook screen discussed in Chapter 7. The top half of the screen lists the available charts in your data directory. The slide show name, with the three-letter file extension SHW, appears in the center of the screen, just below the data directory file list. Below that is the current slide show list as it is built. The bottom of the screen displays the description of the slide show.

To modify the slide show description, press the Tab key once. The cursor moves to the description so that you may edit it as though you were editing a line of text in a word processor. To return to the slide show list, press the Tab key again.

When the cursor is back on the slide show list, you can press the up and down arrows and the PgUp and PgDn keys to select the next chart for the list. When the correct chart name appears on the list, press Enter to select that chart and continue building the slide show. A slide show can contain up to 90 charts. When the slide show list is complete, press F10 (Continue) to return to the Slide Show menu.

To practice creating a slide show, use six of the text charts created in Chapter 4 for a slide show designed to accompany your new product presentation. These charts are listed as follows:

TITLECHT:	A title chart to start the presentation
SIMPLCHT:	A simple list describing customer needs
BULETCHT:	A bullet list describing the new product's benefits

TWOCOL: A two-column chart comparing customer need and product benefit

FREEFORM: A free-form chart detailing the new product promotional plan

ORG: An organization chart diagramming the sales force for the new product

Begin by starting a slide show. To start a slide show, follow these steps:

1. Select the Slide Show Menu option from the Main menu and press Enter.

2. Select Create Slide Show from the Slide Show menu.

3. Enter *newprod* as a slide show name and press Enter.

4. Enter *New Product Presentation* as the slide show's description and press Enter.

The Create/Edit Slide Show screen appears, as shown in figure 9.18.

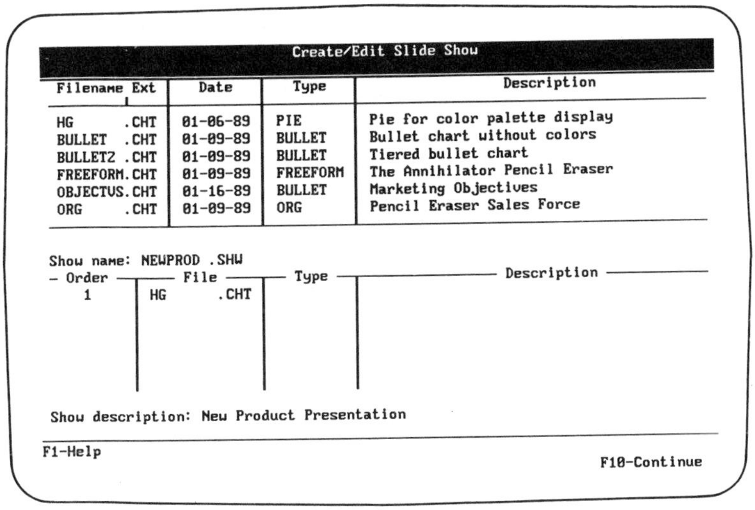

Fig. 9.18.

The Create/Edit Slide Show screen for NEWPROD.

Select the six charts to include in the slide show by following these steps:

1. Use the up or down arrow and PgUp or PgDn keys to highlight `TITLECHT.CHT` on the chart list at the top of the screen and press Enter.

2. Highlight each chart to be included in the slide show one by one, pressing Enter to add each chart to the slide show. The Create/Edit Slide Show screen appears as shown in figure 9.19. If you accidentally add an incorrect file, you need to return to the Slide Show menu and choose Edit Slide Show. You find complete information about editing slide shows in the next section, "Editing a Slide Show."

3. Press F10 (Continue) after you add all six charts to the slide show list.

The Slide Show menu reappears.

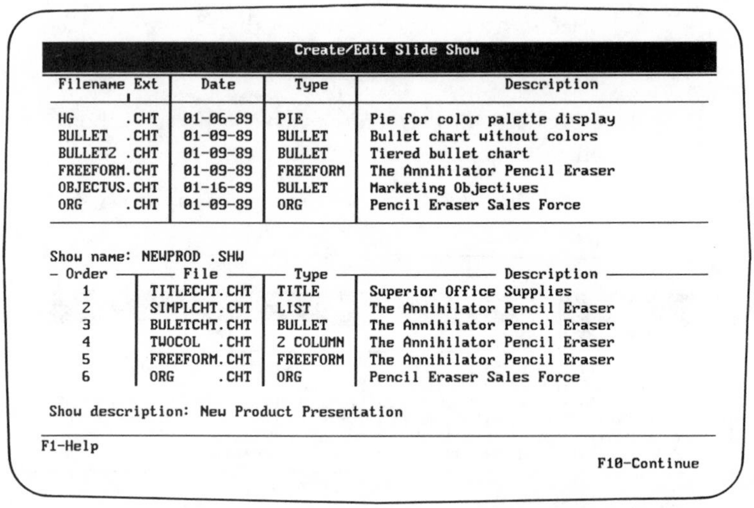

Fig. 9.19.

The Create/Edit Slide Show screen with six charts added.

```
┌─────────────────────────────────────────────────────────────────────┐
│                      Create/Edit Slide Show                          │
│  ███████████████████████████████████████████████████████████████████ │
│  Filename Ext    Date    Type          Description                   │
│                                                                       │
│  HG      .CHT  01-06-89  PIE       Pie for color palette display     │
│  BULLET  .CHT  01-09-89  BULLET    Bullet chart without colors       │
│  BULLET2 .CHT  01-09-89  BULLET    Tiered bullet chart               │
│  FREEFORM.CHT  01-09-89  FREEFORM  The Annihilator Pencil Eraser     │
│  OBJECTUS.CHT  01-16-89  BULLET    Marketing Objectives              │
│  ORG     .CHT  01-09-89  ORG       Pencil Eraser Sales Force         │
│                                                                       │
│  Show name: NEWPROD .SHW                                              │
│  ─ Order ──── File ───    ─ Type ─     ───── Description ─────        │
│      1      TITLECHT.CHT  TITLE     Superior Office Supplies          │
│      2      SIMPLCHT.CHT  LIST      The Annihilator Pencil Eraser     │
│      3      BULETCHT.CHT  BULLET    The Annihilator Pencil Eraser     │
│      4      TWOCOL  .CHT  2 COLUMN  The Annihilator Pencil Eraser     │
│      5      FREEFORM.CHT  FREEFORM  The Annihilator Pencil Eraser     │
│      6      ORG     .CHT  ORG       Pencil Eraser Sales Force         │
│                                                                       │
│  Show description: New Product Presentation                          │
│  ─────────────────────────────────────────────────────────────────  │
│  F1-Help                                               F10-Continue   │
└─────────────────────────────────────────────────────────────────────┘
```

You can now press Esc to return to the Main menu. The slide show you have created is saved on disk. Unlike Harvard Graphics charts, you need not specifically save a slide show after you finish assembling the slide show list. The new slide show is saved each time you add a new chart. The slide show you just created, NEWPROD, remains the current slide show until you select another slide show by retrieving it from disk. If you select Edit Slide Show from the Slide Show menu, the NEWPROD slide show list reappears.

Editing a Slide Show

After you complete a slide show, you can return to the slide show list and make several modifications. You can delete charts, add new charts, or rearrange the order of charts on the list.

To retrieve a slide show from disk, follow these steps:

1. Select the Slide Show Menu option from the Main menu and press Enter.

2. Choose Select Slide Show from the Slide Show menu and press Enter. Harvard Graphics displays the slide shows stored in the current data directory, as shown in figure 9.20.

3. Highlight the slide show you want to retrieve by moving the cursor with the up and down arrows or type the slide show file name after the Filename prompt at the top of the screen and press Enter. In this case, highlight NEWPROD.SHW and press Enter.

```
                          Select Slide Show

  Directory: C:\HG
  Filename:  TEST    .SHW

  Filename Ext |  Date  |  Type  |           Description
  ─────────────┼────────┼────────┼──────────────────────────────────
  TEST    .SHW | 01-17-89 | SLD SHOW |
  BUILD   .SHW | 01-15-89 | SLD SHOW | Demo of building text charts
  HGACCESS.SHW | 01-06-89 | SHOW   |
  LISA    .SHW | 01-13-89 | SHOW   |
  NEWYORK .SHW | 01-13-89 | SLD SHOW | New York & Vancouver show
  SOFTSEL .SHW | 01-06-89 | SHOW   |
  TEMPLATE.SHW | 01-06-89 | SHOW   |
  FUNNGAME.SHW | 01-09-89 | SLD SHOW | Fun and Games Slide Show
  NEWPROD .SHW | 01-17-89 | SLD SHOW | New Product Presentation
  SOSRAP  .SHW | 01-13-89 | SLD SHOW | SOS Revenues Area w/projected 1989
  GROW    .SHW | 01-13-89 | SLD SHOW |
  GROWBARS.SHW | 01-13-89 | SLD SHOW | SOS Expenses with Growing Bars
  RUNLINES.SHW | 01-13-89 | SLD SHOW | SOS Expenses with Running Lines
  BITMAP  .SHW | 01-15-89 | SLD SHOW |
  MENUSHOW.SHW | 01-15-89 | SLD SHOW | Screenshow with User Menu
  ────────────────────────────────────────────────────────────────
  F1-Help        F3-Change dir
                                              F10-Continue
```

Fig. 9.20.

The Select Slide Show screen.

The Slide Show menu reappears. NEWPROD, the slide show you selected, is the current slide show.

To edit a slide show, choose Edit Slide Show from the Slide Show menu. When you do, Harvard Graphics displays the Create/Edit Slide Show screen for the current slide show. When you choose to edit NEWPROD, notice that NEWPROD.SHW reappears in the middle of the screen (see fig. 9.21).

When you edit a slide show, you can cycle among three activities by pressing the Tab key. When the Create/Edit Slide Show screen first reappears, you can add new charts to the slide show list. When you press the up or down arrows, the highlight moves on the chart list at the top of the screen. Press Enter to add a highlighted chart to the list at the bottom of the screen. Press the Tab key again

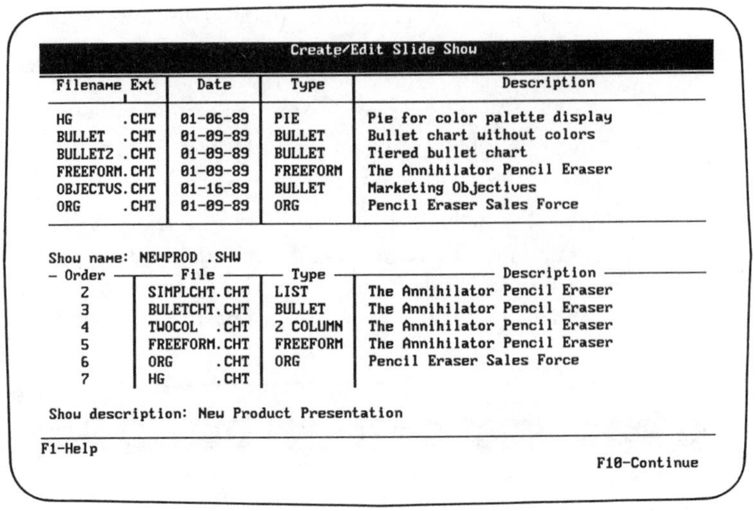

Fig. 9.21.

The Select Slide Show screen showing NEWPROD.

```
┌──────────────────────────────────────────────────────────────────────────┐
│                          Create/Edit Slide Show                            │
│ ┌──────────────────────────────────────────────────────────────────────┐  │
│ │ Filename Ext  │   Date   │   Type   │          Description            │  │
│ │ HG      .CHT  │ 01-06-89 │ PIE      │ Pie for color palette display   │  │
│ │ BULLET  .CHT  │ 01-09-89 │ BULLET   │ Bullet chart without colors     │  │
│ │ BULLET2 .CHT  │ 01-09-89 │ BULLET   │ Tiered bullet chart             │  │
│ │ FREEFORM.CHT  │ 01-09-89 │ FREEFORM │ The Annihilator Pencil Eraser   │  │
│ │ OBJECTUS.CHT  │ 01-16-89 │ BULLET   │ Marketing Objectives            │  │
│ │ ORG     .CHT  │ 01-09-89 │ ORG      │ Pencil Eraser Sales Force       │  │
│ └──────────────────────────────────────────────────────────────────────┘  │
│   Show name: NEWPROD .SHW                                                  │
│  - Order ──────── File ──────┬──── Type ───┬──── Description ──────────    │
│      2        SIMPLCHT.CHT   │ LIST        │ The Annihilator Pencil Eraser │
│      3        BULETCHT.CHT   │ BULLET      │ The Annihilator Pencil Eraser │
│      4        TWOCOL  .CHT   │ 2 COLUMN    │ The Annihilator Pencil Eraser │
│      5        FREEFORM.CHT   │ FREEFORM    │ The Annihilator Pencil Eraser │
│      6        ORG     .CHT   │ ORG         │ Pencil Eraser Sales Force     │
│      7        HG      .CHT   │             │                               │
│                                                                            │
│   Show description: New Product Presentation                               │
│  ────────────────────────────────────────────────────────────────────    │
│  F1-Help                                                                   │
│                                                         F10-Continue       │
└──────────────────────────────────────────────────────────────────────────┘
```

so that you can carry out a second activity, deleting charts or rearranging their order. Pressing the up- or down-arrow keys moves the cursor on the slide show list in the lower portion of the screen. Pressing the Tab key a third time enables you to edit the slide show description. The cursor rests on the description, awaiting your edits. To cycle among these three options, continue pressing the Tab key.

To delete a chart, press the Tab key until the highlight appears in the slide show list in the lower portion of the screen only. Position the cursor on the chart name to delete and press Ctrl-Del. Try deleting the chart called ORG from the slide show list.

Before you press Tab again, you can rearrange the order of the charts in your slide show list by positioning the cursor on the chart to move up or down the list and press Ctrl-↑ or Ctrl-↓. Try highlighting FREEFORM.CHT and moving it up the list and then back down to the bottom of the list. Figure 9.22 shows FREE-FORM.CHT moved to the top of the list. The charts in the slide show are renumbered to reflect their new order.

To add a chart, press the Tab key until the highlight appears in the chart name list at the top of the screen. To add ORG back to the slide show list, highlight the chart name ORG and press Enter. Now press F10 (Continue) to return to the Slide Show menu.

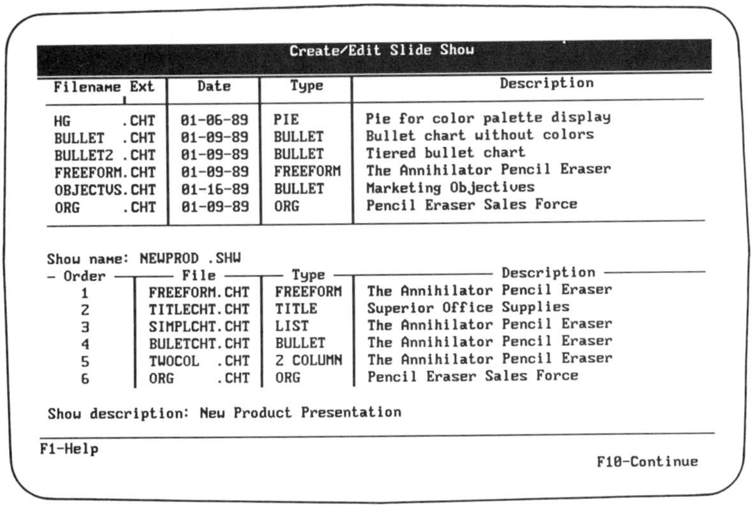

Fig. 9.22.

FREEFORM.CHT moved to the top of the list.

In addition to charts, you can add several other types of files to a slide show. If you add another slide show file name, the slide show branches to the second slide show and begins displaying its files. If you add a template name or a bit-mapped file, you can create certain special effects for screenshows. You read about these effects later in this chapter.

Displaying a Slide Show

To display a slide show, select Display Screenshow from the Slide Show menu. Later, you learn that screenshows are slide shows with transition effects. Even though the slide show you created has no transition effects added, Harvard Graphics still considers it a screenshow if you choose to display it on-screen. When you choose Display Screenshow, Harvard Graphics begins showing the current slide show (in this case, NEWPROD.SHW).

Just as you must press the advance button on a slide projector to view the next slide, you may press any key while displaying a screenshow to view the next chart on the list. After you have viewed all the charts in the slide show, Harvard Graphics returns to the Slide Show menu.

To display a series of charts in a presentation, you almost certainly will want to add a few interesting transition effects between charts. You can read detailed information about the variety of stunning transitions available for screenshows later in this chapter.

Editing Chart Data in a Slide Show

As you view a screenshow, you may notice charts that need alterations. You can quickly return to the data screen of a chart for modifications by pressing Ctrl-E while the chart is in view on-screen. After you have completed modifying a chart's data or its options, you must return to the Main menu, save the chart on disk, and select Display Screenshow from the Slide Show menu again to restart the show.

Suppose, for example, that as you display NEWPROD, you realize that one of the entries on the second chart, the simple list, reads "Long-lasting" rather than "Longer lasting." To correct this error, display NEWPROD.SHW and press Ctrl-E when the simple list appears on-screen. The data screen for SIMPLCHT appears. Correct the word, save the chart, and return to the Slide Show menu to select and display NEWPROD.SHW again.

Printing a Slide Show List

While NEWPROD is still the current slide show, you can print a list of its contents. To print a slide show list, choose Produce Output from the Main menu. Then choose Print Slide Show List from the Produce Output menu. Figure 9.23 shows the printed slide show list for NEWPROD.SHW.

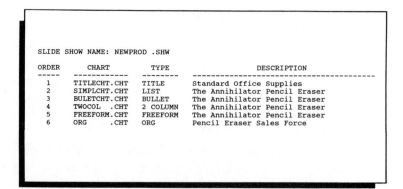

Fig. 9.23.

The printed slide show list for NEWPROD.SHW.

```
SLIDE SHOW NAME: NEWPROD .SHW

ORDER      CHART       TYPE               DESCRIPTION
-----   ------------  --------   ----------------------------------------
  1     TITLECHT.CHT  TITLE      Standard Office Supplies
  2     SIMPLCHT.CHT  LIST       The Annihilator Pencil Eraser
  3     BULETCHT.CHT  BULLET     The Annihilator Pencil Eraser
  4     TWOCOL  .CHT  2 COLUMN   The Annihilator Pencil Eraser
  5     FREEFORM.CHT  FREEFORM   The Annihilator Pencil Eraser
  6     ORG     .CHT  ORG        Pencil Eraser Sales Force
```

Printing Practice Cards

Another task made possible by slide shows is printing practice cards for a presentation. Practice cards hold notes about the charts in a slide show or screenshow and images of the charts themselves. You can create one practice card for each of the slides in a slide show. As you give a speech, you can refer to these cards as you describe the information conveyed by each chart. Each card holds your notes about the chart and a printed copy of the chart.

To create practice cards, follow these steps:

1. Retrieve from disk the slide show or screenshow for which you want to make practice cards, thus making it the current show.

2. Select Make Practice Cards from the Slide Show menu. The Practice Cards screen appears (see fig. 9.24). The cursor rests in an open area under the current slide number, chart name, and chart description.

3. Type your notes about the chart and then press PgDn or F10 (Continue) to create a practice card for the next chart in the show.

4. Press Esc when you have created all the practice cards you need.

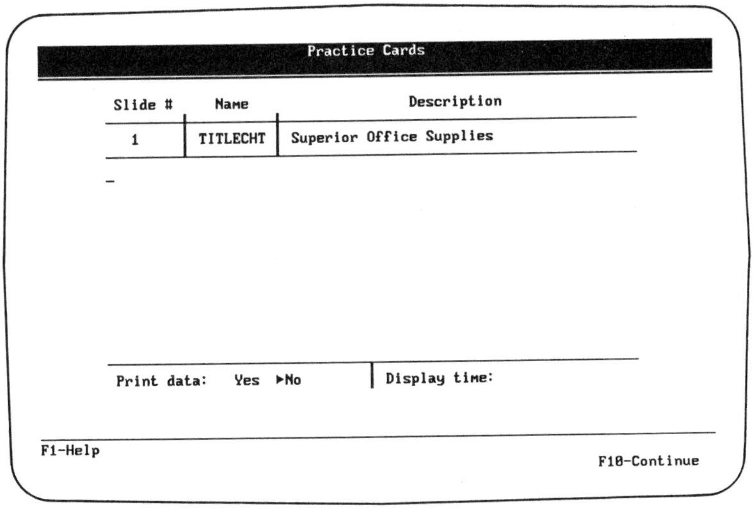

```
                         Practice Cards

         Slide #    Name          Description

            1      TITLECHT    Superior Office Supplies

            _




         Print data:   Yes  ►No    │ Display time:


 F1-Help                                        F10-Continue
```

Fig. 9.24.

The Practice Cards screen.

When you type a practice card note, you can precede an item with a bullet point by pressing Ctrl-B, selecting a bullet style from the Bullet Shape overlay that appears, and pressing Enter before typing the note text.

Try creating a practice card for the first slide in NEWPROD.SHW by following these steps:

1. Make sure that NEWPROD.SHW is the current slide show. You may need to choose NEWPROD from the Select Slide Show screen (accessed from the Slide Show menu) to be certain.

2. Select Make Practice Cards from the Slide Show menu.

3. Press Ctrl-B to make a bullet, choose the round bullet shape by pressing the space bar to highlight it, and press Enter.

4. Type a space, type *Welcome*, and press Enter twice to skip a line.

5. Press Ctrl-B again to enter another round bullet. For the note, type *Introduce myself* and press Enter twice to skip another line.

6. Enter another round bullet, type *Purpose of the presentation* as the next note item, and press Enter twice.

7. Press the space twice to indent and enter a hyphen bullet followed by *Introduce new product*.

8. Enter two more hyphen bullets with the following lines of text: *Describe marketing plans* and *Describe sales force organization*. (Figure 9.25 shows the completed practice card for slide number 1.)

Fig. 9.25.

The Practice Cards screen for chart 1.

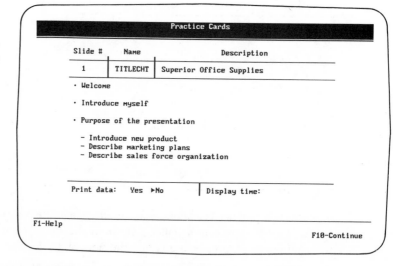

9. Press PgDn to create a note for slide 2.

10. Complete the second practice card as shown in figure 9.26.

11. Press Esc to return to the Slide Show menu.

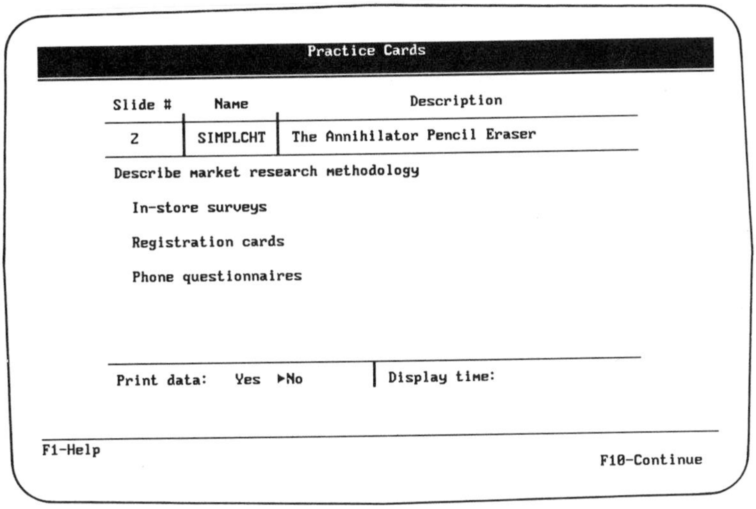

Fig. 9.26.

The Practice Cards screen for chart 2.

After you enter a note for a practice card, you may want to go to a specific slide in a presentation to enter a new note or modify an existing note. To jump to a specific slide, press the Tab key until the cursor is on the slide number, enter a new slide number, and press Enter. You can easily determine slide numbers by printing a slide show list before making practice cards.

To print a page with the chart data after each practice card, press the Tab key to move the cursor to the Print data prompt at the bottom of the screen and change its setting to Yes. By default, the setting is No. To alter the amount of time the chart displays before the next slide appears, press Tab once again to move the cursor to the Display time field. In this field, you can enter a number of minutes and seconds, such as *1:30* (1 minute and 30 seconds), to display the current chart during the show. Later, you learn that you can add a display time for a chart when you add screenshow effects. That display time and this display time are the same. Change one and the other changes.

The practice cards you make are saved with the slide show. The next time you select the same slide show, the practice cards are retrieved, too. To edit the current practice cards, select Make Practice Cards from the Slide Show menu again.

When you complete practice cards for the charts in a slide show, you can print them by choosing Print Practice Cards from the Produce Output menu. Harvard Graphics prints the practice cards for the current slide show. Practice cards display the slide number, chart name, chart description, note, and display time on the top half of the page and the actual chart on the bottom half of the page. Figure 9.27 shows the practice card for chart #1 of the NEWPROD slide show.

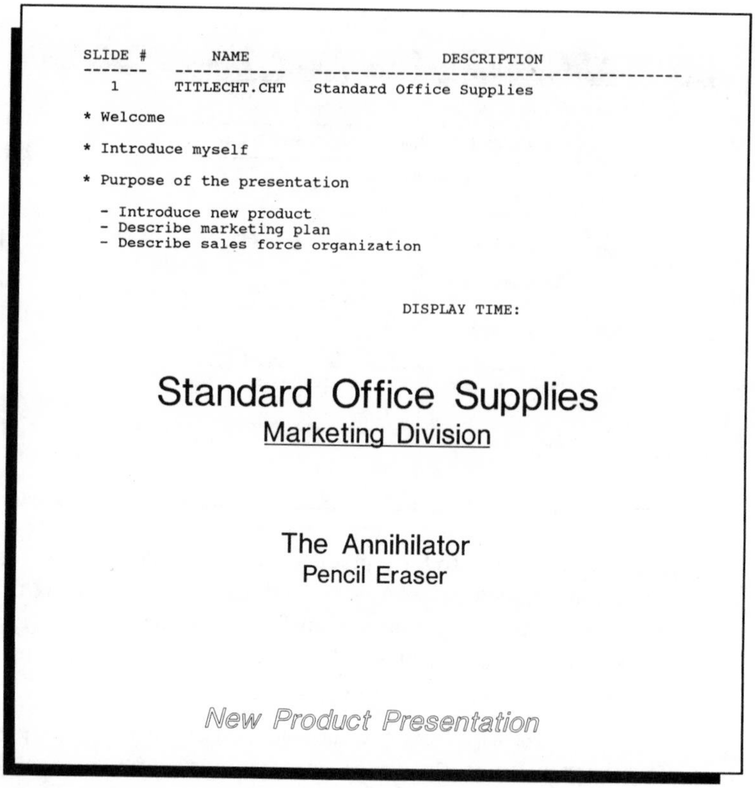

Fig. 9.27.

The practice card for NEWPROD slide 1.

```
SLIDE #        NAME                    DESCRIPTION
-------     ------------    -------------------------------------
   1        TITLECHT.CHT    Standard Office Supplies
* Welcome

* Introduce myself

* Purpose of the presentation

   - Introduce new product
   - Describe marketing plan
   - Describe sales force organization


                                DISPLAY TIME:
```

Standard Office Supplies
Marketing Division

The Annihilator
Pencil Eraser

New Product Presentation

To print practice cards, follow these steps:

1. Select Produce Output from the Main menu.

2. Select Print Practice Cards from the Produce Output menu.

3. Select a print quality from the Practice Cards Options overlay that appears by pressing the space bar and Enter. Figure 9.28 shows the Practice Cards Options overlay.

4. Select Printer 1 or Printer 2 and press Enter.

5. Choose a range of practice cards to print by entering a starting slide number and ending slide number at the From slide and To slide prompts and press Enter.

Try printing the practice cards you created for the first two slides in NEWPROD.SHW by following these steps:

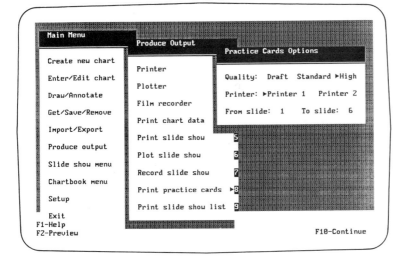

Fig. 9.28.

The Practice Cards Options overlay.

1. Select Produce Output from the Main menu.

2. Select Print Practice Cards from the Produce Output menu.

3. Set Quality to Standard at the Practice Cards Options overlay.

4. Choose Printer 1.

5. Press 1 at the From slide prompt and 2 at the To slide prompt and press Enter.

Using Slide Shows for Batch Printing

To print, plot, or record a series of charts, you can assemble them into a slide show even if you have no intention of displaying them on-screen. Make a slide show with all the charts you want to send to an output device and choose Print Slide Show, Plot Slide Show, or Record Slide Show from the Produce Output menu.

For more information about producing output using this option, see "Printing a Series of Charts" earlier in this chapter.

Screenshows

A screenshow is a slide show designed expressly for display on a PC screen. Of course, you also can project a screenshow in an auditorium or large room with a special computer screen projector that projects a computer monitor's image onto a large screen.

To create a simple screenshow, you add special transitions between the charts of a slide show. These effects are much like the transitions between scenes of a television program. Like the special effects available to the editor of a film, an entire arsenal of wipes, fades, and other transitions to liven up slide shows is at your disposal.

But screenshows offer even more. By keeping in mind the transition effects available when you create the charts of a screenshow, you can use special techniques to build text charts line by line, make the bars of a bar chart grow, move the lines of a line chart across the screen, and add the slices of a pie one by one.

Adding Effects To Create a Screenshow

To create a screenshow, you must first assemble a slide show. While that slide show is the current slide show, you can add screenshow transition effects.

To add special transitions between the charts of the NEWPROD slide show you created earlier, select NEWPROD by choosing Select Slide Show from the Slide Show menu. Select Add Screenshow Effects from the Slide Show menu. If you choose Add Screenshow Effects before you select a slide show, Harvard Graphics displays the slide show list so that you can select a slide show first. The Screenshow Effects screen appears, as shown in figure 9.29.

The Screenshow Effects screen contains eight columns. The first three display the numbers, names, and types of charts in the slide show. The next five columns let you add transitions between charts. These five columns perform the following actions:

❏ Draw determines the effect used to display that chart.

❏ Dir determines the direction for the draw effect.

❏ Time determines the display time for the current chart.

❏ Erase determines the effect used to erase that chart.

❏ Dir determines the direction for the erase effect.

```
                        Screenshow Effects

          Filename      Type   | Draw  | Dir | Time | Erase  | Dir

          Default              | Replace|     |      |        |

      1   TITLECHT.CHT   TITLE  |       |     |      |        |
      2   SIMPLCHT.CHT   LIST   |       |     |      |        |
      3   BULETCHT.CHT   BULLET |       |     |      |        |
      4   TWOCOL  .CHT   2 COLUMN|      |     |      |        |
      5   FREEFORM.CHT   FREEFORM|      |     |      |        |
      6   ORG     .CHT   ORG    |       |     |      |        |



    F1-Help
    F2-Preview show          F6-Choices    F8-User menu    F10-Continue
```

Fig. 9.29.

*The Screenshow
Effects screen.*

Under the column titles, near the top of the screen, is a row labeled `Default`. In this row, you can enter a choice to use for any blank entry in a column. At the moment, the default for the `Draw` column is `Replace`. If you leave an entry blank in the column, Harvard Graphics uses `Replace` as the Draw effect for that chart.

To view the choices available for a column, position the cursor in the column and press F6 (Choices). If the cursor is in the `Draw` column, pressing F6 displays the effects available for drawing the chart, for example. Figure 9.30 shows the Transitions overlay for `Draw`. If the cursor is in the `Dir` column, pressing F6 displays an overlay showing the available directions for the direction effect. Try positioning the cursor in each of the columns and pressing F6 to see the available choices for that column. Press Esc after pressing F6 to remove the Transitions overlay. To erase an effect in a column, position the cursor on it and press Ctrl-Del. You also can replace an effect by entering a new effect over the current effect.

Try experimenting with the available transition effects by moving the cursor down the `Draw` column and picking a transition from the Transitions overlay for each chart. If you want, start with the `Replace` choices shown in figure 9.31. Then press F2 (Preview Show) to display the screenshow. Because the `Time` column is blank, you must press a key or click the right mouse button to advance to the next chart in the show. Later, you can try entering a time (in minutes and seconds) to display the chart on-screen before advancing to the next chart.

When the screenshow is finished, Harvard Graphics returns to the Screenshow Effects screen. To interrupt a show as it displays and return immediately to the

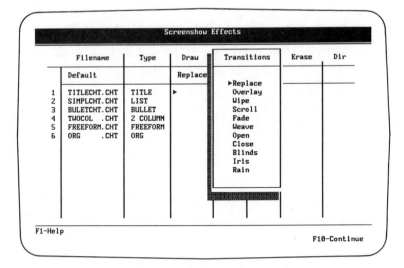

Fig. 9.30.

The Transitions overlay for Draw.

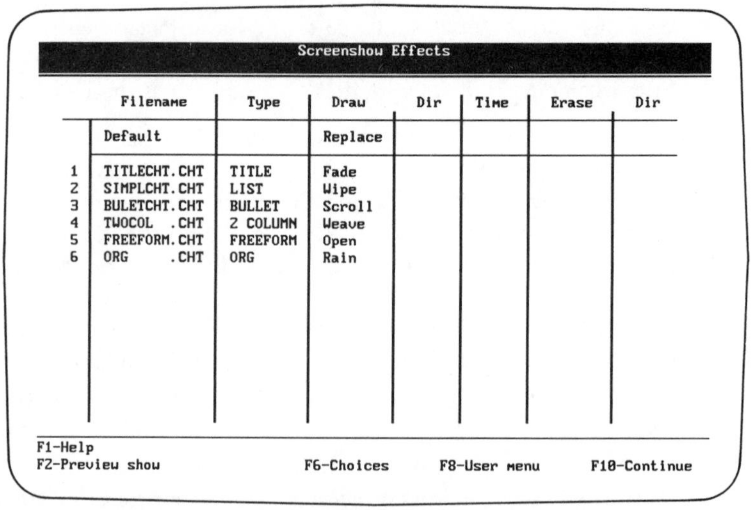

Fig. 9.31.

The Screenshow Effects screen.

Screenshow Effects screen, press Esc. To start a show on a particular chart, position the cursor in the chart's row before pressing F2 (Preview Show).

If you know the name of the transition or the direction you want to use, you can type the first one or two letters and move to the next column to set. For example, you can type *wi* and Harvard Graphics automatically fills in Wipe when you move to the next column.

Already, the screenshow is far more exciting than the simple slide show you created earlier. But you can fine-tune the show by adding complementary Erase effects to the Draw effects you used for certain charts. For example, erasing a chart with Iris Out leads well into drawing a chart with Iris In. If you omit an Erase effect, Harvard Graphics uses the default. If you have not supplied a default Erase effect, the program uses the Draw effect for the next chart to replace the current chart.

Try the effects shown in figure 9.32. Notice the use of Wipe Up, Wipe Down, Open Left, Close Left, Iris Out, and Iris In to erase and draw successive charts. In addition, notice that the default time is 1 second in figure 9.32. To advance to the next chart before the time you have chosen is expired, press Enter or click the right mouse button. To move from chart to chart as quickly as possible, you can use a time of 0.

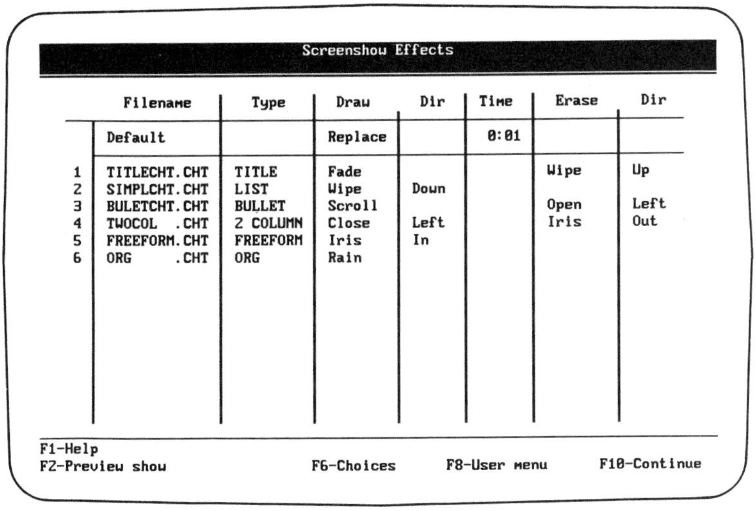

	Filename	Type	Draw	Dir	Time	Erase	Dir
	Default		Replace		0:01		
1	TITLECHT.CHT	TITLE	Fade			Wipe	Up
2	SIMPLCHT.CHT	LIST	Wipe	Down			
3	BULETCHT.CHT	BULLET	Scroll			Open	Left
4	TWOCOL .CHT	2 COLUMN	Close	Left		Iris	Out
5	FREEFORM.CHT	FREEFORM	Iris	In			
6	ORG .CHT	ORG	Rain				

Screenshow Effects

F1-Help
F2-Preview show   F6-Choices   F8-User menu   F10-Continue

Fig. 9.32.

The NEWPROD screenshow.

When you complete the screenshow, press F10 (Continue). Harvard Graphics displays the Slide Show menu. To return to the Main menu, press Esc. The screenshow transition effects are saved with the slide show as you build the show. There's no need for you to issue a specific command to save the show with its effects. But because the effects are saved with the slide show, you must assemble a second slide show with the same charts to display them with different transition effects.

The available Draw and Erase effects are as follows:

- ❏ Replace switches from one full-screen chart to the next.

- ❏ Overlay displays the next chart on top of the current chart. Both charts are then visible.

- ❏ Wipe sweeps up, down, left, or right across the chart. The default is Right.

- ❏ Scroll pushes the chart onto the screen to the right, left, up, or down. The default is Up.

- ❏ Fade fades the chart onto the screen gradually down the screen or all at once. The default is all at once. Use Down to have the new chart gradually fade down the screen.

- ❏ Weave joins two halves of a chart swept in from the left and right side of the screen. The direction setting has no effect.

- ❏ Open reveals the screen from the center out. The visible portion of the chart expands in a straight line vertically or horizontally. The default is Up. Setting Direction to Right opens the screen horizontally.

- ❏ Close closes the screen from the edge in. The visible portion of the chart contracts in a straight line vertically or horizontally. The default is Up. Setting Direction to Right closes the screen horizontally.

- ❏ Blinds brings the next chart into view in stripes that either move down or across the screen. The default is Down. Set Direction to Right for stripes that roll across the screen.

- ❏ Iris reveals the chart from the center of the screen growing outward. The default is Out. To close the screen from the edge in toward the center, set Direction to In. Left and right are not valid directions with Iris.

- ❏ Rain paints the screen from the top down in small drips. The direction setting has no effect.

Special Techniques for Animating Charts

That screenshows let you animate the transitions between charts alone makes them worth their salt. But they provide even more appealing effects. Special techniques enable you to animate the actual charts in a slide show in addition to transitions between charts. The following sections describe some of the best of these techniques for making charts take shape right before your audience's eyes.

Adding Text Chart Items

A technique that provides an interesting alternative to presenting a fully composed list of text items on-screen is to add the items on a text chart one by one, highlighting each as it appears and causing the items already present to recede into the background.

To build a text chart on-screen line by line, create the complete chart first. Remove items from the bottom up one by one, saving each new slightly diminished chart as a separate file. When you build a slide show, add the individual text chart files in reverse order using fade or overlay for a transition. Successive text items will seem to appear one by one.

To make the newest addition to the chart stand out as the chart is built step by step, highlight the last item in each of the charts you save as you dismantle the original chart.

To try this effect, create a bullet list by filling out the Bullet List data screen and the Size/Place overlay so that they match the screen shown in figure 9.33.

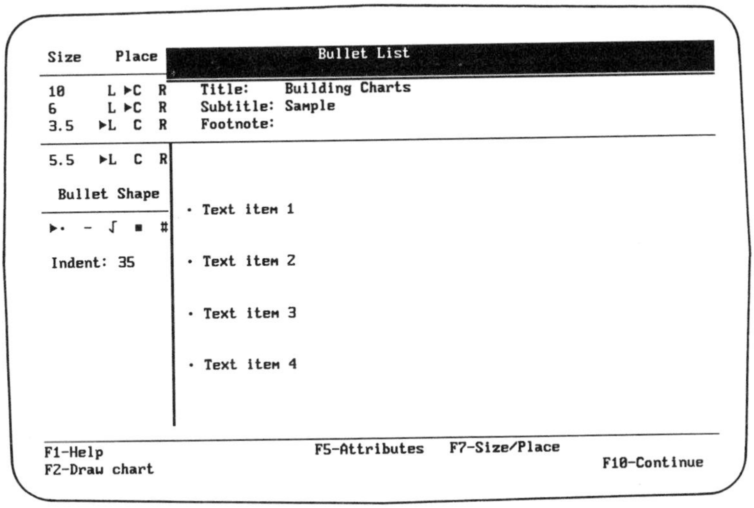

Fig. 9.33.

Bullet List data screen showing Size/ Place overlay.

To be sure that the text aligns properly on successive charts, left-justify the lines of text and use Indent to move them to the center of the screen. In this case, a setting of 35 works perfectly. If you right-align text, the text shifts horizontally based on the current longest line on-screen. When you remove a long line from a text chart as you use this technique, the remaining text shifts to the right, ruining the consistency between charts. Figure 9.34 shows a right-aligned text chart before the last lines are removed. Figure 9.35 shows the same chart after two items are removed. Notice that the remaining lines are shifted horizontally in the second chart.

Using the F5-Attributes feature, set the last item of the chart in yellow and the earlier items in red. Color the title any way you want. Save the chart as

Fig. 9.34.

Before removing the last two items of right-aligned text.

The Annihilator Pencil Eraser
Product Benefits

- Double-ended design

- Brazilian rubber fabrication

- Rubber formula A-27 produces easily removed ball-shaped flecks

- Rubber formula A-27 lasts 70% longer.

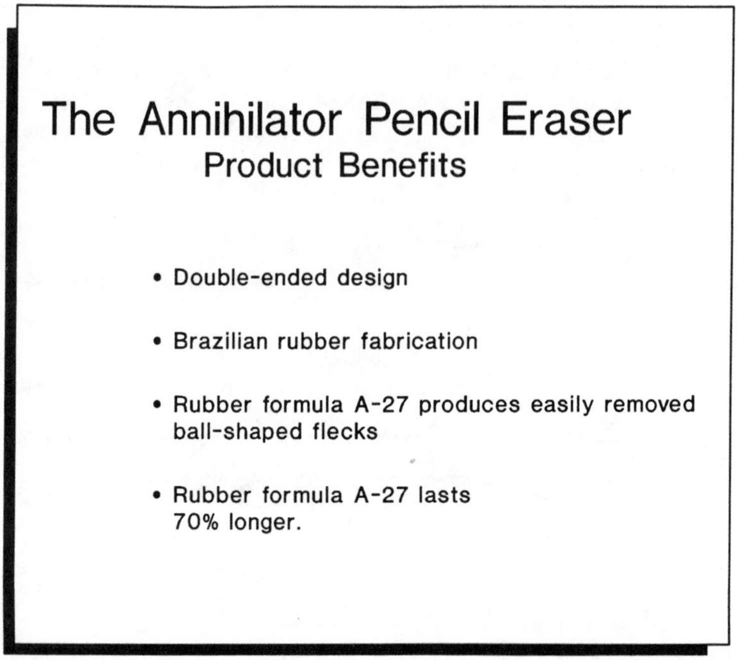

Fig. 9.35.

After removing the last two items of right-aligned text.

The Annihilator Pencil Eraser
Product Benefits

- Double-ended design

- Brazilian rubber fabrication

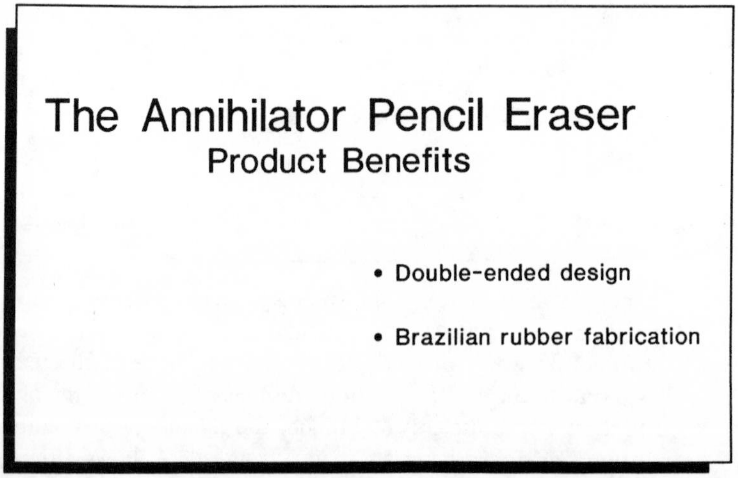

BUILD5. Because BUILD5 is the current chart, select Enter/Edit Chart from the Main menu to review the data screen. Delete the last item by pressing Ctrl-Del with the cursor on that line and color the new last item yellow. Save the revised chart as BUILD4. Repeat the same procedure, removing lines one by one, and creating BUILD3, BUILD2, and BUILD1 showing only the titles.

On the Slide Show menu, select Create Slide Show and add BUILD1, BUILD2, BUILD3, BUILD4, and BUILD5 to a slide show named BUILD, as shown in figure 9.36. Enter *Demo of building text charts* as the description. With all five charts included in a screen show, press F10 (Continue) to return to the Slide Show menu.

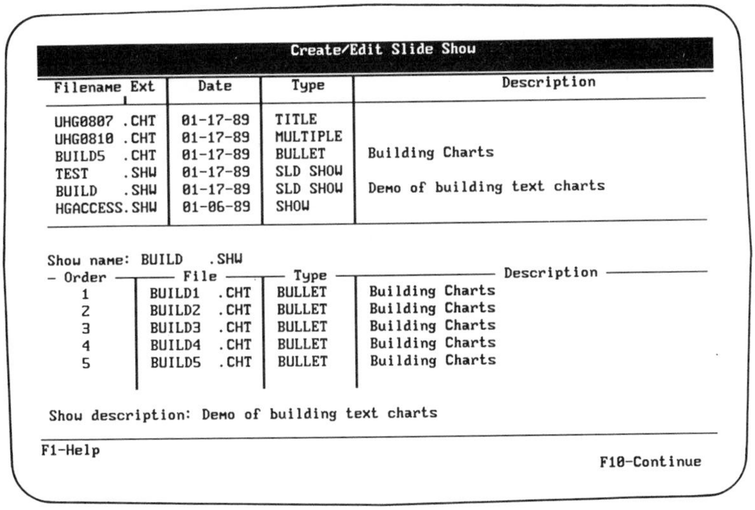

Fig. 9.36.

The BUILD slide show.

Select Display Screenshow from the Slide Show menu. The current screenshow, BUILD, appears. Because you have added no display time yet, you must press Enter repeatedly to cause each new screen to appear.

To place the finishing touches on your screenshow, select Add Screenshow Effects from the Slide Show menu. Replace the current default Draw transition (Replace) with Fade. Position the cursor at the top of the flist of charts and press F2 (Preview Show) to view the screenshow with its effects.

For even more pizzazz, bring all five charts into Draw/Annotate and add additional highlighting to the last text item on each chart. Currently, the last items are yellow, and all the other items are red. You may want to try enclosing the last item in a box or highlighting it with colorful arrows.

Adding Graph Chart Series

You can animate the appearance of graph charts as well. One of the easiest and most striking effects is to add series to a graph chart one by one. To add series, you follow much the same procedure as adding text items to a text chart one by one. First, create and save the completed chart with all series. Then remove a series and save the revised chart. To remove a series from view in a graph chart, you can set Display to No for that series on the first Titles & Options page, or you can use the @Clr calculation at that series as discussed in Chapter 5. @Clr removes the entire series of data so that the graph's data screen does not contain uncharted data. Continue until only a single series remains. When you display the charts in reverse order in a screenshow, each new series seems to add to the series already in view.

Using the data from the Superior Office Supplies Revenue chart you created in Chapter 5, create an area chart to try this technique. Use the chart entitled SOSRPROJ as it has four series—three of actual data and the fourth projected by means of a calculation.

To animate an area chart, follow this procedure:

1. Select Get Chart from the Get/Save/Remove menu and retrieve SOSRPROJ.CHT. Figure 9.37 shows this chart.

2. Press Esc twice to return to the Main menu.

3. Select Create New Chart from the Main menu and Area from the Create New Chart menu.

4. Make sure that the Keep current data query is set to Yes.

5. Press F2 (Draw Chart) to preview the chart and make a note of the y-axis minimum and maximum values. These values are 0 and 200,000, as shown in figure 9.37. The minimum and maximum y-axis values are important when you begin removing series. As you remove series, the maximum Y value of the data left on the chart may change. As a result, the y-axis may readjust to fit the remaining data. To avoid this, you must set the chart's minimum and maximum Y-axis values manually. By making note of the y-axis minimum and maximum values when all the data is in place, you know what to enter for y-axis minimum and maximum values on the third Titles & Options page for the area chart, later in this procedure.

6. Press Esc to return to the Area Chart Data screen.

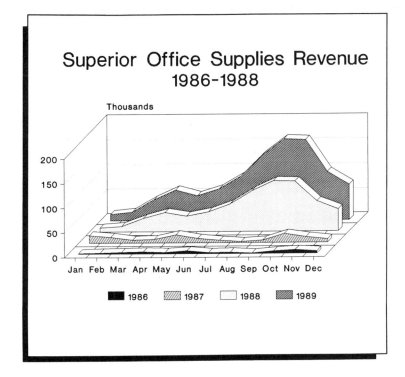

Superior Office Supplies Revenue
1986-1988

Thousands

200

150

100

50

0

Jan Feb Mar Apr May Jun Jul Aug Sep Oct Nov Dec

■ 1986   ▨ 1987   ☐ 1988   ▨ 1989

Fig. 9.37.

The SOSRPROJ chart.

7. Modify the subtitle so that it reflects all four years of data (1986-1989 rather than 1986-1988).

8. Press F8 (Options) to view the first Titles & Options page. Notice that Display is set to Yes for Series 1 through Series 4.

9. Press PgDn to view the second Titles & Options page and set Chart enhancement to None. Animating the adding of series to a three-dimensional chart with this technique is not particularly effective. As you add new series in a three-dimensional chart, the depth of the chart increases. This breaks the continuity between successive charts that makes the animation effect so impressive.

10. Press PgDn once more to view the third Titles & Options page.

11. Set the Y1 Axis Minimum Value to 0 and the Maximum Value to 200,000, as shown in figure 9.38.

12. Press F10 (Continue) and F2 (Draw Chart) to preview the area chart.

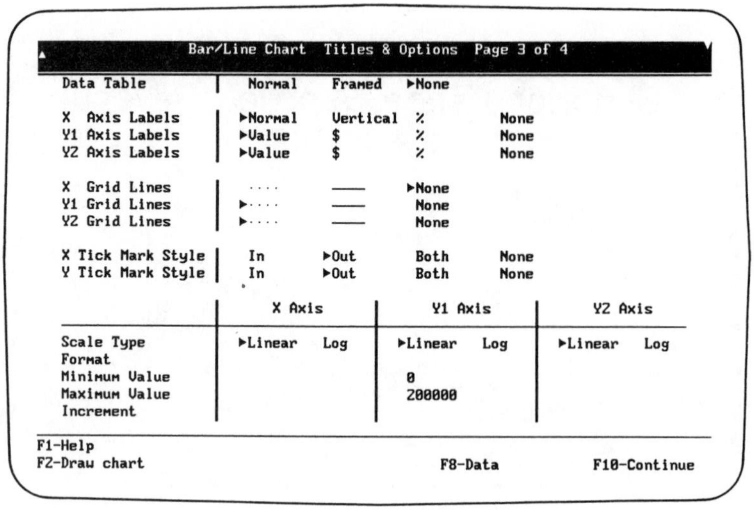

Fig. 9.38.

The third Titles & Options page showing y-axis minimum and maximum values.

```
┌─────────────────────────────────────────────────────────────────────┐
│               Bar/Line Chart  Titles & Options  Page 3 of 4           │
│  ▲                                                                    │
│    Data Table     │ Normal    Framed   ▶None                          │
│                   │                                                   │
│    X  Axis Labels │ ▶Normal   Vertical   %      None                  │
│    Y1 Axis Labels │ ▶Value    $          %      None                  │
│    Y2 Axis Labels │ ▶Value    $          %      None                  │
│                   │                                                   │
│    X  Grid Lines  │  · · · ·  ───────  ▶None                          │
│    Y1 Grid Lines  │ ▶· · · ·  ───────   None                          │
│    Y2 Grid Lines  │ ▶· · · ·  ───────   None                          │
│                   │                                                   │
│    X Tick Mark Style │ In    ▶Out     Both      None                  │
│    Y Tick Mark Style │ In    ▶Out     Both      None                  │
│                                                                       │
│                     X Axis          Y1 Axis         Y2 Axis           │
│    Scale Type     │ ▶Linear   Log  │ ▶Linear   Log │ ▶Linear   Log    │
│    Format                                                             │
│    Minimum Value                     0                                │
│    Maximum Value                     200000                           │
│    Increment                                                          │
│                                                                       │
│  F1-Help                                                              │
│  F2-Draw chart                         F8-Data        F10-Continue    │
└─────────────────────────────────────────────────────────────────────┘
```

Next, begin removing series and saving the incremental charts:

1. Save the current chart as SOSRAP4, for "Superior Office Supplies Revenue Area Projected, chart 4."

2. Select Enter/Edit Chart from the Main menu to return to the Area Chart Data screen.

3. Press F8 (Options) to display the first Titles & Options page.

4. Set Display for Series 4 (1989) to No.

5. Press F10 (Continue) to return to the Main menu and save the chart as SOSRAP3.

6. Select Enter/Edit Chart from the Main menu again to return to the Area Chart Data screen.

7. Press F8 (Options) to display the first Titles & Options page.

8. Set Display for Series 3 (1988) to No, too. Now set Display for Series 3 and Series 4 to No.

9. Save the chart as SOSRAP2.

10. Return to the data screen and the first Titles & Options page again.

11. This time, set Display for Series 2, 3, and 4 to No. Only Series 1 (1986) will be displayed.

12. Save this chart as SOSRAP1.

Now you have created four charts that you can add to a slide show by following these steps:

1. Choose the Slide Show Menu option from the Main menu.

2. Choose Create Slide Show from the Slide Show menu.

3. Enter *sosrap* as the slide show name and *SOS Revenues Area w/projected 1989* as the description and press Enter.

4. On the Create/Edit Slide Show screen, add the charts SOSRAP1, SOSRAP2, SOSRAP3, and SOSRAP4 to the SOSRAP slide show. Press F10 (Continue) to return to the Slide Show menu.

Finally, you should add screenshow effects to create the effect of adding a new series one by one:

1. Select Add Screenshow Effects from the Slide Show menu.

2. Use Wipe as the default Draw effect and Up as the default Draw direction by positioning the cursor in the Default row under Draw, choosing Wipe from the overlay summoned with F6-Choices, positioning the cursor in the same row under Dir, and choosing Up from the Transitions overlay.

3. Enter :02 as the default time so that the show proceeds automatically. Figure 9.39 shows the completed Screenshow Effects screen for SOSRAP.

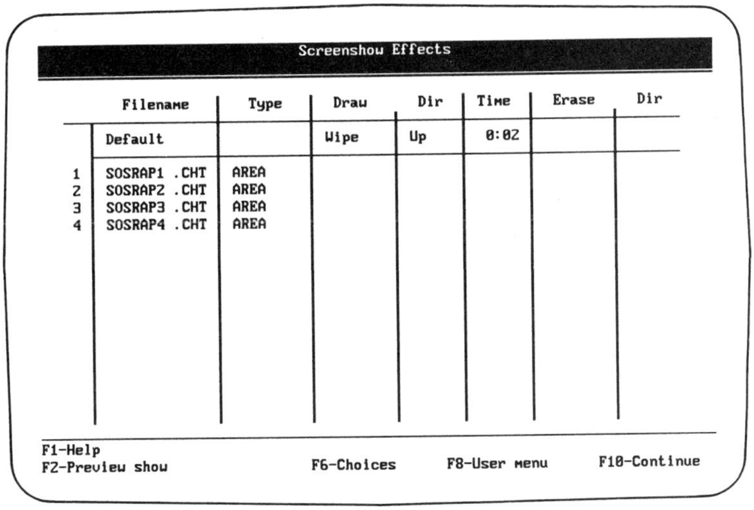

Fig. 9.39.

The completed Screenshow Effects screen for SOSRAP.

Now that the screenshow is complete, press F2 (Preview Show) to see the completed effect.

Try other Draw effects but avoid Weave, Overlay, and Scroll. Weave and Scroll move the entire chart on-screen, ruining the illusion that the chart is changed only by the addition of a new series. Selecting Overlay as the Draw effect causes each new legend to overwrite the preceding legend. Because the legends change as each new series is added, the result is a blurred mess where a clean, clear legend should be.

Making Bars Grow

To make the bars of a bar chart grow, use Wipe Up as the screenshow transition effect between two slides. The first slide hides the bars by displaying them in the color black. The second slide shows the bars in full color. As the second slide wipes up across the first, the full-color bars seem to grow on-screen.

To try this technique, follow these steps:

1. Retrieve the chart entitled SOSEXPEN created in Chapter 5. Figure 9.40 shows the SOSEXPEN chart.

2. Press Esc to view the chart's data screen and F8 (Options) to view the first Titles & Options page.

3. Press PgDn twice to view the third Titles & Options page.

4. Set Y1 Grid Lines to None. In a moment, you will be setting the bars to black. If Y1 Grid Lines are showing, the black bars hide portions of the grid lines on-screen, lessening the effect.

5. Press PgDn to view the fourth Titles & Options page.

6. Set Color for Series 1, 2, 3, and 4 to 16 (black).

7. Press F10 (Continue) to return to the Main menu.

8. Save the chart as SOSEXP2.

Now build the slide show and add the screenshow effects by following this procedure:

1. Select Create Slide Show from the Slide Show menu.

2. Name the slide show GROWBARS and enter SOS Expenses with Growing Bars as the description.

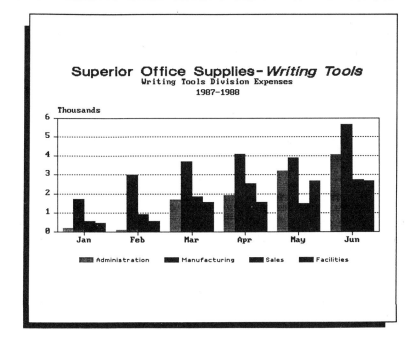

Fig. 9.40.

The SOSEXPEN chart.

3. Add SOSEXP2 to the GROWBARS slide show.

4. Add SOSEXPEN to the GROWBARS slide show.

5. Press F10 (Continue) to return to the Slide Show menu.

6. Select Add Screenshow Effects from the Slide Show menu.

7. Enter 0:00 as the default time.

8. Use Wipe as the Draw effect for the second chart in the slide show, SOSEXPEN.

9. Use Up as the direction for the Draw effect for SOSEXPEN.

10. Enter 10:00 as the time for SOSEXPEN so that the last image remains on-screen until you press Enter.

11. Move the cursor to the top of the Screenshow Effects screen and press F2 (Preview Show) to view the screenshow. Figure 9.41 shows the completed Screenshow Effects screen for GROWBARS.

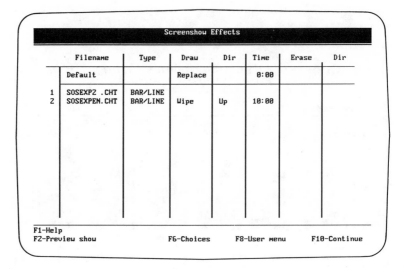

Fig. 9.41.

The completed Screenshow Effects screen for GROWBARS.

Inside the figure:

Screenshow Effects

	Filename	Type	Draw	Dir	Time	Erase	Dir
	Default		Replace		0:00		
1	SOSEXP2 .CHT	BAR/LINE					
2	SOSEXPEN.CHT	BAR/LINE	Wipe	Up	10:00		

F1-Help
F2-Preview show   F6-Choices   F8-User menu   F10-Continue

Making Lines Run

Just as you can make bars grow, you can make lines run across a line chart. To achieve this effect, display a succession of charts, each with an additional data point for each series. Use Wipe Right as the transition effect. The lines on your line chart appear to extend across the screen point by point from left to right.

To try this technique, follow these steps:

1. Retrieve the chart SOSEXPEN. Its y-axis minimum and maximum values are 0 and 6,000, respectively. You need to enter these values later on the component charts of the screenshow, as you did earlier when animating the area chart.

2. On the first Titles & Options page of SOSEXPEN, set Type for all four series to Line.

3. For a dramatic effect, set Bar style to Overlap and Bar enhancement to 3D on the second Titles & Options page.

4. Save the chart as SOSEXPL ("SOS Expenses Line").

5. Return to the SOSEXPL Bar/Line Chart Data screen by choosing Enter/Edit Chart from the Main menu.

6. Delete the four series data for June, but leave the word Jun in the X Axis column.

7. Set the Y1 Axis Minimum Value to 0 and Maximum Value to 6000 on the third Titles & Options page.

8. Save the chart as SOSEXPL5.

9. Select Enter/Edit Chart from the Main menu again.

10. Delete the data for all four series for May, but leave the word May in the X Axis column. The X Axis column now has May and Jun with no data in the series columns.

11. Set the Y1 Axis Minimum Value to 0 and Maximum Value to 6000 on the third Titles & Options page.

12. Save the chart as SOSEXPL4.

13. Continue removing data for all four series month by month and setting the Y1 Axis minimum and maximum values on the third Titles & Options page until you have saved SOSEXPL3, SOSEXPL2, and SOSEXPL1. SOSEXPL1 should have data for January only.

14. Return to the Main menu and select the Slide Show Menu option.

15. Select Create Slide Show from the Slide Show menu.

16. Name the slide show RUNLINES and enter *SOS Expenses w/Running Lines* as the description.

17. Add SOSEXPL1 to the slide show first.

18. Add SOSEXPL2 to the slide show second.

19. Continue until you have added SOSEXPL3, SOSEXPL4, and SOSEXPL5.

20. Complete the slide show by adding SOSEXPL.

21. Press F10 (Continue) to return to the Slide Show menu.

22. Select Add Screenshow Effects from the Slide Show menu.

23. Set the default time to 0:00.

24. Set the Draw effect to Wipe and the direction to Right for SOSEXPL2 through SOSEXPL5 and SOSEXPL.

25. Set Time for SOSEXPL to 10:00 to ensure that it remains on-screen until you press Enter.

26. Position the cursor at the top of the Screenshow Effects screen and press F2 (Preview Show) to watch RUNLINES in action. Figure 9.42 shows the completed Screenshow Effects screen for RUNLINES.

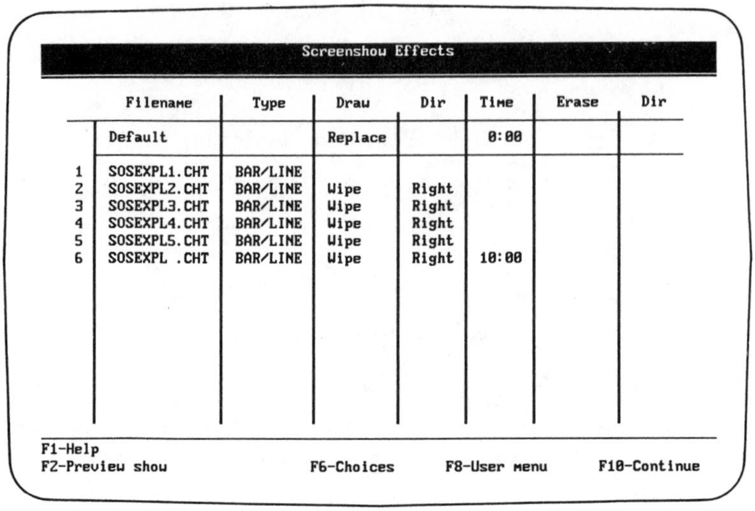

Fig. 9.42.

The completed Screenshow Effects screen for RUNLINES.

You may be surprised that the first chart in the screenshow has data for the month of January, but the screenshow seems to start without any visible lines. Because the chart uses lines, the first chart, with data for only one month, appears blank. The lines appear when they can connect data for at least two months.

Using a Template in a Screenshow

Ordinary templates, the same templates used to format charts automatically, gain special powers when they are incorporated into screenshows. Any annotations, logos, and footnotes they carry appear on all subsequent screenshow slides. In addition, their title, subtitle, and footnote text attributes and color settings rub off on the settings for subsequent charts. By setting a template's title to underlined and italicized, for example, and placing the template as the first slide in the screenshow, you automatically can underline and italicize all the titles in the following screenshow charts whether they are text or graph charts. These settings stay in effect until the screenshow reaches another template with different settings, assuring consistency in formatting among subsequent slides. Templates also affect slide shows because they are considered screenshows as soon as you display them on-screen.

To place the company logo at the top right corner of all slides in a screenshow, for example, create a chart with the company logo in the top right corner. Save the chart as a template and incorporate the template as the first slide when you create the slide show that becomes a screenshow. Because the logo is on a template preceding other charts, it will remain on the screen as chart after chart appears. With this technique, you also can draw a border or add a footnote to appear on all charts in a screenshow. Even if some of the charts in a presentation were created for other occasions, you can use a template's footnote to add the same date to all charts to make them look custom-made for the current presentation.

If you adjusted the overall size and placement of the chart on the template by using the F7-Size/Place feature at the Main menu, all subsequent charts in the screenshow appear in the same size and placement. This makes it easy to leave a space to one side of all charts for a company logo or special text annotation.

To see the effect of a template on a preexisting screenshow, create a template that has three effects for NEWPROD.SHW, the screenshow you created earlier. The three effects of the template are as follows:

1. Format the titles of the charts.

2. Add the presentation date as a footnote.

3. Add a symbol that appears on all charts.

Begin by creating the template with the following steps:

1. Create a simple list.

2. Enter *Superior Office Supplies* as the title, *Presentation* as the subtitle, and *June 12, 1989* as the footnote.

3. Use the F5-Attributes selection to underline the subtitle and set it to color number 9 (royal blue).

4. Use the F7-Size/Place selection to set the title to size 8, the subtitle to size 6, and the footnote to size 3.5.

5. Press F10 (Continue) to return to the Main menu.

6. Pull up the chart in Draw/Annotate mode and add the envelope, paintbrush, and pen symbol from the Office symbol library to the right and below the titles. The completed chart is shown in figure 9.43.

7. Save the chart as a template with the name NEWPROD. On the Save Template overlay, set Clear Values to No.

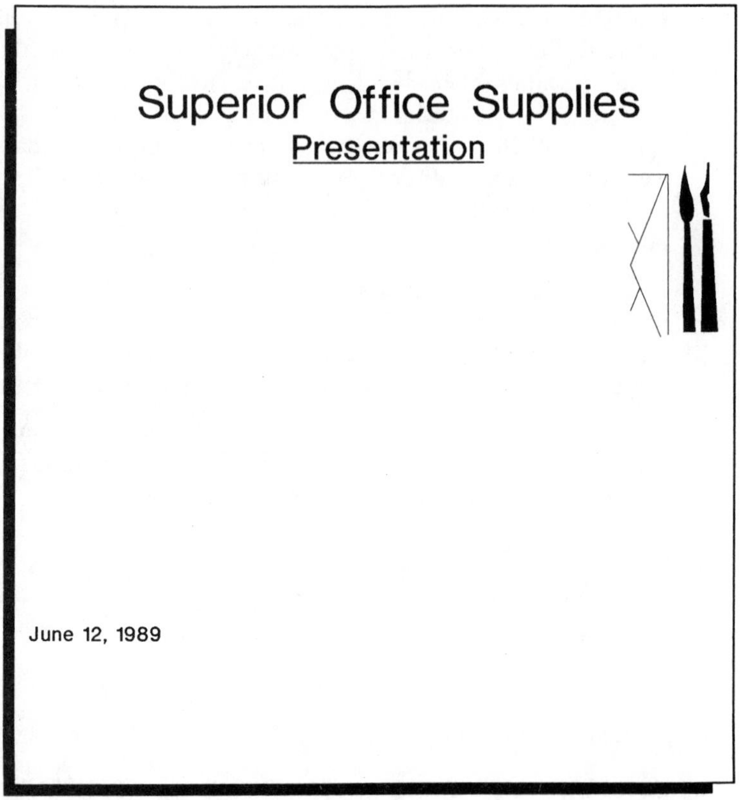

Fig. 9.43.

The NEWPROD template.

Superior Office Supplies
Presentation

June 12, 1989

Next, include the chart in the NEWPROD slide show by following these steps:

1. On the Slide Show menu, choose Select Slide Show.

2. Select NEWPROD.SHW from the Select Slide Show screen.

3. Choose Edit Slide Show from the Slide Show menu.

4. Highlight the name of the template you created, NEWPROD.TPL, and press Enter to add it to the end of the NEWPROD slide show.

5. Press Tab to move the cursor to the slide show chart list in the lower half of the screen.

6. Highlight NEWPROD.TPL and press Ctrl-↑ to move it to the top of the slide show.

7. Press F10 (Continue) to return to the Slide Show menu.

8. Select Display Screenshow from the Slide Show menu.

The templates you add to a screenshow do not actually appear on-screen when you display the screenshow, but their effects are certainly visible. As the screenshow displays, notice that all titles and subtitles are sized similarly, all subtitles are underlined and in blue, and the envelope, paintbrush, and pen symbol appears on all charts. Notice also that the presentation date appears in the footnote of every chart. If the chart already had a footnote, the template's chart displaces the chart's footnote. However, the template has little effect on the first chart in the show, a title chart. The title chart displays the symbol added in the template, but because the title chart has no formal title, subtitle, and footnote, the template's title, subtitle, and footnote formatting has no effect on the title chart. In fact, because title charts lack titles, subtitles, and footnotes, a title chart template inserted into the middle of a screenshow interrupts the effect of an earlier template in the show, turning off the earlier template's formatting effect.

Incorporating Bitmaps into Screenshows

To add the finishing touches to a screenshow, you can use a file from a popular paint program, such as PC Paintbrush Plus, Publisher's Paintbrush, or Dr. Halo, as the background to a chart or group of charts. Paint programs produce bitmapped files, and acceptable file formats have a file extension of PIC or PCX. You can purchase libraries of PCX format files from a number of companies. Marketing Graphics Incorporated (MGI) of Richmond, Virginia, offers an excellent collection of PCX images. Because many scanners produce graphic files with PC Paintbrush format (PCX), you can scan a photo or drawing and use it as the background to a screenshow. What could be more effective than scanning a picture of a product and superimposing on it a graph chart showing sales figures?

To import a bit-mapped file into a screenshow, select the file when you create the slide show. If you use Overlay to draw the next chart in the show, the chart appears superimposed over the bit-mapped image. To display the next chart in the show, you will need to use a transition effect other than Overlay to avoid seeing both charts on-screen at the same time. That effect removes the bitmap unless you replace the current chart with the same bit-mapped file once again. To have a bit-mapped image display as the background to all the charts of a screenshow, then, you must include the bit-mapped image as every other file in the show. Figure 9.44. shows the Screenshow Effects screen for a screenshow that displays the file SUPERIOR.PCX as a constant background throughout the show.

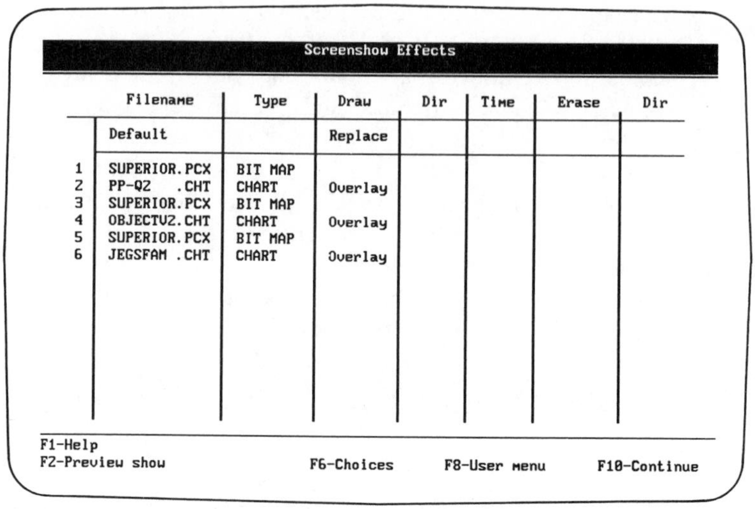

Fig. 9.44.

*Screenshow Effects
screen with
SUPERIOR.PCX
included.*

	Filename	Type	Draw	Dir	Time	Erase	Dir
	Default		Replace				
1	SUPERIOR.PCX	BIT MAP					
2	PP-QZ .CHT	CHART	Overlay				
3	SUPERIOR.PCX	BIT MAP					
4	OBJECTV2.CHT	CHART	Overlay				
5	SUPERIOR.PCX	BIT MAP					
6	JEGSFAM .CHT	CHART	Overlay				

Screenshow Effects

F1-Help
F2-Preview show   F6-Choices   F8-User menu   F10-Continue

For a bit-mapped image to be compatible with the current screenshow, you must have used the same type of graphics card to create both the bit-mapped image and the Harvard Graphics charts. For example, you can use two different machines to create the files as long as both have EGA cards installed, CGA cards installed, or both have VGA or monochrome graphics cards. IBM PS/2 computers have built-in VGA, so you should create both charts and bit-mapped files on another PS/2 or on a PC with a VGA card. The same rule applies if you use a clip-art PCX file or a scan-in image to create a bit-mapped file.

To display full-screen in the background of a chart, a bit-mapped file should be created in landscape orientation and should fill the screen.

When you incorporate bit-mapped images in screenshows, you may notice that the colors of your charts change when displayed following a bit-mapped image. Bit-mapped images almost invariably use a different color palette from the Harvard Graphics default color palette. When the bit-mapped image displays, it changes the color palette in use. Harvard Graphics then displays the chart that follows in the altered color palette. You may need to adjust the colors of the charts in your show to compensate for this effect by adding a Harvard Graphics palette file (PAL) into the screenshow after the bit-mapped file to reset the Harvard Graphics color palette. Designer Galleries, a Harvard Graphics accessory available from Software Publishing Corporation, offers a number of professionally color-coordinated palette files.

Circular or Continuous Screenshows

Just as you can embed template files in screenshows, you can include another screenshow in a screenshow list. When Harvard Graphics reaches a screenshow file name as it works its way down the list, it branches to and begins displaying that screenshow. With this in mind, you can combine smaller screenshows into one longer presentation by adding the name of each successive screenshow in the presentation to the end of the prior screenshow list. Combining individual screenshows to create a longer screenshow is necessary when you want to create a screenshow with more than 90 files or create an interactive screenshow, a presentation that the viewer can control. If you want to branch to another slide show, enter another slide show name as the last entry. When the first slide show reaches a second slide show name, the second slide show takes control. Remaining entries in the first slide show list are ignored.

By making two screenshows refer to each other, as shown in figure 9.45, you can create a circular or continuous screenshow. You also can create a continuous screenshow by including the name of the current screenshow file at the end of a screenshow. Harvard Graphics begins the same screenshow over again. To interrupt a continuous screenshow, press Esc.

Interactive Screenshows

For a variety of applications, letting the viewer choose the portions of a screenshow he or she wants to see can be invaluable. Viewers may enjoy a presentation more if they feel it is at their control. But more importantly, viewers can select the information they want to learn, leaving other information for a later viewing. With this capability, screenshows make rudimentary computer-based training (CBT) possible within Harvard Graphics.

To create an interactive screenshow, you need to combine a number of smaller screenshows into one large screenshow by listing the screenshow names when you create the initial slide show. Then you need to create a menu of choices and corresponding keystrokes from which the viewer can choose. Next, you need to inform Harvard Graphics about which screenshow within a screenshow to display based on the key the viewer presses.

Try this by creating an interactive screenshow composed of screenshows you have created earlier in this chapter: GROWBARS, RUNLINES, and NEWPROD. To create the interactive screenshow, you need to carry out these four steps:

Fig. 9.45.

*A continuous
screenshow made
from two
screenshows.*

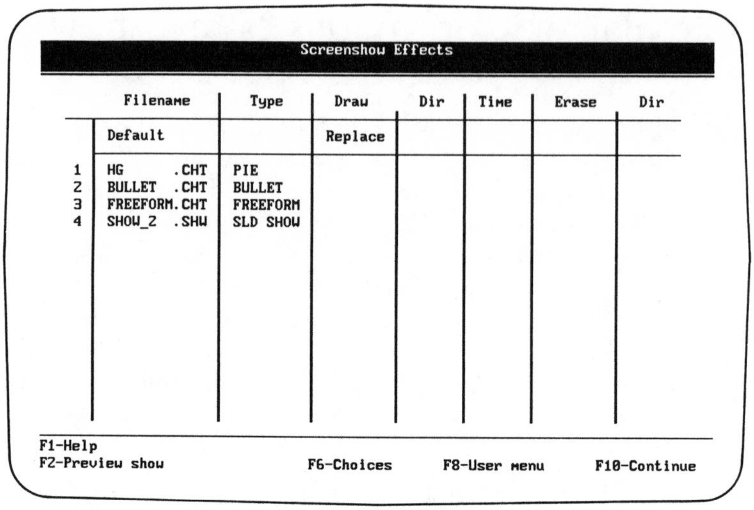

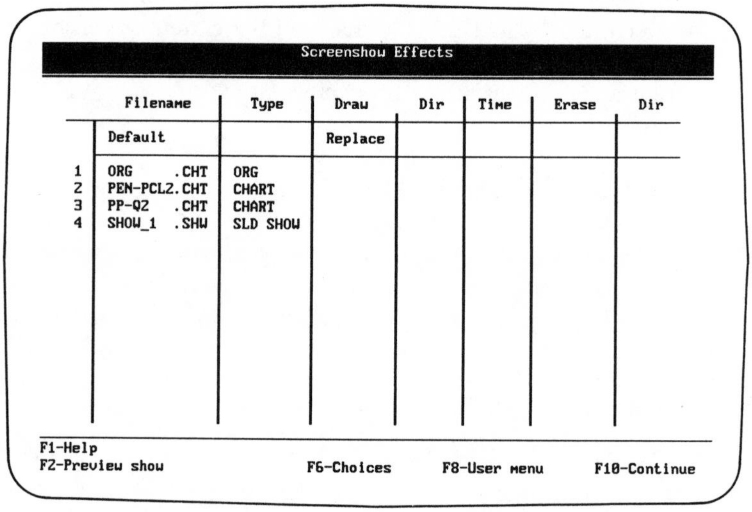

```
                        Screenshow Effects

         Filename        Type    Draw   Dir  Time  Erase   Dir

         Default                  Replace

     1   HG      .CHT    PIE
     2   BULLET  .CHT    BULLET
     3   FREEFORM.CHT    FREEFORM
     4   SHOW_2  .SHW    SLD SHOW




 F1-Help
 F2-Preview show          F6-Choices    F8-User menu    F10-Continue
```

```
                        Screenshow Effects

         Filename        Type    Draw   Dir  Time  Erase   Dir

         Default                  Replace

     1   ORG     .CHT    ORG
     2   PEN-PCL2.CHT    CHART
     3   PP-Q2   .CHT    CHART
     4   SHOW_1  .SHW    SLD SHOW




 F1-Help
 F2-Preview show          F6-Choices    F8-User menu    F10-Continue
```

1. Create a Text Chart menu.

2. Create a master screenshow composed of the Text Chart menu file and the three screenshow files.

3. Fill out the User Menu overlay to match screenshows with viewer keypresses.

4. Add the master screenshow name to the end of each of the component screenshows so that the viewer returns to the Text Chart menu after viewing any screenshow.

Create a free-form Text Chart menu by completing the Free Form Text data screen so that it matches figure 9.46.

```
                         Free Form Text

              Title:    Superior Office Supplies
              Subtitle: Menu
              Footnote:


                         To see:                Press:



                         SOS Revenues              1
                         (bar chart)

                         SOS Revenues              2
                         (line chart)

                         SOS New Product           3
                         Information



 F1-Help                      F5-Attributes   F7-Size/Place
 F2-Draw chart                                      F10-Continue
```

Fig. 9.46.

The MENU1 Free Form Text data screen.

Save the text chart as MENU1.CHT.

Next, create a slide show named MENUSHOW with four slides: MENU1.CHT, GROWBARS.SHW, RUNLINES.SHW, and NEWPROD.SHW. When the slide show is complete, choose Add Screenshow Effects from the Slide Show menu. Figure 9.47 shows the Screenshow Effects screen.

Position the cursor anywhere in the line where the viewer choice should begin—on line 1, which has MENU1.CHT—and press F8 (User Menu). A two-column User Menu overlay appears. In the left column, enter the user keypress. Valid keys are any of the number or letter keys. In the right chart, enter the line number that keypress causes the screenshow to jump to. Fill in the User Menu overlay so that it resembles the overlay shown in figure 9.48.

If a user presses 1 on the keyboard, the screenshow jumps to slide 2, the GROWBARS screenshow. If a user presses 2 on the keyboard, the screenshow jumps to slide 3, the RUNLINES screenshow, and so on. If *slide 1* is entered in the right column next to a blank keypress, the screenshow jumps to the first slide, the menu, if the viewer presses any other key.

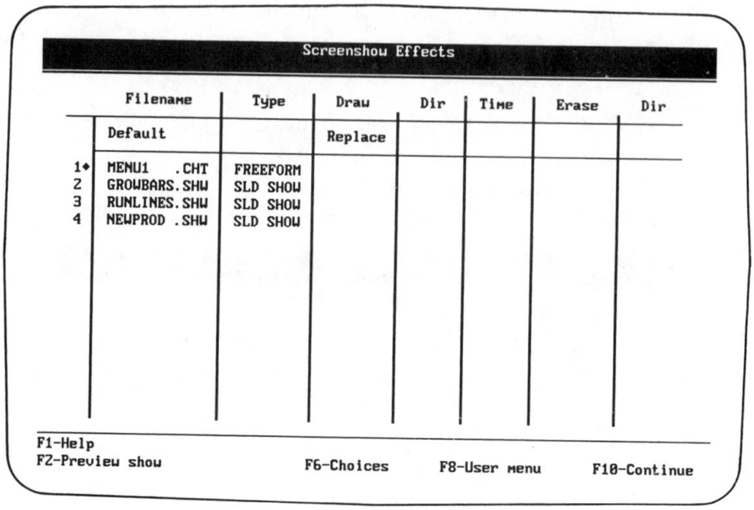

Fig. 9.47.

The Screenshow
Effects screen.

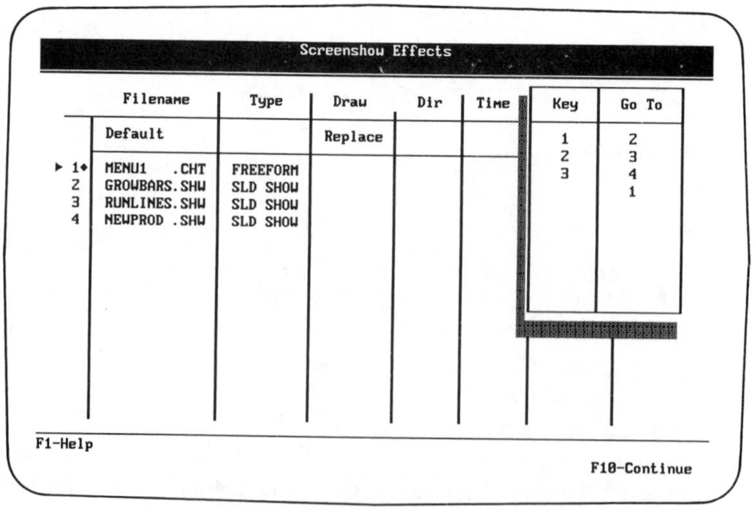

```
╔══════════════════════════════════════════════════════════════════╗
║                        Screenshow Effects                          ║
╟──────────────────────────────────────────────────────────────────╢
║        Filename      Type      Draw    Dir   Time   Erase    Dir   ║
║       ┌─────────────┬────────┬───────┬─────┬──────┬───────┬──────┐ ║
║       │ Default     │        │Replace│     │      │       │      │ ║
║       ├─────────────┼────────┼───────┼─────┼──────┼───────┼──────┤ ║
║   1♦  │ MENU1  .CHT │FREEFORM│       │     │      │       │      │ ║
║   2   │ GROWBARS.SHW│SLD SHOW│       │     │      │       │      │ ║
║   3   │ RUNLINES.SHW│SLD SHOW│       │     │      │       │      │ ║
║   4   │ NEWPROD .SHW│SLD SHOW│       │     │      │       │      │ ║
║       │             │        │       │     │      │       │      │ ║
║       │             │        │       │     │      │       │      │ ║
╟──────────────────────────────────────────────────────────────────╢
║ F1-Help                                                            ║
║ F2-Preview show          F6-Choices    F8-User menu    F10-Continue║
╚══════════════════════════════════════════════════════════════════╝
```

Fig. 9.48.

The User Menu
overlay for
MENUSHOW.

```
╔══════════════════════════════════════════════════════════════════╗
║                        Screenshow Effects                          ║
╟──────────────────────────────────────────────────────────────────╢
║        Filename      Type      Draw    Dir   Time ║ Key    Go To   ║
║       ┌─────────────┬────────┬───────┬─────┬──────╫─────┬────────┐ ║
║       │ Default     │        │Replace│     │      ║  1  │   2    │ ║
║       ├─────────────┼────────┼───────┼─────┼──────╢  2  │   3    │ ║
║ ▶ 1♦  │ MENU1  .CHT │FREEFORM│       │     │      ║  3  │   4    │ ║
║   2   │ GROWBARS.SHW│SLD SHOW│       │     │      ║     │   1    │ ║
║   3   │ RUNLINES.SHW│SLD SHOW│       │     │      ║     │        │ ║
║   4   │ NEWPROD .SHW│SLD SHOW│       │     │      ╚═════╧════════╝ ║
║       │             │        │       │     │                      ║
╟──────────────────────────────────────────────────────────────────╢
║ F1-Help                                                            ║
║                                                      F10-Continue  ║
╚══════════════════════════════════════════════════════════════════╝
```

Position the cursor at the top of the screenshow list and press F2 (Preview Show) to display the screenshow. Choose from the menu that appears. Notice that the master screenshow displays the screenshow you chose and then stops. To cause the screenshow to return to the menu after displaying each component screenshow, you must add the master screenshow's name at the end of each of the component screenshows. To do this, call up each of the individual screenshows with Edit Slide Show, add MENUSHOW.SHW to the end of each slide list, and press F10 (Continue).

Now, try the screenshow again and note that the menu reappears after each screenshow displays. If you press any key other than 1, 2, or 3 at the menu, nothing appears to happen. To display an ending slide when the viewer presses any key other than the keys on the menu, enter the slide's number next to the blank keypress on the User Menu overlay. Harvard Graphics signals that slide 1 on the MENUSHOW screenshow has a user menu by placing a diamond next to the slide number on the Add Screenshow Effects screen.

Exporting to a File

If your goal is to incorporate a Harvard Graphics chart within a document or graphic produced by another program, you can export the chart to a file in one of three formats: Computer Graphics Metafile (CGM), Encapsulated PostScript (EPS), or Hewlett-Packard Graphics Language (HPGL). With another program, you can import that CGM, EPS, or HPGL file.

Exporting a Computer Graphics Metafile

To export a file in CGM format, you need to install VDI device drivers in your computer's CONFIG.SYS file according to the instructions in Appendix D of the Harvard Graphics users' manual. These instructions guide you in adding two device drivers, META.SYS and GSSCGI.SYS. After the drivers are installed and you have rebooted your computer, follow this procedure to export a CGM file:

1. Select Import/Export from the Main menu.

2. Select Export Metafile from the Import/Export menu.

3. Enter a name for the export file on the Export Metafile overlay. Harvard Graphics adds a file name extension of CGM. You may enter a different extension.

4. Select Yes or No at the Use Harvard Graphics Font prompt. Yes causes the program to use a Harvard Graphics font in the CGM file. Because the resulting CGM file is larger, it takes longer to create. No causes Harvard Graphics to use the Metafile font when the program creates the CGM file. The Metafile font depends on the program used to import the Metafile later.

When you import a CGM file into another program, colors, patterns, and line styles may vary from your choices in the Harvard Graphics original file. You may need to use that program's capabilities to adjust those aspects of the image.

Exporting an Encapsulated PostScript File

To export a file in Encapsulated PostScript (EPS) format, you must have either of two files in the directory in which you installed Harvard Graphics: HGPROLOG.PSC for black-and-white PostScript printers or HGPROLOG.CPS for color PostScript printers. Exporting to an EPS file works best with a PostScript printer, although other programs can use EPS files to create graphics for non-PostScript printers.

To export an EPS file, follow this procedure:

1. Select Import/Export from the Main menu.

2. Select Export Picture from the Import/Export menu.

3. Enter a file name and an extension for the exported file. The typical file name extension for EPS files is EPS.

4. Select Standard or High for Picture Quality. Standard uses PostScript fonts in the EPS file. High uses Harvard Graphics fonts and creates a larger EPS file that takes longer to convert and print.

5. Select Encapsulated PostScript as the format and press F10 to create the EPS file.

Exporting a Hewlett-Packard Graphics Language File

The Hewlett-Packard Graphics Language (HPGL) is the standard for communications between software packages and plotters. To export a file in HPGL format, follow this procedure:

1. Select Import/Export from the Main menu.

2. Select Export Picture from the Import/Export menu.

3. Enter a file name and file name extension for the HPGL file. (Recommended extensions are PLT or HPG.)

4. Select Standard or High at the Picture Quality prompt. Standard picture quality uses built-in plotter fonts. High picture quality causes the plotter to reproduce the fonts used in Harvard Graphics.

5. Select HPGL at the Format prompt and press F10 to create an HPGL file.

If you plan to export an HPGL file, use any Harvard Graphics font except Executive and Square Serif when you create the chart. When you use High picture quality, Harvard Graphics creates these two fonts in the HPGL file by generating filled polygons. This process creates a large HPGL file that takes a long time to print.

Chapter Summary

In this chapter, you learned the myriad of techniques you can use to present Harvard Graphics charts. The next chapter is up to you. Remember that you can learn to use a program by reading a book such as this, but you can only master it with experience. Good luck.

Adding Flair with Symbols

As mentioned in Chapter 7, symbols in Harvard Graphics are collections of individual objects that form predrawn images. Some examples include collections of people, countries, cities, buildings, currency signs, vehicles, and figures such as arrows and stars.

These images are stored in symbol files, with the extension SYM, and each symbol file has many different symbols from which you can choose. After you choose symbols, you can work with them—change their sizes, stretch their shapes, move them, copy them, and so on.

This appendix contains an alphabetical listing of all the symbols included with Harvard Graphics. The fill from many of these symbols has been removed so that the symbols are more viewable. To make the symbols on your screen appear exactly the same as those presented here, you can also remove the fill.

A special utility called Business Symbols is available in addition to the Harvard Graphics symbols listed here. The Business Symbols utility includes more than 100 additional specialized symbols. For more information about symbols and how to use them, turn to Chapter 7, "Drawing with Harvard Graphics: Draw/Annotate."

Fig. A.1.

The ARROWS.SYM file.

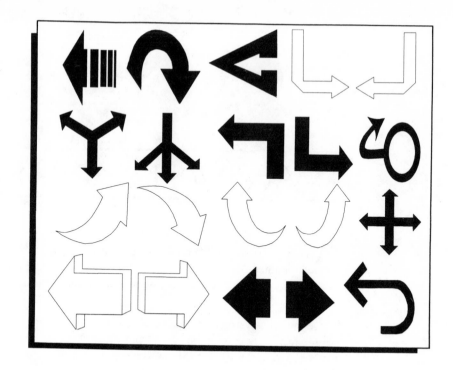

Fig. A.2.

The BUILDING.SYM file.

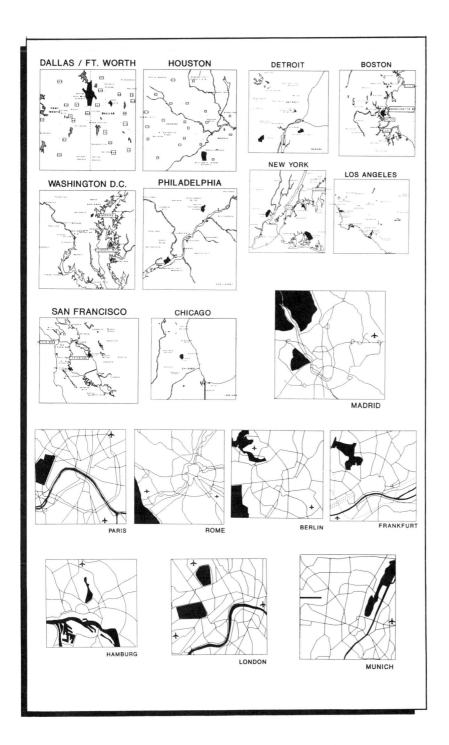

Fig. A.3.

The CITIES.SYM file.

Fig. A.4.

The COUNTRY.SYM file.

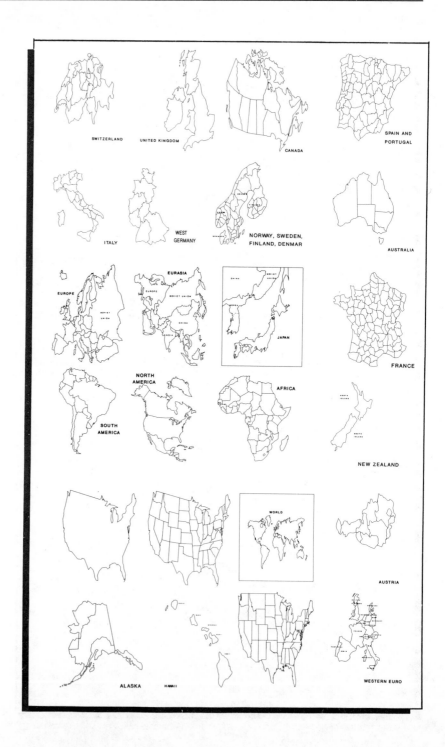

Fig. A.5.

The CURRENCY.SYM file.

Fig. A.6.

The FLOWCHAR.SYM file.

Fig. A.7.

The
FOODSPRT.SYM
file.

Fig. A.8.

The
GREEKLC.SYM
file.

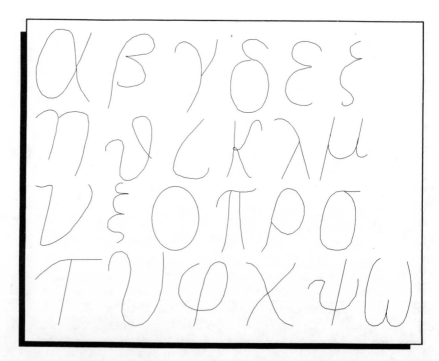

Fig. A.9.

The GREEKUC.SYM file.

Fig. A.10.

The HUMAN.SYM file.

Fig. A.11.

The INDUSTRY.SYM file.

Fig. A.12.

The MISC.SYM file.

Fig. A.13.

The OFFICE.SYM file.

Fig. A.14.

The PRESENT.SYM file.

Fig. A.15.

The STAR.SYM file.

Fig. A.16.

The TRANSPT.SYM file.

Index

P

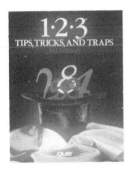

1-2-3 Tips, Tricks, and Traps, 3rd Edition

by Dick Andersen

Covering all releases of Lotus 1-2-3—including 2.2 and 3—this updated version of a Que classic presents hundreds of tips and techniques. Covers 3-D spreadsheet capability, new graphics features, and enhancements to the database and command language.

Order #963
$22.95 USA
0-88022-416-9, 550 pp.

Using WordPerfect 5

by Charles O. Stewart III, et al.

The #1 best-selling word processing book! Introduces Word-Perfect basics and helps readers learn to use macros, styles, and other advanced features. Also includes **Quick Start** tutorials, a tear-out command reference card, and an introduction to Word-Perfect 5 for 4.2 users.

Order #843
$24.95 USA
0-88022-351-0, 867 pp.

1-2-3 Release 3 Workbook and Disk

by Marianne Fox and Lawrence Metzelaar

A complete hands-on tutorial, perfect for individual or classroom instruction! This workbook/disk set contains a series of exercises covering spreadsheets, databases, graphics, printing, and the macro capabilities of 1-2-3 Release 3.

Order #1036
$29.95 USA
0-88022-498-3

Using Paradox 3

by Walter Bruce

Using Paradox 3 is the complete guide to Borland's unique database management program. This comprehensive text for beginning and intermediate users explores how to record a sequence of commands as an easy-to-use script, the program's multiuser capabilities, and the Paradox Application Language.

Order #859
$24.95 USA
0-88022-362-6, 450 pp.

1-2-3 Release 3 QuickStart
Developed by Que Corporation

More than 100, two-page illustrations help you learn the fundamentals of 1-2-3 Release 3. This is an award-winning graphics
based approach to 1-2-3 worksheets, reports graphs, databases,
and macros.

Order #973
$19.95 USA
0-88022-438-X, 450 pp.

1-2-3 Release 3 Business Applications
Edward M. Donie

The new Que book/disk combination contains a series of ready-
to-run business models. The text incorporates Release 3 features,
including 3-D spreadsheets and enhanced graphics.

Order #972
$39.95 USA
0-88022-439-8, 550 pp.

WordPerfect Tips, Tricks, and Traps, 2nd Edition
*by Charles O. Stewart III, Daniel J. Rosenbaum,
and Joel Shore*

A series of helpful tips and techniques on style sheets, keyboard
mapping, macro commands, integrated text and graphics, and
laser printers makes this the perfect resource for experienced
WordPerfect users. Covers WordPerfect 5.

Order #851
$21.95 USA
0-88022-358-8, 650 pp.

Using Ventura Publisher, 2nd Edition
by Diane Burns, S. Venit, and Linda Mercer

This is a comprehensive text for all levels of Ventura Publisher
users. You'll learn both program basics and design fundamentals
as you progress step-by-step into more advanced skills. Dozens
of detailed example documents are presented, and the new features of Ventura Publisher 2.0—including the Professional Extension—are highlighted.

Order #940
$24.95 USA
0-88022-406-1, 800 pp.

1-2-3 Database Techniques

by Dick Andersen

Concepts and technques to help users create complex 1-2-3 database applications! With an emphasis on Release 3 features, this book introduces database fundamentals, compares 1-2-3 with traditional database programs, offers numerous application tips, and discusses add-in programs.

Order #835
$22.95 USA
0-88022-346-4, 450 pp.

Using Computers in Business

by Joel Shore

This text covers all aspects of business computerization, including a thorough analysis of benefits, costs, alternatives, and common problems. Also discusses how to budget for computerization, how to shop for the right hardware and software, and how to allow for expansions and upgrades.

Order #1020
$24.95 USA
0-88022-470-3, 450 pp.

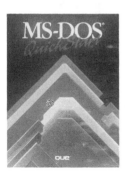

MS-DOS QuickStart

Developed by Que Corporation

The visual approach to learning MS-DOS! Illustrations help readers become familiar with their operating systems. Perfect for all beginning users of DOS—through Version 4.0!

$21.95 USA
Order #872
0-88022-388-X
350 pp.

Using Professional Write

by Katherine Murray

Quick Start tutorials introduce word processing basics and helps you progress to advanced skills with this top-selling executive word processing program. Also contains a section on macros, easy-to-follow examples, and printing tips. Using Professional Write with other programs also is discussed.

Order #1027
$19.95 USA
0-88022-490-8, 400 pp.

More Computer Knowledge from Que

Lotus Software Titles

1-2-3 QueCards	21.95
1-2-3 for Business, 2nd Edition	22.95
1-2-3 QuickStart	21.95
1-2-3 Quick Reference	7.95
1-2-3 Release 2.2 Quick Reference	7.95
1-2-3 Release 2.2 QuickStart	19.95
1-2-3 Release 3 Business Applications	39.95
1-2-3 Release 3 Quick Reference	7.95
1-2-3 Release 3 QuickStart	19.95
1-2-3 Release 3 Workbook and Disk	29.95
1-2-3 Tips, Tricks, and Traps, 2nd Edition	21.95
Upgrading to 1-2-3 Release 3	14.95
Using 1-2-3, Special Edition	24.95
Using 1-2-3 Release 2.2, Special Edition	24.95
Using 1-2-3 Release 3	24.95
Using 1-2-3 Workbook and Disk, 2nd Edition	29.95
Using Lotus Magellan	21.95
Using Symphony, 2nd Edition	26.95

Database Titles

dBASE III Plus Applications Library	21.95
dBASE III Plus Handbook, 2nd Edition	22.95
dBASE III Plus Tips, Tricks, and Traps	21.95
dBASE III Plus Workbook and Disk	29.95
dBASE IV Applications Library, 2nd Edition	39.95
dBASE IV Handbook, 3rd Edition	23.95
dBASE IV Programming Techniques	24.95
dBASE IV QueCards	21.95
dBASE IV Quick Reference	7.95
dBASE IV QuickStart	19.95
dBASE IV Tips, Tricks, and Traps, 2nd Edition	21.95
dBASE IV Workbook and Disk	29.95
dBXL and Quicksilver Programming: Beyond dBASE	24.95
R:BASE User's Guide, 3rd Edition	22.95
Using Clipper	24.95
Using DataEase	22.95
Using Reflex	19.95
Using Paradox 3	22.95

Applications Software Titles

AutoCAD Advanced Techniques	34.95
AutoCAD Quick Reference	7.95
CAD and Desktop Publishing Guide	24.95
Introduction to Business Software	14.95
PC Tools Quick Reference	7.95
Smart Tips, Tricks, and Traps	24.95
Using AutoCAD	29.95
Using Computers in Business	24.95
Using DacEasy	21.95
Using Dollars and Sense: IBM Version, 2nd Edition	19.95

Using Enable/OA	23.95
Using Excel: IBM Version	24.95
Using Generic CADD	24.95
Using Managing Your Money, 2nd Edition	19.95
Using Q&A, 2nd Edition	21.95
Using Quattro	21.95
Using Quicken	19.95
Using Smart	22.95
Using SuperCalc5, 2nd Edition	22.95

Word Processing and Desktop Publishing Titles

DisplayWrite QuickStart	19.95
Microsoft Word 5 Quick Reference	7.95
Microsoft Word 5 Tips, Tricks, and Traps: IBM Version	19.95
Using DisplayWrite 4, 2nd Edition	19.95
Using Harvard Graphics	24.95
Using Microsoft Word 5: IBM Version	21.95
Using MultiMate Advantage, 2nd Edition	19.95
Using PageMaker: IBM Version, 2nd Edition	24.95
Using PFS: First Choice	22.95
Using PFS: First Publisher	22.95
Using Professional Write	19.95
Using Sprint	21.95
Using Ventura Publisher, 2nd Edition	24.95
Using WordPerfect, 3rd Edition	21.95
Using WordPerfect 5	24.95
Using WordStar, 2nd Edition	21.95
Ventura Publisher Techniques and Applications	22.95
Ventura Publisher Tips, Tricks, and Traps	24.95
WordPerfect Macro Library	21.95
WordPerfect Power Techniques	21.95
WordPerfect QueCards	21.95
WordPerfect Quick Reference	7.95
WordPerfect QuickStart	21.95
WordPerfect Tips, Tricks, and Traps, 2nd Edition	21.95
WordPerfect 5 Workbook and Disk	29.95

Macintosh and Apple II Titles

The Big Mac Book	27.95
Excel QuickStart	19.95
Excel Tips, Tricks, and Traps	22.95
HyperCard QuickStart	21.95
Using AppleWorks, 2nd Edition	21.95
Using dBASE Mac	19.95
Using Dollars and Sense	19.95
Using Excel: Macintosh Verson	22.95
Using FullWrite Professional	21.95
Using HyperCard: From Home to HyperTalk	24.95

Using Microsoft Word 4: Macintosh Version	21.95
Using Microsoft Works: Macintosh Version, 2nd Edition	21.95
Using PageMaker: Macintosh Version	24.95
Using WordPerfect: Macintosh Version	19.95

Hardware and Systems Titles

DOS QueCards	21.95
DOS Tips, Tricks, and Traps	22.95
DOS Workbook and Disk	29.95
Hard Disk Quick Reference	7.95
IBM PS/2 Handbook	21.95
Managing Your Hard Disk, 2nd Edition	22.95
MS-DOS Quick Reference	7.95
MS-DOS QuickStart	21.95
MS-DOS User's Guide, Special Edition	29.95
Networking Personal Computers, 3rd Edition	22.95
Understanding UNIX: A Conceptual Guide, 2nd Edition	21.95
Upgrading and Repairing PCs	27.95
Using Microsoft Windows	19.95
Using Novell NetWare	24.95
Using OS/2	23.95
Using PC DOS, 3rd Edition	22.95

Programming and Technical Titles

Assembly Language Quick Reference	7.95
C Programmer's Toolkit	39.95
C Programming Guide, 3rd Edition	24.95
C Quick Reference	7.95
DOS and BIOS Functions Quick Reference	7.95
DOS Programmer's Reference, 2nd Edition	27.95
Power Graphics Programming	24.95
QuickBASIC Advanced Techniques	21.95
QuickBASIC Programmer's Toolkit	39.95
QuickBASIC Quick Reference	7.95
SQL Programmer's Guide	29.95
Turbo C Programming	22.95
Turbo Pascal Advanced Techniques	22.95
Turbo Pascal Programmer's Toolkit	39.95
Turbo Pascal Quick Reference	7.95
Using Assembly Language	24.95
Using QuickBASIC 4	19.95
Using Turbo Pascal	21.95

For more information, call

1-800-428-5331

All prices subject to change without notice. Prices and charges are for domestic orders only. Non-U.S. prices might be higher.

Que®

Free Catalog!

Mail us this registration form today, and we'll send you a free catalog featuring Que's complete line of best-selling books.

Name of Book _____

Name _____

Title _____

Phone (___) _____

Company _____

Address _____

City _____

State _____ ZIP _____

Please check the appropriate answers:

1. Where did you buy your Que book?
   - ☐ Bookstore (name: _____)
   - ☐ Computer store (name: _____)
   - ☐ Catalog (name: _____)
   - ☐ Direct from Que
   - ☐ Other: _____

2. How many computer books do you buy a year?
   - ☐ 1 or less
   - ☐ 2-5
   - ☐ 6-10
   - ☐ More than 10

3. How many Que books do you own?
   - ☐ 1
   - ☐ 2-5
   - ☐ 6-10
   - ☐ More than 10

4. How long have you been using this software?
   - ☐ Less than 6 months
   - ☐ 6 months to 1 year
   - ☐ 1-3 years
   - ☐ More than 3 years

5. What influenced your purchase of this Que book?
   - ☐ Personal recommendation
   - ☐ Advertisement
   - ☐ In-store display
   - ☐ Price
   - ☐ Que catalog
   - ☐ Que mailing
   - ☐ Que's reputation
   - ☐ Other: _____

6. How would you rate the overall content of the book?
   - ☐ Very good
   - ☐ Good
   - ☐ Satisfactory
   - ☐ Poor

7. What do you like *best* about this Que book?

   _____

   _____

8. What do you like *least* about this Que book?

   _____

   _____

9. Did you buy this book with your personal funds?
   - ☐ Yes   ☐ No

10. Please feel free to list any other comments you may have about this Que book.

    _____

    _____

    _____

QUE

Order Your Que Books Today!

Name _____

Title _____

Company _____

City _____

State _____ ZIP _____

Phone No. (___) _____

Method of Payment:

Check ☐   (Please enclose in envelope.)

Charge My: VISA ☐   MasterCard ☐

American Express ☐

Charge # _____

Expiration Date _____

Order No.	Title	Qty.	Price	Total

You can **FAX** your order to **1-317-573-2583**. Or call **1-800-428-5331, ext. ORDR** to order direct. Please add $2.50 per title for shipping and handling.

Subtotal _____

Shipping & Handling _____

Total _____

BUSINESS REPLY MAIL
First Class Permit No. 9918   Indianapolis, IN

Postage will be paid by addressee

11711 N. College
Carmel, IN 46032

┃┃┃┃

BUSINESS REPLY MAIL
First Class Permit No. 9918   Indianapolis, IN

Postage will be paid by addressee

11711 N. College
Carmel, IN 46032